HITLER'S LAST GAMBLE

HITLER'S
LAST GAMBLE

The Battle of the Bulge

BY

JACQUES NOBÉCOURT

Translated from the French by
R. H. BARRY

SCHOCKEN BOOKS · NEW YORK

Published in U.S.A. in 1967
by Schocken Books Inc.
67 Park Avenue, New York, N.Y. 10016

Library of Congress Catalog Card No. 67–20897

First published in France under the title of
Le Dernier Coup de Dés de Hitler
© 1962 by Robert Laffont

English translation copyright
© Chatto & Windus Ltd 1967

Printed in Great Britain

CONTENTS

40444

MAPS

ILLUSTRATIONS

FOREWORD

THE idea of writing this book dates from as far back as 1953. My friend, Jacques Robichon, whom many readers will know as the brilliant historian of the landing in southern France, struck by the importance and human drama aspect of the battle, suggested to me that for the tenth anniversary of the Ardennes offensive I should 'tell the story of Bastogne'. It soon became clear to me that the subject was much wider than the simple account of a battle. The siege of Bastogne is of course a famous story; the Allies had to pay dearly for their surprise (80,000 men), and heavy sacrifices were demanded of our Belgian allies by this last German effort. Yet the Ardennes offensive—known to American historians as the 'Battle of the Bulge'—seems in fact little more than an incident in the war, something far less fraught with consequences than, for instance, the Allied landing in North Africa in November 1942 or in Normandy on June 6 1944. There can, of course, be no comparison. The Ardennes is apt to get out of perspective because the reverse inflicted on the Allies was so unexpected and the alarm created so great.

Nevertheless its political repercussions, both on the German and on the Allied side, were greater than those of any other single operation of the war. The military events, in the strict sense of the word, only become of interest when viewed against the background of the general strategy of the autumn of 1944. On both sides the offensive provided a vivid illustration of the difficulty of establishing the correct relationship between the political direction of a nation or coalition, and its military instrument. The two sides attempted to solve the problem in very different ways: on the German side was to be seen the absolute autocratic authority of Hitler, riding roughshod over his generals' objections and ending in catastrophe. On the Allied side were two parallel tendencies: the strict discipline of the American military machine with its refusal to trespass into the sphere of overall conduct of the war for which it was not responsible, and the absence of the necessary counterweight of firmness of decision and clarity of purpose on the part of those called upon to assume that overall leadership.

The historian, therefore, who tries to present in complete and logical sequence both the events of the battle and their possible repercussions, finds himself working in that grey area where military adventure and political gamble overlap, where the operational becomes merged into the strategic, and where the wishes of the personalities involved, whether Hitler, Churchill or—to a lesser extent—de Gaulle, were necessarily subordinated to the march of events.

The more I delved into American and German military documents and the more eye-witnesses I interviewed, the greater became my determination to make the attempt. But I could not have succeeded, had I not received much support and encouragement.

First and foremost among those who have taken interest in my work, I would thank M. Paul M. G. Lévy, formerly a member of the Belgian Resistance and war correspondent, now director of the Council of Europe Information Service in Strasbourg. He was the first to realise that there were still certain facts connected with the Ardennes offensive which should be brought to light. As early as the end of 1945, for the first anniversary of the offensive, he published a series of articles in *La Cité Nouvelle*, in which, with considerable moral courage, he put the record straight on some of the legends that had grown up around the offensive; though these legends were dear to the hearts of the Belgians, many of them, particularly the coupling of von Rundstedt's name with the offensive, were legends none the less. I owe a great debt of gratitude to Monsieur Lévy, and I trust that I shall have successfully proved the facts which his passion for the truth led him to uncover.

I am equally grateful for assistance from a number of well-known Belgians who have studied this subject. In particular I would mention M. Marcel Bovy, Professor Emeritus, an ex-lawyer, a lieutenant in the Intelligence Service and a member of the Resistance. His book, *La Bataille de l'Amblève: Les combats sur le front nord du saillant des Ardennes*, is a painstaking and detailed account; he worked closely with G. R. de Lame, representative of the town of Spa at Headquarters First U.S. Army, who himself wrote a book entitled *Spa et les Americains*. These two books, and the correspondence which I had both with Abbé Bovy and M. de Lame, cleared up many important points for me. As regards Luxembourg, Abbé Joseph Maertz permitted me to makeuse of his carefully documented study, *Luxemburg in der Rundstedt Offensive*. I should also mention the great assistance I received in Bastogne from Abbé Joseph Zéler, a Professor at the Seminary; he was good enough to introduce me to other people in the town (it so happened that he did so during the winter of 1954, when the town was under snow as at the time of the battle). M. Léon Jacqmin gave me a vivid description of his administration of the town during the siege and Canon Fécherolle allowed me to use his account of the heroic city's sufferings. At Verviers a fellow journalist, Albert Jacquet, a leader-writer of the newspaper *Le Jour*, was kind enough to let me see his account of his impressions, written under the pseudonym Heagy, when he was unofficial war correspondent attached to the American Army. At Stavelot M. Jean Jacob and at Vielsalm Paulin Evrard were good enough to reply in great detail to all my questions and were of the greatest help to me. I would like to thank them all.

I have naturally used many sources of official and private documents, above all the Service Historique de l'Armée at Vincennes; this was made available to me through the good offices of its director, General de Cossé-Brissac. Not only did he provide me with all discoverable American and French military documents but he gave me the texts, not yet then published, of a study which he had personally compiled as a result of his post-war conversations with various German military personalities. This study was of enormous use to me in my research. It was eventually published in 1955 in Issue No. 2 of the *Revue Historique de l'Armée*, under the title: 'La Contre-Offensive Allemande des Ardennes'. Thanks to General de Cossé-Brissac, I was able to discover a number of documents dealing with this period in still unsorted files of German papers.

As regards Germany, my documentation is primarily the result of research conducted in the Institut für Zeitgeschichte in Munich in March 1954. There I was assisted by Drs H. Krausnick and P. Kluke, who displayed the spirit of co-operation, open-mindedness and insistence upon historical exactitude characteristic of that institution. Finally, M. F. Debyser, Director of the Bibliothèque Internationale de Documentation Contemporaine in Paris, gave me the most friendly welcome and showed the inexhaustible patience which all those engaged in research have come to know. Among German helpers, my thanks go primarily to Professor Dr von der Heydte of the University of Würzburg. He gave up hours of his time, giving me a detailed account, not only of the parachute operation which he commanded, but of the general atmosphere in Germany during the closing months of the war and the German officer's attitude to National Socialism. Through his good offices, I was able to see General Blumentritt and obtain from him confirmation of the views which I had formed.

Thanks to Charles W. David, then Director of the University of Pennsylvania Library, I was able to use the original unpublished texts of the 'Führer Conferences', or at least those of them still extant. Through M. Jean Meyriat, Director of the Document Section of the Fondation Nationale des Sciences Politiques, I was able to study the micro-films deposited there. Both were essential ingredients to a proper presentation of these events, and I would thank Mr David and M. Meyriat for giving me access to them. Finally M. Charles Braibant, Director of the Archives de France, gave me permission to consult micro-films of unpublished documents dealing with the International War Crimes Tribunal, Nuremberg.

The bibliography which the reader will find at the end of the book does not include all the books, articles and studies which I have consulted. Many have in fact been overtaken by two major works recently published —on the political side *The Conferences at Malta and Yalta* published by the State Department in 1955, and on the military side *The O.K.W. War Diary*. For the latter we have to thank Percy-Ernst Schramm, Professor of Contemporary History at Göttingen University; it is the daily record which he compiled as Historian to the O.K.W. (High Command of the

Wehrmacht) during the last two years of the war, and was published at the end of 1961. This book enabled me to correct many of the statements made by other authors who were relying solely on their memory. I must point out that unfortunately I have found many gaps in the documentation, particularly on the influence of military events upon political decisions and vice versa. The conflict of interest generally only came to the surface during unofficial discussions preparatory to a decision. On occasions there is some indication of it in Hitler's conferences, but comparatively little. On the Allied side there is nothing. Neither Roosevelt, Churchill, Eisenhower nor Montgomery kept shorthand records of their unofficial conversations. Moreover, the period was one of such Allied crisis that documents which might produce evidence of the ebb and flow of thought are in most cases still in the secret archives.

In this connection, it would have been of particular interest to be able to consult the record of the meetings of the European Consultative Commission, which was responsible for laying down the future of Germany and in which there appears to have been continual conflict between the political desiderata and the military necessities. On the latter subject the most authentic picture would of course be given by the Minutes of the Joint Chiefs of Staff, the British Chiefs of Staff or the Combined Chiefs of Staff. These would shed much light upon the attitude of Roosevelt and Churchill, but it seems unlikely that they will emerge in our day. There are too many accounts still to be squared and too many people still ready to turn into public prosecutor for either the British or Americans to wish to provide such material for polemics.

In addition to official documents, I have made much use of the press of the period. Its analysis has been the work of Mlle Arlette Marchal, who brought to it her keen perception as a historian and ability as a diplomatic correspondent and proved herself a devoted friend. She has given me much encouragement in writing this work, which in many respects is hers.

Finally, all my thanks go to M. Henri Noguères, who was good enough to cast his expert historian's eye over my manuscript and to criticise it. He made many valuable suggestions on the shades of opinion which I have expressed and contributed greatly to making this account readable. His guidance has been invaluable.

INTRODUCTION

On the evening of December 19 1944 General of the Army Dwight David Eisenhower, Supreme Commander Allied Expeditionary Forces Europe, was in his office in the Trianon-Palace Hotel Annexe, Versailles. He was facing his moment of truth. For the second time in his career the decision was his alone and he knew only too well what was at stake: success or failure. His June 5 decision to go ahead with the Normandy landing had been proved right by events—but only just. Now the boot was on the other leg: three days earlier the Wehrmacht had split the Allied front at an unexpected point, the Belgian Ardennes. Hitler was playing his last card and had staked his all on this offensive. An American army corps had been brushed aside and Liège was threatened. What would happen next? Enemy intentions were still obscure: he might drive on Brussels and Antwerp, surrounding the British and Canadian armies labouring on the Lower Rhine; or he might repeat his 1940 thrust into Champagne via Sedan and then swing back behind the American and French forces holding the Saar and Vosges.

The rupture of the Allied front between Aix-la-Chapelle and Luxembourg came at the end of three months of 'phoney war', a shorter but more savage second edition. The campaign in Europe had opened with the close fighting of the Normandy *bocage*; then had come the victorious armoured charge across France during the splendid summer days of 1944. But in the next phase American soldiers had been faced with the physical and moral attrition of position warfare and now for the last three days they had been tasting defeat. At this very moment many of them were living their last hours or minutes; low cloud had deprived them of their air support; death in a hole in the snow was bringing their lonely adventure to an end. Like their fathers at Bois-Belleau in 1918 the young G.I.s were dying where they stood.

Like them, Eisenhower was alone, facing the decision where and how to stem the tide of this last convulsive German effort, how to turn it into a German catastrophe. Whatever he did other generals would criticise him later; there were as many accounts to be squared as decorations to be exchanged. Controversy was certain, as certain as the Broadway ticker-tape parade awaiting him if he returned victorious; equally certain, however, was the merciless interrogation of a defeated general by a congressional committee at which inexpert senators would consider it their prerogative to pronounce judgment before consigning him to the obscurity of retirement in Gettysburg, Pennsylvania.

For Eisenhower, both his own future and the vindication of his meteoric career were at stake on this particular evening. Four days ago President Roosevelt had asked Congress to grant him the five stars of a General of the Army. This, the highest of all ranks, was confirmation of his claim to be the moral successor to General Pershing, the 'grand old man', still alive at the end of 1944, President Wilson's nominee for command of the 3,000,000 American soldiers who had helped the French and British to bring their exhausting conflict to a victorious end in 1918. Pershing's insistence on the autonomy of his forces and his refusal to 'integrate' them into the Allied armies had cost him many humiliating moments.

This time Eisenhower had insisted upon integration—the wheel had come full circle. But the principle was still in dispute, as was the personality of the Supreme Commander. A reverse in the Ardennes would imply more than the loss of a battle; it would set the seal on the failure of a system and involve the disappearance of its architect.

The greatest sceptics were his American fellow-generals, above all his former chief, Douglas MacArthur, a general like his father before him and a flamboyant character with gold all over his helmet. Although the reward of victory in his island-hopping campaign was the prospect of becoming uncrowned emperor of Japan, he considered himself an exile in the Pacific theatre. MacArthur was the doyen of the American army. Promoted brigadier-general after only fifteen years service, he had been wounded in France in the autumn of 1918 when commanding a division. He had done his utmost to ruin Marshall's career and he had not forgiven Eisenhower for escaping from his clutches, once referring to him as 'the apotheosis of mediocrity'. Yet on December 15 Roosevelt had placed MacArthur on the same footing as Marshall and Eisenhower, proposing the same five-star reward for all three, dissimilar though their careers had been.

Only yesterday Eisenhower's fellow-generals had been his senior officers. Since the North African landing they had of course been 'co-operative'. 'Ike' had managed to assert his position; he had been able to bring his Commanders-in-Chief to heel at decisive moments or when impulsiveness led a man like George Patton to break the rules. But his 'friends' and rivals were only human; they were still flabbergasted at his meteoric career—on average a rise in rank every six months since 1942; they had him under scrutiny and they were not prepared to make allowances. His patience and understanding were held against him, particularly when he displayed these qualities towards the British. There was grumbling in officers' messes: 'Concessions to the spirit of the coalition? More like lack of thought, and spinelessness.' The joke among Patton's young officers was 'Ike? The best general the British have got.'

Nevertheless Eisenhower held the ace of trumps in the person of George Catlett Marshall, Chief of Staff of the U.S. Land Forces, whose battlefield was Washington D.C. General Marshall had picked Lt-Col Eisenhower when the latter was Chief of Staff to the winning side on manœuvres in Louisiana. He accelerated Eisenhower's promotion and finally relinquished to him his own place at the head of the Allied armies in western Europe. Marshall had resigned himself to the position of an American Carnot conjuring up formations, equipment and generals with a wave of the wand. He was a 'Whitehall warrior' with the exterior of a military monk, a thinker in uniform, one of the modest breed of generals who can revive the moral fibre of an army and be the architect of cohesion. Roosevelt had promoted him 'General of the Army' at the same time as MacArthur and Eisenhower.

But now if Ike allowed himself to be beaten in the Ardennes, even Marshall could not save him. Events would then prove that Marshall's three years of unswerving support had been an error.

The British generals would have been no more surprised at Ike's failure than the American. They found it hard to accept their subordination to an amateur who had hardly been under fire and whose knowledge of Europe was confined to American military cemeteries, a sort of senior Imperial War Graves official (Eisenhower had spent some time in Paris bringing the guide to the battlefields up to date). They asked themselves what qualified him for his position and came to the conclusion that it was simply the ratio of forces engaged on the Continent; there were and would always be more American divisions than British.

'Ike seems determined to show that he is a great general in the field. Let him do so and let us all lend a hand to pull him through. But he is no commander, he has no strategic vision, is incapable of making a plan or of running operations when started. Moreover he spends his time playing golf at Reims.' Thus Field-Marshal Sir Alan Brooke, Chief of the Imperial General Staff, working off his ill-humour in the evenings. Depending on his mood, Brooke's feelings towards the Supreme Commander ranged from condescension to fury. He listened to all the gossip. Yet during the war Montgomery was a more ardent golf player than Eisenhower. And what was wrong with golf?

Just behind Brooke (or just in front of him—it was always difficult to tell which was covering which) stood Montgomery. He took good care always to appear both as Eisenhower's principal antagonist and his dearest friend. A harsh-voiced puritan who neither smoked nor drank and had no weakness for the fair sex, Montgomery held that a commander should always be in the limelight; he was by no means so naïve as he pretended when dealing with war correspondents and he made the most of his unusual personality.

The German offensive offered Montgomery yet another opportunity of laying claim to the command of all the Allied Land Forces. Eisenhower was under pressure to yield everything or nothing to him—and the issue at stake was a possible German victory.

* * *

That same night, December 19, Hitler was holding his evening conference in a concrete shelter at Ziegenberg. Early in the month he had left East Prussia for his headquarters in the neighbourhood of Frankfurt; it had been constructed during the winter of 1939-40 but Hitler had never used it. Perhaps this fresh site would produce the new 'miracle of the house of Brandenburg' which the Führer so confidently expected.

Keitel and Jodl were with him in the map room. The former was a sort of Wehrmacht Minister of the Interior; he was the administrator who did not intervene in operations in the strict sense of the word. As Chief of O.K.W. he had been promoted field-marshal in July 1940. Perhaps it was failure to achieve his life's ambition of becoming a farmer which had turned him into a blockhead.

Jodl, a colonel-general, had also held his office throughout the war: Chief of the O.K.W. operations staff (Chef des Wehrmachtführungsstab). He was the man who translated Hitler's strategic decisions into orders. At this point he was in charge only of the fronts facing the British and Americans. The Russian front was the concern of Guderian, Chief of Staff of the Army (Chef des Generalstab des Heeres).

'The enemy is holding on,' Hitler was told by his two advisers. 'In the northern sector of the breakthrough Sepp Dietrich, commanding Sixth Panzer Army, has not yet got through towards the Meuse; he is waiting for his supplies to come up. The Luftwaffe has been unable to operate.'

In the centre Manteuffel, with the Fifth Panzer Army, was surrounding Saint-Vith, where there was still resistance. Two American regiments had surrendered. The spearhead of this army was to drive towards Dinant, by-passing Bastogne both to north and south without attempting to capture the town. American parachute troops were arriving there and the infantry divisions following on behind the armour were to lay siege to the place in proper form. On the southern flank Seventh Army was going on to the defensive.

Hitler could not conceal the twitch which had been worrying him for months. 'On to the Meuse, on to the Meuse' he ordered. 'We must get there tomorrow; we must not give Bastogne time to defend itself.'

It fell to Bastogne that evening to act as the breakwater. By pure chance the American parachute troops had unloaded from their vehicles at that point. Their colonel's orders had been: 'Manœuvre; do not get pinned down; keep away from the built-up area.' Bayerlein, commanding the German armour, was taken by surprise; he was faced by a mobile defence everywhere and discouragement began to set in. He made such meticulous preparations for his attack that MacAuliffe, the opposing commander, was given time to put his defences in order.

Colonel Ewell, commanding the U.S. parachute troops, had established his headquarters in the convent; there during the evening he collected a series of haggard individuals, young soldiers shattered by their baptism of fire who had been wandering for two days with German columns on the move all around them. They reached the American lines in groups of three or four, exhausted and 'shocked' according to the military psychiatrists. They were stuffed with food and sent to sleep it off. Their tribulations left the hard-bitten parachutists of 501 Airborne Regiment unmoved.

There was one man who did perhaps understand their state of mind; he had tried to escape from the fate which threatened them all and to run away from his fear; so this evening he was in a military prison, counting how many days had elapsed since his petition for mercy had been forwarded to General Eisenhower. He was little Eddie Slovik, condemned to death as a deserter: when he came under fire he had left his unit and given himself up to the neighbouring company. His petition was dated December 9 but he was not worried: no American soldier who had deserted simply to avoid coming under fire had been shot since 1864. Eddie had written to the general 'I am yours for victory'. He expected a favourable reply.

From Liège to Paris, from Cherbourg to Bordeaux, all thought of preparations for the first Christmas of liberation had vanished that evening. Liberated Europe was in the grip of fear, subjugated Europe in the depths of despair. The German débacle of the summer, the Russian autumn offensives, the pounding of the Reich's factories and railways by Allied bombers, the optimism of the victors, had all seemed to guarantee an end to the war in the closing weeks of 1944.

Confidence had given way to resigned expectation but there had been no anxiety. And now by launching his unexpected blow on December 16, Hitler had destroyed all these illusions. During the 17th and 18th, the civil population had had no authentic news: for the first time since the landing Allied censorship was intercepting the despatches from the hordes of war correspondents who swirled between Paris and the front.

The truth when it came was that much more brutal. The spectre of the spring of 1940 raised its head; the Belgians began to evacuate once more; the French knew from experience that they still had a few days' grace before they must take to the road.

One of General Juin's officers visiting the Versailles headquarters on December 18 remarked to Bedell Smith: 'What! Aren't you packing your bags?' Whether the question was genuine or facetious it was hardly calculated to advance the French cause in the eyes of Eisenhower's Chief of Staff. Nevertheless it expressed the secret thoughts of the thousands of uniformed men and women shuttling back and forth between the Grandes Écuries of the Palace and the Trianon-Palace Hotel. They were not thinking of the road to Bordeaux via Cande, but that to Cherbourg via Rennes and Granville. The journalists realised that there was panic in the air and they reported accordingly; a snowball reaction set in and the French and Belgian civil population, nerves on edge after four years of occupation,

B

lost their heads. Bedell Smith's bold summarisation of the situation—that the Ardennes offensive had been dreamt up by the press—had some foundation in fact. What he meant was that there were only two men who had kept their heads, Eisenhower and himself. And that was true.

*   *   *

The same evening Albert Camus was drafting his editorial for *Combat*. The galleys of the next edition were already on the marble-topped table in the printing room of the great building in the Rue Réamur; the news they presented was pretty ridiculous: 'The radical party congress proclaims that it is a revolutionary party in a revolutionary country . . . during the draw for the national lottery at the Palais de Chaillot, a Mouézy-Eon comedy entitled *Tout est au Troc* will be staged . . . the new revue at the Casino de Paris is entitled *En plein Jazz*.'
Camus made an attempt to hint at the truth:

All that we can say [he wrote], is that Germany still exists, that she has not been beaten and that the war is not at an end . . . we must never forget that we are at war and that if American lives are being lost at Montjoie, Frenchmen must sacrifice themselves elsewhere . . . this offensive should teach us that a country at war cannot leave its young men to choose as the spirit moves them between volunteering for the forces or lounging round the bars.

General de Lattre de Tassigny, commanding the French First Army, was in his headquarters that evening at the Hotel de la Balance, Montbéliard; he was reading a message which had just arrived from General de Gaulle: 'You should give your troops to understand that they are not in the least "deserted", rather the contrary.'
The previous day de Lattre had written to de Gaulle in much the same way as Albert Camus: 'Among all ranks but particularly among the officers, even at a high level, there is the general impression on that the nation is ignoring them and deserting them. The basic cause of this malaise rests in the apparent non-participation of the country in the war.' A few days later Pierre Hervart commented in *Combat*: 'We are a nation of irresponsible civilians.' All Parisians knew of the war was the sight of American soldiers wandering about; they were good for trade and for the black market which operated between the Opera and the Madeleine.
The French were disturbed about the German offensive primarily because they were certain to be 'mixed up in it' once more. Moreover everybody knew that if the Germans succeeded, many tunes would have to be changed and many decisions re-thought. Albert Camus wrote: 'Imagine for a moment the Germans in Paris once more. We know well enough who among us would close their ranks and continue to resist. We know well enough who would take to their heels and who would prepare

to do another about-turn. These changes of allegiance are bringing this country to collapse.'

On this same December 19 a new newspaper published its second number. Page one carried a three-column headline that in the Ardennes 'the entire front is on the move over a breadth of fifty miles'; alongside it was an appeal for 'a spirit of reform beginning by reforming ourselves'. The previous day the posters announcing the appearance of this newspaper had called for a 'revolution—a legal revolution'. This was enough to give rise to all sorts of suspicions. So Le Monde came into existence, at a time of ferment and stress. Its sense of proportion and its pessimism made it a target of abuse from the beginning.

* * *

Eisenhower was alone; Hitler was alone; the soldiers trying to warm themselves and dry their equipment round their petrol stoves were alone; the prisoners of war were alone; the refugees were alone; there was nothing but loneliness on that December 19. Fear in all its shades of intensity, from doubt to panic, from anxiety to despair was bred and fed by loneliness. It was one of Europe's most dismal days.

* * *

A few hours earlier Eisenhower had taken the measures which would exorcise the spell. At least he hoped he had. He had gone to Verdun to issue his orders for the counter-attack: Patton was to attack the southern flank of the German bulge and eliminate it. But on getting back to Versailles the latest intelligence showed that this decision had been overtaken by events: the Allied front was threatening to split and each half was in danger of being encircled and annihilated.

The northern flank was giving way and disintegrating. Bradley, commanding Twelfth U.S. Army Group, was in Luxembourg and could hardly control the divisions on the distant northern front. Yet that was where the main German effort was being made.

At the tip of the salient there was no definite front. There was nothing to stop the enemy forcing the bridges between Givet and Namur. Montgomery had hurriedly sent forward detachments to cover them, but he considered the situation 'disagreeably vague'.

Eisenhower thereupon took his decision. Montgomery was to take command of the northern front with two American armies, First and Ninth, under his command. Eisenhower forgot that this 'faithful friend' had been harrying him for the last three months for just such an increase in his forces as the first step to overall control of all the Allied Land Forces. Bradley was unwilling to give up a single man to Montgomery but friendship for Bradley did not weigh with Eisenhower. He turned a deaf ear to Patton's howls of rage; he disregarded the furious protests of the American press.

The headlines referred to a 'European Pearl Harbour'. If it was indeed a Pearl Harbour, the time had come for radical counter measures.

To decide to apply such drastic measures Eisenhower must have been acutely conscious of the deterioration in the situation since that day in June when he had given the signal for the invasion of Europe. During these six months the halo of victory had disappeared as quickly as had the military and political rewards to which the world was hoping that victory would lead. Eisenhower was still at the head of the Allied armies, thanks to Marshall's unwavering support and Roosevelt's lack of interest in military problems — even those of strategic importance — which contrasted so strongly with Churchill's attitude.

The fact that the Allies were taken by surprise seemed to show that Eisenhower's critics were right; they had been saying that to fill the post of Supreme Commander it was not enough merely to be better than any boardroom chairman at drafting compromise motions. Montgomery expressed similar views, implying that it was entirely Eisenhower's fault that the war did not end until the spring of 1945: 'When a certain strategy was decided upon it wasn't directed; we advanced to the Rhine on several fronts which were uncoordinated. And what was the German answer? A single concentrated punch in the Ardennes when we had become unbalanced and unduly extended.'

This criticism implied that the Ardennes surprise was the logical sequel to the strategy adopted from late summer onwards. Eisenhower's only retort was a Press Conference statement in October 1958:

It happened to have been my responsibility to conduct the Western invasion and under the authority of the Combined Chiefs of Staff I was given a free hand . . . We won the war in eleven months from the day we landed and I heard no single prediction that the war would be over in less than two years. As a matter of fact Winston Churchill told me that if we captured Paris by Christmastime he would remark that that was the greatest military operation of all time.

This was a dignified reaction in spite of its undercurrent of vexation, but it settled nothing. Eisenhower chose to evade the issue as if the allusion to this period, particularly when made by Montgomery, revived the memory of a quarrel still most distasteful to him.

*   *   *

In Hitler's mind the Ardennes offensive was merely a set piece from a Wagner tragedy. Looked at in retrospect from the Allied side that is indeed all it seems to be, particularly when it is remembered that the Yalta meeting took place a few weeks later.

In the light of the atmosphere at the time, however, the behaviour of all the principal actors on the stage can be explained by one factor: the spectre of the war beginning all over again just when it seemed to be ending. Hitler played deliberately upon this obsession. In Wolfschanze (Wolf's Lair), his East Prussian headquarters, he had been planning ever since early August to strike a violent blow at the Allies before their momentum carried them on to German territory. The initial object of course was to gain time to reconstitute the German forces, but the Führer also dreamt of a spectacular reversal of the situation: he would gain several weeks' breathing space and with his new divisions would drive back to the Channel, sweep across the western front and then return eastwards to settle accounts with the Russians either on the battlefield or at the conference table. Stalin, he thought, might agree to talk, might allow the Third Reich to finish off the United States and above all Great Britain, the enemy number one whom Hitler loathed with the hatred of the rejected suitor.

Some of his generals also dreamt of major changes in the situation which would allow them to avoid the unconditional surrender demanded by the Allies. In contrast to Hitler's line of thought, they imagined that, should the Russians succeed in forcing the lines of the Vistula or Oder during the Ardennes offensive, the Wehrmacht might invite the Anglo-Americans across the Rhine and ultimately defend Berlin with them against the Russians.

All this was no doubt fantasy, but autumn 1944 was a season of fantasy, and of indecision while awaiting a miracle. Hitler knew what he meant by the miracle: disintegration of the Allied camp as a prelude to a change of alliances.

Hitler's entourage became more and more deeply involved in the intrigues which had divided them ever since the seizure of power. His physical deterioration made it easy for Goebbels, the Minister of Propaganda, and the latest arrival, Martin Bormann, Chief of the National Socialist Party Chancellery and successor to Rudolf Hess, to enlarge their authority. Their assurances of loyalty were made only to counterbalance those of Göring and Ribbentrop.

As the Great German Reich went into its decline millions of rebellious foreigners were to be found within its borders. The inmates of the concentration camps, the political deportees, the victims of racial persecution, foresaw an acceleration of that process of systematic extermination which will forever be linked to the name of Germany. Hordes of foreign workers mingled with the population. The prisoners of war felt their courage returning. In spite of bombing, fires, famine and torture a feeling of hope helped this polyglot mass of humanity to survive. The Nazis believed that their secret weapons would win them a last minute victory; their hostages pinned their faith on the speed of advance of the liberators. Everybody thought that the end of the war was near.

*   *   *

The Ardennes offensive was a rude awakening. The surprise lay not so much in the resurgence of German power as in the revelation of Allied weakness. The British and Americans seemed to be so preoccupied with their disagreements that they had forgotten that the war must be finished before they could turn their thoughts to the peace. Since the end of August the problem of the peace had apparently taken priority over all others, yet the confusion of ideas and interests was such that no clear picture emerged. On the rare occasions when the electoral campaign for his fourth term allowed him time to think Roosevelt wondered how the true twentieth-century international order was to be produced. He lent his authority to the wildest schemes often without reading them, certainly without absorbing them.

As a war leader Churchill followed the course of events closely and he made vain attempts to bring Roosevelt down to earth. The fundamental difference between these two characters and their methods of work was reflected on the military level in the quarrel between Eisenhower and Montgomery. The latter added fuel to the fire; he was convinced that only the British, with their experience of European affairs, were fit to direct a conflict in which the United States were more capable of providing troops than solving problems. Eisenhower was a greater pragmatist than Roosevelt but his concept of the basis of his authority as Supreme Commander was a conviction diametrically opposed to that of Montgomery. In his view the United States were called upon to settle the destiny of the entire world; they were giving all their Allies, the British included, the tools of victory; they were therefore best fitted to fix once and for all the destiny of a Continent in which they had no intention of intervening perpetually. 'They were also dangerously sure that they knew what was best for Great Britain and Europe.'*

In mid-August, when operations came temporarily to a halt, the basic disagreement, hitherto plastered over by the necessities of the alliance, came out into the open. The Allies were ahead of their timetable and they did not push on into Germany largely because Eisenhower did not know what line he should take. He marked time, waiting for the directives which Roosevelt could not be bothered to give or even consider. As a result he was criticised for missing the opportunity of taking Berlin, prolonging the war by nearly six months, putting himself in a situation where he risked a major defeat and finally bringing the Allies to the Yalta conference at which the lines of post-war Europe were to be drawn, in a weak posture *vis à vis* Stalin.

Subsequent political events—and the publication of memoirs—have often given rise to accusations such as these. To what extent are they justified? All too often their background is disillusionment over the 'phoney peace' in which we are now living. Marshal Foch's contemporaries were

* L. Woodward, *British Foreign Policy in the Second World War*, p. liv.

equally bitter over the results of the Treaty of Versailles and they re-
proached him for failure to insist on the armistice being signed in Berlin.
Faced with the permanent Berlin crisis, the Korean war and the division
of Germany, many people feel uneasy and impotent and so have been
only too ready to lend an ear to the accusations of Field-Marshal Montgomery or the vindictive statements of General MacArthur. I believe them
to be wrong.

The Ardennes was an effect, not a cause. It came at the end of a dramatic
autumn; it was the last German victory; it was Hitler's last bluff; it was
the first American débacle. So it must be regarded as the final act of a
great political adventure both on the German and on the Allied side.
Many have tried to present it merely as an incident in the struggle, but in
spite of curious lapses of memory on the part of certain of the participants
and in spite of the accumulation of legend, a certain truth emerges which
the ambiguous language of the official accounts cannot altogether conceal.
This truth appears initially only in hazy outline; it has to be unearthed.
It can be discovered, not so much by working out the exact chronological
sequence of events or a detailed painstaking account, as by progressive
reconstruction of the atmosphere in which Hitler clung to his hopes and
Eisenhower reckoned his worries by passing days. As it emerges this truth
reduces the legends of the period to their true dimensions. The problem
is this: was Europe really on the verge of catastrophe in December 1944?
This is the question to which this book will attempt to provide an answer.

Chapter 1

'FATE LEAVES US NO CHOICE . . .'

WHEN Hitler looked at his situation map at the end of August 1944 all he could see were Allied offensives converging on Germany and sagging fronts with occasional gaps which had not been plugged in time. The Wehrmacht was withdrawing in sometimes more, sometimes less good order, in Poland, the Balkans, Italy and France; everywhere the Allied air forces were masters of the skies.

The Russians had launched their summer offensive on June 22. Two months later Marshal Koniev had captured Lwow and crossed the Vistula near Sandomierz, opening the way towards Cracow and Czechoslovakia. At Jassy-Kichinev Tolbukhin and Malinovsky had surrounded twenty-two German divisions with 3,500 guns and 33,000 vehicles; Friessner, commanding the German Army Group South Ukraine, had beaten a hasty retreat. Marshal Antonescu had been arrested and Rumania had changed sides; Bulgaria had declared war on the Reich. The Ploesti oil was gone. The Germans were shortly to be driven from the Balkans and the Soviet armies were on the point of gaining contact with Tito and his partisans. Budapest would soon be in the front line.

In the north the Russian offensive was moving with equal rapidity. Zhukov, Rokossovsky and Chernikovsky reached the borders of East Prussia in July, moved on to the Vistula and halted before Warsaw, where the heroic Polish rising took place. Finland sued for peace on September 4; the German forces in the Baltic area were cut off and annihilated in September and October.

The figures speak for themselves. Along the 1,250-mile front Germany had lost 916,000 men since June 1. Between January and September the number of German divisions had been halved, sinking from 257 to 137; they were faced by 400 Soviet divisions.*

A Month of Disaster in the West

On the western front the débâcle in France did not really begin until the end of July: on the 31st the Americans broke through the German front at Avranches, captured Rennes on August 4, Le Mans on the 9th and Nantes on the 10th. On August 16 the British broke through at Falaise. The Commander-in-Chief, Field-Marshal von Kluge, counter-attacked at Mortain and Domfront but both attacks failed and his forces were in danger of being surrounded. Without waiting for instructions from

---

* In December the ratio of forces on the Vistula front was 9 : 1 in infantry, 6 : 1 in armour, 10 : 1 in artillery and 15 : 1 in other arms.

Hitler he gave orders for withdrawal and then, on August 19, committed suicide. He was the third field-marshal in a month to fall victim to the battle in the West; Rommel had been severely wounded on July 27 and von Rundstedt had been dismissed. Twenty-three corps or divisional commanders had gone and a considerable number of army commanders had been killed or relieved of their commands. Dolmann, commanding Seventh Army, had been killed, Haussner had been wounded, Geyr von Schweppenburg had been 'summoned to Berlin', von Salmuth had been replaced by von Zarger in command of Fifteenth Army in the Pas-de-Calais, where, even at the end of July, Hitler was still expecting the 'real' Allied landing.

The Führer was looking for a man who could take the situation in hand. The July 20 plot had been engineered by officers and according to him it showed

how widespread was the poison in the ranks of the High Command. The field marshals and generals are traitors and they have placed their creatures throughout the signal service. How can I brief the generals commanding on the Western Front on my strategic plan when the information will have reached the Allies before the telegrams arrive in Paris?

Rommel, Rundstedt, Kluge—any one of them could be a traitor or at least have attempted treachery. Hitler put the question to Jodl and his staff on July 31. He was looking for a man.

I do not want any more generals chosen by seniority [he said]. Loyalty is the primary consideration, and the will to fight. I must have brave men; their rank does not matter. I do not want braggarts like the commander in Cherbourg, who say that they will fight to the end and then surrender. Let us have no more generals with handles to their names; they are the first to get themselves captured. Look at Tito. There's a man who has no military background but his determination to fight has earned him his rank of Field Marshal.

The man was found—Field-Marshal Walter Model. He had made a reputation for himself in Russia as a successful commander in defensive operations. Perhaps he would now be able to hold the Anglo-Americans, if not on the Seine, at least on the 1918 line. He was not one of those officers with 'a handle to their name', always ready to surrender. On the evening of July 20 he had been the first to reaffirm his loyalty to the regime. His officers disliked him for his brutality but his military talents were undoubted; the rank and file rather liked this foul-mouthed commander, apparently always in a rage, for he was invariably alongside his men in the most dangerous corners. His undoubted loyalty to Hitler allowed him to criticise and sometimes even to refuse to obey—something which no other general would have dared to do. In August 1943 he had beat a headlong retreat from the Orel salient in spite of the Führer's formal orders to the contrary transmitted to him on more than one occasion via Field-Marshal von Kluge.

And now it was Kluge whom Model replaced on August 17 as Commander-in-Chief West and Commander-in-Chief Army Group B.

Model wasted no time at Army Group B Headquarters at La Roche-Guyon. He had less than ten days to get such German forces as had escaped from the Falaise pocket back across the Seine. Allied fighters were flying up and down the river continuously, machine-gunning the disorganised convoys and even individual vehicles and groups of men. The German forces left in Normandy 240,000 dead and wounded, about the same number of prisoners and more than 2,000 of the 2,300 tanks engaged. In Provence the French First Army and the U.S. Seventh Army had landed and were moving up the valley of the Rhone at a speed calculated to cut off the retreat of the German forces tumbling back from south and south-west France.

The main line of defence had been laid out in 1943 by General Kitzinger; it ran roughly along the line of the First World War front from Abbeville to Besançon via Amiens, Soissons, Epernay, Chalons, Saint-Dizier, Chaumont, Langres and Gray. But if this line was to be occupied, the line of the Seine must be held for seven days and Model had hardly indicated his delaying positions before they were overrun by Allied armour. Paris was outflanked on the east and liberated on August 25.

Between the Seine and the main line of defence a position along the Somme and Oise from Neufchatel to Compiègne was to be held from August 31, but that very day Amiens was taken by the British, who charged on towards Antwerp, driving before them the remnants of Fifteenth Army, six divisions which had hardly fought at all.

During these last days of August Model and Blumentritt despatched numerous appeals for reinforcements to Hitler's headquarters. Their size shows the extent of the disaster; a complete Army had to be reconstituted. On August 24 they cabled: 'Send us reinforcements of at least 30–35 infantry divisions and 12 armoured divisions. The Allies have a total of 61 divisions, all motorised, and they are supported by 16,400 aircraft.'

Hitler's only answer was: 'Hold on where you are.' Model was losing control of his forces and on August 29 summarised the position as follows:

In the eleven armoured and motorised infantry divisions which fought in Normandy there are no more than five to six tanks on the road per division. Give me men and equipment to reconstitute at least eleven regiments. I can form four new formations out of my sixteen infantry divisions but the majority have lost their heavy equipment and the men have nothing but personal weapons. Close support artillery has been reduced to a few isolated guns; armoured divisions have in general only one battery. The men are demoralised by the continuous enemy air superiority. Finally there is no contact whatsoever between Army Groups B and G [in Southern France].

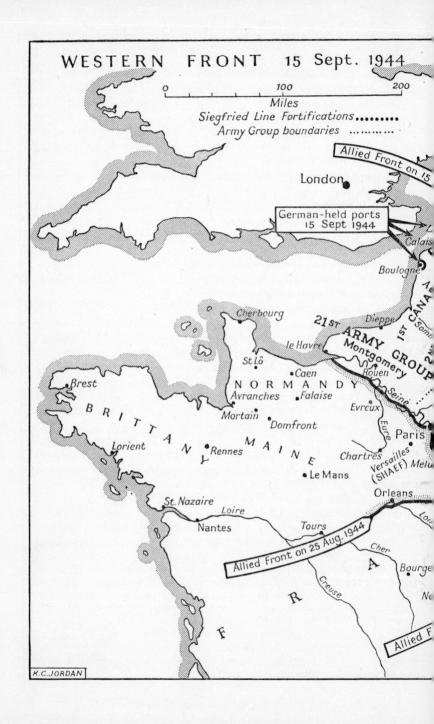

WESTERN FRONT 15 Sept. 1944

0   100   200
Miles
Siegfried Line Fortifications ....
Army Group boundaries ....

Allied Front on 15

London

German-held ports
15 Sept 1944

Calais

Boulogne

Cherbourg   Dieppe

21st   ARMY GROUP

le Havre   Montgomery

St Lô   Rouen

Brest   Caen   Seine

N O R M A N D Y

Avranches   Falaise

B R I T T A N Y   Mortain   Domfront   Evreux

Eure   Paris

Lorient   Rennes   M A I N E

Chartres

Versailles
(SHAEF) Melu

Le Mans

St. Nazaire   Orleans

Loire   Loi

Nantes   Tours

Allied Front on 25 Aug. 1944   Cher

F   R   A   Bourge

Creuse   Ne

F   Allied F

K.C.JORDAN

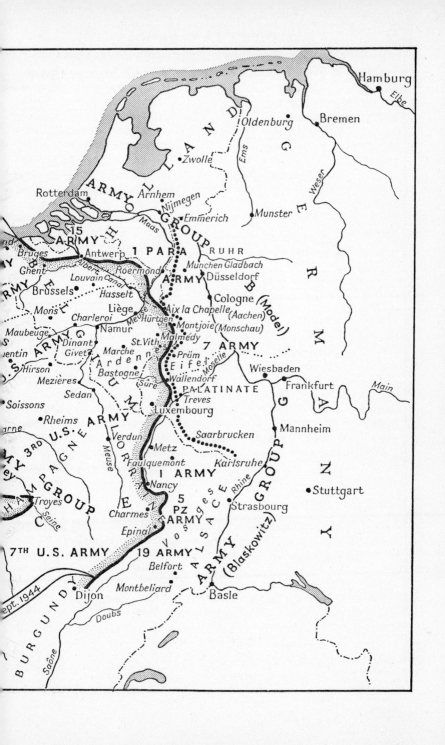

On the borders of Champagne and Burgundy road blocks manned by
Feldgendarmerie and Waffen SS detachments sifted the fugitives and
passed them on to Re-organisation Centres. Divisional artillery was reconstituted by requisitioning farm tractors and anti-tank guns. As for the
Luftwaffe, it was now providing no more than 400 sorties per day, too
dispersed to be effective. Eight hundred aircraft had been sent as reinforcements to the west during August but only 200 managed to get back into
Germany at the beginning of September. The rest were captured on the
ground or failed to return. General Galland, commanding the German
Fighter Force on the western front at this period, later said: 'We were not
beaten in the air but disorganised on the ground, like the French Air
Force in 1940.' Echoing Field-Marshal Model's calls for help, an artillery-
man wrote home: 'I won't stay very long. I really don't know what we are
still fighting for. Very soon I shall run over to the Tommies, if I am not
killed before I get there.'*

On September 4 Model at last announced that he could 'hold the line
Antwerp–Albert Canal–Meuse–Siegfried Line'. But he required 'at least
twenty-five fresh infantry divisions and five or six armoured divisions';
his present fighting strength was no more than ten infantry divisions and
about four armoured divisions'.

Germany's enemies were driving forward on all fronts and it seemed
that the Reich itself would be invaded in a matter of weeks. People asked
themselves whether Hitler would attempt to avert invasion as Ludendorff
and Hindenburg had done in 1918. Perhaps he would sound out each of
the Allies separately in the hope of discovering a crack in the front;
perhaps he would exploit the differences of view between Roosevelt, Stalin
and Churchill. Concocters of diplomatic plans were buzzing round him.

But Hitler lived in a dream. He was obsessed by historical precedents.
He thought only of the 'magnificent opportunity offered him by the coming
winter with its fog, long nights and snow'.†

Hitler in Summer 1944

On July 31 the Führer stated: 'The problem facing Germany is a moral
and not a material one. There can be no question of discussion with any
of the Reich's enemies. This war will not be concluded by negotiations or
tactical manœuvres. It is a struggle to the death, in which one of the
combatants must go under without trace.'

The same day Hitler had given General Warlimont, Jodl's deputy,
orders for transmission to Field-Marshal von Kluge; they laid down that
there should be 'garrisons in the main ports under carefully selected
commanders determined to hold out to the end'.

'I cannot yet tell how the dice will fall,' Hitler had concluded.

* Shulman, *German Defeat in the West*, p. 175.
† See *Hitlers Lagebesprechungen*, Fragment 43, September 1 1944.

The remark was significant: the Allied onslaught was only just beginning and it proved to be unexpectedly violent; yet Hitler only agreed to withdrawal in order to prepare for a long-term offensive rebound. This was therefore the background to the plans for withdrawal and to the establishment of the blocking line upon which Kluge was to hold with 'fanatical determination'; he was also to refuse to be drawn into a war of movement in which Allied air action would increase the Wehrmacht's difficulties.

It seems incredible that Hitler could have counted upon so spectacular a change in the situation. There can be no logical military or political explanation. Perhaps the truth lies in his Jekyll and Hyde personality.

When Hitler was giving his directives to Jodl or Warlimont he was the war lord, the Feldherr. He may have been a self-taught strategist who wasted his own and other people's energies and stifled all independent thought, but he spoke with the authority of a Commander-in-Chief who sometimes had a flash of genius and who was struggling to preserve anything which could be saved from the wreckage; he would go to any lengths to recover the initiative.

But suddenly at the turn of a phrase he would turn into the unbalanced mystic, the believer in myths, a frenzied incomprehensible being. He would become the prophet carried away by his 'mission', all the more dictatorial since the failure of the July 20 plot to bring that mission to an end. Roosevelt too had a habit of calling upon Providence, but Hitler's 'Providence' was something very different. In his case Providence was the evil spirit of that twilight of the gods towards which his colossal gamble was moving. His future was a dream world, real only to him.

'If the German people are to be defeated in this struggle it will be because the people have been found incapable of withstanding the test of history. It will be ripe for destruction.' Thus Hitler to his Gauleiters: at the same time he was preparing the orders which were to set the seal on this destruction.

On the face of it, these apocalyptic hallucinations are hardly compatible with an urge to resume brilliant offensive operations in the west. What did he really believe the future held in store—victory in the field or collapse? His attitude seemed to be governed partly by illusion, partly by ignorance and partly by hatred of his sceptical general staff advisers; there is no knowing which was the dominant factor. At this period, the influence of the party old guard—the original members—was predominant, and for them there could be no retreat from the great adventure. They had been gambling ever since 1933 and this time were prepared to throw double or quits.

The explanation of Hitler's pathological reactions may be far simpler —his premature physical deterioration. He was only fifty-five, but all those who had dealings with him during the summer of 1944 agreed with Skorzeny that he had become 'an old man'. The bomb of July 20 had only

given him superficial injuries: damage to both ear drums, certain distur-
bance of the circulation and a subcutaneous hæmorrhage in the right arm.
Those had soon healed. Basically Hitler's decrepitude stemmed from the
abnormal existence which he had been leading since the outbreak of the war
and the unsuitable remedies prescribed for him by his friend Dr Morell.

The Führer's appearance shocked those who had not seen him for some
time. His left arm continually twitched and could only be restrained by
his gripping it with his right hand. He walked in a slumped posture, almost
shuffling. Even if he appeared to be listening, no one could be sure that
he had heard what had been said, for he was now extremely deaf, at least
in his right ear.

He was having hormone injections, which had become as indispensable
to him as a drug; they produced in him a state of raging excitation. While
in these trances he would prophesy the advent of an irreparable catastrophe
for Germany and with her the entire world. Then the drug would cease to
act. Hitler would appear to be clear in his mind but was in fact prostrate,
far away, taking in so little of what went on around him that he would
greet even the best known members of his own staff several times over
as if they were strangers. Goebbels himself admitted that any serious
conversation with the Führer was becoming increasingly difficult. Sometimes he was not listening because his mind was just drifting, not even
apparently occupied with daydreams of his own; alternatively he was
carried away by his visions and would talk without drawing breath: he
would conjure up pictures of the fall of the Roman Empire, one of his
favourite themes; he would discuss the supply problem, give orders about
dog breeding and launch himself into furious tirades against his oldest
friends.

When he ran out of breath he would hark back to his favourite story:
that of Frederick the Great and how he had been saved by a series of
miracles. Though he remembered only superficial incidents in the story
Hitler likened himself to this legendary hero.

'The longer I study men the more I like dogs,' Frederick is supposed
to have said. This was Hitler's pet remark; he was only genuinely attached
to one living thing, his bitch, Blondi, a shy, savage alsatian. That summer
she had puppies and Hitler looked after them. Blondi loved no one but
her master; she would growl and bark when anyone else came near. One
day when she was disobedient Hitler said bitterly: 'You too, Blondi! You
are like the Generals; you are betraying me.'

Hitler was suffering from continual spasms of pain and cramp in his
stomach, with resulting bouts of giddiness. He shunned all social life;
he literally went to ground. Wolfschanze, the 'wolf's lair', his East Prussia
headquarters, was in a forest near Rastenburg. It consisted of two enclosures
of 'bunkers' (concrete shelters) and huts; one was for the members of the
staff; the other was protected by barbed wire, an embankment and a stake

fence and was closely guarded by the SS. Apart from Jodl and Keitel, who lived and worked there, Warlimont was the only member of the military staff who had regular access to it. In the centre of this camp was another enclosure equally closely guarded; there Hitler lived with one or two faithful followers of whose devotion he was certain. Jodl said at Nuremberg: 'The Führer's Headquarters was a cross between a monastery and a concentration camp.'

Hitler spent his days in a concrete bunker with a 20-foot-thick roof. It was a hermetically sealed box with no window and no outlet to the open air. The air pressure was kept artificially high and it was lit twenty-four hours a day by electricity. The surrounding marshy area together with the half dried concrete produced a damp atmosphere which his entourage found trying. But if those around him protested, Hitler would reply: 'Your wooden huts would not stand up to any form of air bombing. I have no wish to live in them.'

Yet the Führer was only alive because the bomb of July 20 had exploded in one of these huts, where a briefing conference was being held. Had it happened in one of the concrete bunkers none of those present could have survived.

Hitler loved to dilate upon the advantages of a 'natural existence', but he followed no such rule himself. The only one who found it possible to conform to his peculiar timetable was Martin Bormann, the head of the Party Chancellery; he was a late arrival on the scene of the Third Reich but he was now always on hand in an attempt to fulfil his ambition to be the controller of the 'machine'. Hitler did not get up until after 11.0 a.m.; his 'briefing conference' was held in mid-afternoon and at 5.0 p.m. he took a siesta; then began the interminable evening sessions which left his entourage exhausted. At midnight came the 'evening' briefing conference followed by an endless vigil drinking tea and talking spasmodically; eventually in the small hours the Führer would go to bed. He ate little and alone; he never forgot to take his castor oil.

During his leisure moments he read Carlyle and his tales of great men. He would receive Professor Giesler, who would submit to him plans for the rebuilding of Linz, intended as the great artistic metropolis of post-war central Europe. The architect in him would come to life again and the statesman would begin to daydream about his retirement. His associates, however, no longer talked about their retirement; perhaps it was their age —and perhaps it was some vague hope of withdrawing discreetly from the party without attracting attention. Hitler himself was tired of the life which he was leading. On August 31 he said to Generals Westphal and Krebs, who were leaving for the western front:

You realise that this war is no fun for me. I've been cut off from the world for five years. I've not been to a theatre, a concert or a film. I devote my life to the single task of running the war, because I know that if there's not an iron

c

will behind it the battle cannot be won. I blame the general staff for under-
mining the morale of officers who've come here from the front; and when the
staff visit the front it is only to spread their pessimism there.*

The autumn came. Martin Bormann returned to the charge daily in
his attempt to persuade Hitler to take some ten days' holiday in the Ober-
salzberg. The eastern front began to move once more. By October the
Russians were in Augustov, only fifty miles from Wolfschanze. Gun flashes
could be seen in the south-east each evening. Common sense and Hitler's
health both indicated a move to Bavaria.

Hitler's answer was:

I shall not go under any circumstances. My presence is necessary to re-
assure the inhabitants of East Prussia and bolster the morale of the troops.
If I were not there many officers would tend to give up ground too easily.
Once in the Berghof my staff and the headquarters officers would get their
wives along. The effect on the population would be disastrous. I shall only
leave Rastenburg if forced to do so by the military situation.

The whole of Germany lay between Hitler and the western front where
he was proposing to seize the initiative. This clearly did not help the
conduct of operations, but a morbid pre-occupation with his own security
led him to disregard this problem. On the evening of September 17 he
said to Keitel and Jodl: 'We must take these things seriously. We should
not forget that the vile July 20 business might restart ... now here we
have only one SS battalion, responsible to the Reichsführer [Himmler],
and one police battalion. That's all, isn't it?'

Keitel agreed.

Hitler went on:

It is a daunting prospect and we must realise what is at stake: if some
abominable coup should take place ... here am I, here is my entire staff,
here is the Reichsmarschall [Göring], the staff of the Armed Forces, the
Reichsführer, the Minister of Foreign Affairs. What a haul that would be!
It would be worth doing, wouldn't it? If I could sweep up all the Russian
leaders at one stroke I would not hesitate to risk two parachute divisions.

Without even leaving his audience time to register their agreement
Hitler continued:

We must be extremely careful. Suppose someone does the dirty on us. It
would be no good saying afterwards: we suspected it; we knew about it. We
must not take the information we are getting too complacently. It is worth
thinking about. [On July 20] the enemy announced what was going to happen.
In retrospect it all seems like a fairytale. But the enemy was saying to himself:
All is well; we have found the man we want at headquarters. No need to
worry; the Germans will do what is necessary to get rid of the Führer!

* *Hitler's Lagebesprechungen*, Fragment 46.

Obviously such base creatures do exist. And what the enemy is saying now makes one think they have discovered another one . . . our security depends entirely upon the number of men guarding us.*

Hitler's own experience of *coups de main* only increased his obsession. After all, he had contrived to rescue Mussolini.

A number of factors therefore led Hitler to shut himself off from the outside world: his physical deterioration, the mental shock of his officers' treachery, mortal fear of being kidnapped. So his behaviour was the exact opposite of that of the born demagogue: he shunned his people; he gave them no opportunity to express confidence in him or admiration for him; he behaved as if secretly he feared that they might suddenly rise in anger against him. Goebbels and Bormann returned to the charge daily, trying to extract from him some word or gesture to make headlines in the press; but in vain. The Minister of Propaganda was furious to discover, for instance, that over a period of two days the name Hitler appeared in the German press six times, whereas those of Churchill and Roosevelt were mentioned one hundred and four times.

'I shall not speak unless I can announce a military victory,' was Hitler's reply to their objurgations. 'Any speech by me would be depressing unless it had some glorious theme.'

Goebbels was at a loss, saying to his secretary: 'It would not be surprising if the people end by thinking that Hitler is no longer of any political or military importance, that he is an outmoded figure to whom they owe loyalty merely out of habit or long standing affection but who is no longer an object of respect.'

Goebbels' Great Opportunity and the Compromise Peace

Goebbels' complaints may well have stemmed simply from opportunism, from his chagrin at finding that one of the essential ingredients of his hold over the German masses had gone. But the fact that his Führer remained silent did not prevent Goebbels from producing in his weekly article in *Das Reich* apocalyptic prophecies ranging from a dramatic reversal of the fortunes of war to the subordination of Europe to Stalin.

Hitler was now becoming increasingly incapable of imposing his authority on his old cronies and Josef Goebbels no longer believed in him. The Propaganda Minister had shown up well at the time of the coup of July 20. As Gauleiter of Prussia he was the only man in Berlin; he was the only one of the great men of the regime who did not rush off to Rastenburg on the evening of the drama which might have been the end of them all, to assure Hitler of their horror and devotion. Goebbels had not lost his head; he had summoned Major Remer, commander of the Guard Battalion, and had put him into direct touch with Hitler by telephone; then he had

---

* *Hitler's Lagebesprechungen*, unnumbered fragment, September 17.

directed the suppression of the coup. During the decisive hours when the success or failure of the rising was balanced on a knife edge, Goebbels had saved Hitler.

On July 25 Goebbels was nominated 'Reich Plenipotentiary for total war', on the pretext that 'all aspects of public life must be adapted to the requirements of total war in all fields'. His appointment meant that he now had authority in certain matters hitherto the responsibility of Göring. At the same time Himmler took over command of the Home Army in addition to his responsibilities as Minister of the Interior, Chief of Police and Reichsführer SS. The old rivalry between the three men took on new proportions; it did not help preparations for the decisive offensive in the west.

In Goebbels' view total war meant that he should exercise control over commanders and over the supply of men and material to the front; it also meant that he was entitled to intervene directly in the diplomatic field. On August 24 he announced the closure of all theatres and cinemas, a ban on concerts, the introduction of a sixty-hour working week in offices and the cancellation of all holidays. He promised Hitler that he would raise a million men in three months. But he then found himself engaged in a time-wasting battle against actors, who showed a certain reluctance to pay their official homage to the Führer on Goebbels' instructions. One of them wrote: 'I believe in Hitler as firmly as I believe in victory.' It was difficult to take action against so ambiguous a remark. It was equally difficult to punish the popular actor Hans Albers when he was caught selling French brandy at 300 marks a bottle, or the comedy actress Jenny Jugo when she was discovered to have a secret food store.

Settling these trivial details counted for much with Goebbels. In the midst of dealing with them he launched a new campaign to gain control of foreign policy, which he had been trying to wrest from Ribbentrop ever since 1938. In view of the German defeats on the Russian front of autumn 1943 Ribbentrop had been inclined to put out feelers to Stalin to discover what his price would be for an armistice. His pathological hatred for Great Britain had led him to make the same proposal when the Allies landed in North Africa. At the end of 1942 he had urged: 'We must open conversations with Madame Kolontay the Soviet Ambassador in Stockholm. Germany must declare herself ready to abandon her conquests in Eastern Europe as the price of peace in the East.' Ribbentrop returned to the charge after Stalingrad. Hitler's answer was, 'later, after we have scored a decisive success', but he allowed his Foreign Minister to maintain contact in Stockholm via the diplomat Peter Kleist. On August 30 1943, however, when another note from Ribbentrop appeared, Hitler categorically refused any further attempt at contact. Stalin, in his view, was not sincere; he would merely use these conversations to intimidate his British and American allies and force them to open the second front. Nevertheless, however much talk there may have been about war to the death, the dilemma was clear: in the summer of 1944 Germany could only hope for a victorious conclusion to the war if fighting could be brought to an end on one or other of the two fronts. Negotiations were therefore essential. They could be undertaken with the Western Powers, with the object of forming common cause against the Soviet Union and driving the Red Army back into Asia as the Reichswehr had wished to do in 1919. Alternatively Germany could negotiate with the Russians, drive the Anglo-American forces back to the Atlantic coast and then partition the Continent on the lines of the German–Soviet pact of August 1939. The conspirators of July 20, officers or diplomats who had joined the Nazi Party only as a matter of form or who had gradually drifted away from it, had counted upon the first solution; they took it as a foregone conclusion that their supposed future ally was simply waiting for a proposal of this sort. At the root of the other scheme lay the tendency to 'National Bolshevism', not so far removed from the standard 'National Socialism'. In addition it would give Germany the satisfaction of making fools of the Anglo-Americans and a perverted pleasure in pursuing an all-or-nothing policy: a Nazi Europe or a Communist Europe.

'Having gone to war in order to prevent the German armies establishing themselves on the shores of the Atlantic, the British will be taken aback to find Soviet forces there when the conflict ends,' Hitler remarked one day during the winter of 1944–5.

Goebbels, for his part, had always been inclined this way. On April 12 1944 he wrote a memorandum which Martin Bormann intercepted before it reached Hitler. Goebbels considered that it was 'vital to bring the war to an end as quickly as possible on one front or the other'. He therefore advocated an attempt at negotiation, for 'the Western powers will never agree to bring the war in the west to an end and leave us free to strike at the Soviet Union'. Stalin's attitude, however, he considered was anti-British and anti-American. It should therefore not be impossible to make common cause with him against the Western Powers.

To demonstrate Germany's goodwill our negotiators should be able to suggest the extension of the Soviet sphere of influence to cover Rumania, Greece, Bulgaria, Finland and Northern Norway, and Russian absorption of the Baltic States and annexation of the Government General of Poland as far West as the Warta. This would in fact be far more than Molotov had asked for in Berlin in November 1940.

On September 2 1944, when General Oshima, the Japanese ambassador, called on Goebbels to suggest the resurrection of a Berlin–Moscow–Tokyo alliance, Goebbels said: 'The Reich should offer Stalin the Dardanelles, Persia and India.' Oshima replied: 'The Kremlin is not altogether opposed, but before there is any question of an alliance there must be an armistice and peace must be concluded. Japan would willingly act as mediator.'

Stalin was playing this byzantine game with caution. He told the German negotiators in Stockholm: 'Take care; the Japanese are out for themselves and have no wish to be drawn into a war against the U.S.S.R. In fact they have only one object: to ensure that the German and Soviet armies pin each other down as long as possible.'

Goebbels had no inkling that the Japanese were playing a double game. When Oshima left him he dictated a report to Hitler which was nothing less than a plan for a complete reversal of Germany's alliances.*

Its conclusions speak for themselves:

If the situation developed on the lines I have indicated, we should still have certain important trumps in our hand which we could put in the scales without seriously jeopardising the triumph of our cause in the East, which would remain a great accomplishment, unique in history. The German people would greet a change of this nature in the conduct of the war with profound satisfaction. We should be able to gain space for ourselves in the West, and the Anglo-Americans would not hold out for long against the pressure of the new situation. Of course we could not expect from this the victory we dreamed of in 1941 but it would nevertheless be the greatest victory in German history . . . The danger from the East would not disappear altogether but we should be well equipped to face the future . . . We should be abreast of the situation once more. We should breathe freely again; we should be able to go forward, reorganise ourselves and, if need be, strike blows which would be decisive for the outcome of the war.

Ribbentrop was clearly the last man capable of carrying through such an adroit and promising scheme; Goebbels wrote of him:

He will not take advice; he is too conceited even to listen. He is at odds with everybody and the obstinacy upon which he prides himself so frequently means that he has not the necessary flexibility of mind. He considers foreign policy a secret science of which he alone possesses the secret; whenever he condescends to lift the veil, all he does is to produce a second rate leading article.†

Goebbels then painted a picture of the ideal diplomat capable of making

* I found a French translation of this report in the French Army Historical Section. It is undated and I have found no trace of the original German, although this must certainly exist. There seems no doubt that it is authentic. Goebbels suggests that Japan's good offices should be used and this seems to justify relating it to Oshima's visit and dating it in the first few days of September 1944.

M. Maxime Mourin in his book *Les Tentatives de Paix dans la Seconde Guerre Mondiale* gives an exact date, December 21. Without further confirmation this seems improbable. On p. 208 et seq. M. Mourin quotes the report from a copy published in the newspaper *La Presse*.

† At this same period Ribbentrop summoned Schellenberg, the head of the Secret Service, who held high rank in the SS, and ordered him to act upon an idea which Ribbentrop ascribed to Hitler—the assassination of Stalin by a visitor armed with a pistol disguised as a fountain pen! The scheme was never pursued. See *The Schellenberg Memoirs*, pp. 424–5.

the running either with the East or with the West; it was not difficult to guess whom he meant:

> We must have a Foreign Minister possessed of intelligence and flexibility together with energy and tenacity. He should get unambiguous war directives from you, my Führer, and he would then get to work. It would be his duty to dissect the patent disagreements now dividing the enemy camp, exploit them and draw the maximum advantage from them. His aim, which he must pursue pertinaciously, must be to break up the enemy coalition. If he does not succeed at once he must try again. He should be given time to set out his pieces on the chessboard of war. He should have a good staff who know how to speak and persuade. He should weed the defeatists out of the Ministry of Foreign Affairs and so give German foreign policy a sound basis once more. In my opinion it would be no miracle if he succeeded; the miracle would be if he did not succeed.

Lucid though this may appear, its general theme shows that Goebbels was totally ignorant of the true relationship between the Allies. It is true that, at any rate between Churchill and Stalin, there was an underlying mistrust, but this did not prevent both being equally determined to pursue the war against Germany to the end. Goebbels' reasoning was based entirely upon the idea that at this stage of the war Stalin would be interested in reversing the system of alliances. This was a totally unrealistic notion, for in September 1944 the Soviet Union already knew that by carrying on the war she could count, not only on crushing Germany, but also on territorial and political gains out of all proportion to those which the Reich could offer.

Nevertheless some of the problems worrying Hitler were based on the same line of thought as that of Goebbels; time had to be bought and the best use made of it; some local success had to be gained; the British and Americans must first be defeated, but it must never be forgotten that even if hostilities against Russia had to be temporarily suspended, the great reckoning 'with the East' was still to come. In Hitler's eyes, however, Goebbels' scepticism vitiated his reasoning. Goebbels apparently did not believe that the forthcoming 'great blow' promised by Himmler was possible.

Goebbels' memorandum, however, fitted into the zig-zag pattern of Hitler's thinking. Irascible, prone to frenzies of prophecy and taking a morbid pleasure in the unparalleled disasters which he foresaw, Hitler was a master of the art of leaving each one of his advisers thinking that he might agree with him. He was well aware that all leading circles in the Reich thought that the sands had run out. So while continuing to issue orders for new total war measures, Hitler spread soothing rumours: Japan was going to act as intermediary; German diplomats were in touch with the American Government; the ex-Soviet ambassador in Berlin had moved to Stockholm to take up his secret contacts again.

None of this was complete untruth but Hitler made use of these manœuvres as camouflage and bait. At the Nuremberg trial Albert Speer,
Hitler's Minister for Production and Armaments, said:

... Hitler deceived all of us ... He raised hopes that, like Japan, we would
start negotiations in this hopeless situation so that the people would be saved
from the worst consequences. To do this however it was necessary to stiffen
resistance as much as possible. He deceived all of us by holding out to the
military leaders false hopes in the success of diplomatic steps and by promising the political leaders fresh victories through the use of new troops and
new weapons and by systematically spreading rumours to encourage the
people to believe in the appearance of a miracle weapon—all for the purpose
of keeping up resistance.*

The question is whether Hitler was himself clear on what he wanted or
what he could achieve. He was continually shifting his ground and so
continually contradicting himself.

He explained his views on August 31 1944, when he spoke to Generals
Krebs and Westphal before their departure for the western front to help
Model get the situation under control. He blamed the conspirators of
July 20 for thinking that the war could be ended as a result of disagreements between the Allies: 'Some of them thought they could side with
the English against the Russians; others, like Schulenburg [ex-German
ambassador in Moscow], thought they could ally with the Russians against
the English; others—fools!—that they could play off one against the
other. Too naïve altogether! That sort of thing only happens in a Western
thriller.'

Then, without drawing breath, Hitler put forward as his own the theory
he had just been condemning:

The time is not ripe for a political decision. I think during my life I have
given adequate proof that I can win political victories. I don't need to tell
anybody that I wouldn't miss an opportunity to do so. But of course it's
childish and naïve to hope that at a time of severe military defeats a favourable
political moment will arrive. ... The moment will arrive when disagreements
between the allies have become so great that the break will come. Coalitions
have always failed right throughout history. ... I intend to carry on the
fight until there is a prospect of a peace that is reasonable, of a peace tolerable
for Germany which will safeguard the existence of this and future generations.
Then I will sign it.

There was little likelihood of this sort of peace emerging from a compromise. In any case Hitler was no longer in a state of mind to scheme
in an attempt to achieve a position of strength, meanwhile working out
some acceptable basis of negotiation. On September 13 he ordered the
formation of Sixth Panzer Army which was to strike the 'decisive blow'

* *IMT*, Vol. XVI, p. 485.

in the west and so create this position of strength. But at the same time he issued the 'scorched earth order' (he was to repeat it in March 1945 in order to face the victors with a vacuum) which hardly accorded with any intention to negotiate. As a precaution, all industrial installations, power stations and communications in territory still occupied were to be destroyed, as also in the German provinces threatened by invasion, such as 'Alsace-Lorraine', Bohemia and Moravia, Austria and Upper Silesia.*

This monstrous idea, recalling the most hideous catastrophes of history, the crash of empires and the sweep of irresistible invasions, was suggested to Hitler by Bormann, Ley and Goebbels. Germany and Europe were to go down with the Führer and the Party!

To counter this, the moderates, such as Alfred Speer, were forced to encourage Hitler in his determination to strike a 'decisive blow' in the west, recapturing territory which would be of use and not a desert. It was the only argument which they could advance against the 'scorched earth order'. If the great blow failed the inevitable sequel would be chaos and the final ghastly apotheosis, the final scene which in fact took place in the ruins of Berlin at the end of April 1945, though without the Wagnerian splendour of which Hitler had dreamed.

Hitler did not consult his military advisers on subjects such as this, but they were his most ardent supporters in his determination to carry on the struggle. Keitel and Jodl were his blindly obedient executive officers; they were clear-thinking, at any rate in Jodl's case, and acquiescent. They had obeyed Hitler without question for too long now for any thought of rebellion to enter their heads. The remaining officers had been discouraged by the failure of the July 20 coup but they were loyal to their country and had sworn allegiance to the head of state; so they had no choice. Even the most famous of them were prepared to submit to anything, including the humiliating necessity of giving the Hitler salute and the shame of the 'court of honour' at which Rundstedt, Guderian, Jodl and Keitel together with certain other well-known officers were compelled to cashier fellow officers who were implicated in the plot and hand them over to the 'people's tribunal'.

The 'court of honour' sat four times between August 4 and September 15. None of the accused appeared before it; simply on the basis of legal documents it cashiered fifty-five officers, including Field-Marshal von Witzleben, and nine generals, in some cases posthumously.

In spite of all their feelings and in spite of their conviction that the war would end in November, the officer corps from the highest to the lowest refused to embark upon further political adventures. At the Nuremberg trial it was said:

'Certain of the younger members of the officer corps had begun to have

* On this subject see Speer's explanations at the Nuremberg trial, *IMT*, Vol. XVI, pp. 487–8, and the document *Speer-18*.

their doubts. But it was too late. The fate facing Germany in the event of capitulation left the soldiers no other course but to do their duty to the end. In any case theirs was not the decision whether to lay down their arms.'*

This statement sums up the testimony given at Nuremberg by officers representative of different shades of opinion in the Wehrmacht: Field-Marshal von Brauchitsch, who had retired at his own request at the end of 1941, General Halder, who had been dismissed in 1942, Field-Marshal von Manstein, General Warlimont, deputy to Jodl in Hitler's headquarters, and General Westphal, Chief of Staff to Rundstedt on the western front.

The military were resigned. Hitler and the party leaders were intoxicated by their own slogans: 'This is no time for half-heartedness. . . . Willy-nilly we must risk the great adventure and stake double or quits. . . . Desperate situations require desperate remedies'—so Frederick the Great is supposed to have said during the Seven Years War.

So the Ardennes falls into place: it was a desperate remedy, the last throw of the gambler who had lost his all.

* *IMT*, Document *PS 3798* (not in official record).

Chapter 2

THE SPECTRE OF
MISSED OPPORTUNITIES

IN September the Führer gave General Guderian, the new Chief of Staff, a general outline of his plans: there was to be an offensive in the west; it was to take place as soon as possible, so that once a decisive defeat had been inflicted on the Allies the troops involved could be transferred to the Russian front before the frost set in. The move from west to east was to take place at the latest by mid-December. The weather forecast was that the autumn would be prolonged and the Russian offensive, which would not occur before the ground had been hardened by frost, would not therefore come before the New Year.

The reader may well wonder why Hitler decided to initiate a war of movement in a mountainous forested area like the Ardennes during the autumn mud and rains and using hastily reconstituted armoured formations whose fighting efficiency was therefore inevitably questionable. After all, during the summer when the Caen plain had offered an ideal opportunity for armoured operations, Hitler had insisted upon a static defence in which the German armour had frittered away the best of its equipment without achieving anything except to hand the initiative to the enemy.

Old Comrades' Dreams

Hitler's decision bore no relation to the time-honoured rules of strategy. He brushed aside all commonsense objections and based his decision on instinct, his own memories of his soldiering days and an obsession about history repeating itself.

Mein Kampf contains a significant passage in this connection:

It was my luck to be in the first two and the last offensives [of 1918]. They made on me the most tremendous impressions of my whole life; tremendous because for the last time the struggle lost its defensive character and became an offensive as it was in 1914. In the German army's trenches and mine galleries men breathed anew when, after three years of hell, the day for squaring the account at last arrived. . . . For the last time the goodness of God smiled upon his ungrateful children.*

Hitler was always influenced by his old comrade's memories; they were at the basis of much of his sentimentality. The call to 'turn to politics'

* *Mein Kampf*, vol. I, Ch. 7, p. 89. (James Murphy's translation—abridged edition.)

which came to him after the November 11 1918 armistice was similarly in-spired. Throughout the Second World War his disconnected monologues were full of reminiscences of his time as a corporal in the Sixteenth Bavarian Infantry Regiment. He had made no effort to get to know modern conditions of warfare—he had hardly ever been seen at the front. He issued a stream of orders to hold on at all costs even against crushing enemy superiority. He seemed to think that he was commanding the Imperial Army which had fought in Champagne, on the Somme and in Artois. He was a believer in the overriding importance of 'fire power' and set little store by movement.

In November 1944, referring to the Russian front, he said: 'Our losses have been small because we have been holding on where we were. Our greatest losses always occur during these "glorious retreats" which we make in order to regain freedom of manœuvre.'

When Jodl was reporting to him on the fighting in the Aachen salient Hitler asked: 'What was the average width of front held by a division at Verdun?'

Yet this obsession with 'attrition' was pushed completely into the back-ground by the plan for the western offensive. Position warfare was becom-ing almost an article of faith and yet this was the moment chosen by Hitler to launch his armies into an offensive adventure. One wonders why.

Once more the Führer was harking back to the Great War; he wanted a modern version of the March 1918 offensive. His generals were pre-occupied with the existing problem, the war on two fronts. Hitler, however, seemed to think that the relative inaction of the Soviet forces during 1944 had produced a situation similar to that following the treaty of Brest–Litovsk which had left Hindenburg and Ludendorff free to act in France.

The German offensive of the spring of 1918 had been aimed at Amiens as a focal point in the communications between the British and French armies; its main weight had been directed against their point of junction. In 1944 Hitler's objective was Antwerp and he meant to reach it by attack-ing along the dividing line between Bradley's American army and Montgomery's British army. In both cases the object was the same—to seize one of the enemy's vital points, split his front in two and reach the sea, at the same time surrounding the British in a new Dunkirk pocket.

In 1918 Ludendorff had kept his main attacking force and his reserve divisions in the centre, in the area of Maubeuge–Hirson–Mezières, in order to keep Foch guessing until the last moment whether they would attack in Champagne, Artois or in Flanders. They moved up only by night. The final positions were occupied only the day before the attack. All the well-worn security precautions were repeated in the Ardennes operation. Even the Gotha raids on Paris and the firing of 'Big Bertha' were reproduced in the form of the V1 and V2 attacks on Antwerp, London and Brussels.

The directives of December 1944 are reminiscent of those of March 1918: the initial tactical victory was to pave the way for a strategic victory, the recipe given by Ludendorff in his memoirs. Ludendorff had launched forty divisions against twenty-one British. Hitler used thirty against four American. Even by scraping the barrel, however, Hitler could not produce the 100,000 men whom Ludendorff had in reserve. Moreover to Amiens from Saint-Quentin, the starting point for the Somme offensive, the Kaiser's army only had to cover forty miles of comparatively favourable country, whereas to reach Antwerp the Führer's armour had first to cross the Meuse and then cover more than another hundred miles.

Finally in 1918 a German victory might perhaps have led to a freely negotiated peace. In 1944 there was little likelihood that the offensive could lead to a military decision which would pave the way for negotiation. In both cases, however, propaganda managed to convince people that large-scale action might lead to a spectacular reversal of the situation.

Allied commentators were at first hesitant to draw comparisons, but references to the March 1918 offensive appeared during the very first days of the Ardennes operations. General Blumentritt, Rundstedt's Chief of Staff and later his biographer, was right when he wrote: 'When the documents of this period are carefully studied and this bitter struggle between Hitler and Rundstedt is revealed in full, it seems likely that Hitler will be seen to have been thinking in terms of the great March offensive of 1918 in the First World War.'

A Political Offensive

This was therefore the great missed opportunity, the memory of which haunted Hitler. The July 20 plot had spurred him on to look for another opportunity and he was determined not to let it slip. He had promised himself that as soon as he could he would force the officers into line. By an odd process of reasoning he likened them to the civilians who had 'stabbed the Kaiser's army in the back' in 1918. It was clear who the external enemy was; now the internal enemy who had been plotting the overthrow of the regime ever since 1933 and had been sabotaging the war effort, was now to be dramatically unmasked. His object in fact was to set the seal on the National Socialist revolution. The conscription of further classes would bring new blood into the army. Himmler would take care of that, and the Ardennes would be the baptism of fire for this new generation of soldiers whose pride would be their loyalty to the Führer.

Himmler had been given command of the Home Army on July 21, the day after the plot. He had raised forty-three divisions and he kept control of them until the moment they reached the front. The Gauleiters, the heads of the National Socialist party administrative districts, had been instructed to assist him in the creation of a National Socialist army. The Reichsführer SS had long dreamed of being the head of such a force.

Himmler had assisted in the liquidation of Röhm whose aim had been exactly the same—to Nazify the army through the SA; but he had then gone on to set up SS fighting units, the Waffen SS. Though the general staff of the Wehrmacht had incorporated them into regular formations for the 1940 campaign, Himmler had snatched them back again and in 1941 obtained the agreement of Hitler to their development and organisation into divisions. Recruitment for them expanded and the 'racial criteria' demanded for acceptance were relaxed. The Waffen SS then began to take in recruits other than volunteers, chosen from the cream of the army. The cadres transferred from the Wehrmacht to the Waffen SS were in many cases good trainers but were not outstanding soldiers; tactically the junior officers were mediocre. The result was that Hitler's desire to have his élite troops used in the greatest danger spots decimated these formations. They were continually having to be refilled.

The best supplies of winter clothing and the latest equipment were always allocated direct to the Waffen SS but on many occasions the normal army infantry units following on behind them had to make good their errors. The army hated this praetorian guard as much as Himmler hated generals.

In the atmosphere engendered by the failure of the July 20 coup the lukewarm, the hesitant and the outright anti-Nazis among the 60 per cent of the corps of officers characterised by Himmler as 'neither good nor bad' felt no more inclined to volunteer for the Waffen SS than to try and escape from the clutches of the Party functionaries whose duty it was to supervise the Wehrmacht. So although the élite formations had disappeared in battle, the survivors now had a new function: to form cadres for Himmler's new army.

On August 3 1944, after the first conscription of recruits at the end of July, Himmler assembled the Gauleiters at Posen and explained his object.

In my order of the day [he announced] I gave this new army the name of the National Socialist People's Army (Die National-Sozialistische Volks-armee). I asked the Führer—and he agreed—that the divisions thus rising anew should be given the name of People's Grenadier Divisions (Volks-grenadiersdivisionen). I rejected the idea of the Reichswehr and everything to do with it. I had to find a name. I believe that at this moment we are waging a people's holy war; I believe that the army which must win this war, and with which we shall win it, is the National Socialist People's Army; the name indicates unequivocally that this army must be indelibly stamped with the doctrine of National Socialism.

The meeting had been called by Martin Bormann, head of the Party Chancellery, and Himmler was preaching to the converted, for all the

Gauleiters had felt themselves threatened by the near success of the military coup. Himmler gave them a long dissertation on the army's disloyalties. He called upon them to take revenge; he did not go into detail but merely invited them to imitate him, to go round the manœuvre areas and talk to officers in order to re-awaken in them the spirit of honour, obedience, loyalty and tenacity; those they could not convince, they were to denounce and purge. 'About a third or a quarter of the corps of officers is very good . . . fifty to sixty per cent are indifferent—neither bad nor really good. . . . They must have things explained to them without offending them or talking above their heads. The problem is the company and battalion commanders; they form the main body of officers.'

Himmler concluded:

We are going to raise a new army, thirty or forty armoured divisions and the same number of regular infantry divisions. We shall be tireless in organizing and training them from the last boot button to political indoctrination, from anti-tank fighting to ability to spend the night in the open in a temperature of minus forty . . . In addition there will be twelve SS armoured divisions and thirty European divisions, which, as you saw on the Narva, can fight with great dash. Then when weariness is gaining a hold on the other side, will come the time to talk of peace. A new army, fully ready to fight, will give the Führer the arguments and the triumphs which will allow him to dictate the peace.*

Himmler was so determined to deny victory to the army that he even went so far as to revise party theory and lay upon the generals the responsibility for the 1918 defeat, hitherto imputed to the machinations of the 'Reds' in the rear. He made use of the 'old comrades' myth but with some caution; he had no wish to abolish existing organisations; his object was gradually to gain control of them. He counted upon the enthusiasm of the newly recruited classes to carry their elders along.

The political indoctrination of the army had begun well before July 20 1944. Martin Bormann had his own organisation, parallel to that of Himmler; ever since the winter of 1943-4 he had been in control of the 'NSFO' (National-Sozialistische Führungsoffiziere) who were party functionaries attached to the land forces as political commissars. After July 20 he had invested them with the ranks and prerogatives of regular officers. In theory they were supposed to check officers' loyalty to Nazism, but in fact they were working solely to increase Bormann's influence. During this summer of 1944 Himmler and Bormann, though on the surface working hand in glove, were in fact each pursuing their own quest for power, and this involved the elimination of their common enemies, Göring, Ribbentrop, the generals and their creatures.

Many of the events of this period will not really be explicable until the full story of the internal quarrels in Hitler's court is divulged. Martin

* *Vierteljahrshefte für Zeitgeschichte*, October 1953, p. 383 et seq.

Bormann's letters to his wife nevertheless show how deep rooted they were. It is certain that during the last six months of 1944 the political rivalries within Hitler's headquarters exerted a decisive influence on the conduct of the war. General Blumentritt comments: 'On the German side events in the west in 1944-5 can be described in terms of an army fighting a continuously losing battle, abandoned by its political leaders.'

Nevertheless among the recruits, in other words at the bottom level, faith was still alive. The regime had been in power eleven years and many of the young had been brought up entirely under the National Socialist system; political fanaticism sometimes led to acts of heroism in defeat. Hitler once said: 'I have an imperialist navy, a reactionary army and a National Socialist air force'; and in fact the men of the Luftwaffe drafted into the new divisions showed just as much enthusiasm for the war as did the youngsters of the 1946 and 1947 classes who were extracted from the labour service or urban anti-aircraft units and hurled into battle after only six or eight weeks' training.

These boys had no conception of the hardships of an infantryman's life; they found it intoxicating to devote themselves blindly to the service of one man. They were as blindly devoted to Hitler as the children of the Hitler Youth who, a few months later, went into battle at the age of fourteen. Less than a year later, however, they were echoing the cry of a young man a little older than themselves, Wolfgang Borchert, who in the desert of defeat proclaimed: 'We are the generation without ties and without depth. Our depth is the abyss. We are the generation without happiness, without home, without farewells. Our sun is pale, our love is cruel and our youth is without youth. We are the generation without limit, without restraint and without protection.'

Appeal to the Old Guard

There was nothing unexpected in this last convulsive attempt by a totalitarian dictatorial regime to save its skin by ridding itself of an internal enemy with whom previously it had had to come to terms to ensure its victory. Mussolini with his Salo Republic had made a similar attempt to make good the opportunity he had missed through excessive deference to the monarchy after his march on Rome.

But the Wehrmacht was more than just a party to a struggle; it was the framework holding up the whole structure of Germany at war. The crises of 1933 to 1938 had not eliminated the recalcitrants and the purge following the July 20 coup had been partial only. The problem was how to neutralise the army, how even to rouse it in support of Hitlerism. Himmler told the Gauleiters how; the army had to be its own disciplinarian:

The army, thank God, seized the opportunity to liquidate the Berlin Putsch on its own; at the same time Dr Goebbels and I took steps to ensure that

neither the Luftwaffe, the Navy, the SS or the Police fired a shot or intervened in any way. The army's attitude is most significant. When I liquidated
this criminal plot, my object was to get the army to purge itself. That is why
I proposed that there should be a court of honour consisting of certain
marshals and generals and that that court should petition the Führer to strip
Field Marshal von Witzleben of his rank and arraign him before the people's
tribunal.

One of the members of this 'court of honour' was Field-Marshal von
Rundstedt, the personification of military resistance to Hitler and subsequent military submission. Between 1933 and 1938 he had handed in
his resignation three times and eventually, after the invasion of the
Sudetenland, it was accepted. Apparently therefore he had been of the
same way of thinking as Beck, the Chief of the General Staff and leader
of the military opposition, who had resigned in the summer of 1938.
Rundstedt had been recalled to active service for the Polish campaign and
promoted field-marshal during the French campaign, when he had commanded Army Group A, which had attacked through the Ardennes. But
in 1941, while commanding Army Group South in Russia, he had been
dismissed for refusing to order Kleist's army to push forward to Rostov.
Then in the spring of 1942 Hitler had recalled him and made him
Commander-in-Chief in the west. A month after the Allied landing
Rundstedt, in agreement with Rommel, who commanded Army Group B
(Seventh and Fifteenth Armies, on the coast from the Loire to the Pas-de-
Calais), asked Hitler's authorisation to withdraw from the immediate
vicinity of the Allied bridgehead in order to get his armoured divisions
out of range of naval gunfire.

Forwarding the request to Hitler Jodl commented: 'This is an admission
of incompetence and defeat. It is the prelude to the evacuation of all
France.'

Twenty-four hours later von Rundstedt was relieved of his command
and replaced by Field-Marshal von Kluge.

Three weeks later came the drama which ended by breaking Rundstedt;[*]
he was made president of the 'court of honour', thus becoming responsible
for cashiering his rebellious fellow officers—and he accepted, giving the
lie to all his past gestures of independence, turning himself into a yes-man
and giving the Nazis the pledge they required.

His motives remain obscure.

Colonel Bodo Zimmermann, head of Rundstedt's operations section on
the western front, in a memorandum on the 1944 campaign in France
written after the war, described him as follows: 'Rundstedt's vision on all
matters was completely clear; he could judge precisely what was possible
and what was not. . . . He made no secret of his aversion to the representatives of the regime.'

* In 1944 his age was sixty-eight; he died on February 24 1953.

Criticising this monograph, however, General Speidel, ex-Chief of Staff to Rommel, considered this far too kind an estimate. He asked two questions: Why did von Rundstedt accept the presidency of the post-July 20 court of honour? And, why, in December 1944, did he accept command of the Ardennes offensive, when he knew that it was a desperate venture, and not ask to be relieved of his command in the autumn of 1944?

Speidel wrote:

Von Rundstedt's case is most painful and one can only think that by this time his mental and physical powers must have been impaired. General Beck's judgement of him was much harsher.

In his view Field Marshal von Rundstedt had not the courage of his convictions; moreover on July 4 he had given Field Marshal Rommel his word that he would never again accept a command from the 'Bohemian corporal'; he did not keep it.

So on September 1 the old field-marshal presented himself once more to Hitler. Hitler needed him for his impossibly risky western offensive. He had to have a military man to make war and he had to have a field-marshal to give the army confidence. The return of Rundstedt would appear to the army as a guarantee that the Party would cease interfering in military matters and that Germany would be defended on the Rhine by sane military methods instead of the senseless improvisations and crazy orders which had led to the withdrawal from France. On his side Hitler knew that Rundstedt would keep to the general staff rules, would restrict himself to his job of military technician and take no hand in political developments.

So Rundstedt resumed his position as Commander-in-Chief in the west, Walter Model continuing to command Army Group B. The latter was solidly loyal; Hitler had no fear of being let down by Model; his estimate of the military situation would not be tinged with politics. If he protested, it would be on technical grounds only. If any of his generals became too impulsive or let their tongues run away with them Model would refer pointedly to recent court martials. On September 5 his Chief of Staff, Speidel, was relieved by General Krebs and transferred from the Army Group headquarters to the Gestapo cellars in Berlin. There was now nothing left of the military opposition which had centred around Rommel.

Von Rundstedt and Model were an ill-assorted pair, an old gentleman and a freebooter. Montgomery's Intelligence Section made the apt comment:

To bring back the Old Guard implies that the situation is desperate and since little can be done about it, it may mean that the Old Guard is to take the blame. The return of von Rundstedt is reminiscent of the description of the role of cavalry in modern war: 'to add distinction to what would otherwise be a vulgar brawl'. The re-appointment is interesting as exhibiting muddle and desperation: but (unlike the cavalry) it doesn't really make much difference. The task of C-in-C in any German theatre has degenerated to that of local Chief of Staff to Hitler, and liable to dismissal as much for carrying out quaint orders as for protesting against them. Only Model, it is said, has found the solution: neither to implement nor to criticize but to promise.

Stabilisation of the Western Front

On September 1 therefore Hitler received Field-Marshal von Rundstedt and his Chief of Staff, General Westphal, to explain to them what he expected them to do; this was to stabilise the western front and prepare to recapture the initiative.

In my view the situation is as follows [he told them]. The Allies have no ports and their lines of communication are over-extended. They will be forced to halt. Before they have established a front it should be possible to cut off the heads of their armoured columns, particularly the one advancing in Champagne. So attack from Nancy and Neufchâteau towards Reims.

In the meanwhile you will prepare for the defensive battle on the Reich frontiers, based on the following essential principles: the Netherlands are to be retained; not an inch of German territory is to be abandoned; the Allies are to be prevented from using Antwerp and resistance is therefore to be kept up as long as possible at the mouth of the Scheldt; the Allied air bases are to be held as far as possible from the heart of Germany, and the Ruhr and Saar are to be protected.

Hitler was insistent on keeping the 'strong point' of the Netherlands. He considered it of great economic and military value, whereas von Rundstedt looked upon it merely as a political hostage, perhaps of value for negotiations with the Allies. But the Führer's intentions were capable of a quite different interpretation: holding the enemy away from the frontiers of Germany might be intended to maintain the Wehrmacht as close as possible to Great Britain, with the V1 and V2 launching sites still aimed on London, the Dutch aerodromes only a few minutes' flying time from the British coast and the Pas-de-Calais still unusable by the Allies.

These orders indicate the expectations upon which Hitler's hopes of a reversal of the situation were based: entry into service of new aircraft, command of the North Sea by midget submarines, continuance of the flying-bomb attack on England and finally an offensive aimed at Antwerp and the Flemish coast.

The Führer was well aware that if the operation was to succeed it would require considerable resources: with the Allied front on the line Belfort–Vosges–Metz–Liège its left flank could not be broken by anything less than two highly equipped armies. Full scale air cover would be essential to protect them as they crossed the Rhine and Meuse as the Wehrmacht did not have available river crossing equipment on anything like the Allied scale.

Rundstedt admitted to his Chief of Staff that the whole concept was fantastic: maintenance of the Dutch bridgehead, he said, could not be justified by any purely strategic consideration; it would require far too many men. Any forces in Holland would be unable to manœuvre and would be in danger of being trapped if the Allies forced the Rhine at the Nijmegen bend; as on the Atlantic Coast, this would be another case of large numbers of men being captured without a fight.

No Such Thing as the Rundstedt Offensive

Throughout the autumn Field-Marshal von Rundstedt sent report after report to Hitler protesting against the offensive.

At the Nuremberg trial Göring said: 'The Führer planned the whole thing himself. Both the plan and the concept were his alone.'

At the outset of his period of imprisonment von Rundstedt himself protested against 'the fact that this stupid operation is sometimes called the "Rundstedt offensive".' In his testimony at Nuremberg, during his interrogation by Major Shulman of the Canadian Army Intelligence Service and in more intimate discussion with the American psychologist Gilbert, he used almost identical expressions:

My entire general staff training revolted against an operation of this sort. If old von Moltke thought that I had planned this offensive he would turn in his grave . . .
My lack of resources was such that I could not countenance the idea of this counter offensive. Our forces were far, far too weak for such immense objectives . . . . With our Luftwaffe knocked out we had to move only at night, whereas Patton could wind up his tanks and move day or night right into our positions. Our man-power was all shot too. All we had was the run-down old men who could not fight and foreigners who kept deserting. And Hitler kept hollering 'Hold your ground'! Like Bastogne, just to mention one name. It was absolute madness! And that was the man who wanted to be considered a great field general! He did not know the first thing about strategy! All he knew was bluff!*

These strictures might be suspect were there not innumerable witnesses to confirm Hitler's anger and contempt at the army's conduct of operations. Since the failure of the Russian campaign he had imposed upon his staff methods of control analogous to those of the Party. Acknowledged experts were downgraded to mere executive staff officers whose duty was simply to obey. General Heilmann, commanding 5 Parachute Division,

* See Gilbert, *Nuremberg Diary*, pp. 342-3.

recalled—apparently as if it was accepted practice—that 'in the sixth year of the war it had become customary for the highest level to issue instructions in the greatest detail to the lower echelons.'

Blumentritt had no doubt as to Hitler's intention: 'If the plan for the offensive succeeded he would be the saviour; if it failed Rundstedt would be saddled with the responsibility.' Success would be political, defeat would be military. The Party would boast of having prodded the army into capturing Antwerp; any hesitation or any opportunity offered to the enemy would be ascribed to the generals.

From Hitler's point of view this particular gamble undoubtedly came off. In spite of his protests, the name Rundstedt became firmly linked with th s operation in the history of the war. The Belgians, for instance, connect the man and the operation so closely that they frequently refer to 'before Rundstedt' or 'after Rundstedt'.

The connection dates from the autumn of 1944. Allied caricaturists and the military commentators put the old field-marshal on a pedestal as a symbol of Germany at war, as the personification of the power which had surprised them, terrorised them and defeated them. As soon as the offensive was launched everyone agreed without further thought that it bore the stamp of Rundstedt; power was ascribed to him which he never possessed. On December 18 1944 the war correspondent of *Combat* in all good faith wrote: 'Hitler no longer has anything to do with the strategy and it is the army alone which now decides. Himmler and Goebbels have grasped this and when the army makes a demand or a request they obey without argument. If von Rundstedt requires men, Himmler and Goebbels strip the country.' The majority of military writers would have agreed with this estimate unquestioningly.

Oversimplified though this view was, the man became even more closely identified with the operation after the German withdrawal. In January 1945 the full scope of the devastation and criminality wreaked in the Ardennes was revealed to the Belgians; examples were more numerous and more atrocious than in 1914 or in the rest of occupied Europe. Von Rundstedt was held fully responsible for the offensive; all crime and extortion was therefore laid at his door.

For four years the Belgians had suffered under the Gestapo, the SS and the Wehrmacht and they drew little distinction between them. They could not be expected to try to puzzle out the internal struggle between the army and the Party, or to allocate responsibility for crime according to the colour of a uniform. Their judgment of Field-Marshal von Rundstedt stemmed from this period. But they were unconsciously proving the accuracy of Hitler's calculations: the Führer let loose all his wrath upon the head of Rundstedt; the French and Belgians accused him of the most odious crimes. His name came to typify the crisis of the German officer corps, the bitter hatred between Party and army and the consternation of the occupied nations faced by an unexpectedly resurgent enemy. One wonders whether he really deserved quite so much.*

* The fact remains, however, that Field-Marshal von Rundstedt kept his mouth shut when the crimes committed by Sepp Dietrich's men became known. This had been his long established policy, as witness a document dated September 1941: he was at the time commanding Army Group South in Russia and he gave orders that no Wehrmacht unit was to become involved in 'the inquiries and actions against circles hostile to the Reich' (i.e. communists, Jews, etc.). These were the 'exclusive task of the special security police and SD commandos'. Similarly the members of the Wehrmacht were ordered not to take action or participate in 'the extortions practised by the Ukrainian population against the Jews'. They were forbidden either to watch or to photograph 'the execution of measures taken by the special commandos'.

This document is quoted by Leon Poliakov and Josef Wulf in *Das Dritte Reich und Seine Diener* published in Berlin in 1956. It shows at the very least that Rundstedt was determined 'not to get into trouble'. He knew what was going on but preferred to shut his eyes to the facts. The question is whether Rundstedt was of a character to deserve to be made to carry the responsibility for all the war crimes committed against Belgian civilians and American soldiers during the Ardennes offensive. In fact he was too far removed from the criminals in the administrative hierarchy. So far as I know, there is no proof that he ever condoned, still less ordered, these crimes and brutalities. He said nothing; he did not 'wish to know'.

Chapter 3

THE GERMAN 'MIRACLE OF THE MARNE'

AMONG the other instructions given by Himmler to the Gauleiters was to comb through all those in reserved occupations in industry, civil defence and the Party organisation; his object was to hunt out and send to the front those in hitherto exempt occupations, some of whom had successfully concealed themselves ever since the beginning of the war.

In the first six months of 1944 an initial 'skim off' had produced 1,000,000 additional men for the Wehrmacht. Goebbels was hoping to find a further million before the end of the year, but this was little more than wishful thinking; the loss of the occupied territories meant that there would be no further foreign workers available and 7,000,000 of them had already taken the place of Germans mobilised into the forces.

The million men dug out by the Gauleiters were hardly enough to fill the gaps. By July the High Command of the Wehrmacht had abandoned any attempt to form new units. Far from being able to make good the losses, it had been forced to disband those regiments and divisions which had suffered most heavily in action. The average strength of infantry divisions had fallen from 17,000 to 12,500.

During the first fortnight of July, after Army Group Centre's débacle on the Russian front, Hitler had ordered the formation of fifteen new divisions and then a further three. Of these eighteen formations two were sent to the west in September, one to Norway and the fifteen others to the eastern front. On September 2 he ordered a further twenty-five new divisions to be raised; they were to form an operational reserve in the rear of the western front and were to be ready for action by October or November.*

Priority for the West

Of these forty-three divisions, therefore, twenty-seven were available for the final offensive effort in the west. They were christened 'people's divisions'. Their strength was in theory 10,000 men but those used in the

---

* The O.K.W. War Diary gives the following information on manpower and forces on the western front. September 29: nearly 600,000 dead, wounded and prisoners; September 6: thirteen infantry divisions (including the four in the Atlantic Coast 'fortresses'), three armoured divisions and two armoured brigades fit to fight. Army Group B, however, had no more than 100 tanks on the road (*K.T.B./O.K.W.* IV I, pp. 376 to 377).

Ardennes were seldom over 8,000. They were given numbers from divisions destroyed in August, Hitler having insisted that the latter should continue to be shown in the order of battle.

Because of the part they were to play in the offensive, these divisions were given the best of everything. Their proportion of automatic weapons and artillery was high but transport was not on the same lavish scale; they had only horses or bicycles. In addition to these infantry divisions the following units were raised for the western front: twelve brigades of motorised artillery, ten brigades of multi-rocket launchers—the weapons known in Europe as 'Stalin organs'—ten anti-tank battalions and twelve heavy machine-gun battalions.

During the summer the factories turned out 1,500 tanks. Hitler allocated them all to the west. In spite of Allied bombing German industry had contrived to increase production of artillery and assault guns; all these too went to the west as equipment for the spearhead of the great offensive, which was to consist of the freshest armoured divisions and ten new armoured brigades, each organised around a Panther battalion of some forty tanks.

Guderian, the new Army Chief of Staff and Inspector General of Armoured Forces, got no change. He did not under-estimate the value of taking the offensive in the west, but it was his job to hold the Russians, particularly in the Balkans and the Carpathians. He was just rubbing his hands over one success: in spite of Hitler's aversion to fortified lines, which he considered a concession to his generals' pusillanimity, Guderian had obtained his agreement that the Reich's eastern frontier fortifications from Konigsberg to Breslau should be rehabilitated. They were to be manned by 100 fortress battalions and 100 batteries, reinforced later by anti-tank, machine gun and engineer units.

By the middle of August Guderian had concentrated his fortress troops for training. Seventy-five battalions had already been formed. Then came an order from Supreme Headquarters that all were to move to the west forthwith.

To equip his hundred batteries Guderian demanded the allocation of the Polish, French, Russian and Czech artillery equipment which had been held in depots for five years. Jodl's only answer to this request was the immediate despatch to the west of every gun above 50 mm for which more than fifty rounds could be made available. To stop the Russians Guderian was left only with light artillery and guns for which no more than a few rounds could be provided.

Von Rundstedt re-assumes Command

When Field-Marshal von Rundstedt left for the west on September 5, the Reich's land forces consisted of 327 divisions and brigades, including thirty-one armoured divisions and thirteen armoured brigades. After the drain of the August battles, however, these were paper figures only; the situation maps and the strength tables showed that in fact the fronts were held by 252 divisions and fifteen to twenty brigades. In addition there were fifty-five divisions provided by the Reich's Allies, the Finns, the Hungarians and the Bulgars, all of whom were on the point of defection. In any case the satellite divisions were only half the strength of a German division.*

Of this total von Rundstedt had available forty-nine infantry divisions, fourteen armoured divisions and four armoured brigades. 25 per cent of these formations were of normal strength; a further 25 per cent below strength but fit to fight; the remaining 50 per cent were worth nothing.

These forces were distributed as follows:

In Holland, Fifteenth Army was holding the mouths of the Meuse and Rhine. Alongside it the newly formed First Parachute Army guarded the right bank of the Albert Canal.

Between Brussels and Sedan was Seventh Army, but on its right was a gap into which the British had penetrated in the direction of Ghent, Antwerp and Hasselt.

Between Sedan and Charmes First Army was attempting to cover Nancy.

These formations made up Army Group B under the command of Field-Marshal Model.

---

* Dr Cole in *The Lorraine Campaign*, pp. 29–30, gives the following detailed figures for German forces on October 13 1944 from an O.K.H. strength return:

The Wehrmacht (i.e. the armed forces as a whole) was theoretically at a strength of 10,165,303 officers, N.C.O.s and men distributed as follows:

Army and Waffen SS: 7,536,946
Air Force: 1,925,291
Navy: 703,065

The land forces included:

The Field Army (Feldheer): 3,421,000 men.
The Home Army (Ersatzheer): 2,387,973, men, including sick, wounded in hospital, medical personnel, territorials, air force ground personnel and recruits under training.
Waffen SS: 207,276.

In addition to these figures there were 1,500,000 men in the Luftwaffe ground formations, the Allgemeine SS, the police and foreign volunteer units. The last belonged either to the army (in the case of Spaniards, Italians and French) or to the Waffen SS (in the case of Indians, Arabs, Flemings, Walloons, British and French) or to the 'Eastern Auxiliary' formations (Osthilfsfreiwillige).

The greater part of the field army was concentrated on the eastern front: 2,046,000 men out of 3,421,000.

Between August 1 and September 1 strength on the western front (France, Belgium, Netherlands) fell from 770,000 to 543,000, but this does not take account of reinforcements, which kept the total in the region of 700,000.

Further south was Army Group G commanded by General von Blasko-
witz. This included:

XLVI Corps, holding territory from Charmes to south of Epinal;
Nineteenth Army, covering Epinal to the Swiss frontier.

From the outset Field-Marshal von Rundstedt had only restricted authority over these forces; all legal powers were reserved to Hitler's own staff
(an important point in this period of demoralisation). In many cases his
authority was restricted purely to the tactical employment of the formations concerned; this applied, for instance, to the new Army Group H
consisting of the formations occupying Holland which was constituted an
autonomous front on November 10; it applied also to those land forces
which did not belong to the army, such as the Waffen SS, the Parachute
formations which remained under Luftwaffe command, the Luftwaffe
divisions and the territorial units in the Münster, Wiesbaden and Stuttgart
military districts; the latter were only available to von Rundstedt in the
event of large scale enemy airborne operations. The four divisions isolated
in the Atlantic ports were under command of the Navy. Third Air Fleet,
later the 'Luftwaffe Western Command', worked only 'in co-operation'
with the Commander-in-Chief. It controlled the firing of the V1s; the
V2s were under command of Himmler. Rundstedt only learnt of the targets
for these weapons after firing had begun.*

The field-marshal, however, had one advantage as compared to his
predecessors and his own position prior to the Allied landing: he had no
political responsibilities other than those directly connected with the conduct of the war. Gauleiter Sauckel, for instance, who was responsible for
recruiting forced labour, had no representative at his headquarters, for
there could be no question of deporting workers from an operational zone
which in any case included a decreasing proportion of occupied territory.
There was no call for Rundstedt to issue orders or requirements to the
French and so Abetz, previously German ambassador in Paris, had no
liaison officer at his headquarters. The appointment of von Stolzmann as
Ribbentrop's representative with Commander-in-Chief West was purely
a matter of form.

In his first report, dated September 7, von Rundstedt said: 'Six weeks!
I must hold for six weeks.' He estimated that Eisenhower had fifty-four
divisions and 2,000 tanks. In fact on September 1 the Allied Supreme
Commander had only thirty-seven divisions in Belgium and eastern France
(twenty American, twelve British, three Canadian, one French, one Polish);
on September 15 these were augmented by the six French and three
American divisions of Sixth Army Group moving up the Rhone valley.
Von Rundstedt had practically nothing with which to oppose them; there

---

* The first V1 was launched on London at 1.20 a.m. on June 13 1944. A total of
2,400 were eventually fired. The first V2 was launched at 6.40 p.m. on September 8.
1,115 were eventually fired. Neither had the smallest influence on operations.

were only 100 tanks in the whole of Army Group B and his reserve consisted of 9 Panzer Division, which was very weak, one battalion of heavy tanks and two brigades of assault guns already in the line at Aix-la-Chapelle.

Rundstedt sent a telegram: 'To protect the Rhineland–Westphalia industrial area I must have at least ten infantry divisions and all the armour available, whatever the consequences elsewhere may be.'

The lightning Allied advance on Liège (liberated on September 8) and the Ardennes produced a direct threat to Aix-la-Chapelle and the Ruhr. Commander-in-Chief West realised this only too well and was apprehensive of the follow-up to this offensive, but Hitler refused to admit the seriousness of the situation.

On September 7 he instructed von Rundstedt 'before all else rehabilitate the Rhine defences'.

The Value of the Siegfried Line

As early as 1943 Hitler had ordered a study of the Rhine line. On August 20 1944 he had laid down that the 'West Wall', called the Siegfried line by the Allies, should be rehabilitated. In his capacity as Commander-in-Chief of the Home Army Himmler was in charge of repairing the forts; in his capacity as Minister of the Interior he supervised the Gauleiters who were responsible for the completion of the job.

The Siegfried line was in a state of complete dilapidation, as were the defences of the Rhine bridges. No one could find the files or the plans of the forts. Himmler initiated a period of feverish but ill-directed activity, the effects of which Simon, the Rhineland Gauleiter, made sure were felt throughout the hierarchy. Flimsy works were constructed, of no military value of any sort. The civilian authorities and innumerable party functionaries meddled in the business and their decisions frequently conflicted with the requirements of the army engineers. To put an end to these squabbles Hitler relieved Himmler of his powers. Rundstedt, who fell heir to them, immediately began reorganising the Rhine bridgeheads and the old fortified sectors of the western front. But he was overwhelmed with other responsibilities and very soon left it to the police or the Party authorities to continue their supervision of the work.

The Siegfried line at least had the merit of being there. It had been constructed in 1936 and stretched from Basle to Roermond (opposite the Maastricht appendix); even when the 1940 campaign began it still did not cover the entire Reich frontier. It then had to take second place to the Atlantic Wall; equipment was removed from the forts already completed, as it was from those of the Maginot line.

The Saar sector was the most heavily protected; in certain areas there were more than forty forts per square kilometre, as Patton found in the autumn. On the right bank of the Rhine between Basle and Karlsruhe the

line was 800 yards deep; two lines of forts protected the approaches to
Cologne. The line ended at München–Gladbach–Roermond on the Belgo–
Luxembourg frontier.

But the West Wall had now been neglected for four years and its
defensive potential was no longer high. It was doubtful whether the forts
were sufficiently strong to stand up to 1944 air bombing. The 37-mm guns
which had been adequate for anti-tank and anti-aircraft purposes in 1939
were no longer effective and the turrets had not been designed to accom-
modate 75- or 88-mm guns. The machine-gun loopholes were intended for
the 1934 machine gun and did not fit the 1942 models. Though the fire
plans had been carefully worked out, they proved to be partially useless
owing to lack of signal facilities. Finally men were not available to provide
the garrison intended (ten per pillbox). Each Division had to hold twenty-
five miles instead of the regulation five miles.

Then came another idea, the rehabilitation of the Maginot line in the
Faulquemont area, already considered by the Army High Command in
October 1941. The plans proved so complicated that early in September
the garrison commander at Metz requested the originals from Supreme
Headquarters. Hitler did nothing about this request until November, by
which time the moment had long since passed.

On September 10 200,000 workers arrived on the Siegfried line to assist
the fortress battalions in putting the pillboxes in order. Five days later
von Rundstedt issued an order implicitly admitting how far the enemy had
advanced:

'1. The West Wall is of decisive importance in the battle for Germany.

'2. I order that the West Wall and each individual pillbox should be
held to the last round.'

But the troops too often went to ground in these 'mouseholes', as
Rundstedt nicknamed the pillboxes. On October 31 an order from General
von Knobelsdorf, commanding First Army on the Saar, laid down that

garrisons of permanent fortifications are to come out into the open, set
up listening posts and outposts and reply to fire directed against the gun-
ports. . . . The reprehensible habit of waiting until the enemy is within
grenade range cannot be tolerated under any circumstances. When the
enemy is moving to attack or to re-organise, no one is to remain in the pillboxes; every man must go to his battle station.

Early in December a new order laid down: 'The struggle within the
West Wall must be conducted outside the pillboxes.'

The Fight Against Time

Six weeks was therefore the period during which von Rundstedt must
hold the Allies at arms length if he was to prepare his withdrawal to the
Siegfried line, or rather the general line from Zwolle (on the Zuider Zee)
via Arnhem along West Wall and the western slopes of the Vosges to

Belfort. His plan presupposed the evacuation of Holland; this would free the forces there and allow him both to strengthen his defence line and concentrate the available tanks as a mobile reserve near the Cologne gap.

Rundstedt said to his staff: 'We are in no position to withstand a prolonged static war. Wherever the allies concentrate their forces they will break through. For us there can be no question of military victory or of winning the war. Our only hope is to hold on long enough to allow some development on the political front to save Germany from complete collapse.'

His political concept was a simple one; in accordance with German staff college rules it stemmed from the intentions he attributed to the enemy: Montgomery and Eisenhower would do all in their power to reach Berlin before the Russians and stop the Russian army pushing too far west of the Oder. There were therefore two points at which they might break through the German front:

Either north of the Ruhr via Aix-la-Chapelle; or towards Frankfurt-on-Main via Trier.

Von Rundstedt was soon given the answer on the feasibility of the second operation—and he was in luck. On September 11 the leading elements of 5 U.S. Armoured Division took certain of the Siegfried line forts by surprise and crossed the Sure at Wallendorf, north-west of Trier. All available German forces counter-attacked for eight successive days to prevent the Americans reaching the 'gate of the Moselle' leading to the Rhineland and the Palatinate via Trier. The American combat command was eventually driven back across the Sure.

General Westphal, von Rundstedt's Chief of Staff, says in his book:* 'If the enemy had thrown in more forces, he would not only have broken through the German line of defences which were in process of being built up in the Eifel but in the absence of any considerable reserves on the German side he must have effected the collapse of the whole west front within a short time.'

This local success was reassuring, but it did not reduce the field-marshal's anxiety over the other possibility: a break-through towards the Ruhr, accompanied by a major airborne operation by the six Allied Airborne Divisions located in Great Britain and hitherto unused.† Initially von Rundstedt expected airborne operations in the Oldenburg area (west of Bremen), then near Belfort and finally in rear of the Siegfried line. In fact, as events proved, all his forecasts were wrong.

But once again luck was with him; a captured document showed him that the parachute operation was to take place in the Rhine bend, in the area Emmerich–Nijmegen–Arnhem.

* *The German Army in the West*, p. 174.
† Only three were operational, the British 1 Airborne, the American 82 and 101 Airborne and 1 Polish Brigade.

The Allied parachute troops were dropped on September 17. They were met by 9 and 10 SS Panzer Divisions, which had unexpectedly moved into the area to re-organise. Moreover, contrary to von Rundstedt's expectation, the operation was not combined with a frontal offensive.

These were two successes for the Germans. Nevertheless Rundstedt knew only too well that they were due neither to some stroke of strategic genius on his part nor to any superiority of forces. At Wallendorf the Allies had been unable to push across the Sure. At Arnhem they had lacked drive, but in mid-September they were still perfectly capable of breaking through the Siegfried line at any moment; its whole seventy-five-mile front was held by only seven or eight battalions.

General Speidel's comment is:

The halting of the allied pursuit was a German variation of the 'miracle of the Marne'. . . . Had the allies held on grimly to the retreating Germans they could have harried the breath out of every man and beast and ended the war half a year earlier. There were no German ground forces of any import-ance that could be thrown in and next to nothing in the air.

Speidel's view is confirmed by Westphal: 'In September 1944 *any* strong combined operation of enemy armour and parachutists might have resulted in a break through on a strategic scale . . . north of Trier . . . and . . . on the lower Rhine. . . . German resistance could have been extin-guished in the same year.'

General Blumentritt, Westphal's predecessor and von Rundstedt's friend and biographer, takes the same view: 'If the allies had concentrated the main weight of their offensive in Belgium and had broken through, nothing could have stopped them.'

On the Allied side the pause in the offensive in Belgium roused similar passions. The British official history* considers that the three weeks from August 15 to September 5 'were among the most dramatic of the European war, equalling in intensity those of May and June 1940'.

The drama the history refers to lay in the field of the general conduct of the war and of the political ends served by military operations. These ends have frequently been judged in the light of post-war developments; it is tempting to imagine that the cold war might have followed an entirely different course had Eisenhower's forces swept through the thin German front and had Montgomery been the first to arrive in Berlin and Bradley in Saxony. The fate of Berlin would not have been in the balance and the Soviet zone would not have extended to the Elbe.

Two questions are pertinent: first, did the Allies really possess the resources to break through the German front and drive on to Berlin? This is primarily a war game problem, which must necessarily remain hypothetical. The real question is this: assuming that the resources did

* John Ehrman, *Grand Strategy*, Vol. V, p. 377.

exist, did Eisenhower have the right to try? Did Roosevelt's and Churchill's political instructions authorise him to run this risk? Did they even leave it open to him to do so? Did they preclude his trying?

Whatever the answers to the questions, the military inaction of end-summer 1944 must be regarded as the origin of the catastrophe which so nearly occurred in December. But the responsibility for Eisenhower's inaction does not lie with him; it lies at the higher level, that of the 'Big Two'. No instructions of any sort were issued. Roosevelt and Churchill were not in agreement on policy for the immediate future and so left the military commanders in a vacuum. Neither the Combined Chiefs of Staff nor the Supreme Commander could plan their line of action.

Chapter 4

'THE THOUSAND-YEAR REICH'

HITLER had promised his people 'a thousand-year Reich' but after eleven and a half years of Nazi rule Germany was beginning to wonder whether the time limit had not already been reached. Every other day the official newspaper *Das Reich* carried long lists of those who had 'fallen for the Führer'; the endless lists of promotions and decorations and Goebbels' weekly ruminations on the destiny of nations were poor compensation. Hardly a night passed when Allied bombers did not return to pound the ruins. From Hamburg to Munich, from Aix-la-Chapelle to Vienna and Prague, no German could sleep in peace. Nerves were on edge; morale was being sapped.

In the early years the Reich had been expanding but now, as they withdrew to their own frontiers, the German armies brought back with them a flood of foreigners whose fate became bound up willy nilly with that of the German civilian population.

Germany the Prison Camp

This Germany was little better than a vast concentration camp. No one knew exactly how many men were behind barbed wire. Millions had been deported into Germany; many had disappeared without trace; others were still hoping but were not in fact destined to see the end of the war or return to their homes.

Early that summer Himmler, the Reichsführer SS, had ordered Adolf Eichmann, a lowly lieutenant-colonel and according to his own statement no more than a bureaucrat, to set down the number of Jews whom he had collected and massacred. It appeared that 4,000,000 had been liquidated in the concentration camps and 2,000,000 done to death by the SD (Security Police) Commandos. Himmler was disappointed; he had hoped that the figure would be well over 6,000,000. In addition there were the regime's internal enemies who had been filling the concentration camps ever since 1933; from 1940 onwards their numbers were swelled by the resisters, accused of political or racial crimes. The figure of 20,000,000 has been given for prisoners of all types, some of whom passed through the fifteen main concentration camps before being distributed into the 900 forced labour camps.

Determination to survive, the sole mainstay of resistance to this barbarism, was inevitably sapped by these long autumn weeks of waiting. Michel de Boüard, Dean of the Literary Faculty of Caen University, was at the time one of the leading spirits of resistance in Mauthausen concentration camp; his description of the prisoners' reactions is as follows:

When we heard of the allied landing in June 1944 many of us thought that the war was at an end. Since one had to pin one's hopes on some imaginary date, we first thought of 15 August. Disappointed in this, we became more cautious but even the most sober estimates counted upon Christmas at home. Christmas brought the news of the German counter-offensive in the Ardennes. I was in the camp hospital at that time. The blow was shattering. I saw the last spark of life go out of hundreds of men. They gave up hope.*

So the Ardennes at least brought Hitler this one terrible and generally unrecognised victory. That it was a victory was confirmed by the figures; during the second fortnight of December 1944 and early January 1945 the death rate in the concentration camps suddenly multiplied by ten. The link between cause and effect seems obvious; either the prisoners' spirit had been broken as Professor Boüard states: alternatively the SS guards, seeing the last hope of victory disappear and defeat staring them in the face, had indulged in a final outburst of sadism.

It is not known whether there was a similar reaction in the prisoner of war camps or the huts into which the 7,000,000 foreign workers were crammed. There can be no doubt, however, that many must have been discouraged by this final German effort. The foreign workers were completely cut off from their homes; they owed no allegiance to the emigré 'authorities' in Germany, though in some cases these authorities' officials did try to take care of their fellow countrymen. So Belgians, Frenchmen, Italians, Danes and Poles, left to their own resources, had reached a sort of live and let live *modus vivendi* with the German population. The Gestapo and the 'birds of paradise' (the Nazi Party officials) kept an eye on any movement which might savour of preparation for rebellion. The Allies were still far away and seemed to have no wish to make use of this unorganised mass of humanity to the rear of the German front.

In the kaleidoscope of nationalities characteristic of Germany in the final stages of the war, certain political leaders were still trying to play some part, though probably without much conviction. They were recognised as representative authorities neither by their fellow countrymen, who were either prisoners or had been conscripted to forced labour, nor by the various German authorities whose duty it was to carry on some sort of a foreign policy, in spite of the fact that all links to the greater part of the outer world had now been broken. In the eyes of the Reich Government the Italian armistice, the loss of Rumania and Bulgaria, the Finnish armistice and the evacuation of France and Belgium had not cancelled the 'alliances' concluded with the Governments of these countries during

* *Revue d'histoire de la Deuxieme Guerre Mondiale*—special edition on the German concentration camp system, July to September 1954, p. 80.

E

Germany's victorious period. During the autumn of 1944 there was a flurry of diplomatic activity in Berlin and 'liberation committees' were formed, aping the 1940 emigré governments in London. These shadowy authorities were in theory given control of political and clandestine military activities in the territories 'occupied' by the Americans, the British and the Russians. They were not responsible for protection of the foreign workers held in the Reich with the exception of the Italians, who were looked after by Mussolini's government at Salo which had diplomatic representation in Berlin. The French were another exception. Laval had resigned before the Government moved from Paris, first to Belfort and thence to Sigmaringen. There was now a 'French governmental commission' including Darnand, Déat and Luchaire, under the chairmanship of Fernand de Brinon which in theory had some responsibility for the prisoners of war and civilian workers. In fact Scapin's office (for prisoners) and Bruneton's (for civilian workers) operated more or less independently of the Sigmaringen 'government'. In addition the members of the 'Chantiers de Jeunesse' (labour organisation) who had been drafted into Germany for forced labour, managed to preserve a degree of independence and remain firmly organised under their own leaders.

With a French 'government' in Germany the struggle between Paris and Vichy begun during the last year of occupation became more bitter. Supported by Himmler and Goebbels, Jacques Doriot formed a species of autonomous republic on the island of Mainau in Lake Constance, apparently expecting to be recognised as the sole representative of the French political authorities. The emigré leaders spent their autumn in a savage battle over the distribution of 'ministerial portfolios'. For the military who had been lured into this venture only one course was open: enlist in the German army and follow it down the road to perdition in its senseless final battle.

The same events which threw the inmates of the concentration camps into the depths of despair aroused crazy hopes in Sigmaringen 'government' circles. A well-known writer declared: 'Our bags are packed. In a week's time I shall be sleeping in Paris. We have reached the culminating point of the collaborationist curve.' Others, though thinking it likely that the German plan would succeed, were more pessimistic or perhaps more far sighted. One of them wrote: 'France will be ground down as never before: new battles of annihilation will take place in our country compared to which earlier struggles will seem like child's play. What sort of welcome will our fellow citizens give us? Even more important, what sort of riff-raff are we to be mixed up with as we return?'*

The most conspicuous of Nazi Germany's remaining foreign henchmen was the Belgian quisling, Degrelle, commanding 28 Waffen SS Division, named Wallonia. He was scheduled to take over the administration of

* Robert Aron, *Histoire de Vichy*, p. 726.

Belgium under the Gauleiter Grohé. During a 'press forum' held in Vienna on December 12, three days before the Ardennes offensive, he showed what the emigrés were really thinking. No one present had an inkling of forthcoming events and Dr Dietrich, the Reich press chief, proclaimed: 'Europe cannot exist without Germany. Europe is now no longer possible without a National Socialist Germany. Germany's European programme will substitute the clear light of a historical concept for the dim desires of the people of Europe.'

In reply to this pathos Marcel Déat gave an exposé on the origins of the war, tracing them back to February 6 1934 and the 'seizure of power' by Gaston Doumergue. But when Degrelle's turn came he did not mince his words.

I wonder whether intellectually the Germans will ever be able to come to terms with Europe . . . the majority of our friends now here present have already lost their countries, abandoned to the enemy; those countries have made real sacrifices for the great German Reich. That is why we demand: tell us at last what we are fighting for, not merely what we are fighting against! After the war Europe must have some definite objective. What is it?*

The Germans in a Stupor

The German man in the street had given up asking this question long ago. He continued to put up with the hardships of the war only under the pressure of the police machine, even more severe now that the Party was in control. At the end of September the American press published the Morgenthau plan, producing exactly the effect which Eisenhower feared. Goebbels had only to publish extracts from the Allied press and reproduce or invent letters to *The Times* to reduce the population to despair. There was now no further argument: any result other than victory would turn the Germans into a nation of serfs, fed from soup kitchens for as far ahead as anyone could foresee. The illusion that they might be 'reasonably' treated by the Anglo-Saxons had vanished. The average German was not interested in war guilt; he did not think of the vast damage inflicted on Europe by German invasion and tyranny. For him a single explanation covered everything: the Allies had quite clearly learnt nothing from the 'errors' of the Treaty of Versailles. They had no understanding of the reasons for the crisis which had sown the seed of Hitler's dictatorship in the interwar period.

The nation was ruined, cities were flattened, refugees were streaming in all directions, there was an army of war wounded and innumerable families had lost their bread winner, 'fallen for the Führer'. In the immediate post-war period political stability and rapid rehabilitation of the country's industrial resources would be essential. The Germans thought back to

* Peter Kleist, *Auch Du warst dabei!*, p. 377.

the spectre of the 1920s and the unemployment and inflation following the 1918 Armistice. Even if they had to pay reparations once more it was surely as much in the Allied interest as in that of the Germans that the debtor should not be completely bankrupted.

The conclusion to which all these vague hopes led was that if there could not be a compromise peace, Germany should at least be left with a certain measure of autonomy after her unconditional surrender. That would allow Germans to liquidate Hitler and his government and then the country could proceed. But the plans now ascribed to the British and Americans, and confirmed by their war propaganda, swept away all these ideas. If the great metallurgical and chemical combines and even the smaller Black Forest industries were to be razed to the ground, if the population of the frontier areas was to be deported into the interior of the country and if the Fatherland was to be divided, what was the good of going on looking for a political solution? Since surrender would mean the loss of everything, the only solution was to fight to the bitter end and even beyond, while still clinging to the hope that somehow those who survived would be given an opportunity to re-create their country.

So the Germans were driven back on to nihilism. They became increasingly bitter as they found that they were the target of a hatred, the reason for which they only partially understood. They were submerged by a flood of foreigners who, though they might be sharing their fate, were crowding out their country. The Germans therefore just lived from day to day. Material shortages increased now that the occupied countries which had provided supplies were lost. Danish and Dutch butter had vanished and German butter cost 100 marks a pound instead of 2 marks. The cigarette started on its career as a medium of exchange which was to reach such heights in later years. A pound of coffee cost 1,000 marks and an egg 5 marks. The existence of numerous types of bank notes, differing according to the theatre of operations, and the increasing rapidity of circulation of money meant that a system of barter became normal commercial and banking practice and inflated the price of anything of value. The first death sentences for black market activities were pronounced at the end of 1944, but even so the Government was powerless to prevent a deterioration of standards.

Along the Kurfürstendamm, the Berlin Bond Street, the repercussions of the withdrawals in the west were more noticeable than those of the disastrous defeats in Russia. The defection of Italy meant that there were no more Italian shoes; when Paris was liberated by the French and the Allies, that was the end of the supplies of hosiery and scent which had given Germans a nostalgic reminder of luxuries they had never known. For a year now there had been no issue of dresses or overcoats against clothing coupons, all stocks of clothing being reserved for war wounded. The sticky cakes so beloved by Germans were controlled by the Reichskonditor

('Reich confectioner') a euphemism for I. G. Farben, the great chemical firm which produced synthetic butter, eggs and cream.

There was therefore just as much hardship in Germany as in the liberated countries. But justice was about to be done; the Germans were not yet at the limit of their privations, whereas for the rest of Europe liberation had set free those moral and spiritual forces upon which recovery depended.

The Myth of New Weapons

By 1942 the days of territorial conquests were over and their place in German propaganda was taken by promises of the remarkable results to be anticipated from the use of 'secret weapons'. Since, however, they were always 'in course of preparation' and never seen to get any further, the Germans became sceptical; on their side the Allies, confident in the results of their air bombing, felt they had little to fear from any new German inventions.

The arrival of the first V1s on London on June 13 1944 and the first V2s on Paris and London on September 8, aroused fear on one side and hope on the other. People began seriously to think that the consolidation of the front in the autumn would give Germany time to initiate mass production of the new type of submarines, of 'flying bombs' and even of the atomic bomb. The prototypes of the new weapons were perfected at about the same time as the counter-offensive was being planned, so Hitler had the additional argument that these weapons would soon be in production and provide him with the necessary tools to reverse the fortunes of war. All that was necessary according to him was to gain a few weeks; this could best be done by capturing Antwerp, splitting the Allied front and embarking on a new campaign in France. These were the objects laid down for the Ardennes offensive.

As early as the autumn of 1944, Germany did in fact possess the weapons capable of turning the tables. The Mark XXI submarine had been in existence since 1943; it could travel at 16 knots and remain submerged for long periods at great depth. In addition there was the Mark XXIII which was smaller but more flexible. Then there was the Messerschmidt 262 jet fighter, and finally the rockets. All these weapons would be in service in the near future and, if used in a concentrated fashion, would have constituted a major danger to the Allies. 120 Mark XXI submarines and 61 Mark XXIII's had been launched before the end of the war and at Bremen the British found miles of railway wagons loaded with pre-fabricated parts. They were just a year too late—perhaps even only three months. Had they been in service in the Atlantic and the Channel during the winter of 1944-5 they would have been a most serious threat to the Allied supply line.

German air strength was rising at a rate only dimly suspected by the

Allies. At the end of the war they found on a Norwegian aerodrome a number of 4-jet Heinkel bombers capable of a two-way bombing mission to New York; the raid was planned for May. The German aircraft industry had expanded at an incredible rate since 1943. During 1944 40,600 aircraft of all types were produced, three times the 1942 figure in spite of Allied superiority in the air. Allied bombing, intense though it was, had not been able to prevent war production in all fields being tripled; tank production between April and December 1944 was in fact five times that of 1942 and the maximum figure was reached in December (598, as against 100 per month in 1942).

But Allied bombing was concentrated on the vital points in the war economy—oil refineries and communications. Rumanian oil was now no longer available and the production of synthetic petrol fell catastrophically: in January 1944 150,000 tons of aviation fuel were produced but in December only 26,000 tons.

The Luftwaffe was hamstrung just as much by theoretical disagreements and squabbles among the High Command as by the Allied bombing. The Messerschmidt 262 had been on the drawing board since 1938. It was the first jet fighter in the world and in trials had reached a speed of 550 m.p.h. at 27,000 feet; but from the autumn of 1940 until early 1943 Hitler had held up production. Finally, eighteen months later, he was convinced and authorised production, but only on condition that the fighter was converted into a high-speed bomber. The first squadron became operational in October 1944 and the first wing in November. The ratio of losses was immediately reversed, two Allied escorting fighters being shot down for one German, instead of two German for one Allied.

But between June and October the Luftwaffe had lost an average of 500 aircraft per week. The commander of the fighter force, General Galland, had contrived somehow to reconstitute a reserve of 700 aircraft. He was planning to strike 'a major blow' (der grosse Schlag) by large-scale interception of enemy raids. Hitler wished to force him into using the new aircraft immediately and piece-meal. Galland refused to abandon his plan unless production of fighters was stopped and turned over to anti-aircraft weapons.

In September and October Himmler became involved in the argument. The Focke Wulf 190 and Messerschmidt 109 had been equipped with new and heavier armament and a controversy started on the role of fighters— whether they should be used to intercept the American and British bombers or in a ground attack role. Nevertheless Galland continued to prepare for his 'major blow'. By November 12 he had assembled eighteen fighter squadrons or 3,770 aircraft, of which 3,000 were available to take part in the proposed operation. But on November 2 120 fighters had been lost. Although fifty American bombers had been shot down, this confirmed Hitler in his opposition and he finally vetoed the 'major blow'. A propor-

tion of the units held ready for it were transferred to areas immediately
to the rear of the western front.

Galland had no notion of the background to this decision and was simply
left bemoaning the dissipation of his force. The units were divided between
the air defence of the Reich and ground attack tasks in support of the
Ardennes offensive, but no clear directives were issued. The thousand
Me. 262s, against which the Allied air forces had no defence and which
could therefore have scored an easy victory, were left unused for lack of
fuel, runways and trained pilots.

The atomic bomb was the only one of all the 'secret weapons' capable in
itself of producing a complete change in the balance of forces. But the race
between the American and German scientists was not as close as the
Americans imagined. In August 1942 the German scientists had stated that
it would be two years before they could produce an operational weapon.
The government decided that two years was too long, that the war would
be ended by that time and that they would not tie up war potential in an
enterprise the results of which were uncertain. Work was finally stopped
in June 1943 when the stocks of heavy water in Norway were destroyed.
The German scientists were reduced to studying the construction of
atomic piles.

The struggle between the Wehrmacht and the Party was naturally
particularly severe in the field of new weapons. The generals looked for
material effect and so advocated the massive employment of the new
weapons on the battlefield or against long range military targets. The
political leaders, on the other hand, were primarily pre-occupied with their
psychological effect. In the autumn of 1944, for instance, Goebbels and
Ley, the head of the Labour Front, were considering denunciation of the
Geneva Convention and the simultaneous use of two gases, tabun and sarin,
against which there was no protection. By November three factories were
in production and they had not been affected by bombing. Goebbels' plan
was only scotched at the end of December when Speer, the Minister of
War Production, heard of it and cut off the supply of raw material.

The possible use of rockets for terror attacks was more obvious and
Himmler managed to get complete control over the V2. SS Obergruppen-
führer Kammler was in charge of their manufacture and employment and
SS Standartenführer Berg was responsible for propagandising their results;
he presented them as 'retaliatory weapons' (Vergeltungswaffen—whence
the title V weapons). In this case too Speer, with the support of the
military, attempted to stop development on economic grounds—a jet
fighter could be constructed for the price of a single V2.

Unfounded though it was, the myth of the new weapons produced a
sort of hysteria on the Allied side and it reached a new pitch of intensity
when, in late autumn, Goebbels suddenly put a stop to the propaganda
campaign. In fact it had become clear that the change in the situation

anticipated from the large-scale use of these weapons was unlikely to come soon. Hope was therefore fading. Goebbels calculated that a period of mystery would revive curiosity and increase the anxiety of the Allied press, which was still putting forward fantastic estimates of the German lead in research.

On October 22, for instance, the *New York Times* announced that Hitler had ordered all work on the V2 to be abandoned and efforts concentrated upon the V3; this was said to be a missile carrying an atomic bomb 'double or quadruple the power of an ordinary bomb' and capable of reaching the United States.

The profusion of articles such as this goes some way to explain the fear which gripped the world when the Ardennes offensive broke. On December 19, for instance, the *Daily Mail* headline was: 'Secret weapon, background to Nazi push' and on January 3 the same paper produced a banner headline: 'U.S. told: V bombs in 30 days. New York and Washington probable targets.'

Their psychological effect was undoubtedly the greatest achievement of these secret weapons until they became one of the main post-war armaments of the great powers. The flood of false rumours issuing from the Ministry of Propaganda penetrated down to the lowest fighting echelon and even reached the German prisoner of war camps in the United States. In November 1944 an enquiry conducted by the 'psychological warfare division' showed that 53 per cent of German prisoners believed that these secret weapons would change the outcome of the war, 64 per cent thought that Hitler would save Germany and 51 per cent were certain that the Allies would be thrown back into the sea.

It is true that prisoners must have something to believe in, so the validity of these figures is relative only. One story does, however, seem to prove that in Germany itself the secret weapons legend restored men's courage and increased their fanaticism. In November 1944 150 pilots drafted into the Waffen SS agreed to man a V1, guide it to its objective and blow up with it. Speer produced technical arguments to prove the futility of these weapons and Hitler agreed that these pilots, who had been christened 'self sacrifice volunteers', (Selbstopfer or SO Männer) should be returned to their units.

Here too there was deception and it was the worst of all. The idea had been mooted by Göring and Goebbels on the lines of the Japanese Kamikaze. But Colonel Baumbach, the leader of this band, had to admit that many of the self-sacrifice volunteers did not really understand what their job consisted of. At most they imagined that they had been picked for particularly dangerous operations, such as the rescue of Mussolini. Colour was lent to this idea by the fact that a certain number of the pilots had been persuaded into volunteering by Skorzeny, the expert in the organisation of especially dangerous coups.

Chapter 5

THE ALLIES—PEACE ROUND THE CORNER

EISENHOWER: 'Wars are won through public opinion.'
MONTGOMERY: 'Give people victories, and they will not worry about who's won them.'

A FEW days after the opening of the Ardennes offensive on December 16, the *Daily Mail* published a double cartoon entitled, 'Awakening'. The first picture showed 'John Wishful Thinking' sitting happily in bed and Father Christmas arriving with his sack over his shoulder to give him the stockingful of peace for which he had asked. The second picture showed von Rundstedt emerging from the sack and finishing off the trusting John.

It is true that this sudden German effort took the Allies by surprise at the very moment when they were preparing to accept victory as a Christmas present. Nevertheless, even though the 'Rundstedt' offensive fell like a thunderclap, it did not come out of a clear sky. Ever since the summer the British and American press had been giving public opinion gradually to understand that difficulties were increasing. The bitter inter-Allied disagreements were proof. In the staffs in London, and even more in Washington, where there had been far more wishful thinking, certainty of victory by the end of the year was ebbing. A feeling of disquiet began to grow in the Allied camp, vaguely at first and then with increasing precision, as people began to realise that, because they were not aiming at the same peace, the three great Allies were now no longer fighting the same war. Anglo-American disagreements had increased during the summer. The liberation of Europe meant that decisions had to be taken. The Russian advance in the east posed the necessity for negotiations with Stalin and he was evasive. With peace on the horizon some precise political thinking was necessary and that was not to Roosevelt's taste.

'Peace around the corner' was, therefore, the background to an incipient crisis; it became acute during the first fortnight of September and again in December, when political differences were accentuated by the reverses suffered in the Ardennes. The leaders made it their business to reforge the solidarity of the alliance, but the press on either side of the Atlantic conducted a battle of words more violent than any since the outbreak of war. Though there were lulls from time to time, from early August to September the crisis was more or less continuous.

Eisenhower the Centre of the Conflict

When summer 1944 ended one man, Dwight David Eisenhower symbolised Allied military achievements since the Normandy landings. Organisationally he was a middleman between the political direction of the war and the military responsible for waging it. At the summit the global conduct of the war was in the hands of Roosevelt and Churchill. On operational matters each was advised by a national Chiefs of Staff Committee. The task of working out a common strategy was the responsibility of the Combined Chiefs of Staff, who also directed all Allied operations. This organisation had been formed in Washington in January 1942. It was a combined committee consisting of the U.S. Chiefs of Staff and the British Military Mission under Field-Marshal Sir John Dill. Decisions could only be taken with the agreement of the British Chiefs of Staff in London. It was a ponderous system, only to some degree alleviated by the fact that relations between Field-Marshal Dill and General Marshall, Chairman of the U.S. Chiefs of Staff, were excellent.

Once Combined Chiefs of Staff (C.C.S.) directives had been approved, they came back to the National Staffs for transmission to the various Commanders-in-Chief which each controlled. The members of the C.C.S. were, therefore, to some extent performing a dual function, that of both 'legislature' and 'executive'. It was perfectly possible for them to find themselves responsible for implementing a directive to which they had been opposed at the drafting stage, but discipline, their common background of general staff training and their loyalty to the alliance prevented them re-opening the question. Theoretically it was a simple system and in many cases it worked well in practice, but it was nevertheless a complicated piece of machinery. With the profusion of interlocking authorities, the machine tended to become clogged when an urgent situation requiring rapid action arose.

Neither Churchill nor Roosevelt were inclined by nature or habit to pour oil on troubled waters. On all matters strictly within their province the President gave a completely free hand to his 'military technicians'. Political considerations, however, naturally on occasions directly affected operational planning, and even the Chiefs of Staff and members of the government (the Secretaries of the Army and Navy) were frequently kept in ignorance of the political requirements considered overriding by Roosevelt. He listened primarily to Harry Hopkins, an advisor without specific responsibility, or to Henry J. Morgenthau, Jr, the Secretary of the Treasury. Then he would take action and leave the military to find out from the press what he had done. As far as Churchill was concerned, he made no secret of the fact that he enjoyed taking a direct hand in operations, however small, and he frequently did so with disturbing effect. He harked back to his experiences in the Boer War or Kitchener's Egyptian

Campaign as a young Hussar officer. He would frequently send orders on matters of detail direct to Alexander or Montgomery, by-passing the Chiefs of Staff. On these occasions it fell to General Ismay to calm down the Chief of the Imperial General Staff, Sir Alan Brooke, who then had painstakingly to water down the Prime Minister's over-ambitious ideas.

The differing methods of the Big Two were reflected at the executive level and magnified by the fact that British and American military traditions were different. This gave rise to continuous friction. Once the task had been given and the objectives laid down, American commanders gave their subordinates a free hand, and the latter frequently took the bit between their teeth and got on with their job without worrying too much about keeping their exact place in the general scheme of things. The British on the other hand considered in Churchill's phrase that, 'the general may well not be up to his job, which has often been the case'. They therefore insisted on 'the higher level staffs and highest governmental authorities' exercising 'a certain measure of direction and control', sometimes down to the lowest levels.

This being the psychological and political climate, it was not surprising that the nomination of a Supreme Commander for the expeditionary forces in Europe led to months of doubt and hesitations.

In many ways Eisenhower's appointment had been the best of a bad job. He was a proxy rather than a Commander-in-Chief. His position was very different from that of Foch in the closing months of the First World War; moreover the two men were very different, both in temperament and military ability. Eisenhower—at any rate at this period—was so acutely conscious of his limitations that he declared that if Marshall became Supreme Commander, he was quite ready to take over command of an Army Group parallel to Montgomery.

The Eisenhower legend was largely based upon the ability as conciliator, arbiter and diplomat which he showed as Supreme Commander. These qualities may have been painted in overglowing colours, for he showed all the faults associated with those qualities. He could switch from patience to brutality; he was quite capable of sending staff officers back to their units if they failed to get on with their opposite numbers of the other nationality. But faced with Montgomery, who was getting directives from London, he would continuously refer matters to the Combined Chiefs of Staff. He was by nature inclined to weigh the pros and cons. He was continuously asking for advice and, when given it, was hesitant to translate it into orders. As his Chief of Staff, however, he had chosen the rugged General Bedell Smith, nicknamed 'The Barker' by his staff, who was an adept at transforming his commander's intentions into orders and forcing him to take a firm line. The two formed a remarkable team. Bedell Smith even acted as a mouthpiece for Marshall. The latter, with immense tact and highly confidentially, would give guidance in the form of suggestions, which Bedell Smith would use to influence day-to-day decisions.

Churchill and Roosevelt might well have been better advised to choose as Allied Supreme Commander someone more spirited, a commander with a more intimate grasp of the political implications of the various phases of the campaign. Clemenceau and Lloyd George, after all, had been just as totalitarian in their concept of the function of government in war but they had preferred a commander who had to be restrained rather than urged on and so had chosen Foch. A Commander-in-Chief's sense of discipline after all did not need to be that of an N.C.O. However, this was the way it had worked out, and Eisenhower's nomination clearly rested on the conviction that he would never 'make a scene'. At the end of 1941 he had said that his greatest ambition was to retire as a colonel commanding a tank regiment and this remark was admiringly quoted as proof of character. One wonders whether it really deserved as much. It might just as well have been taken as a disturbing indication of timidity and lack of self-confidence. Weighing up all the arguments, however, Marshall, Roosevelt and Churchill decided that it was proof of a capacity for sober judgment of possibilities. It must be admitted that their decision was justified by events, for in spite of all the pressures which converged upon him, Eisenhower retained his sense of proportion. He adjusted himself to developments and would only force an issue in the last resort.

The Shy Supreme Commander

Most of the great captains of history have preferred to shut themselves away and wrestle with their problem alone, emerging only at the moment when they have had to give the word 'Go'. This was not Eisenhower's way. In July 1944 he had gathered round him an immense headquarters of nearly 5,000 people; even the twenty-four members of his personal staff had some 200 direct subordinates. This was a long way from General Marshall's idea of a team of some twenty specially chosen officers, not unlike Marshal Foch's staff in 1918. Churchill made fun of it, saying that the staff should be able to provide a 'devoted battalion' of 1,000 officers to undertake all the most desperately dangerous operations.

The core of this Anglo-American world was Eisenhower's little 'private family', a friendly circle in which rank did not count. The centrepiece of it was a hatchet-faced Irish girl—with a firm chin, piercing eyes but a sensual mouth and ironically quivering nostrils. Kay Summersby had been a London model who had joined the A.T.S.; when Eisenhower first came to England she had happened to be detailed as his driver, and this she remained, becoming one of the few civilians in Supreme Headquarters. In October 1944 she was made a second lieutenant in the W.A.C. (the U.S. women's organisation) and became the Supreme Commander's private secretary. In February 1945 she was promoted lieutenant and became his A.D.C.

She was up in all the secrets and sat at the head of the table in Eisenhower's personal mess. Brooke was thunderstruck one day to see her apparently playing the mistress of the house and Winston Churchill, the guest of honour, being placed on her right. John Moaney, the coloured sergeant, who was later Eisenhower's personal valet in the White House, waited at table. 'Mickey', Sergeant MacKeogh, the general's orderly, was a sort of mascot to him. Their relationship resembled that between 'an indulgent uncle and a nephew anxious to please'.*

This ultra-democratic 'family existence' suited the Supreme Commander's tendency to paternalism which was to be seen when he visited the troops. He would invariably taste their food, showing that he took a real interest in the minor annoyances of military existence; he by no means invariably found the food good and the G.I.s appreciated that. Nevertheless the Supreme Commander's popularity had its ups and downs. After the tension of the spring and summer of 1944 he spent a quiet autumn living like any other householder, either at Saint-Germain in the house which von Rundstedt had occupied, or in the caravan located some distance from Supreme Headquarters. He was criticised for not being seen sufficiently often at the front.

Eisenhower had plenty of charm, with his blue eyes and natural smile—the smile only became fixed during the 1952 presidential campaign. At the end of the war the general picture of him was that of a simple, uncomplicated individual, a general who did not go in for hair-splitting and had difficulty in bringing himself to send men to their death. He was the antithesis of the impetuous war leader; he resembled more the head of the personnel department. His personal charm was the secret of his success as a high level mediator. For this reason he preferred to meet people and talk to them rather than write memoranda or issue instructions.

Nevertheless, Eisenhower was a shy man, and so was often torn between the desirability or necessity of giving expression to his thoughts and translating them into orders on the one side, and the fear of committing a solecism on the other.

Depending on which of these two sides to his character was uppermost at the time, he could be forceful or reticent, obstinate or ready for any compromise, naïve or secretive; sometimes he would shun crowds, at others he would be eager to hear them cheer him; but invariably as an alibi he would use a series of moral statements verging on the platitudinous.

He disliked paper work and detail. He seldom used his pen or read files; he insisted upon oral reports and refused to read anything larger than a page and half. The contradictory sides to his make-up meant that he had

* Marquis Childs, *Eisenhower, Captive Hero*, p. 73.

a natural tendency to indecision. The personality of his Chief of Staff was, therefore, of even greater importance than in a normal military organisation; Bedell Smith became the thinker, the arbiter and the chief tactician of the 'cotton wool brigade'* the small political and military staff which became so adept at protecting the general from outside influences—and, if necessary, at forcing him to decide.

Bedell Smith was exactly the man for this job, and the mere fact that Eisenhower chose him proved that the Supreme Commander was a shrewd judge with a highly developed regard for his personal convenience.

One of the most valuable members of the Supreme Commander's entourage was the naval attaché, Captain Harry Butcher; he ran the household, combining the roles of administrator and organiser of the Supreme Commander's free time and simple pleasures; his primary job, however, was to maintain relations with the war correspondents.

Eisenhower had first met him in 1926 at the house of his brother Milton, when Butcher was editor of a farming newspaper dealing primarily with fertilisers. He then took over the Washington office of the C.B.S. Radio network, an experience which stood him in good stead when Eisenhower asked for him as 'naval aide' to the Supreme Commander. Butcher became one of Eisenhower's most effective propagandists.

The word 'propagandist' may sound too strong, but the English term 'public relations officer' has too much of a publicity connotation. No general had ever before been 'sold like a brand of soap'. This, nevertheless, is what Butcher set himself to do. He was a fine mixture of tact and indiscretion. He made the most of Eisenhower's dislike of the cine-camera and his insistence on keeping the details of his private life out of the press; yet Butcher met the demands of American public opinion to know something about this imperturbable American, this 'average man', the unpretentious child of the Middle West, the John Doe who had turned into the greatest general in the world. All this was some compensation to the United States for the humiliations inflicted on Pershing by an ungrateful Europe a generation earlier.

Generals—in many cases wrongly—are said to have an almost pathological aversion to journalists; but Eisenhower had the intelligence to trust Butcher and, via him, the news technicians. It was a clever move, flattering to the journalists, and it paid off handsomely. The trust placed by the Supreme Commander in the journalists bound them to him, whereas had he adopted an attitude of defiance or shown any signs of hostility, they would have been quite prepared to publish without discrimination anything which they could 'fish up' out of Supreme Headquarters. Eisenhower put

* The phrase 'cotton wool brigade' was coined by the Alsop brothers in the autumn of 1957, to denote President Eisenhower's staff. It is an apt description, though clearly not quite to the same degree, of General Eisenhower's 1944–5 entourage.

them on their honour, and so produced a self-censorship more effective than any other restriction.

Nevertheless, during these months preceding the final victory a section of the American press can rightly be accused of being irresponsible. Some of the correspondents had hitched their star to the more spectacular generals; they made the most of their clashes and added fuel to the fire of the anti-British campaign which stemmed from the raging hostility of Patton to Montgomery, for instance. It is only fair to say, however, that their British counterparts were just as bad and never missed an opportunity of voicing British discontents. The war leaders were, of course, primarily responsible, for the newspapers got their stories only from those who wished to tell them. Eisenhower was modest and deplored the fact that because of his position he was always in the limelight, whereas men like Hodges, Bradley, Gerow and many others were left out in the cold simply because they were attending to their business as commanders. Whatever the reasons for this ballyhoo, in retrospect it is deplorable; the smallest disagreement became an international matter, and commanders felt the weight of public opinion whipped up by the press bearing on them so heavily that it sometimes even influenced the conduct of operations. By the end of August there were 980 war correspondents accredited to Eisenhower; he could hardly be expected to remain immune to their influence.

Such was the position of the Supreme Commander and the atmosphere in which he had to work. It shows how many were the rocks through which he had to navigate from the time of the Allied landing to the Ardennes. For a sensitive man like Eisenhower, allergic to the assertion of his authority, the pressures were severe.

In addition to these pressures, the events of the autumn reinforced Eisenhower's tendency to inaction and the beneficiary was Hitler. As agreed before the landing, the Supreme Commander took over operational command of all forces at the beginning of September. As American Theatre Commander he controlled all the American air and land forces in Great Britain and on the Continent. As Supreme Allied Commander he commanded the following groups:

Field-Marshal Montgomery's Twenty-first Army Group (British), which consisted of First Canadian Army and Second British Army and held the northern sector of the Allied front.

Twelfth U.S. Army Group commanded by General Bradley, which consisted of U.S. First Army (Hodges) on the eastern frontier of Belgium, U.S. Third Army (Patton) in Lorraine and along the Saar, and U.S. Ninth Army (Simpson) initially in Brittany, moving to southern Belgium in October and into the line at Aix-la-Chapelle in November.

Sixth Army Group (American and French) commanded by General Devers. This consisted of U.S. Seventh Army (Patch) in northern Alsace,

French First Army (de Lattre de Tassigny) in southern Alsace and 2 French Armoured Division (Leclerc).

Eisenhower's tactical air forces consisted of the Ninth U.S. Air Force and the Second British Tactical Air Force with a total of 3,728 American and 5,104 British fighters. At the Quebec Conference at the end of September it had been decided that he should have no control over the heavy bomber forces, R.A.F. Bomber Command and the U.S. Strategic Air Force, but in case of emergency he was authorised to ask for action by these forces in direct support of ground operations.

Finally in reserve he had General Brereton's First Airborne Army consisting of XVIII U.S. Airborne Corps (Ridgway), the British Airborne Corps (Browning) and the U.S. IX Troop Carrier Command.

The Italian front was not under Eisenhower's command but under that of the British general, Maitland Wilson.

Eisenhower's total forces consisted of twenty-three infantry divisions and the equivalent of seventeen armoured divisions; of this total seventeen were British and twenty-three American. They were faced by forty-one German divisions, five of which were shut up in the Atlantic ports, whilst two were still withdrawing from western and south-western France. These figures do not, however, give a true picture, for the Allies were in fact the stronger by two to one in men, twenty to one in tanks and twenty to one in guns. The Luftwaffe had little more than 600 aircraft against the Allied figure of nearly 9,000.*

From One Extreme to the Other

Looking back after the 'six mad weeks of the break-through' (to use Bradley's phrase) no one was more surprised than the Allies at the speed at which events had moved. In the light of the severity of the first ten days' fighting in Normandy the forecast of the planners at Supreme Headquarters on June 17 had been that the Belgian frontier would not be reached before December 23 and the German frontier north of Aix-la-Chapelle not before May 2 1945. It was thought that the final battle would then be very rapid and June 1 1945 was estimated as the date on which the German forces would surrender.†

But the first Siegfried line fort had been captured on September 11, seven months ahead of schedule.

Plotters and prophets never like to see their forecasts belied by events. In this case they swung from one extreme to the other and indulged in blind optimism based on over-hasty superficial appreciation. During the second fortnight of August, the intelligence summaries of all the various armies, both British and American, were more or less unanimous: the Germans had not merely been beaten into a jelly, they were disintegrating.

* Figures from Cole, *The Lorraine Campaign*, p. 2 et seq.
† See Pogue, *The Supreme Command*, p. 257.

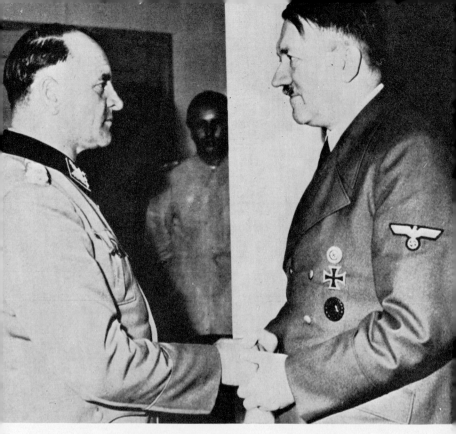

1(*a*) General Sepp Dietrich received by Hitler, 1944

(*b*) Field-Marshal Walter Model

2(a) A German patrol in no-man's land

(b) General von Manteuffel in late summer 1944

On September 8 the Combined Chiefs of Staff Joint Intelligence Committee in Washington, which was always inclined to paint a rosy picture, concluded that the German armies would surrender piecemeal and that it was 'improbable that any organised resistance under the German High Command could continue beyond December 1 1944 . . . it might perhaps end even earlier.'

The only discordant note came from Colonel Koch, G.2 to Patton's U.S. Third Army fighting in Champagne and on the borders of Lorraine. He said:

The enemy has been able to maintain a sufficiently cohesive front to exercise an overall control of his tactical situation. His withdrawal, though continuing, has not been a rout or mass collapse. It must be constantly kept in mind that fundamentally the enemy is playing for time . . . it can be expected that the German armies will continue to fight until destroyed or captured.*

For once this warning voice was echoed—and authoritatively. Winston Churchill too did not believe in an early German collapse. On the *Queen Mary* on his way to his meeting with Roosevelt in Quebec he warned the British Chiefs of Staff against exaggerated optimism, reminding them of 'the German onslaught in March 1918'.†

Might it not be that history would repeat itself? Churchill had given a vivid picture of German recovery: 'a monster of seemingly unfathomable resources and tireless strength, invulnerable—since slaughter even on the greatest scale was no deterrent.‡

These words from *The World Crisis* refer to the June 1918 surprise attack along the Chemin des Dames. Churchill had then been Minister of Munitions and he could still remember only too vividly the problems which had worried him at the time—the preservation at all costs of the Channel ports and the maintenance of liaison between the French and British armies. At the beginning of September 1944, the major ports from Antwerp to Bordeaux were still in German hands. This was one of the reasons for Churchill's pessimism as opposed to the combined staff's optimistic forecasts. As for splitting the American and British forces, Hitler was the only person who seriously considered the idea just at this moment. In his heart of hearts, however, Churchill may not altogether have excluded this possibility.

Eisenhower also was sceptical. He was not worried about historical precedents in which he had not been personally involved—in 1918 he was commanding an Armoured Training Centre at Gettysburg, at the age of twenty-seven—he simply added up the balance sheet of practical possibilities. Whether the Germans were on the verge of disintegration or not,

* Pogue, op. cit., p. 245.
† Churchill, Vol. 6, *Triumph and Tragedy*, p. 131.
‡ Churchill, *World Crisis 1916–18*, Part II, p. 458.

F

the Allies were incapable of dealing them the decisive blow which would accelerate the process.

The planners had been too intent on working out exact forecasts and had not allowed for the necessary flexibility; supplies and rearward services had not kept pace with the fighting troops. The stocks which, according to the plan, should have been established in Normandy during the summer, had been run down. The distance between the depots and the units to be supplied increased daily and the bridgehead transport resources were quite unable to cope with the demand. The necessity of operations to reduce the German garrisons in the ports had to be envisaged even though the port installations would be destroyed in the process. Antwerp had been captured on September 4, Le Havre on the 12th, Brest on the 19th. But by then it was already too late to gear up the enormous machine feeding the units at the front. There was only one solution—to free the mouths of the Scheldt. But in fact the Germans maintained a stubborn defence there into November, denying the Allies use of the port of Antwerp. On September 8 Churchill brought the British Chiefs of Staff down to earth with a note which said: 'It is difficult to see how 21st Army Group can advance in force to the German frontier until it has dealt with the Germans at Walcheren and to the north of Antwerp.'*

Eisenhower had been wrestling with the same problem for weeks. His staff's intelligence summaries left him cold, and had it been possible to confine their echoes to Supreme Headquarters, their effect would have been small. But as a result of calculated 'leaks' the British and American press was indulging in a wave of wild unthinking optimism. The war correspondents were carried away by their enthusiasm and the victorious generals encouraged them to make much of the distances they had covered, the towns they had captured and the courage of their soldiers. Eisenhower was horrified at the tone of the American press. Criticism of British delays was punctuated by headlines and editorials extolling the G.I.s and their leaders. The result was a curious mixture of euphoria and bitterness; American public opinion was in danger of becoming convinced that the end of the war would only be a question of weeks, if only the British could be persuaded to go all out.

Ike warned the war correspondents on several occasions, advancing weighty technical considerations, reminding them that the lines of communication were stretched to the limit and that in the near future any further advance on a broad front would become almost impossible even against minor opposition. He gave bouquets to Allied co-operation and made much of the difficult task accomplished by Montgomery in the battle for Caen, pointing out that by pinning the enemy down he had enabled Patton to break through at Avranches. At the same time he pointed out to the British that the march of American troops through Paris had none of

* Churchill, *Triumph and Tragedy*, p. 171.

the political implications which they imagined and on which they commented so bitterly.

The Supreme Commander clung to his theory of 'the advance on a broad front' decided upon before the invasion of Normandy. The question now was whether to adhere to this theory or take advantage of the opportunity offered by the speed of the German withdrawal. This was the basis of the strategic and personal dispute which up to the time of the Ardennes offensive raged between Eisenhower and Montgomery, the latter supported by Brooke.

On September 1 Montgomery was promoted field-marshal. But this did little to console him for a bitter disappointment. For the first phase of the landing and during the battle of Normandy, he had been Commander-in-Chief of all Allied Land Forces, and he considered that both efficiency and logic demanded that he should so continue. Eisenhower, he said, 'should not descend into the land battle and become a Ground C-in-C'.*

The necessity for unified land control seemed to Montgomery so great that he stated that he was quite prepared to serve under the orders of Bradley, commanding Twelfth U.S. Army Group, 'if public opinion in America was involved'.†

Eisenhower was all the less inclined to agree with this reasoning in that, quite apart from his natural ambition, Montgomery made no secret of his desire to bring about a radical change in the plans worked out for the assault on Germany.

In Eisenhower's view, before the decisive offensive was launched, Antwerp must have been captured, the Allies must be in control of the mouths of the Rhine and behind the front the forces which had landed in southern France on August 15 must have effected a junction with the right flank of the armies coming down from Normandy, thus completing the clearance of France. Only then could an attempt be made to encircle the Ruhr both from north and south.

Even before the end of the Normandy battle however, Montgomery was thinking of a bold manœuvre which he terms in his memoirs, 'a Schlieffen plan in reverse'. His idea was that his Twenty-first Army Group, supported by Hodges' U.S. First Army, should break the line of the Rhine between Antwerp and the Ardennes and drive on Berlin. To support this offensive logistically all other operations in France would be stopped and all other forces immobilised; the operation would rely for its effect upon a concentrated blow. But Bradley and his Twelfth U.S. Army Group were also moving forward fast; they considered that their momentum would carry them to Metz and the Saar, and open the road to Frankfurt. These would be spectacular returns for the American war effort and Eisenhower felt that he could not sacrifice them, however impressive the

* Montgomery of Alamein, *Memoirs*, p. 268.
† *Idem*, p. 269.

British plan might be—a point of view which Montgomery refused to grasp. Even if Eisenhower had been a Napoleon, had contrived to concentrate all his available resources, step up the output of his swollen lines of communication and supply troops in the heart of Germany from Cherbourg, Washington would never have allowed the Supreme Commander to take the gamble. Marshall's and Eisenhower's hands were tied by an overall war policy, the details of which were kept secret from them.

Montgomery harried the Supreme Commander incessantly, withdrawing only to return to the charge, but he was wasting his time. Finally Eisenhower, with the agreement of General de Guingand, Chief of Staff Twenty-first Army Group, whose tact was a major factor in reducing friction, laid down his objectives. The line of the Rhine in the north and the German frontier in the centre should be made good; an offensive should be launched towards the Saar in the south, and minor operations should be carried out in preparation for future major offensives.

So autumn was a gloomy period, characterised by the Canadian battle for the mouths of the Scheldt, the fruitless struggle for a bridgehead at Arnhem, and position warfare in the Aix-la-Chapelle salient and the Forest of Hürtgen. The situation was reminiscent of the 1917 battles of attrition. Montgomery made use of the parallel in his personal crusade. Supreme Headquarters' latest plans, he said, had resulted in a strategic set-back; an attempt must be made to restart the war of movement in the spring by concentrating maximum force at a single point. Since the Allied front was divided by the Ardennes, he suggested that to north and south of this point there should be one Commander-in-Chief—Bradley in the south and himself in the north. U.S. Ninth Army should thus be under his command and he would be responsible for the offensive against the Ruhr.

On December 7, after Churchill had brought pressure to bear on Roosevelt, Montgomery made a last attempt at a meeting in Maastricht with Eisenhower, his deputy, Air Chief-Marshal Tedder, and Bradley. As if all the arguments of the last three months amounted to nothing, they discussed once more a synchronised offensive both in the north and south and unification of command of the land forces. Eisenhower ended by giving way to some extent. The main effort in early 1945 would be north of the Ruhr; Bradley was to divide his forces into two groups separated by the Ardennes massif; there the hundred-mile front was to be thinly held by four divisions. On Bradley's right Patton was to attack from Lorraine towards Frankfurt; on his left Simpson's Ninth Army would support Montgomery's offensive.

This was a paper compromise only, and the basic differences remained. Open crisis had been avoided for the moment, but since press comment was inevitably a few days behind events, the German offensive became linked in the public mind with this change in the Allies' operational plan. Eisenhower was pictured as having been worsted by Montgomery.

Chapter 6

ALLIED POLICY IN THE DOLDRUMS

THERE must have been some reason for Eisenhower's obstinate refusal to seize the unexpected opportunities with which the fortunes of war presented him in the summer of 1944. He has always avoided answering this question. His loyalty to Roosevelt even after his death must have been based on something more than mere caution. At the time Churchill was not similarly inhibited. On August 6 he wrote to Harry Hopkins: 'I am grieved to find that even splendid victories and widening opportunities do not bring us together on strategy.'

The Big Three had, however, been quite prepared to count their chickens before they were hatched; in January 1944 they had set up the European Consultative Commission. But diplomats work slowly, and Roosevelt refused to admit that strategy might also include military operations. Six weeks after the landing, therefore, Eisenhower was completely ignorant of the political principles upon which he should work. He could not plan the best line of entry into Germany unless he knew the procedure authorised for an eventual enemy surrender and, still more important, unless he knew whether there were any overriding considerations, other than operational, governing his junction with the Soviet army.

What To Do with Germany

The European Consultative Commission did no more than lay down in broad outline the peace-time organisation for the administration of Germany and the division of the country between the three victorious powers, the starting point being the moment at which the Civil Affairs Organisation took over from military authorities, which was to be as quickly as possible.

The exact meaning of the words 'as quickly as possible' was of course a point of vital interest to the Supreme Commander but one on which he was totally in the dark. Roosevelt had thought that insistence upon unconditional surrender would enable him to 'avoid discussing the future of Germany' (Richard Crossman's apt phrase in the House of Commons on October 26 1945). On November 28 1943 at the Teheran Conference Stalin himself had

questioned the advisability of the unconditional surrender principle with no definition of the exact terms which would be imposed on Germany. He felt that to leave the principle of unconditional surrender unclarified merely served to unite the German people, whereas to draw up specific terms, no matter how harsh, and tell the German people that this was what they would have to accept, would, in his opinion, hasten the day of German capitulation.*

In the light of the collapse of German resistance in Tunisia and then of the Italians, Eisenhower made no less than three requests to the Combined Chiefs of Staff for a public statement explaining the terms of surrender and setting out clearly the arrangements for the future of Germany. In his view, this would offer the German generals some definite future whereas surrender pure and simple could be nothing but a policy of despair. A cease-fire would have something to offer instead of a complete blank to which even a continuance of the struggle might appear preferable. Goebbels' propaganda would be deprived of a 'golden' theme of which it would not fail to make use. Eisenhower begged for some definite directive in December 1943, in April 1944 and again in August. At that stage of the German withdrawal, a few days before the capture of Paris, he advocated a psychological offensive which he considered might lead to local surrenders and increase confusion in Model's armies. German units surrounded in the Normandy pockets might not have tried to fight their way out so furiously.

But in August Roosevelt had refused to make any political gesture.† In November Eisenhower made a fourth attempt, but Roosevelt was not to be moved, and this time was supported by Churchill. The Prime Minister argued that the Germans would take any such move merely as proof of weakness on the part of the Allies, who were at the time in a difficult position. It would be better, he said, to make the explanations after an indisputable victory.

Eisenhower could not therefore use the traditional weapon of psychological warfare, although it might at the time have had a considerable effect upon the German officer corps which was suffering the wave of repression following July 20. The Supreme Commander was also hampered in his preparations for the Rhine crossing operation. Inevitably he had to take account of the future division of Germany. Personally he was opposed to carving up the country into zones of occupation and would have preferred an integrated military government for all Germany. In any case in mid-August he did not know whose forces were to occupy the north-west of the country; it seemed inconceivable that when the fighting was over, the

* Sherwood, *White House Papers of Harry L. Hopkins*, Vol. II, p. 777.

† On July 25 the European Consultative Commission had in fact agreed on a draft text for the surrender terms. Roosevelt approved it on August 8 but was probably not in a position to communicate it to Eisenhower pending Churchill's and Stalin's agreement. The Commission did not receive the official American approval until September 9, that of London until October 21 and that of Moscow until as late as December 14. In any case no use was made of the draft when the German surrender occurred; certain parts of it were incorporated in the Declaration of Assumption of Authority in Germany by the Allies on June 6 1945. (*See* Conferences at Malta and Yalta, p. 110 et seq.)

British and American armies with their enormous supply services would, contrary to all common sense, carry out a gigantic general post. It seemed more than likely that the layout initially adopted for the offensive would become permanent.

In face of opposition by Churchill, Roosevelt continued to demand that the North German coast and ports be occupied by the Americans in order to ease the problem of shipping forces home for demobilisation.*

By August 17 Eisenhower had lost patience with the vacillations of the diplomats and military 'experts' of the European Consultative Commission. He sent Roosevelt an ultimatum: he was going to decide the question without regard for political considerations and proposed to move into Germany with the British Twenty-first Army Group on his left. The Americans would therefore later occupy Germany south of the Main and the British north of it.

The Consultative Commission did not make up its mind to sign the protocol laying down the boundaries of the occupation zones until September 12—and even then without allocating the northern zone. Between August 17 and September 12 came Montgomery's insistence on the drive into the Ruhr. The Ruhr was essential to the British economy on two counts: German coal and steel would allow it to recover its lost markets, and German heavy industry would be dealt an irreparable blow. The reasons Montgomery gave were military, but they were inevitably considered against this background. Eisenhower's refusal to agree with him stemmed to some extent from his aversion to taking into account 'political considerations' of this nature. Nevertheless, at the Quebec Conference a month later Roosevelt ended by accepting British occupation of the Ruhr.

There remained the question of Berlin. If Eisenhower had given the capture of Berlin as an objective for his forces, he would have been forced, all technical objections notwithstanding, to agree to Montgomery's proposals. The first question was whether he was justified, after all their exertions since June, in calling upon his troops for an additional effort merely in order to win the race to which the Soviet armies would clearly have challenged him. From the military point of view the answer depended upon an accurate estimate of available resources. From the political point of view the question was raised with certain embarrassment and without any real emphasis; although its importance was amply proved by the post-war crisis, it was never examined in detail. Only a small proportion of the documents which could throw light upon the discussion have been published.

The question is whether there ever was a discussion. Once the September 12 protocol laying down the occupation zones and fixing the Berlin Statute (Tripartite at this period) had been issued, the affair was settled.

* Also, as he confided to Stalin during their first private meeting at Yalta on February 4 1945, to prevent the U.S. lines of communication crossing France.

In theory at least the nationality of the army which captured the German capital would in no way affect its occupation. The Western Powers knew that their sectors in Berlin would be surrounded by the Soviet zone.

During the discussions in the European Consultative Commission between January and September 1944 the U.S. State Department representatives were the only ones to see matters clearly. Philip Mosely, the senior representative on Ambassador Winant's staff, could not manage to get agreement to a corridor linking Berlin to the Western Zones. He was opposed, not so much by the Soviet representatives, as by his colleagues from the War Department. They stated that they were convinced that the Soviet forces would advance to the Rhine and that it was therefore useless to conclude an agreement on zones of occupation. *A fortiori* their strategic planning made no allowance for the capture of Berlin; they were as pessimistic as the planners who had drawn up the 'forecast' timetable for operations in the west.

The fact that the Allies were six months ahead of schedule as a result of the German withdrawal may have given rise to the idea of capturing Berlin as a bargaining counter in future negotiations. Eisenhower first gave evidence of some such idea on September 15, three days after the conclusion of the agreement on the division of Germany into zones of occupation; he wrote to Montgomery: 'Clearly Berlin is the main prize . . . It is my desire to move on Berlin by the most direct and expeditious route . . . in one co-ordinated concerted operation.'* But between these two sentences the Supreme Commander referred at length to secondary objectives at which the Allied forces should aim, 'should the Russians beat us to Berlin'; he mentioned Hanover and Hamburg, Augsburg, Munich, and a thrust towards Leipzig–Dresden.

Replying three days later, Montgomery rejected these operations and placed all his emphasis on 'the main prize'. He said: 'I consider that as time is so very important we have got to decide what is necessary to go to Berlin and finish the war; the remainder must play a secondary role.' Replying on September 20 Eisenhower adhered to his plan for the offensive, saying. 'Specifically I agree with you in the following: my choice of routes for making the all-out offensive into Germany is from the Ruhr to Berlin . . . when we get to the Rhine, the next concern of Bradley's will be to put a strong fully equipped Army on his left to accompany you to Berlin.'†

On the face of it, these were unambiguous assurances; their object, however, was to give Montgomery the impression that he was right in principle and at the same time serve as an excuse for failing to put these principles into practice. Moreover Eisenhower never subsequently referred to these letters, either in his memoirs or during the later controversy

* Montgomery, *Memoirs*, pp. 277–8.
† *Ibid.*, pp. 279–81.

during his presidency when he was accused of having deliberately neglected Berlin. 'I knew', he said, 'that any pencil-like thrust into the heart of Germany such as he [Montgomery] proposed, would meet nothing but certain destruction. This was true no matter on what part of the front it might be attempted. I would not consider it.'*

His reaction to certain of Churchill's proposals in the summer of 1944 undoubtedly gives a pointer to his attitude to the political aspect of a possible offensive on Berlin. Early in August Churchill had pressed him to cancel the landing in southern France in favour of an operation in the Balkans or against the Brittany ports. In his book, Eisenhower says:

The Prime Minister may have thought that a post-war situation which would see the western Allies posted in great strength in the Balkans would be far more effective in producing a stable post-hostilities world than if the Russian armies should be the ones to occupy that region. I told him that if this were his reason for advocating the campaign into the Balkans he should go instantly to the President and lay the facts, as well as his own conclusions, on the table. I well understood that strategy can be affected by political considerations, and if the President and the Prime Minister should decide that it was worth while to prolong the war, thereby increasing its cost in men and money, in order to secure the political objectives they deemed necessary, then I would instantly and loyally adjust my plans accordingly. But I did insist that as long as he argued the matter on military grounds alone I could not concede validity to his arguments.†

One wonders whether Churchill had hopes similar to those of Montgomery on the operational level. He was 'very anxious to forestall the Russians' in central Europe, but apparently only in 'certain areas', primarily Hungary and Austria.‡

In September he was pessimistic over the prospects of an early offensive and it was perhaps for this reason that he did not make too much of the Berlin problem during the Quebec Conference. The Combined Chiefs of Staff report simply proposed to 'penetrate deeply into the interior of Germany' and Churchill does not even mention the subject in his memoirs. Like all the others actors in this phase of the war he preserved an embarrassed silence; in the 1950s no one re-opened the argument about the origins of the Berlin crisis. The German capital might well have been a bargaining counter prior to September 12 1944, but it seems as if the Western Powers had no wish to consider it as such. Subsequently their hands were tied by agreements and they had no opportunity for political action.

In London there was evidently more appreciation of the possibilities still open to Eisenhower before the Civil Affairs Administrators in charge of the occupation took over. The plans worked out in the autumn of 1944 for the reorganisation of Germany were in fact based on the assumption that

* Eisenhower, *Crusade in Europe*, p. 335.   † Eisenhower, *op. cit.*, p. 311.
‡ Churchill, *Triumph and Tragedy*, p. 131.

'Anglo-American forces would reach Berlin before the Russians' and that Berlin would be administered as an 'integrated military district' until the arrival of the Russians. Only then would the national sectors function independently.*

This extract from the British Official History of the War shows the background thinking of the Foreign Office at the time, and the Foreign Office controlled the political division of the Civil Affairs Organisation.†

The final decision was Roosevelt's. He was undoubtedly aware of the possibilities but purposely shut his eyes to them. He had resisted Churchill's urgings for an offensive into Austria, citing 'purely political and internal considerations' and saying that 'Overlord could not have survived the slightest setback if it had become known that sizeable Allied Forces had been landed in the Balkans'. *A fortiori* to immobilise the American armies in favour of an almost entirely British offensive on Berlin would have affected his chances in the presidential electoral campaign, now (late summer 1944) in its final and most critical weeks. He was opposed to the establishment of any zone of influence in Europe and was convinced that like himself 'Uncle Joe' Stalin would remain faithful to his Teheran promises; he thought that if only he could talk to him privately and as man to man all misunderstandings would disappear. In his deteriorating state of health Roosevelt slipped back into the indecision which was the undoing of many of his earlier and bolder initiatives.

Stimson, the Secretary for War, and the State Department now began to press for the issue of some directive on the conditions to be imposed on Germany. On September 5 therefore, Roosevelt approved the plan for 'Pastoralisation' dreamt up by Henry J. Morgenthau Jr and got it hurriedly approved by Churchill during the Quebec Conference.‡

In the atmosphere of the time Morgenthau's ideas were understandable but this did not alter the fact that they were totally unrealistic. The Morgenthau Plan had only one result but it was fundamental: added to the demand for unconditional surrender it lent additional force to Goebbels'

* F. S. V. Donnison, *Civil Affairs and Military Government North West Europe*, p. 255.

† The British Chiefs of Staff went even further. In a Memorandum dated September 9, they expressed the opinion that the Allies should 'be on their guard against a Russo-German collaboration and that in the event of Russian hostility, we should need German help'. They continued that the Russians had no intention of allowing a unified Germany to rearm unless they could dominate it subsequently. The dismemberment of Germany would therefore enable the western portions to be kept within the western European orbit. The Foreign Office considered the Chiefs of Staff argument as 'fantastic and dangerous'. (See Woodward, *British Foreign Policy in the Second World War*, p. 469).

‡ The 'Morgenthau Plan' was based upon the fact that Germany's military strength depended upon her industrial potential; its object therefore, was to reduce the latter to the 'essential minimum' and to develop German agriculture in order, in Morgenthau's words, 'to return Germany to a pastoral way of life'.

propaganda: more than ever the struggle was one of life and death. Eisenhower's headquarters made no secret of the fact that in face of such statements of principle, even though they were subsequently watered down by Roosevelt, it would be difficult to break German morale.

Under these circumstances, the mere thought of risking a set-back by openly entering upon a race for Berlin against the Russians (for there could be no doubt that this was what such an offensive really meant), was anathema to Roosevelt. It ran completely counter to his concept of his duty which was to pave the way for full employment for the American workman, design the organisation of the United Nations, and leave the military—the technicians—to win the war, since they knew how to do so. Above all, influenced by his wife, he was opposed to any involvement in European affairs. His entire policy consisted of avoidance of action, postponement of major decisions on the post-war period, and rejection of any initiative which could disturb the course of events, whether pre-determined or not. His ambition was to 'usher in the true twentieth century'; disinterested though this attitude may have been, it did not give Eisenhower much guidance on his short-term objectives. Moreover, it implied a rigid respect by the Allies of the unwritten agreement on non-intervention in European affairs.

Robert Murphy, political advisor to SHAEF in August 1944 and so particularly concerned with the German problem, has recently produced evidence which confirms the above analysis.*

According to him the division of Germany along the line of the Elbe was thought to be the best solution and the one most rapidly attainable, since at the time it was expected that the Soviet offensive would reach the Rhine and 'even penetrate into France'. The idea was supported by the British and by many Americans, particularly 'the military and the President'. According to Mosely, however, it was the U.S. military who were the first to be convinced of the scope of the Soviet offensive.

Murphy has also stated that, as regards Berlin, neither the diplomats nor the politicians were anxious to reinstate it as the capital, considering it as the home of Nazism. Eisenhower apparently considered that the conquest of Berlin would cost 100,000 men and refused to take any initiative in the matter. In the end Roosevelt left the question entirely in the hands of the Supreme Commander. Murphy added: 'The civil authorities were in disorder as a result of President Roosevelt's poor state of health. The military, therefore, had to take decisions which had major political implications.'

All these personal statements throw some light upon the problem, but the argument on responsibility is still open and we shall not get at the truth until the original documents, still carefully concealed, are made available.

* During a lecture in New York in May 1962. It will be noted, however, that particularly on the subject of the division of Germany along the Elbe he is not so definite as in his memoirs, *Diplomat among Warriors*, Chapter 16.

From Blind Optimism to Depression

So the Americans were about to swing from one extreme to the other. Since the end of the summer their press, with encouragement from Washington, had kept them in a state of exaggerated optimism. They were far removed from any theatre of war; they were not afflicted either by general mobilisation or by restrictions; they were still living a peace-time existence. They had never had any idea of the real dangers of war and they thought the contest was over. Vast though it was, their war effort was remarkably limited compared to the Germans' total war and the British national war. They had never had to face mobilisation of the total resources of the nation, nor deprivation of the basic liberties which enable every citizen to decide his own future. Yet even so, the American economy was the backbone of the Allied war effort.

Early in September it looked as if the struggle was practically over. The administration slowed down war production and allocated an increased percentage to the Pacific. In the war factories the unemployment factor reappeared, and the American workman lost no time in going off to look for a job in industries unconnected with the war. The business world became less willing to accept military orders and began to prepare for reconversion. A big Chicago firm went so far as to refuse to fulfil orders from the War Department and when sanctions were taken against it on December 28, there were violent protests against Government severity.

In this atmosphere of psychological relaxation came the realisation that neither the Russians nor the British were keeping to the unwritten agreement regarding non-involvement in Europe and that sooner or later the United States would have to intervene. The threat of civil war in Belgium and Greece, London's refusal to accept Count Sforza as a member of the Italian Cabinet, the new partition of Poland, the meeting of Churchill and Stalin in October all made it look as if the British were everywhere and the Americans nowhere. Caught up in the presidential election, the Americans felt that events had got ahead of them and they were the victims of Allied chicanery. The press fulminated against their partners' bad faith and tried to make out that London and Moscow were hatching some plot behind the back of the United States.

Americans had thought that there were lofty sentiments behind the policy later christened by the *Economist* that of the 'noble negatives'—the policy of non-intervention with the object of non-involvement. The *New York Times* congratulated itself that the American concept of war was 'unusual'. 'Britain, Russia, and other European nations see war as an instrument of politics, but for the United States it is something purely and narrowly military—to win the war and then go home. The British and the Russians want to win the war in such a way as to further their policies.'

On many occasions the London *Times* lent colour to this interpretation, praising the Russians for trying to ensure the security of their western frontier—'and it would be foolish as well as somewhat hypocritical to consider the insistence on this right as the symptom of an aggressive policy.' The American newspapers were indignant at such cynicism, but *The Times* replied: 'If regional understandings represent power politics, the United States, like M. Jourdain, has since 1823 been writing prose without knowing it.'

The American press was so busy reproaching its ally for 'reconstituting the old Power Bloc', the central European and Mediterranean ambitions of which had finally prevented the war being ended 'on the anniversary of Pearl Harbour' (according to the *Army & Navy Journal*), that it had no time for an objective re-examination of the basic conditions governing the war in Europe. It simply hinted that victory was still some way off. As reasons for the stiffening of enemy resistance it cited the myth of the Siegfried line, the insurmountable obstacle which their G.I.s had nevertheless pierced at Aix-la-Chapelle, and the moral recovery of the German people. From this it was a short step to the conclusion that nothing had been settled at all and ever longer lists began to appear of German units which had moved up to the front since the beginning of October. After three weeks to a month of gloomy news about Allied shortages of ammunition, equipment and motor tyres resulting from the bad weather, communications difficulties and the falling level of production, one of the best informed military correspondents, Hanson Baldwin, announced on December 16 (the very day on which the Germans attacked in the Ardennes) that in the west Hitler had available a hundred divisions against sixty Allied.

So American public opinion swung—with no half-way house—from excessive confidence to panic. Hitler's seizure of the initiative occurred at the very moment when the American people's state of mind pre-disposed them to an unreasoning over-estimate of the Reich's potentialities.

Then during the first days of the offensive the Supreme Commander clamped down a complete black-out on all news, putting the journalists into a fury. The stories which the war correspondents fed to the radio networks and the teleprinters became completely unreasoning.

What of France?

France had imagined that liberation would immediately lead to a golden period of plenty; though disappointed, she continued to find it difficult to realise that the war was still in progress. Pen friend organisations were still flourishing and courses on twelfth-century French literature recommenced at the Sorbonne. Apart from those who had relatives involved, the nation as a whole seemed determined to forget that there were still more than a million Frenchmen in concentration camps and German prisoner-of-war camps. The French had no conception of the extent to which they were despised by their Allies. The only one to realise it was General de Gaulle. He journeyed to Moscow, looking for a counterweight to the haughty British and Americans, but found that he was simply treated as the representative of a conquered nation.

The American press did nothing to raise its readers' opinion of France; after two days in and around the Ritz Mrs Clare Booth-Luce noted that: 'Frenchwomen do not look as though they had suffered very much. Fur coats and exotic hair-do's are to be seen everywhere in Paris.' Frederick Crawford, an American businessman, who had been despatched on a mission to France, described the situation quite simply:

The Resistance consists largely of Communists, teenagers and ex-criminals. If you carried on your business for the Germans but did not enlarge it you were considered a patriotic citizen. If you carried on your business for the Germans, enlarged it and made a profit—you were a collaborator. And recently, if you fell out with your trades union, you were a collaborator.

It is only fair to add that the *New York Herald Tribune* protested against this as being a superficial impression. 'Mr Crawford', it said 'has been in a dream world in which the Germans were merely deficit financiers and patriotism a crime against collaboration.'

Many Frenchmen may have been unable to understand why they could not simply go back to the summer of 1939, but nevertheless French soldiers were holding the Vosges. They formed an army—or rather a collection of military units—of 200,000 to 300,000 men, as divorced from their country as were the G.I.s from their home states in America. De Lattre with the French First Army and Leclerc with the 2 French Armoured Division performed prodigies in welding together soldiers from Africa, boys from the Chantiers de Jeunesse and the Equipes Nationales on the one hand and the men of the Free French Forces, the French Forces of the Interior and the F.T.P.* on the other. It was only in these squadrons and companies, with their variegated headgear but standard battle-dress blouse that men could exchange reminiscences of their exploits in the Resistance or on one of the Allied fronts without coming to blows. The French First Army was re-creating France.

In the eyes of the Allied High Command, however, these soldiers who had just moved up the Rhone and Saône and were now getting ready to liberate Alsace were fit for nothing more than police duties. The views of the Supreme Command and those of the French government were poles apart on the use to be made of the French Forces of the Interior. In General de Gaulle's view they should be accepted without reservation into the Allied forces, be completely re-equipped, and used to augment the French First Army and so form the basis of the post-war French forces.

* Franc-Tireurs et Partisans, the French Left-Wing Resistance Organisation.

Eisenhower refused to equip more than the expeditionary forces; he was only authorised to provide equipment for the battalions and commandos capable of taking an early part in the fighting. Anything more than that depended upon the decision of the Combined Chiefs of Staff and ultimately upon Roosevelt and Churchill. Eisenhower was pre-occupied with the question of law and order in the rear areas and so demanded the formation of security units to undertake Gendarmerie tasks and protection of the lines of communication. In addition, talking to French visitors, he would ask for 'service units' to ease the task of the enormous organisation already clogging the American rear areas.

When the offensive came to a halt at the end of October and the manpower crisis developed, Eisenhower weakened slightly. He agreed that two additional French divisions should be equipped, but the de Gaulle government still demanded eight. The argument had not been settled when the Ardennes offensive came. The Allies did at least, however, give the French government *de jure* recognition, on October 23, after the enlargement of the consultative assembly. Eisenhower had supported the State Department in overcoming Roosevelt's hesitation, a fact which should be recognised, even if his motives were not entirely altruistic. Top-level military negotiations nevertheless remained as difficult as ever.

To sum up this short outline of the state of affairs on the Allied side. It would clearly be a gross exaggeration to say, as Blumentritt did of their German counterparts, that Eisenhower and Montgomery were 'officers abandoned by their political chiefs'. There was no question of abandonment, but SHAEF (Supreme Headquarters Allied Expeditionary Force) and the Allied capitals were wrestling with different problems. In day to day matters Eisenhower contrived to get his integrated staff to work well without too many clashes of personality or too much friction; he managed to keep control of such turbulent personalities as Patton and Montgomery. But this success was largely offset by the difference in concept at the top level. On the one hand was Churchill, determined to be a war leader in the full sense of the word; on the other Roosevelt, by nature disinclined to take any direct interest in the course of operations. The happy mean was difficult to strike. Churchill pursued the traditional British policy of seizing upon any long-term change in the European balance of power, Roosevelt took refuge behind the traditional military policy of his country and refused to look further than the end of the war. But the Americans had five armies with an enormous organisation in the field, as against two British. Their view inevitably carried more weight.

It is always difficult to hold the balance between the politician and the military, but in this case the problem took on a new dimension. Eisenhower may have been no Foch, but Roosevelt was even less of a Clémenceau. Hitler spurred on his generals and rode them on a tight rein; by contrast the Allied chariot was driverless. Inability to seize the unexpected opportunity offered during the summer was the precursor to the shock of the Ardennes offensive; the whole American machine, lacking a realistic war philosophy and over-prone to wishful thinking, was taken by surprise.

3(a) British parachutists on patrol beyond the Meuse

Officers of Supreme Headquarters: General Bedell Smith (Chief of Staff), Captain
ry Butcher (aide-de-camp), General Eisenhower, Air Chief-Marshal Sir Arthur
Tedder (Deputy Supreme Commander)

4(a) The German vanguard on the first day of the offensive

(b) A warning notice on an abandoned German car

Chapter 7

THE 'UNLIKELY ARDENNES . . .'

'We were not unmindful that in 1940 Hitler had broken through this same unlikely Ardennes front to overrun France'—BRADLEY

IN Hitler's headquarters there was a certain major whose sole job was to keep the O.K.W. War Diary. Oddly enough—for armies do not generally make use of specialist qualifications—he was an expert. In civil life Major Percy E. Schramm was Professor of Modern History at the University of Göttingen. He had the gift of looking at things from two different points of view, that of the present and that of the day when he and his colleagues would be able to consider it all from a distance and write the history of what had actually happened. Schramm's summaries in fact explained rather than described the course of events. He was torn between his loyalty as a German officer and his personal feelings—his daughter-in-law, Elisabeth von Thadden, had been executed after the plot of July 20. So he buried himself in his office among his mountains of files on operations planned or in progress. In the whole of the headquarters there was probably no one who knew so much of the truth regarding the Führer's last hopes. Every office kept him abreast of the development of its work—in most cases not knowing what its neighbour was doing. So he was indeed at the focal point of decision and implementation. In September 1944, Major Schramm was told to get from Liegnitz, where they had been deposited with the Reich Central Archives, all documents concerning the preparation of the western offensive in 1940. The pretext was the issue of a brochure commemorating the campaign which had brought Germany to complete triumph in a month. In fact the documents were needed to help in the preparation of the new offensive, which was intended to take the whole world by surprise and re-establish the position prior to the recent disasters.

From 1940 to 1944

As already mentioned, Hitler was determined to 'take advantage of the winter's long nights and bad weather', to launch a counter-offensive at a time when the Allies would be unable to use their mobility and conduct an elastic defence. On September 6 he approved Jodl's initial appreciation on the implementation of this proposal. Jodl's conclusions were that nothing could be done before November 1 and then only on two conditions: first, that the front should be kept as far to the west as possible and secondly that an immediate start should be made on the withdrawal of the units to be re-constituted and trained for the counter-offensive.

Similarities between 1940 and 1944 were remarkable. A superstitious

G

being like Hitler no doubt realised them and perhaps thought them a good omen, disregarding the changes in the strength and capabilities of the opposing forces. Just as in 1940, in early autumn 1944 his determination rode roughshod over the doubts and hesitations of staff officers who thought themselves military experts. On September 27 1939, Hitler had made light of their fears; the Polish campaign being over, they were instructed to draw up a plan for an operation to roll up the French and British fronts in November. On October 10 he had given an outline of it in the Reich Chancellery: 'This is a question of life and death and it determines the direction we must take: the German armies will break through on a broad front between Luxembourg and Nijmegen, will by-pass Antwerp to the west and proceed to cut off the Belgian and British armies.'

The generals had been horrified at the prospect of embarking on a war of movement against their enemy of 1918. They objected that operations would be hampered by fog, that the days were too short, that it was difficult to concentrate the forces in time, that supplies were still lacking and that the armoured forces would only be able to advance slowly, the area being intersected by rivers.

In any case, they said, nothing could be done before November 25. Hitler had ridden straight through their objections. Although he had not yet become the intuitive strategist unhampered by rules, which in the eyes of his technicians his later successes proved him to be, he insisted on the principle of offensive action. On October 25 1940 he changed the area of the break-through to south of Liège in the direction of Reims and Amiens. In December he had elaborated the plan to include an airborne operation on the left bank of the Meuse to seize all the bridges between Namur and Dinant and hold them for the advance of XV Armoured Corps which was to cross the Ardennes.

The plans on which the French campaign of the spring of 1940 was fought were frequently modified before being finally fixed at the end of January. But the following dates should be remembered: October 10 and October 25; these were the dates of the major decisions. The general intention should also be remembered: to cross the Ardennes and seize the Meuse bridges preparatory to an advance towards Brussels or the Somme. These two dates were to come up again in 1944. As far as the area of the offensive is concerned it seems more than likely that thoughts were turning in this direction before any real examination had been made.

Why the Ardennes?

It was Jodl who was responsible for translating Hitler's strategic ideas into action. He was now working on 'the desperate venture, the sortie from a fortress threatened with starvation'—to use his own words of 1946. Beside him was a major whose job it was to draft the Wehrmacht communiqué, Ritter von Schramm (no relative of the historian referred to

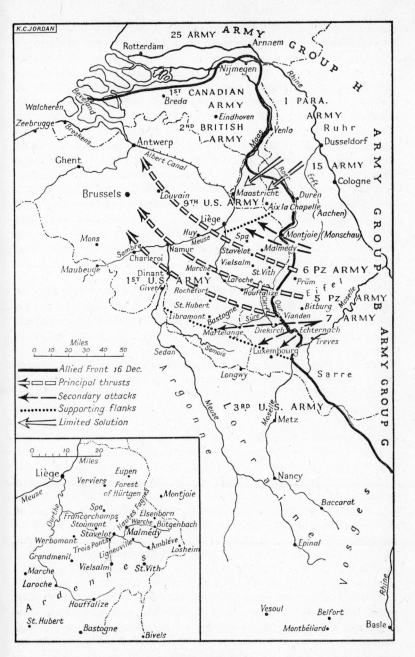

German Plans

above). In addition to the official communiqué, Major von Schramm frequently wrote editorials on the situation in the *Völkischer Beobachter*, the official and widely-read Nazi Party newspaper. It seems probable that he was made a member of Jodl's staff not only to ensure that he had first-hand information, but also to write these editorials as a guide to public opinion.

It looks as if the part he played on this newspaper was more than that of a mere reporter. In any country at war, particularly under a totalitarian regime which is approaching its end and knows it, official newspapers do not publish anything which is not intentional. Everything is angled on 'psychological warfare' or 'maintenance of morale', which comes to the same thing. On September 10 the *Völkischer Beobachter* published a geographical survey of the Ardennes, calling it 'a most difficult military obstacle, offering a resolute defender numerous possibilities for delaying action'. The article was unsigned; it made no reference to the speed with which German troops had forced this obstacle in 1940—perhaps due to the fact that at the time Rundstedt was attempting to stabilise the situation west of the German frontier.

Three days later, on September 13, came another unsigned article emphasising the importance of the Hautes-Fagnes plateau, a desolate moorland in the northern Ardennes near the German–Belgian frontier. On October 4 and 5 followed two articles signed by Major von Schramm containing the following ominous remarks: 'We know what we have lost in the West and what we have to defend . . . once fresh preparatory measures have been taken, we shall move westwards again to meet the enemy.' He went on to describe the natural strength of the Ardennes line: on the south the valley of the Sure, in the centre and north the wooded heights bordering the Eifel and the Hautes-Fagnes plateau. These were described as excellent defensive positions. The Aix-la-Chapelle gap was given as the sector most vulnerable to an enemy break-through.

Major von Schramm knew what he wanted to say:

1. We are going to resume the offensive.

2. It is useless to attack in the Ardennes since they are too easy to defend.

3. We must restrict ourselves to an operation to clear the enemy out of the Aix-la-Chapelle sector and free the small area of German territory now occupied.

The intentions of the various German personalities involved, however, were not all as simple as that. Although, with good or ill grace, they accepted the principle of the counter-offensive, they still disagreed upon the area. The general staff, represented by von Rundstedt, wished to restrict the operation to the clearance of the Aix-la-Chapelle salient. Hitler, however, had already selected the Ardennes. So, although von Schramm's articles of October 4 and 5 on the surface supported the restricted commonsense military view, they in fact contributed to a vast camouflage operation by which Hitler deceived his own military leaders for three weeks and the Allies for more than two months.

Success in the preservation of secrecy had been a major factor in surprising the French High Command in May 1940. The point on which the main weight of the German offensive would fall had been concealed up to the last moment. By the time French forces had reached the Meuse between Givet and Namur, the German armoured divisions were already in sight of the Semois and the French had been surprised while still on the move. But this had happened in the spring and French general staff theory had been that the Ardennes were impassable. Only two demolition lines had been prepared prior to the offensive, to be defended by delaying detachments from the Chasseurs Ardennais.

Guderian's break-through at Sedan had shown up the fallacy of the theory of the Ardennes 'fortress'. But four years later no one imagined that the same blow would be repeated. The American generals may have been inexperienced on the battle field but they had almost certainly studied the 1940 operation. Patton had read Guderian and Rommel—that was obvious from the way in which he handled his tanks. He and his fellow generals must inevitably have refought—and won—the Anglo-French battles of May 1940 in their war games. They knew where the main roads ran, where obstacles could be by-passed, the run of the valleys and where they could be crossed.

Tired though the American divisions were after the summer campaign of 1944, they still had sufficient resources, it seemed, to bring the Germans to a halt in a few hours, for the latter had nothing like the transport resources of 1940 available. Even if the Panzers had adequate supplies of fuel they would still be operating in snow and mud or on slippery roads. Instead of being able to skim across the country in a cloud of dust they would get bogged down.

Today these objections seem obvious and it is surprising that they were not brought out in the German staff memoranda. There is no indication, however, that they were ever set out in detail. They certainly seemed obvious to the Allied commanders. The latter may have been haunted by the precedent of May 10 1940, but they left the Ardennes out of account in their final appreciation. So between the two opponents it was all square: at the end of August the Allies did not carry out the offensive expected by the Germans; in December the German counter-offensive did not fall where the Allies were anticipating it.

Once more therefore the question must be asked: why the Ardennes? The answer is that of all the various possibilities this was the least likely. As Jodl pointed out in a conversation with Bedell Smith, Hitler's stroke of genius was to take the same theoretical data and use them as a basis for a second operation differing radically from the first: the first surprise attack—at the point chosen for the offensive—would be followed by a second wave which would drive through to the objective once the break-through had been achieved. The Allies would be left wondering whether the objective was Sedan, the Semois or Reims. In fact it was to be Antwerp.

But we must go back to early October. The 1940 files had arrived in German Supreme Headquarters and Hitler had laid down the area for the offensive. Studies of the ground made in 1940 proved that the easiest approach route led through Luxembourg and southern Belgium.

The Basic Plan

On October 8, Jodl submitted to Hitler five plans, offering him a choice of various points of impact along the entire western front; in none of them, however, was any special emphasis laid on the Ardennes.

Of these five plans, three envisaged offensives in the area of Lorraine and the southern Vosges, all conceived as pincer movements to encircle and destroy parts of U.S. Third Army or First French Army. Hitler was in fact apprehensive lest de Lattre should receive new reinforcing units to stiffen the Allied front.

The objective of the first proposed operation was Longwy, one of the pincers starting from central Luxembourg and the other from Metz.

The second plan was for two offensives starting from Metz and Baccarat and converging on Nancy.

The third, on the Alsace and Burgundy borders, was for two attacks starting from Epinal and Montbéliard, with Vesoul as objective.

Hitler discarded these plans as being too similar to the unsuccessful counter-offensives of the second fortnight of September. He had learned his lesson. Moreover the objectives of the proposed operations in the Vosges-Lorraine sector did not seem to him sufficiently ambitious.

Jodl, however, submitted two other offensives in the northern sector of the front: one to start from the area of Venlo (west of the Ruhr) directed at Antwerp; the other was to start from northern Luxembourg in a north-westerly direction and then swing northwards to meet a secondary offensive launched south-westwards from the area north of Aix-la-Chapelle.

It was from these two proposals that the final plan emerged. It had two advantages: it would cut off the British Twenty-first Army Group and parts of U.S. Ninth Army, now at a standstill in front of Aix-la-Chapelle. These would be surrounded north of the Albert Canal and the pressure on the Ruhr eased as a result. The 1940 files showed that on November 23 1939, Hitler had said to his Army commanders: 'The Ruhr is our Achilles heel. Continuance of the war depends upon possession of this area. If England and France move through Belgium and Holland towards the Ruhr, we shall be in a situation of very great peril.'

The proposed offensive, however, offered another advantage in addition to the protection of the 'Achilles heel'—the capture of Antwerp before Crerar's First Canadian Army under Montgomery had succeeded in clearing its approaches. Throughout October a high-class German division protected against armour by floods had been disputing every inch of ground in the Zeebrugge–Breskens pocket; the coastal batteries on Walcheren and Beverland had been keeping the channel closed. The hope was that these units, which had apparently been abandoned to their fate in this vital area, would be able to hold the Allies long enough for the mobile forces advancing from the east to join up with them.

Rapid action was clearly necessary and D-Day was fixed in principle for the second fortnight of November. The offensive was to be carried out by three armies under Army Group B (Model) as follows:

On the right Sixth Panzer Army (consisting of four armoured divisions) was to force the crossing of the Meuse on either side of Liège, clear the area Maastricht–Liège and move north on Antwerp.

In the centre Fifth Panzer Army (including two armoured divisions) was to cross the Meuse between Fumay and Namur and drive on Antwerp, throwing out a protective screen to cover Sixth Panzer Army against the American divisions which it was anticipated would move up from the south and west in an attempt to cut its communications between Antwerp and Dinant.

On the left, Seventh Army would cover the operation as a whole between the Meuse and the Semois and maintain contact with the Moselle front.

When Fifth and Sixth Panzer Armies had crossed the Meuse (on D plus two in theory) the British forces would presumably swing round to meet them on the line of the Albert Canal. The German forces still fighting in Holland would then take them in the rear.

In addition to the above mobile forces six further armoured divisions were held in reserve; Model was also in theory to have sixteen Volksgrenadier divisions by November 20, four further divisions in early December and two so-called 'parachute' divisions formed of ground personnel from the Luftwaffe and Navy but in fact trained neither to jump nor to fight as infantry. Their training was not due to be completed until November 15. In addition the following were made available to support the operation:

12 brigades of 'people's artillery',
14 groups of army artillery,
10 brigades of rocket launchers,
16 groups of assault guns and anti-tank guns.

In all, therefore, there were between thirty-two and thirty-six divisions plus the corps troops. The infantry divisions were distributed: nine to Sixth Panzer Army, seven to Fifth Panzer Army, seven to Seventh Army; the remainder were in reserve.

The two break-through armies were commanded by men who could not possibly have been less alike; they typified the warring tendencies within the German army.

Sixth Panzer Army, formed for this offensive on September 13 from the remnants of the armoured formations withdrawn from the battle in the west, was commanded by Sepp Dietrich. He was a Bavarian butcher-boy who had served in the Reichswehr after the First World War and joined the National Socialist Party in 1928. He had been the leader of the public meeting strong-arm squads which had formed the original core of the SS. During the 'night of the long knives' on June 30 1934 he had been in command of the SS guard battalion and had been personally responsible for the shooting in Munich prison of six leaders of the rival organisation, the SA. The SS guard battalion had later turned into the Leibstandarte Adolf Hitler, an élite of the élite and Hitler's bodyguard. Sepp Dietrich had continued his military career in Normandy, where he had commanded the I SS Armoured Corps; it had been cut to pieces.

Sepp Dietrich had no aptitude for the subtleties of staff work, but as a trainer of men he undoubtedly possessed certain qualities. He apparently felt himself in a sufficiently strong position to crack frequent jokes (in a restricted company of course) about Himmler's mediocre strategic and physical attainments. This did not, however, apparently affect his steadfast loyalty to the Reichsführer SS. From 1930 onwards he had staked his career on Himmler and for the freebooter turned general the gamble was now paying off. His army was now to make the main attack and it would indeed be a victory for him and his SS if he could lead it to Antwerp.

The neighbouring commander, who was reduced to the role of supporting Sepp Dietrich, was his almost exact opposite. General Hasso Eckart von Manteuffel, son of a family famous in Prussian military history, was only forty-seven years old. He had been born in Potsdam, the home of the German military tradition, had entered the army as a cadet in the Ziethen Hussars and become a member of the Reichswehr show-jumping team. He had not, however, wasted his time mourning the disappearance of the cavalry but had become an armoured enthusiast by 1935. Although he had never entered the Holy of Holies, the great General Staff, he had risen in three years of war from command of a regiment to that of a Panzer Army. He was a wizened little man with fine clear-cut features, the typical 'German aristocrat' without the rough exterior of the professional soldier. Both in Russia and Tunisia he had shown himself an excellent strategist.

To qualify for a major command on the western front in late summer 1944 Hitler demanded from his generals both technical competence and complete political reliability. One wonders on what grounds Manteuffel was chosen. He was certainly extremely popular with the troops, who recognised his personal courage—undoubtedly a valuable factor. More important still, however, his name had never figured during the enquiry conducted by the Gestapo on the military and civil opposition movements, only part of which had been uncovered by the July 20 plot. There were several explanations for Manteuffel's attitude. He was far away in North

Africa and Russia. He was a sceptic and a clever man. He may have placed a very strict interpretation on his oath to the Führer. Whatever the reason, however, for someone of his background he had achieved a distinct *tour de force*: he was marked down as belonging neither to one camp nor the other—nor even to the third, that of the Allies.*

Hitler Conceals His Plans

For nearly three weeks Hitler managed to keep Field-Marshal von Rundstedt totally in the dark regarding not only his intentions, but the reasons for his preparations, even though they profoundly affected the whole structure of the western front. It is an incredible fact, but it is true. At the same time it is typical of Hitler's methods as a war leader. The field-marshal commanding on the western front was expected to obey like any drummer boy, to carry out orders without asking why or if he did ask, to put up with evasive replies. General von Buttlar-Brandenfels, head of the O.K.W. operations staff and therefore a vital cog in Hitler's planning, put it quite clearly during the Nuremberg trial. He stated: 'I do know that in the zone which was proposed for the offensive [the Ardennes] there had already been troop movements ordered by the Supreme Command before the Commander West, who was responsible, was informed and that he, therefore, made frequent enquiries of us asking for an explanation of these movements.'†

This seemed so extraordinary that counsel for the defence, Dr Laternser, returned to the charge, but von Buttlar-Brandenfels reiterated: 'Commander-in-Chief West was only informed subsequently' of movements of formations within his command.

Model, commanding Army Group B, was no better informed, but the explanation given to both commanders seemed plausible and coincided with their own forecasts; in their view 'the focal point of the Western Front' (Blumentritt's words) was the Aix-la-Chapelle sector. It was here that they expected the Allied offensive to be resumed and in fact on October 18, Eisenhower partially gave way to Montgomery's urgings and agreed to resume the offensive in the north in early November. On

---

* General von Manteuffel returned to public life after the war. In 1953 he was elected to the Bonn Federal Parliament as a Free Democrat Deputy and nominated Secretary of Defence a year later. In 1957, however, he was not re-elected and he subsequently suffered a humiliating, though perhaps not unduly severe experience—in August 1959 the Karlsruhe court sentenced him to eighteen months imprisonment for having executed a nineteen-year-old soldier. The incident had occurred in the Ukraine in January 1944. The boy had failed in his duty of defending his position during a Russian attack and had been sentenced to two years imprisonment by Court Martial. Manteuffel had ordered his summary execution and in his defence had cited Hitler's instructions laying down that 'order was to be maintained at all costs'.

† *IMT*, Vol. XV, p. 572.

October 12 Hitler informed von Rundstedt and Model that new formations would be located in the Cologne area as reserves immediately available to counter the Anglo-American offensive. They might either forestall it or wait for it to develop. Everyone found this an adequate explanation for the increased troop movements and the build-up of stocks of fuel, ammunition and equipment to a level well above that required for static defence. The concept of the 'plan of deception' was clearly set out in an order dated November 5:

A large scale enemy offensive is expected to be aimed at the area Cologne–Bonn. To take this offensive in flank, two forces are being prepared, one north-west of Cologne and the other in the Eifel. The latter will as far as possible be concealed. The former will be made to appear as the more important. The Luftwaffe will be deployed on similar lines.

The Allies, as we shall see, fell into the trap completely. For more than a fortnight, however, Rundstedt also felt that dealing with Hitler's head-quarters was like 'tilting at windmills', in the words of his Chief of Staff, Westphal. The front was crumbling and both Rundstedt and Westphal were crying out for fresh forces, whereas the orders issuing from East Prussia laid down that units were to be withdrawn.

On October 15 they received 150,000 reinforcements, which did no more than make good their losses. They asked for at least eight infantry and three armoured divisions or alternatively for authorisation to withdraw the right flank behind the Waal and so make available seven more or less fresh divisions. Even in the Aix-la-Chapelle sector their appeals were only grudgingly met. Keitel, who was responsible for allocating equipment, was unable to understand why, with the front static, more fuel and ammunition should be required in this area than elsewhere.

Rundstedt and Westphal began to fear that the Alsace front would crack under American and French pressure. They cabled: 'Send at least two of the reserve divisions to Army Group G. Two made available today will avoid the loss of four tomorrow.' Hitler refused; Alsace, he replied, must be defended with the divisions already available. Finally, in November he allowed Rundstedt one division for reinforcement, but it was then too late; shortly thereafter the French First Army reached the outskirts of Belfort and 2 French Armoured Division captured Strasbourg.

In mid-October Rundstedt reported, '80,000 men have been withdrawn for Sixth Panzer Army. Where are they? Why not use them as soon as they have been organised into units.'

Hitler's only reply was to withdraw Manteuffel's Fifth Panzer Army for re-organisation, leaving only a small proportion on the Aix-la-Chapelle front. Rundstedt still did not know why.

In eastern Germany Sepp Dietrich was busy reforming the first four divisions of his army. In spite of opposition from the Waffen SS officers,

two-thirds of his staff were drawn from the Wehrmacht and the gaps in
the SS Panzer divisions (1, 12, 2 and 9) were filled by N.C.O.s and men of
the regular forces. Even Dietrich's Chief of Staff, General Kraemer, was
a regular; as a face-saver he was given the corresponding SS rank.

Early in November Sixth Panzer Army (it did not receive the title of SS
until January 1945) moved into the great Westphalian training camps. Its
allocation of tanks from O.K.W. was double that of the normal armoured
divisions and a high proportion of the arms, equipment and ammunition
on the way to the eastern front had been diverted to it.

Training had to be begun almost from scratch. In recent years all ranks
had become unaccustomed to offensive warfare and were ignorant of the
lessons of recent experience on the combined employment of the various
arms of the service. Experienced drivers were required for the new tanks—
in many cases they were too new and went into the attack with inadequately
run-in engines. Trained drivers had, however, frequently been drafted into
the ranks when their vehicles were destroyed during the Normandy fighting
or the retreat across France, and been killed as ordinary infantrymen.

Notwithstanding the call-ups of the summer, further efforts were made
to winkle out any man capable of carrying a rifle or anti-tank weapon.
Even the Party organisation was affected and forced to reduce activity.
No more recruits were to be had from the 1946 and 1947 classes, so on
October 10 Arthur Axmann, the Hitler Youth leader, announced that
70 per cent of the 1948 class youngsters had volunteered for military service
and would be called to the colours. Early in December Rundstedt protested against the despatch to the west of these boys of barely sixteen.

Hand in hand with these crisis measures went a psychological 'indoctrination' campaign conducted by the *Völkischer Beobachter* in a rising
crescendo. Everything was grist to the mill: the glorious future opened up
by the Volksgrenadier divisions, the fate in store for Germany under the
Morgenthau plan, the part which scientific inventions would play in
modern warfare. The climax was reached on October 19 when a red banner
headline announced that: 'To commemorate the Battle of Nations [Leipzig
1813] the Führer announces the formation of the Volkssturm.'*

The Volkssturm was in fact a levee *en masse* or local militia, comprising
all men from sixteen to sixty 'capable of bearing arms in defence of the
Fatherland'. It was strictly controlled by the National Socialist Party
organisation. Militarily it was under command of Himmler in his capacity
as C.-in-C. of the Home Army, politically and administratively under
Martin Bormann.

In principle this German Home Guard was entirely divorced from the
Wehrmacht. Bormann and Himmler invariably refused to give the military

* The actual date of the decree was September 25 and those of the ensuing political directives September 27 and October 12. See the article entitled 'Der Deutsche
Volkssturm 1944–1945' in *Wehrwissenschaftliche Rundschau*, April 1960, p. 209.

any information about it, even when fighting was taking place on German territory and the Volkssturm was directly involved.

The Fight for a 'Limited Solution'

Hitler was of course eventually compelled to widen the circle of the initiated; at the least the commanders on the western front had to know what was the purpose of all the movements taking place. Jodl and his staff had worked feverishly to get the main lines of the operation established before von Rundstedt was informed and so give him no chance to argue. It was now the end of October, so there was only a bare month before the period which statistics showed was likely to be the rainiest in western Europe, that ending on November 25. During that period it was anticipated that rain and moonless nights would prevent the Allied air forces observing and interfering with movement behind the front. The key man in this decision had been Lieutenant-Colonel Schuster, the head of the Meteorological Service, who had been responsible for choosing the date May 10 1940; the question was whether his luck would hold once more.

So on October 24 von Rundstedt's and Model's Chiefs of Staff, Generals Westphal and Krebs, arrived at the Führer's headquarters. There they learnt the reason for Supreme Headquarters' silence. Hitler himself gave them the astounding news and sketched out the main lines of the proposed operation; Jodl then followed with instructions in complete detail for its execution.

Arrangements were made to keep the operation secret even from the historian. No record of these conversations was made; the O.K.W. War Diary contains not a word on the subject. Written orders were not to be issued until after the return of Westphal and Krebs to C.-in-C. West headquarters in Coblenz. Their interview with Hitler can therefore only be reconstructed from von Rundstedt's and Westphal's memoirs.*

What the Führer had to say to the two generals has already been revealed: he intended to regain the initiative, to attack in the Eifel where the enemy was weak and drive on Antwerp, splitting the enemy front in two. Up to the time of the offensive von Rundstedt was to conduct a defensive battle all along the western front with the forces already available to him. 'Any adjustments to the Front will only be accepted if their object is to improve the position from which the offensive will start or re-group units holding too wide a front.'

All newly constituted formations were to be devoted to the offensive,

---

* Generals Westphal and Blumentritt have both given long accounts of this interview. The latter, however, must have got his information from von Rundstedt, in whose biography the account appears. Von Rundstedt's account was obviously based on the report from Westphal, his Chief of Staff. The latter is therefore in fact the only source, since Krebs, the other general present at the interview, died at the end of the war.

which was to be entirely in the hands of Army Group B under Field-Marshal Model. He was to keep the Aix-la-Chapelle battle going, while at the same time working out the plan of movement and issuing the orders for the offensive. Göring had promised 3,000 fighters to support the attack. (Eventually this number was reduced by half, including 100 jets.)

Meanwhile Keitel had been busy assembling, moving and distributing stocks of fuel for tanks and aircraft. According to the initial plan fuel consumption from the start of the offensive to arrival at Antwerp would be of the order of 17,000 tons. Rumanian oil had been lost for nine days at the end of September and synthetic petrol production had been brought to a standstill by Allied air attacks; only a month's consumption was available for the Wehrmacht as a whole. Keitel nevertheless hoped to reach the required figure by cutting down allocations to other fronts. He was helped by the bad weather; although oil refineries were now priority targets for the Allied air forces they received only 10 per cent of the total bomb tonnage dropped on Germany in October and November. This was, however, to some extent offset by the damage to railways, which threw the weight on to road transport and so increased fuel consumption.

Krebs and Westphal were flabbergasted by their interview with Hitler and the additional details given them at headquarters. They pretended not to realise that the decision had been taken down to its smallest detail. They put forward certain objections even to Hitler himself. Their argument ran:

We are very pleased to learn that at last reinforcements will be made available for the Western Front. The general idea of resuming the offensive is welcome in principle, but we cannot in so short a time judge the chances of success of the plan. At first sight it raises a number of questions. How will the situation evolve before the start of the offensive? Will there be an adequate number of fresh forces available? Whatever the figures given, will the Luftwaffe be in a position to support the ground operations effectively? If worthwhile results are to be achieved, air superiority must be gained at least over the area of the main offensive effort and this will require several days of air fighting.*

Eventually the two generals gave Jodl the real background to their objections: the date of November 25 was far too soon and it would never be possible to reach the final objective, Antwerp, with the resources envisaged. They then left for Coblenz to make their reports.

On November 1 Jodl despatched the final order to Westphal; it included a note in Hitler's own handwriting: 'The intention, organisation and objective of this offensive are unalterable'. In theory this note should have been the final word for von Rundstedt as for any other field-marshal, but he was determined to try to get more realistic ideas adopted. In his heart of hearts he was opposed to any form of offensive. He did not see that he could do more than carry out the instructions he had received on

* See Westphal, *German Army in the West*, p. 179.

October 12: to remain on the defensive and be prepared to take in flank any Allied movement across the Roer. Making counter-proposals to a Hitler plan was always a risky business and there was little likelihood that they would even be considered. The only hope was to accept the Führer's basic principle of recapture of the initiative, not to propose another operation but to change in apparently minor respects the one he had already worked out in complete detail.

This was the genesis of the 'limited solution' as opposed to the 'major solution'. In spite of his loyalty to Hitler, it was Model who worked it out, Rundstedt doing no more than approve it. From this point on Rundstedt gave the impression of washing his hands of the whole enterprise.

On November 3 Jodl arrived at the Headquarters of Army Group B to brief the assembled generals on Hitler's hopes for the operation and to convince them. Model, Manteuffel and von Rundstedt produced a long list of objections. Their argument ran:

We naturally approve of the Führer's general concept; but one must be realistic: Antwerp is far too distant an objective to be captured by the forces available. Even supposing we get there, our flanks would not be strong enough to resist Allied counter-attacks. It is no good aiming at an objective from which it will be necessary to withdraw as soon as it had been captured. The offensive could achieve no more than a temporary suspension of Allied traffic through Antwerp with little subsequent effect upon their supply position. Would it not therefore be more prudent to proceed by stages? In the first phase the three armies available would attack from north of Aix-la-Chapelle to Luxembourg, break through the enemy front, reach the Meuse, capture Liège and then, moving north from Namur and south-west from Maastricht, surround the enemy forces in the Aix-la-Chapelle salient. Only when this had been done, and provided the American divisions surrounded were put out of action rapidly, could the second phase be envisaged, that of a move on Antwerp. If all went well Eisenhower would lose ten to fifteen divisions, in other words 25 per cent of American strength in Europe. This would be a lesser victory than the capture of Antwerp but a less risky operation. The reinforcements envisaged would be adequate for the 'limited solution' provided they could be brought up to their assembly areas quickly. If the Allies attacked before preparations had been completed all decisions must be postponed.

On November 4 Model and Manteuffel set all these ideas down on paper in a memorandum.

The reply arrived the very next day straight from Jodl: 'The Führer has decided that the operation is unalterable in every detail.'

The trains bringing Sixth Panzer Army to the western front were already on the move (it required some 800, more than for the entire 1940 campaign!) but the argument went on between the obstinate Hitler and his generals, determined not to attempt the impossible. It continued throughout the month of November. Even Sepp Dietrich was talked round by his

Chief of Staff, Kraemer, and convinced of the advantages of the 'limited solution'; he was won over by the psychological argument that exhausted or inexperienced men would be more likely to fight to regain a portion of their own territory and that it was therefore better to clear the Aix-la-Chapelle salient rather than charge off towards an objective far away in the west.

The date of course had to be postponed, since it proved impossible to complete the concentration by November 25. It was finally fixed for December 10. On November 16 Jodl appeared once more, this time at Rundstedt's headquarters in Coblenz to indoctrinate the commanders. He seemed to them to be almost convinced of the wisdom of the limited solution; he promised to put the point once more to Hitler, though he did not hold out much hope of shaking the latter's determination. It seems doubtful whether the Chief of the O.K.W. operations staff was sincere. More probably he was simply pretending to agree with the views of his audience in order to cut short a discussion which he knew to be useless. The statements which he made a year later to the American interrogators suggest that for the sake of peace and quiet he was adopting a middle of the road position between the modest but realistic expectations of his western front colleagues and the strategic dreams of his Supreme Commander. It was his job nevertheless to translate these dreams into operational orders. He said:

We should have . . . started concentric attacks on Aachen from Monschau, Maastricht and Central Holland and crushed your forces in the Aachen pocket, their supply lines having been cut . . . It is difficult to say whether we could have destroyed the forces in the pocket or whether you could have supplied them by air using your entire air force. But at all events it would have made a terrific impression on political, military and public opinion. But even with captured fuel and supplies I doubt if we could have reconquered France. . . . All the same it would have been a big setback for you and you would have required many months to recover from it. You had many divisions in the United States not yet ready.*

The November paper arguments were, however, overtaken by events. On November 16 Eisenhower resumed the offensive in the Roer sector, supported by 2,500 aircraft. The Germans were well entrenched; they had had two months to prepare their defensive position in the Hürtgen Forest and the mining villages and they lost no ground. Nevertheless four infantry and nine armoured divisions earmarked for the Ardennes offensive were drawn into this battle of attrition.

Both sides compared this phase of the war to the 1916 fighting. Under a fearful artillery barrage infantry waited in their foxholes for the attacking waves of enemy infantry and tanks, just as they had done in Champagne and Verdun, on the Somme or in Flanders during the Great War. During the autumn of 1944 the village of Hürtgen changed hands fourteen times,

* Robert Merriam, *Dark December*, p. 30.

the Forest of Hürtgen eighteen times and the village of Vossenack twenty-eight times. As in the Argonne or the Côtes de Meuse, woods which appeared on the maps become no more than areas of tree stumps pockmarked by shell holes. On both sides the line was held by second-rate troops, the higher class troops being kept in immediate reserve and used for local attacks in a vain attempt to break through and get this immobile front on the move once more. There were many individual acts of heroism but on the American side the G.I.s were becoming discouraged; they were bogged down in mud and rain and facing an enemy whose artillery suddenly began once more to hammer them continuously. Little did they know that the Fritz in the foxhole opposite probably belonged to a battalion most of whose men were deaf or suffering from some stomach disease. Little did they know that for the first time since the dark days of 1918 the German High Command had had to take severe measures to suppress the first signs of a wave of desertion for which this time no defeatist propaganda from the rear could be held responsible.

An O.K.W. note dating from the end of November speaks volumes. It asked for returns of 'desertions, court martial sentences and executions for cowardice since September 13 1944. Figures are to be given for N.C.O.s and men; officers are to be given by name.'

In spite of all these sacrifices Hitler persisted in his daydreams. At the end of November he returned to the Reich Chancellery and was operated upon for a polyp on the vocal chords. Every day, however, brought its setbacks and its new problems. Throughout the first fortnight of December, right up to the day before the offensive, last minute adjustments were found necessary.

Chapter 8

THE LURE OF WINTER

FIELD-MARSHAL VON RUNDSTEDT was now definitely 'out of the hunt'. His signature may have appeared on the orders and counter-proposals which flew back and forth during the last days of November between his headquarters in Coblenz and the Reich Chancellery where Hitler was installed; but it was Field-Marshal Model and his Army Commanders who took over all technical preparations and carried on the struggle to keep the offensive within the bounds of common sense. Old Rundstedt was weary of arguing, but nevertheless he fulfilled the role for which Hitler had recalled him: he saved Hitler's face. There can be no other explanation for his presence at Ulm on October 18 for the funeral of Field-Marshal Rommel; he must have known that Rommel had committed suicide on the Führer's orders. Rundstedt's caution cloaked each successive stage of the Wehrmacht's abdication.

On December 2 a stubborn quartet, Model, Manteuffel, Sepp Dietrich and Westphal, presented itself at the Reich Chancellery, armed with all the technical arguments, for a last attempt to get Hitler to agree to objectives which could be reached by the forces available. Rundstedt was not with them; Hitler registered momentary surprise at the absence of the field-marshal; then his optimism reasserted itself (all those who met him during the first fortnight of December agreed that he was confident and in good form) and he swept Model's arguments aside. In spite of the supply difficulties, he said, in spite of the inadequate training of the assault units, and in spite of the reduction in the air support promised by Göring, they would be victorious—on one condition: that his original plan was carried out to the letter.

Manteuffel was prepared to let events settle the argument over final objectives. He attacked Hitler on the tactical details of the first phase up to the Meuse. Only when the line of the Meuse had been made good could further objectives be decided. He set out his concept of the attack, differing considerably from the plans laid down by Hitler.

Manteuffel's argument was that the three-hour preliminary bombardment would simply put the enemy on the alert. If the attack went in at 11.00 a.m. as laid down, the German forces would be at the mercy of the enemy artillery for several hours beforehand; perhaps also of his fighter bombers, since the bad weather forecast by the meteorologists was a chancy business. The more inexperienced units and those composed either of very young soldiers or old men might well be disorganised in their assembly areas.

H

A forty-five-minute bombardment would be enough provided it was directed on vital points. It should take place at night and its targets should be the American headquarters, signal centres, batteries and 'stop-lines' at cross-roads. With their command system thus disorganised the American forward positions would be over-run before they had either the time or the opportunity to give the alert.

H-hour should be put forward to 5.30 a.m. by which time the German assault units could be to the rear of the American outposts. Under cover of the artillery preparation they would have infiltrated deep into the American positions and would then attack in the artificial moonlight produced by A.A. searchlights directed on to the low clouds. The British had recently used this method in the Arnhem bridgehead. American sentries were usually asleep at first light and so surprise could be guaranteed.

Finally, by putting H-hour forward all available hours of daylight could be used for the advance of the armoured divisions; they should follow close up behind the infantry and exploit the break-through immediately.

Hitler had previously laid down that the artillery preparation should be spread all along the front, but he now agreed that it should be concentrated on defined objectives as suggested by Manteuffel. One of the reasons for the latter's suggestion was, no doubt, the danger of which his subordinate commanders had warned him during the previous weeks: the artillery preparation might well be more dangerous to the Germans than to the Americans. According to General Heilmann, commanding 5 Parachute Division, the Werhrmacht gunners were shooting nothing like so well as they had in the early war years; the 'shorts' would inevitably spread panic among the infantry, the majority of whom had never taken part in an attack or followed a creeping barrage.

Hitler finally announced that during the first few days of the offensive the Luftwaffe would be able to make between 800 and 1,000 sorties daily, thus ensuring relative air superiority. He relied on bad weather to keep the Allied air forces on the ground. He did not, however, explain how it would nevertheless be possible for the German jet fighters to take off.

Meticulously Prepared 'Improvisation'

On the ground preparations were not proceeding at all as Hitler imagined. D-Day was postponed from December 7 to 10, then 13 and finally 16, but this was not enough to make the limited forces at Model's disposal fully effective. Allied intelligence summaries presented a very false picture of the situation, either through pessimism induced by the surprising German recovery or because of a tendency to place too much credence in information issuing from the Reich; they consistently over-estimated German strength. The German High Command was in fact carrying out a very well-managed operation of deception, passing false information to the Allies via double-agents and foreign workers in Germany. It was so successful that in the first week of December, Twelfth U.S. Army Group Intelligence estimated that there were 1,300 tanks concentrated behind the Roer and in the Eifel. In fact on D-Day for the offensive Fifth and Sixth Panzer Armies had no more than 800 between them, and these were unevenly distributed; tank strength in Sepp Dietrich's four armoured divisions was double that in Manteuffel's; on December 16 Dietrich's divisions were at full strength whereas the three armoured divisions of Fifth Army were only 60 to 80 per cent of establishment. When one of these three formations left the Saar front for its assembly area it left all its anti-tank guns behind for the relieving division, moving with only twenty-five tanks, ten anti-tank guns, one strong artillery group, about half its anti-aircraft and one motorised infantry regiment; in addition the division was practically devoid of transport and tank-carrying vehicles.

This division was in the area of Bitburg. At the end of November 5 Parachute Division belonging to Seventh Army also arrived in the area from Holland. It was in little better shape; only one of its three regiments was fit for battle; the other two were still being formed, back in Oldenburg. A report on this division dated December 1 stated that it was 'fit for defensive operations under certain conditions'. The question was what these conditions were. Most of its personnel came from the air force and two of the colonels commanding regiments had never taken part in an infantry attack; the artillery was manned by anti-aircraft personnel who did not know how to engage ground targets; the division was almost completely without heavy equipment, wireless sets and transport; its anti-tank group had lost its guns in an air attack during the move up to the assembly area; finally its signals equipment had been routed to another division in error and never caught up again. The paper strength of the division was 20,000 men, but on D-Day only approximately half were present. The only units fit to fight were one regiment, one engineer battalion and a brigade of assault guns allotted in support instead of the artillery which the division did not possess. Yet Model said to General Heilmann the divisional commander: 'The parachute troops will find their way forward; I am confident of their courage.'

In fact Model was trying to conceal his lack of resources behind an optimism which deceived no one. The instances quoted above were no exceptions. In any case even if all petrol-driven vehicles from tanks to light cars had been available, Model could not have supplied them. By mid-December only 7,000 of the 17,000 tons of fuel 'scratched up' for the offensive had arrived in the Eifel, although the remaining 10,000 did arrive by D-Day.

It is true that Allied air action delayed the movement of fuel by both road and rail, but in addition Keitel was distributing it very sparingly indeed. He held up the movement orders, fearing that the fuel would be used prematurely in local operations. The situation was aggravated by the fact that at the lower levels people did not know why the fuel stocks were being built up and so, although the tankers had reached the right bank of the Rhine near Cologne, the services refused to move them to the Eifel. Then from Christmas onwards the weather in the operational area cleared, Allied fighter-bombers were everywhere and movement became difficult.

The theoretical fuel consumption tables drawn up by O.K.W. therefore proved wrong from the outset. The armoured formations in fact had only two days fuel available. The question was how far they could get in that time. Rapid success was clearly essential. Jodl calculated on the armour being able to cover 125 miles, disregarding one of the lessons of the Russian front that ice and snow reduced the average distance travelled per day to 30 miles. The commanders at the front were more realistic; they estimated that in two days they would not do more than 60 miles.

The available fuel was, therefore, just enough to get to the Meuse. Beyond the river and for the move on Antwerp the armour was forced to assume that it would capture imaginary American petrol dumps. In the last analysis this was the supposition upon which the success of Hitler's whole ambitious plan depended; in other words the hard facts of the situation had pronounced inexorably in favour of the 'limited solution' put forward by the generals—reach the Meuse first and then see!

During the first fortnight of December a hundred trains per day moved into the Rhineland carrying the units and their equipment. The Allied tactical air forces had not been able to do serious damage to the Rhine-land bridges and all those over the Moselle except one were still intact. The only delays arose from damage to the railway signal system.

Particularly strict concealment orders were issued to units moving up into the line. They were to move by night only and lie up by day in woods and built-up areas; no vehicle movement was allowed within 5 miles of the front to ensure that the enemy was not alerted by engine noise. Artillery was brought up to within 4 miles of the front on December 10 and then either man-handled into position or horse-drawn. As soon as the guns were in position wheel marks were carefully erased. The armoured divisions moved up to their assembly areas by night in stages, starting on December 12; their movement was covered by low-flying aircraft to hide the noise of the tank engines. The final infantry moves took place on the night of December 14; they also covered their tracks as they went. Many of the assault units did not reach their final positions until the night December 15–16, when they superimposed themselves on the Volks-grenadier divisions holding the line. These measures of strict secrecy were enforced right up to the last moment. Even the operation's code-name, 'Wacht Am Rhein' (Watch on the Rhine), was designed to deceive; it gave the impression of a purely defensive operation to guard against a possible Allied break-through at Aix-la-Chapelle. On December 4 the name was changed to 'Herbstnebel' (Autumn Mist) already used in September for the evacuation of the Po Plain.

The 'Autumn Mist' was pretty thick. In the first fortnight of November the only people in the three armies concerned who were allowed to know the real reason for the movements then in progress were the Army Commander, his Chief of Staff, the Head of the Operations Section, the General's A.D.C. and one clerk. All had had to sign statements (the first being Krebs and Westphal on October 24 after their interview with Hitler) recognising that it would be a court martial offence to divulge even the smallest fraction of their activities. The neighbouring Army Group commanders were only let into the secret at the last minute. General Student was not warned until December 8 that certain units of his Army Group H were to carry out a subsidiary operation from the Roermond area. On the same day he was instructed to detail one of his parachute officers, Lieutenant-Colonel von der Heydte, for a parachute operation behind the American lines, but was unable to tell him where the operation was to take place.

Starting on December 1, divisional commanders were gradually put in the picture, but as late as December 10 Bayerlein, commanding the Panzer Lehr Armoured Division which formed part of the second wave, still did not know what was in the wind. The lower level commanders, therefore, found themselves carrying out seemingly senseless orders, since they did not know their real object. Reconnaissance patrols were forbidden; absolute wireless silence was imposed in rear of the front; visual signalling was restricted; the laying of fresh telephone lines was forbidden. They were only let into the secret gradually: regimental commanders three days before the attack, battalion commanders two days and company commanders the evening before D-Day.

The few staff officers in the know were overwhelmed by matters of detail. They had to supervise the positioning of the artillery and anti-aircraft without letting the overall layout be known; they had to act as couriers, but were not allowed to use liaison aircraft because of the January 1940 precedent when two officers carrying plans for the western offensive from Münster to Cologne by air had forced-landed in Belgium. The last to be informed were the 'camouflage officers' in the villages in the rear of the front whose job it was to get the new units under cover and direct them to their billets; all road-signs were strictly forbidden and no one except reinforced detachments of traffic police was allowed to guide the units.

This insistence on secrecy cost the lives of a number of German airmen shot down by their own anti-aircraft; the latter knew nothing of the offensive, were not expecting to see the Luftwaffe suddenly reappear in force on the western front and were convinced that anything which flew must be either American or British. In the eyes of the staffs this was no more than a minor annoyance; once they had been let into Hitler's game they were intent on preserving the secrecy of the operation up to the last moment.

The Nazi Party, on the other hand, did not think that a series of vague promises was enough to raise the morale of the public or justify the call-up of the Volkssturm. The first to give a hint of his intentions was Hitler himself; on Magda Goebbels' birthday on October 28 he told her that there would be a great military victory before Christmas and that it would change the course of events. On the pretext of giving 'confidential' information to their subordinates, the Gauleiters broke all the rules of military security and in fact gave them a general outline of the plan. Field-Marshal von Rundstedt was flabbergasted when he heard that Simon, the Rhineland Gauleiter, had given full details of all he knew over the loud-speaker to a public meeting at Bitburg. Bitburg being only some 12 miles behind the front was clearly an area in which Allied intelligence agents were liable to be operating.

The most likely potential agents were the foreigners who had been incorporated into the Wehrmacht: Alsatians, Poles, Luxembourgers, Slavs. Orders were issued for them to be moved to other fronts, provided the units concerned were not too seriously affected.

It was questionable, however, whether the morale even of the Reich Germans was all that good. An order of the day signed by Hitler and dated November 25 was significant; it seemed more than likely to spread demoralisation:

This battle will decide whether the German people shall continue to exist or disappear. It demands complete devotion from each one of us; from the soldiers it demands that courage which defies death; from all it demands unshakeable pertinacity; from commanders it demands unyielding authority. These qualities will enable us to re-establish a desperate situation.

Should a unit commander be isolated and feel incapable of continuing the struggle, he will first ask his officers, then his N.C.O.s and finally his men if any one of them is prepared to take over his responsibilities and continue to fight. The commander will then transfer to this man, whatever his rank, the duties of commander. At the same time the new commander will be given the appropriate prerogatives and privileges.

The object of this order was to inspire every man to fight 'without thought of withdrawal'; clearly, however, it was calculated to raise doubts about the confidence and energy of the established hierarchy. It could be read as heralding some reorganisation giving preference to Nazi Party members within the forces and so, although on the face of it intended to reinforce discipline, its effect was exactly the reverse. But there was another document, the purpose of which was even more obscure; it was issued by O.K.W. 'for officers only—not to be distributed below Divisional Headquarters'. It is dated late 1944, not long before the Ardennes offensive. It is so extraordinary that extracts are worth quoting:

Every officer has the duty of saving himself in emergency. The view of many junior officers that they must never leave their men alone in the hour of danger is in need of correction.

Every member of the Wehrmacht must realise that it is of paramount importance to save the officer corps for the reconstruction of the Fatherland. The German officer is too valuable to be sacrified, especially in hopeless situations. That he should save himself by withdrawing is in the interest of the country.

It was the German officer corps that almost achieved world dominance for Germany in the first assault of 1914–18. It was this same officer corps that rebuilt Germany for this second attempt at world leadership. That this second attempt might also fail was foreseen. The present trend of the war compels us to exercise the utmost economy of officer material.

. . . In order to prepare, from a technical point of view, for the third un-avoidable trial of strength for the leadership of the world we have need of our officers. Manpower we have been able to find in quantities at all times.

For this reason care must constantly be taken to maintain the officer corps at its present strength. Nevertheless certain company commanders must at the same time be detailed to stay with their troops and in case of necessity to sacrifice themselves as well. Examples of this sort are necessary for the maintenance of the troops' morale. Divisional commanders will nominate junior officers to die the hero's death.*

This document is so extraordinary that one is attempted to doubt its authenticity. It is the sort of thing which might have been put out by the Allied Psychological Warfare Branch, to raise doubts on this point of honour within the Wehrmacht. If it really was issued by O.K.W. it would be valuable evidence of the thinking of certain sections of the great German General Staff. They were evidently looking further than the immediate lost cause. If they really were basing their hopes upon the permanency of the officer corps, the twelve years of the Nazi regime had evidently taught them nothing. Governments might come and go but the great German General Staff would remain to ensure victory at the third attempt. This document is almost too good to be true. The fact that in the post-war period total silence has been preserved on the subject, both by the Germans and the Allies, may be interpreted either way—as evidence of mystification or complicity.

The Front Line

The German private soldier knew nothing of all these plans; he was just a tiny particle of the pool of strategic manpower, plodding about in the

* The translation given here is that which appeared in Second British Army Intelligence Summary, No. 111, September 1944. The document was also re-produced in Ninth U.S. Air Force Intelligence Summary, No. 113. Since this book was first published it has come to light that this series of German documents ended in July 1944. It follows therefore that this document must have come from other sources. It may have been a psychological warfare operation—Trans.

mud and snow with no notion of what the future held in store. On the 'quiet' sector where Fifth Panzer Army was to attack, the front had remained almost static since the end of September. The American line of foxholes facing the Germans in the Siegfried line ran east of the main Saint-Vith–Luxembourg road, so as to protect the heavy guns firing on the German fortifications; the Germans made probing raids from time to time.

A 'no man's land' 3–4 miles wide ran down to the Our valley below the German positions. The Allies kept it patrolled, occupying the main villages for a few hours at a time, just long enough to collect information. On several occasions the Germans had removed Luxembourg hostages in face of brave resistance by the local militia.

In this frontier zone between Belgium and Luxembourg a number of German dialects were spoken and so the German intelligence service had no difficulty in infiltrating agents, some of whom had already lived in the area during the occupation. At Walferdingen, for instance, the former Gestapo representative reoccupied his old room, the key of which he had kept when he left in September. He now used it as an observation post and, entirely unnoticed, checked the movement of American convoys on the Luxembourg–Ettelbruck road.

Summarising the Intelligence situation after the war, Bradley's (Twelfth U.S. Army Group) Intelligence Section considered that 'the Germans' intelligence concerning our dispositions was as usual excellent'.*

This was a somewhat flattering estimate the primary object of which was retrospective justification of the decisions of U.S. Twelfth Army Group; it bore little relation to the truth as seen through German eyes. All reconnaissance patrolling had been stopped from the end of November lest prisoners be taken who, even though they knew nothing of the plan, might talk and give something away to alert the Americans. The German commanders therefore knew little of the enemy facing them.

They did not, for instance, know of the unit moves which had taken place within U.S. First Army in Luxembourg between December 10 and 15. In many places when the German troops arrived, battery positions and strong points at cross-roads were found to be unoccupied. Often too when the German assault troops entered the villages between the Our and Clerf, they encountered no more than American advance parties; this sector of the front had been quiet for months and units had moved off before the relieving units arrived, taking their equipment with them. The Fifth Panzer Army's advance across northern Luxembourg was considerably eased by these great gaps and one wonders whether the German High Command knew of them. It seems doubtful.

General Heilmann, commanding the German 5 Parachute Division, told an interesting story of his reconnaissance for his attack, made

* Twelfth Army Group, *Final After Action Report*, Vol. III, G.2, p. 25.

with his engineer battalion commander. He stated that the Americans kept the Our Valley under observation. All he knew was that he would have 28 U.S. Infantry Division opposing him—nothing more. A few days before the offensive, in an effort to offset the shortage of river crossing equipment, one of his units by chance discovered a culvert known to no one other than the fortress battalion holding the sector. The battalion had been careful not to tell the newly arrived parachutists about it, for the culvert led to the Luxembourg bank of the river and the men of the Siegfried line garrison used to pay discreet visits to the farms there. Every night an American patrol would move through this culvert with clockwork regularity, reach the edge of the fortified area and return unmolested the same way. Heilmann decided to use it for the first wave of his attack. This incident shows that in this sector at any rate German reconnaissance had been less than thorough. The German soldier's only knowledge of the enemy with whom he was now to try conclusions was as a pursuer. The battles of Lorraine and the Forest of Hürtgen had shown that the Americans could fight. No one knew, however, how they would behave in face of a violent offensive, whether they would be able to do without their colossal supply system or whether the infantry would still retain its dash once deprived of the support of the other arms. The G.I.s faults and failures were well known and were exaggerated in order to raise the morale of the 'Landser' soldier; the American, he was told, would avoid hand-to-hand fighting, did not like fighting at night and did not know how to look after himself, particularly in rainy weather; his armour did not venture off the road and kept up a continuous chatter over the radio of which advantage should be taken. The last point at least was true and the Germans made the most of it in the Ardennes, as they had already done in Lorraine.

This estimate of American psychology was given in a brochure distributed by Field-Marshal Model. He then went on to describe the enemy layout: 2 or 3 miles to the rear of their outposts the Americans had organised a system of 'hedgehogs' in echelon; they were well sited, strongly held and mutually supporting. They were backed up by armour and artillery. Behind these were located combat groups of two or three companies of infantry supported by troops of tanks; they could intervene within six hours from the start of an attack.

The German orders were issued from December 10 onwards; they laid down that the mobile formations should follow immediately behind the initial attack, by-pass the U.S. strong points and push on without delay. The strong points were to be mopped up by the infantry following behind.

The armoured spearhead of Fifth Panzer Army consisted of XLVII Panzer Corps commanded by General von Lüttwitz. 'By-passing the strong points' meant to him that he must not waste time in front of Bastogne. His two armoured divisions would by-pass the town which would then be taken by the Volksgrenadier. On December 2 Manteuffel had prophesied to Hitler that there would be a siege of Bastogne; it was a vital point in the road system, he said, and would undoubtedly be the objective of any American counter-attack against the southern flank of the pocket. But his forecast made little impression on Hitler, so little that, far from reinforcing Seventh Army, which was responsible for covering the left flank of the operation against any counter-attack from the south, he cut it down.

Hitler's Final Speech to the Generals

Since November 20 Hitler had been in Berlin but on December 10 his special train arrived in the Frankfurt area. He installed himself in a head-quarters in the Chateau of Ziegenberg west of Bad Nauheim, the code name of which was Adlerhorst (Eagle's Eyrie); it had been constructed during the winter of 1940 but had not in fact been used during the French campaign.

On December 11 Hitler held his final conference with the Army Com-manders and their Chiefs of Staff. Once more Westphal, speaking for von Rundstedt, attempted to get the scope of the offensive reduced. He made no attempt to change the final objective but suggested that a definite time limit be laid down; if, by night fall on D + 1, the leading troops had not reached the Meuse south-west of Liège and established bridgeheads across the river, it should be admitted that the offensive had failed and it should be called off.

Jodl's reply was: 'This first phase must last five or six days.'

No very firm decision seems to have been taken, for on the evening of December 18 Rundstedt apparently thought that he was entitled to ask for the offensive to be called off immediately. In the event Hitler refused and insisted upon the continuance of an offensive, the result of which was to fritter away the best of his remaining armour.

At the December 11 conference Sepp Dietrich, when his turn came, asked for a further postponement, saying that his units were not yet ready. It was agreed that the date should be put back from December 14 to 15; the very next day it was again postponed to December 16. Brandenberger, commanding Seventh Army, protested against the inadequacy of his equip-ment, saying that his army had had a raw deal compared with the two attacking armies. Hitler would have none of it.

At 6 p.m. next day, December 12, all commanders down to divisional level, some thirty generals in all, were summoned to the Führer. It was dark when they left Coblenz, whence they were taken in a bus which twisted and turned through side roads to prevent its occupants knowing where they were going. On arrival at Ziegenberg they were made to deposit their arms and brief cases before going into the conference room. The walls were lined with SS guards who kept their eye on all those present. Bayerlein, commanding the Panzer Lehr Division, recorded that: 'No one in the audience dared move or even take his handkerchief out of his pocket'; Hitler seemed to him 'ill and downcast'—a different impression from most other observers.

It was hardly the right atmosphere for one of Hitler's set speeches, of the type which in earlier years would have held the Nuremberg crowd spellbound. The generals were inured to such Hitler antics; this was not the way to overcome their scepticism.

Hitler spoke uninterruptedly, extempore and without notes for two hours. Only a few pages of the stenographic record of this interminable harangue have survived; they give the first part of the speech which traced the development of German history as background to the forthcoming offensive:

The Treaties of Westphalia did not prevent Germany occupying the predominant position in Central Europe which destiny has prescribed for her. If the British Empire had never come into existence, if the United States had been German instead of British, if France had never reached the position of preponderance which she occupied. . . .

It was a confused series of inconsequent statements. Hitler jumped from the Treaties of Münster to parliamentary democracy; he traced all Germany's misfortunes to her encirclement in the wars of the twentieth century; he described Churchill as the instigator of the 'Holy War' against Germany. He then justified his decision to launch a preventive war, saying that the German lead in armaments, though definite, had been insufficient to allow him to wait further than 1939.

From the technical point of view, he went on, Germany was now in a position of inferiority as compared to her enemies, but in order to win the war the essential point was to convince the enemy that he could not achieve ultimate victory. He might make territorial gains but the price he would have to pay would be so terrible that he would become demoralised and convinced that in spite of his victories the war would continue, since Germany refused to accept any idea of surrender. If he found that he was faced by a people and an army still united

one day his nervous energy will collapse. What will happen was what happened to Frederick the Great in the seventh year of his war and which can be accounted his greatest success. People may say: Yes, but then the situation was different. It was not different, gentlemen; at that time all his generals, including his own brother, were near to despairing of success. His prime minister and deputations of ministers from Berlin appeared and begged him to put an end to the war since it could no longer be won. The steadfastness of one man made it possible for that battle to be carried through and the miracle of a change in the situation eventually to be accomplished.

This politico-historical dissertation went on for a further twenty minutes before Hitler came to the real subject of the meeting: the offensive in the west. He recalled that in 1940 he had been the only one to insist upon offensive action and the result had been a triumph. This time, he continued, there was one major difference: they knew the enemy's fighting capacity but, apart from the Luftwaffe, there was little difference in the relative strength of forces. Units on both sides were tired but the Americans had just lost 240,000 men in three weeks. The German tanks made good their lack of numbers by their quality.*

Once they had broken through the American front all the German troops would find in the rear areas were bank clerks dressed as American officers. The enemy had no reserves. Surprise and bad weather were the two essential conditions for the success of the offensive. The Luftwaffe would not, however, be able to give support except in the area of the breakthrough; over the front as a whole it would be best not to count upon air support. It would be available in double measure later.

Hitler concluded:

If the offensive succeeds I will take a modest back seat and leave the laurels of victory to the generals. If it fails it will be my responsibility alone. But success will enable us to free fresh reserves in Norway, cross Belgium and continue into France. For several months now the war industries have been working for nothing else but this operation and the Eastern Front has gone short. But it will not be possible to concentrate so much equipment a second time. If we fail we face dark days. . . .

Once more Hitler described the main outline of the operation and finally Field-Marshal von Rundstedt felt that he must say a few words to assure Hitler of the generals' loyalty. 'We are staking our last card,' he said. 'We cannot fail.'

This was perhaps the only statement of the day with which all those present would have agreed without question. All had their reservations and many may have been thinking on the line of Speer's remark at Nuremberg: 'He deceived us all. . . .'

Treatment of Partisans and Prisoners

During the early days of the offensive numerous crimes were committed in the area overrun by the SS armoured divisions—eighty American prisoners were shot in cold blood at Malmédy and nearly a hundred Belgian civilians were murdered at Stavelot, Bande and Forêt. It is therefore pertinent to ask what instructions had been issued on this subject prior to the offensive.

On September 1 1944 O.K.W. repeated and elaborated upon an instruction dated June 29 1939 setting out the principles for the treatment of

---

* *Hitler's Lagebesrechungen*, Fragment 28, the text of which ends here. The account of the remainder of the meeting is from that of General Heilmann commanding 5 Parachute Division who was present.

prisoners of war and civilians in occupied territory. The taking of hostages had meanwhile become standard practice and during the four years of German occupation of Europe various forms of extortion had been practised by the occupation authorities.

The German High Command may therefore have thought it advisable to remind its troops of the necessity for respecting these principles; they could then, if necessary, be invoked against the Allied forces when they entered German territory. The 1939 directive forbade molestation of the civilian population, looting, rape and the destruction of industrial installations. Spies were not to be executed on the spot but taken to the rear; prisoners were only to be shot if attempting to escape. Similar treatment was prescribed for guerillas and inhabitants of occupied territory caught redhanded carrying out 'reprehensible acts'.

The September 1944 directive laid down—rather late in the day in view of the number of summary executions of 'partisans' all over Europe—that local militia and volunteer formations were to be treated as soldiers and not as guerillas provided that their members wore some badge visible from a distance, were carrying arms openly, were under control of a responsible commander and observed the laws and usages of war. Prisoners captured in battle were to be sent to the rear by the most expeditious means.

These orders were the theory and it was laid down that they were to be repeated every three months. The question is what happened in practice.

Sixth Panzer Army's operation order dated December 8 stated unequivocally: 'Action by armed civilians must be anticipated. These civilians in general belong to the movement known as the Resistance Movement. It is likely that roads will be mined and charges placed on railways and bridges. Headquarters, telephone lines and convoys etc. must be guarded . . . Resistance by armed civilians must be broken.'

Sixth Panzer Army was composed primarily of SS units and this order was signed by Sepp Dietrich. It should be read in conjunction with the strict instructions given in September by Martin Bormann to all Party authorities on the control and surveillance of prisoners of war; these instructions were that under no circumstances were prisoners to be left with the army. The general idea was the same in both cases; under the guise of military necessity the object was to instil terror; at the very least terror was admitted as a possible method. The vagueness of the terms of the order was certainly sufficient to open the door to the use of terror.

After the war, both at the Nuremberg trial and at that of the SS personnel accused of the Malmédy murder of American prisoners, the prosecution maintained that formal orders had been issued for the massacre of prisoners. Field-Marshal von Rundstedt denied this. But Jodl admitted: 'It could never have been issued through military channels. It could have been issued only through the Police—that is to say Himmler or the S.S.'*

* *International Military Tribunal*, Vol. XV, p. 417.

Had such an order been given it would undoubtedly have been issued at least to divisional level and copies must inevitably have been found. But apparently this was not the case.

The general atmosphere of the time, however, led to complete absence of scruple towards prisoners of war and civilian hostages, at least on the part of those who considered this offensive primarily a political operation. On December 14 Sepp Dietrich, commanding Sixth Panzer Army, held a meeting of unit commanders to issue final orders. He made no mention of collecting points for prisoners of war and one of those present, thinking he had forgotten, asked: 'And the prisoners? Where shall we put them?'

'Prisoners? You know what to do with them,' Sepp Dietrich retorted.

At his trial before the American Military Tribunal in Dachau for the Malmédy massacre, Sepp Dietrich maintained that this Pontius Pilate reply merely meant that the Hague Conventions were to be respected.

Ten years later, however, I had the opportunity of interrogating a Wehrmacht colonel who had been present at this conference. His reply was quite definite: 'Addressed to the generals and senior officers of the Waffen S.S. and in the atmosphere of the time, a phrase of this nature could mean only one thing: get rid of the prisoners. And that is the way it was interpreted.'

The colonel continued:

In fact the Americans were at fault in condemning to death only those who committed the crimes and not Sepp Dietrich. He was the man really responsible for the Malmédy massacre and for the way in which 1 S.S. Panzer, the Leibstandarte Adolf Hitler, shot down civilians throughout their advance, particularly at Stavelot. The least that can be said is that the commanders were letting their men run riot.

According to General Westphal, von Rundstedt only heard of the incident through the Allied radio on December 19. Both at the time and later before the American Military Tribunals the defence of the SS accused was that the Allies were exaggerating the incidents in order to keep up a campaign of hate.

Accusations such as this did not come very well from the German High Command, for on December 15 O.K.W. issued an order of the utmost cynicism:

From now on the maximum number of reports of Anglo-American atrocities will be made. If material is inadequate, commanders should not be deterred by the fact that, if information is somewhat exaggerated, denials may be issued locally by the units concerned. The object is to obtain propaganda effect. During the First World War enemy propaganda produced complete inventions of this nature—for instance, that children's hands had been hacked off.*

---

* The reference number of this order is O.K.W./Ag Nr 725/44 gKs v. 15-XII. I found it in the French Army Historical Section with a covering note to the

To cover up their own misdeeds the Germans proposed to say that Belgian civilians had been murdered by the Americans! To say the least of it this clearly does not show any tendency to excessive scruple! In any case it is clear that no attempt was made to curb the reactions of men fighting desperately for a lost cause, of soldiers enraged at the discovery that they had been deceived.

In the evening news bulletin of December 13 General Dittmar, the German radio military commentator, described the situation on the western front as follows:

The main feature is that for the first time for a long time the High Command has freedom of action. This applies principally to the sectors in which decisive action of extreme importance may take place; it is due to the fact that there is no longer that sense of inferiority in men and equipment which has so far frequently governed command decisions. The course of events has not as yet forced the German High Command to throw its operational reserves into the battle. Moreover, violent though the fighting has been, it has not affected German strength to the point of depriving it of the possibility of launching vigorous counter-attacks at the vital point of the front.

The next day the French General Staff Public Relations Office, published this statement without comment. It is easy now to read between the lines of General Dittmar's statement. But the question was whether the Allies were sharp-witted enough at the time to puzzle out his real meaning.

Commander-in-Chief West from Army Group G (on the Saar and Alsace front). After quoting this order the Chief of Staff of Army Group G added: 'We propose nevertheless to keep strictly to the military Court of Enquiry procedure and to base any reports on documents of undoubted validity in case the proceedings should later be published as diplomatic documents.' In the Chief of Staff's view the O.K.W. order 'definitely trespassed into the propaganda field'.

Chapter 9

'NOTHING TO REPORT . . .'

'There is nothing to report on the Ardennes Front'—GENERAL
WHITELEY, Eisenhower's Assistant Chief of Staff Operations,
addressing Senior Air Force officers on December 15 1944.

CIVILIANS are apt somewhat tactlessly to ask generals how they come to
be taken by surprise and allow the home front to get a fright. The civilian
cannot conceive that great military headquarters could ever be subject to
illusions similar to his own. If staff officers do not know, he thinks, who
does? The question is whether anybody on the Allied side really did know
anything in the first fortnight of December; or rather whether there was
anybody with sufficient imagination to piece together the jigsaw puzzle of
innumerable snippets of information and perceive that something unfore-
seen was likely to happen. It is the intelligence officer's business to work
out and classify the various hypotheses upon which enemy action may be
based. If the generals take no notice, the intelligence officers wash their
hands of the matter, saying that they have done their duty. If the operations officers discard certain solutions, one of which subsequently proves
to have been the best, they also wash their hands, saying that the ultimate
responsibility is that of the general. The general of course has many other
matters to consider, the arrival of reinforcements, logistics, the situation
in the rear areas, and of course the decisions taken in the stratosphere by
the leaders responsible for the overall conduct of the war.

In this chain of interlocking authorities, responsibility for failure or
surprise inevitably becomes nebulous; the Commander-in-Chief may well
say, as did Eisenhower, that 'the blame falls upon him alone'; a subordinate
may maintain, as did Hodges of U.S. First Army, that his staff alone had
forecast everything but no one had listened. Neither should be taken too
literally.

Eisenhower's Worries

There is no doubt that the Allied command was guilty of lack of foresight; an objective appreciation, however, must take account of the
Supreme Commander's state of mind and of the other matters worrying
him during these winter days, as he travelled round the front and to and
from headquarters, defending himself against the press campaign which
was accusing him of failure to look the facts of war in the face.

Eisenhower was wrestling with a problem which could well be decisive
for the whole future of the campaign—the manpower crisis. It had first
raised its head in Canada during the summer; to fill the gaps caused by

the battle of attrition round Caen, General Stuart, the Canadian Army Chief of Staff, had had to disband first a division and then an infantry brigade before being allowed to call for reinforcements from home. Very few volunteers were coming forward. The Canadian Minister of War made a tour of Europe and on his return proposed the mobilisation of certain classes. The result was a riot in Montreal and the prime minister, Mackenzie King, was forced to take refuge in compromise: only 16,000 men would be called up on November 23. No more than 9,700 appeared; the rest vanished, the Ministry of War stating euphemistically that 'this could hardly be termed desertion'.

A further factor came into play, subsidiary perhaps but indicative of an unhealthy state of mind in American public opinion. People began to cast up the balance sheet of United States and Commonwealth forces available; this showed that of 20,000,000 men mobilised, 2,000,000 were in the 'European theatre of operations' (western Europe and Italy), and of these 900,000 were in rear services. The fighting units consisted only of some eighty divisions (14,000 men each) of which Eisenhower had approximately sixty.

The local offensives of November had produced no more than 'nibbles', reminiscent of the Argonne and Verdun, but their cost had been 3,000 men per day, 90,000 per month. As against this, reinforcements amounted to 53,000. Even these included eighteen-year-old recruits called up under protest, and soldiers 'skimmed off' the Air Force; they had hardly been licked into shape and had no combat experience. The fall in American strength was not due to losses in battle alone; after five months of exhausting campaigning the G.I.s were only too ready to be 'referred for examination' by the military psychiatrists and the latter were very apt to diagnose 'combat fatigue', requiring treatment. Others deserted. To put an end to the wave of desertion, Eisenhower rejected Private Slovik's plea for mercy. He was one of forty soldiers condemned to death for desertion; a poor little fellow from Detroit, brought up in the years of the great depression and incapable of adapting himself to army life. Eddie Slovik was the only deserter shot. No American Commander-in-Chief since Lincoln had given such an order. The pitiless necessity of making an example, no matter who the victim, was proof of Eisenhower's anxiety over the crisis in morale.

In Washington Marshall was searching for some method to make good the lack of manpower. By December 7 he had been driven to the conclusion that the only expedient was to divert to Europe reinforcements intended for the Pacific theatre. The effect of this measure could not be felt, however, in time to meet the German offensive rebound.

In the five weeks prior to December 15 Twelfth U.S. Army Group had suffered 64,000 battle casualties and another 12,000 had been evacuated with frost-bitten feet; the divisions in the line were at only 78 per cent strength in infantry. The situation was worst in Patton's Third Army which was later to carry out the most effective counter-attack, taking the German offensive in flank. Twice, on December 6 and 13, infantry units were reinforced by transferring 5 per cent of the manpower in the rear services (excepting medical units and those composed of coloured personnel). Even this produced no more than 6,500 men.

Until fresh troops arrived from the United States, Eisenhower could not contemplate more than the battles of attrition on the Saar and around the Aix-la-Chapelle salient which he states in his memoirs inflicted losses on the Germans double those of the Americans. All he could do was to secure, slowly and at heavy cost, the jumping-off positions for the major operations which would later bring him to the Rhine. Accordingly, on December 13, U.S. First Army went into the attack against the four Roer dams, the capture of which was essential to prevent the communications of any force moving up to the Rhine opposite Bonn being cut. R.A.F. bombers had attacked them four times in waves of 180 aircraft, but had not succeeded in destroying them. It was now hoped that the American infantry would achieve the object by capture.

In spite of the optimism of the Combined Staff in Washington, and in spite of the illusions to which certain members of his entourage were prone, Eisenhower realised quite clearly the price he might well have to pay for concentrating his forces in two selected sectors, leaving the rest of the front weak. When Harry Butcher told him on October 30 that he proposed to put the Luxembourg short-wave radio station at the disposal of war correspondents, Ike replied that this sector was very thinly held and that the Germans might well attack there.

In his book Eisenhower states that he and Bradley had decided at this period to play for high stakes and to accept the possibility of an enemy offensive in this area, knowing that it would not be able to reach the Meuse and would be caught between the American forces from north and south. It would be a good opportunity to finish off the bulk of the German armies in the west. This argument is too obviously *post hoc* and is intrinsically unconvincing. According to Harry Butcher's diary, on December 5 Eisenhower put no faith at all in a possible German offensive; he was counting upon the bad weather, the floods and the mud keeping the Germans bogged down on the defensive for some time yet.

Information Available to the Allies

The Army and Supreme Headquarters intelligence summaries, both daily and periodical, show that plenty of information was available to the American generals at all levels; from the outset, however, they fell into Hitler's trap. As early as October they knew that fresh Panzer armies had been formed and moved, first to Westphalia and then to the Cologne plain; they were convinced they knew why. Hitler, they thought, was preparing an operation known as 'Watch on the Rhine', the object of which was to take in flank an Allied offensive across the Roer towards the Rhine.

During the last week of November, when the Allied offensive in the Aix-la-Chapelle area had failed, the Germans appeared to divide the strategic reserve which they had concentrated in the Cologne area and reinforce both halves. Supreme Headquarters' G.2 Order of Battle of November 30, identified twenty-five divisions including four Panzers and announced the arrival of Sixth Panzer Army immediately to rear of the front. It concluded:

This would indicate that the German High Command considers the situation in the Geilenkirchen-Julich-Düren sector very serious. It would seem that every effort is being made to delay use of the armoured reserves as long as possible. . . . Volksgrenadier divisions continue to arrive as required, and six of them have appeared during the past fortnight. These are low-class divisions and their role appears to be to bolster the front or to enable tired and depleted units to be relieved. In most cases they are in fact located in quiet sectors.

The possibility of a German offensive did not appear as a serious possibility in First and Third U.S. Armies' forecasts until December 10. Summarising enemy activity over the preceding month, Colonel Dickson, First Army G.2, concluded:

The enemy's armoured reserve appears to be quartered along the railroads, generally in a semi-circle from Düsseldorf to Coblenz with Köln as a centre point. He has brought up and continues to bring up Army and Corps artillery formations and to build up his fighter and fighter-bomber strength on the Western Front. It is plain that his strategy in defence of the Reich is based on the exhaustion of our offensive, to be followed by an all-out counter-attack with armour between the Roer and Erft.

Colonel Dickson then asked himself what von Rundstedt would be trying to do to counter the imminent Allied operation, which 'must be considered the greatest threat to a successful defence of the Reich'. His answer was: 'Make good the Siegfried Line, recapture the forts lost in the Aix-la-Chapelle area, accepting defeats in the south rather than compromise his hope of a decisive success in the north.'

In his view the enemy attack would come in the northern sector of the Allied front and fall primarily upon Second British Army and Ninth American Army. On December 15 he cited statements by prisoners supporting his view that the attack would take place between December 15 and 25, the capture of Aix-la-Chapelle having been promised to the Führer as a 'Christmas present'.

For two months all the American intelligence experts had been mesmerised by the theory that Aix-la-Chapelle must be the objective. They wrote off as unimportant certain reports to the contrary, definite though they were. On December 14, for instance, Colonel Dickson reported as follows:

A German woman, whose statements are believed reliable according to VIII U.S. Corps, has given the following information of her observations behind the German lines during the three days beginning 10 December. She saw many horse-drawn vehicles, pontoons, small boats, and other river-crossing equipment coming from the direction of Bitburg and moving west through Geichlingen (opposite Vianden). In Bitburg she overheard some military personnel saying it had taken three weeks to get there from Italy; there were also troops in the town with grey uniforms and black collar patches. She also stated that she had seen many artillery pieces both horse-drawn and carried on trucks.

These units in fact belonged to Fifth Panzer Army which was to cross northern Luxembourg. But Colonel Dickson laid no special emphasis upon this information, merely commenting: 'Really interesting information. The arrival of fresh units is confirmed by prisoners' statements and air reconnaissance. The presence of a large number of engineer units with bridging equipment suggests the preparation of an offensive rather than a defensive action.'

This was indirectly confirmed next day by a report from VIII U.S. Corps holding the Ardennes front. It reported a change in the behaviour of enemy units opposite the corps, suggesting the arrival of fresh troops. There was considerably less patrol activity, but vehicle traffic opposite the southern flank of the salient formed by the American front on the Schnee Eifel was incessant. This was the road along which next day the German armoured columns were to start their drive on Saint-Vith.

The Americans infiltrated their own OSS agents through the German lines; moreover, the population, particularly in Luxembourg, was friendly and gave them every assistance. Definite indications of preparations for an offensive filtered across the Our. Strict though the German camouflage measures were, they could not entirely conceal the concentration of fresh units and there were many statements by Luxembourgers which should have alerted the Allied command well ahead of time. During the night November 27–28, for instance, some of the inhabitants of Bivels, near Vianden, had been swept up by a German patrol and interrogated by a Luxembourg citizen who had gone over to the enemy in September. He had told them: 'We shall be back in Luxembourg in a week and in Verdun shortly after that.'

The prisoners managed to escape and as they moved along the eastern bank of the Our they observed the first fresh German forces moving up. When they reached their homes the local militia took them along to the Americans. Although the remark quoted above proved to be partially untrue, their statements ought to have been checked. Apparently they were not.

At Bastogne, where the headquarters of VIII U.S. Corps was situated, the entire population was expecting a German offensive. Light signals were said to have been seen and Germans in civilians clothes observed laying out dropping zones for parachute operations. The headquarters was warned by the Belgians but apparently did not take the information seriously. It may well have been thought that this was merely an outbreak of 'spy mania', inevitable at this period and in this area. Nevertheless, all this information from the population of the frontier area should not have been disregarded. After all they knew their own country. Enquiries to check their stories might have been complicated but should have been made; they would at least have confirmed the information arriving through military channels.

One of the leading inhabitants of Bastogne during the battle told me: 'American casualness prior to the offensive was only equalled by their toughness once it had been launched.'

During the period from November 17 to December 16 there were ten days on which weather was so bad that aircraft were grounded and navigation instruments useless. Nevertheless, in general terms air reconnaissance did its job well. Practically every day signs of increasing activity to the rear of the German front were reported. The tracks of road convoys were visible in the snow and no camouflage could entirely conceal the rows of tanks lying up in the woods. The increase of both day and night rail traffic was even more obvious and practically every sortie brought back fresh confirmation. On December 6 a night-fighter squadron even located the battery of fifty searchlights in the Kaiserslautern area which Manteuffel intended to use to produce artificial moonlight for the start of his attack. The air force was quite clear on the conclusion which should be drawn from all these movements observed during the first fortnight of December: the bulk of the reinforcements crossing the Rhine were moving, not towards the Aix-la-Chapelle salient, but in a more southerly direction.

Last-minute leakage of information was, as always, inevitable. In this case it was clear beyond doubt. Three instances will suffice. During the night of December 13–14 a runner from 17 SS Security Company was captured. He was carrying a message from divisional headquarters to a unit in the line: 'Last night's message ordering a withdrawal was in error. Remain where you are and prepare for a counter-attack which is being planned.'

The same night 422 U.S. Infantry Regiment, which had just taken over in the Schnee Eifel massif, captured a German patrol. The patrol leader was carrying von Rundstedt's order for the attack which had just been distributed to units. It was forwarded at once to regimental headquarters where it disappeared into the jungle of 'official channels'. In the same area a Polish deserter warned that an offensive was imminent. It would be launched, he said, before dawn on some day between December 15 and

Christmas. This information, however, only arrived at the American head-quarters at Saint-Vith at the same time as the news of the attack.

There can be only one conclusion; with the mass of information arriving from all the sources available to them the Allied commanders ought to have been able to discern ample evidence that the target of the German offensive was not merely the Saar or the Roer. Moreover there was one man who did realise the situation; amid all the conflicting theories he was the only one who maintained that some operation was pending in the Ardennes. This was General Strong, Chief of Eisenhower's Intelligence Division, and so the most senior of all the intelligence officers. He had been British Assistant Military Attaché in Berlin before the war and then head of the German Section in the War Office. He guessed Hitler's intention and realised that Hitler's views would prevail over those of the military technicians. He maintained that five or six consecutive days of bad weather would be enough for Hitler to launch an offensive.

But this intelligent assessment ran counter to the ideas held at all levels in the fighting formations. Moreover the good work done by air reconnaissance was largely offset by lack of liaison between the army and air head-quarters; responsibilities and powers were not clearly defined and the best use was not, therefore, made of the results of reconnaissance sorties.

'A Calculated Risk'

At the Allied staff conferences held every morning intelligence officers usually elaborated verbally upon their theories regarding enemy intentions. Their statements were not recorded and they were usually wrapped up in somewhat imprecise—if not contradictory—language, so that whatever happened the officers could say later that they had been right. We shall therefore never know how strongly those who supported the idea of an Ardennes offensive pressed their point of view. Clashes of personality unfortunately also increased scepticism and distorted people's conclusions. At headquarters of First U.S. Army, for instance, Colonel Dickson had hit upon the truth, but he was at loggerheads with the Chief of Staff, the Head of the Operations Section and with General Sibert, Head of G.2 at the headquarters of Twelfth U.S. Army Group.

Sibert was therefore inclined to scepticism and he confirmed his immediate master, Bradley, in his view that the Germans would not attack in the Ardennes. Bedell Smith, Eisenhower's Chief of Staff, however, was convinced by General Strong's arguments and told the latter to put his view across in detail to Bradley. He did not feel that he could issue Bradley with a definite order since it could not be based upon absolute certainty. Strong had a forty-five-minute interview with Bradley but could not shake him. Bradley stated that he realised the danger and was proposing to make certain movements of divisions to guard against the possibility.

In his memoirs Bradley stated that he was taking a 'calculated risk'. The

Ardennes operation did not seem to him 'the most rational'. He had a
choice between carrying out a winter offensive and maintenance of 'a
secure defence everywhere on the Allied line'. He had chosen the offensive.
'Nothing less than an unequivocal indication of an impending attack in
the Ardennes could have induced me to quit the winter offensive.' But
the single fact that Twelfth U.S. Army Group had not a single unit in
reserve to guard against this 'calculated risk' shows that he did not really
believe in any such possibility. The excuse was thought up subsequently.

Supreme Headquarters' thoughts were turned primarily to Alsace and
in particular to the situation around Strasbourg and the Colmar pocket,
which Eisenhower had ordered should be eliminated by December 14.
Eisenhower's aim was to shorten his front in the Vosges, and he tended
to imagine that von Rundstedt must be thinking along the same lines, that
they must both be living in the same pure strategic atmosphere and basing
their calculations upon reasonable employment of the available resources.
In fact he should have reckoned (as did Strong) not upon the rational,
'traditional' reactions of von Rundstedt but upon those of Hitler. The
Allied High Command was indulging in wishful thinking. This was what
lay behind the remark by General Whiteley, Assistant Chief of Staff
Operations at SHAEF, on December 15, when he told a conference of
Allied air force commanders at Versailles that there was nothing to report
from the Ardennes sector.

The press had no reason either to pat itself on the back for any particular
prescience. It is true that its impressions were gathered primarily in
London and Washington rather than 'on the ground', in other words from
sources even more prone than those of SHAEF to believe that which suited
their own preconceived ideas. The most interesting comments were those
of Liddell Hart, who likes to think himself the father of modern strategy,
and Hanson Baldwin, his *New York Times* rival. Both of them were clearly
dependent on their respective war departments.

On November 20 Liddell Hart gave a vague hint in the *Daily Mail* to
the effect that the Germans had managed 'to pull out their panzer divisions
for refitting' implying that any future counter-offensive would therefore
have greater punch.

Similar warnings were sounded at this period in other British newspapers but they were the exception, drowned in a flood of articles the
general tenor of which was that the Germans were at the end of their
tether.

There was not a word of such gloomy prophecies in the American press,
and Hanson Baldwin seemed to have no such idea in his head. Even on
the British side they did not sound like cries of alarm; they did not sound
like voices crying out in the wilderness of scepticism. Their pessimism did
not carry conviction and its wording lacked force. Their implicit warning
note became perceptible only after the event, like a tiny stroke of a black

brush on a grey background. Too much importance should not be attached to them.

Amusingly, as soon as the offensive had been launched, Liddell Hart unashamedly took advantage of the journalist's permanent stand-by, the short memory of his readers. His article of December 10 was headed: 'Attack should be no surprise to the Allies'. It continued:

The place Rundstedt has chosen for his counter-stroke provides, too, no reason for surprise. Indeed it is more surprising that the Allies themselves made so little attempt to penetrate this sector between Eupen and Trier instead of concentrating their efforts in the lowlying area around the north of Aachen with its numerous water courses and towns.

The course of events was, in fact, a source of satisfaction to the 'great professor', for whatever they did his disciples on both sides were bound to prove him right—the German generals had long been studying his theories on armoured warfare. The attack showed once more that 'the area was more accessible to tanks than was commonly supposed, particularly according to the hidebound thinking of French General Staff circles'. The defence showed that he had been right in saying earlier that there were 'several possible Thermopylae'* in the Ardennes. Finally Hitler had failed to adopt his idea of clearing the way for the armour by an airborne operation—according to Liddell Hart the only way of dealing with defiles and bottle-necks.

After all this it would be good for the master to interrogate his pupils once the war was over; both sides would sit at his feet.

To return to General Bradley's 'calculated risk'—it is of interest to see upon what this was based:

On December 16 General Hodges' First U.S. Army was holding the Luxembourg front up to Geilenkirchen (opposite Cologne).

On his left (to the north) VII U.S. Corps was taking part in the offensive launched on December 13 against the Roer and Erft dams.

In the centre, V U.S. Corps was also involved in this operation. In fact, it was directly facing the German Sixth Panzer Army. VIII U.S. Corps, with headquarters at Bastogne, was spread out all along the Ardennes over nearly a hundred miles, as far as the southern border of the Grand Duchy of Luxembourg. It consisted of the following:

14 Cavalry Group.

106 Infantry Division: this had arrived direct from England and had never been under fire until it went into the line on December 10.

28 Infantry Division: a tough veteran unit which at this time was also in line in northern Luxembourg.

9 Armoured Division: which had just detached a combat group to V Corps.

* *The Defence of Britain*, p. 219.

4 Infantry Division: holding the junction of the Our and Moselle in the area of Echternach.

The majority of these units were taken by surprise whilst still taking up their positions. Their signal system had not been established and their strong points were in many cases only semi-equipped, the weapons having been removed by the previous units. Since nothing seemed very urgent in this area, no one had been in a great hurry to replace these weapons. The positions themselves had not in all cases been reconnoitred in detail.

The staffs may have been quite unsuspecting, but the men in the line were put on the alert by the increase of engine noise to the rear of the German lines. The outposts of one of the regiments of 106 Infantry Division, for instance, situated on the south-eastern flank of the Schnee Eifel, dominated the entire enemy road network. The Polish deserter's statement referred to above reinforced its colonel's conviction of the significance of these movements. With his battalion commanders, he drew up plans for a counter-attack to meet the threatened offensive. It was no good; manœuvre was impossible: 'There are no routes for withdrawal,' he concluded. 'You must hold on where you are at all costs.'

Although these men had never been under fire before, in fact they held out for three days before being over-run. More than anything else it was the performance of the American infantryman which was the glorious page in the history of the Ardennes offensive.

The night of December 15-16 began uneventfully for the 75,000 American soldiers between Monschau and Echternach. It was just a normal night of snow and ice, the cold accentuated by lack of sleep—just the usual initiation to the hardships of war. The veterans who had come down from the Hürtgen Forest had spent many such nights. The newly arrived thought that their worst exertions were over. All slept the sleep of tired men after a last glass of beer at the soldiers' canteen.

They did not hear the muffled tramp of 250,000 German soldiers moving into line on the other side of the stream or at the foot of the slopes opposite. They did not realise the significance of the purr of a thousand tank engines or the roar of lorries coming up over the last miles of snowy, straw-covered road. They did not know that 2,000 guns were now in position pointing westwards. Snow was falling bringing down a great blanket of silence. The guys opposite, huddled in the cement pillboxes of the Siegfried line, it seemed to them, hadn't even got the wits to light a fire! Tomorrow was definitely not going to be the day on which those damn German bastards came out of their holes!

Chapter 10

DECEMBER 16

AT last the German troops had been let into the secret that lay behind their long period of waiting. At the very last minute they moved up to the front and at dawn on December 16 1944 they went forward. Sepp Dietrich's Order of the Day read:

Soldiers of Sixth Panzer Army! The great moment of decision is upon us. The Führer has placed us at the vital point. It is for us to breach the enemy front and push beyond the Meuse. Surprise is half the battle. In spite of the terror bombings, the Home Front has provided us with tanks, ammunition and weapons. They are watching us. We will not let them down.

With the opening of the artillery barrage all along the front of Sepp Dietrich's army at 5.30 a.m., the Ardennes offensive becomes a matter of straight military history. The picture is of a series of overcast days with falling snow and men feeling their way forward in search of an invisible enemy. It was no spectacular military clash, but it had its drama. I propose to deal only with those phases during which the outcome still seemed to hang in the balance, though it is doubtful if it really ever did so. Even this short account of the course of events will show that, panic-stricken though the Americans were and violent though the German punch was, the legends which fear has built up around this offensive have little basis in fact.

The Northern Sector of the Front

Some idea of the ground over which the battle was to be fought is essential, though the picture must be a somewhat abstract one, similar to that of the German staff officers at Coblenz or Ziegenberg, as they pored over the contours and variegated colours of the staff maps. In rough terms the German front line overlooked a deep cleft running generally north and south formed by the valleys of the Sure and Our. Fifty-five miles to the west lay the first major obstacle—the Meuse, which was to be reached on D plus 3; it ran from south to north, turning almost due east at Namur through Huy and Liège. Approximately midway between these two lines was the river Ourthe, winding through a deep valley in a general south-north direction and joining the Meuse at Liège.

Between the Ourthe and the Our a line of hills runs in a general north-easterly direction, topped by the towns of Bastogne and Saint-Vith, the two focal points of the Ardennes' road system. The high ground is shaped like an arrow, the eastern tip of the arrow-head being formed by the Schnee Eifel massif on the left-hand (eastern) bank of the Our, the point

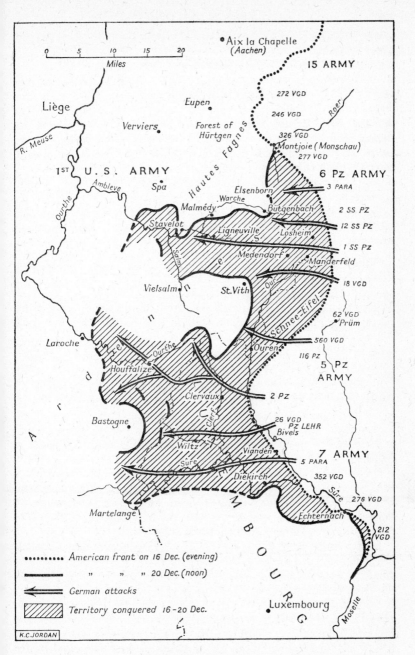

The First Four Days

Map labels:

Aix la Chapelle (Aachen)

15 ARMY

272 VGD
246 VGD
326 VGD
Montjoie (Monschau)
277 VGD

Liège

Eupen

Verviers

Forest of Hürtgen

Hautes Fagnes

R. Meuse

1ST U.S. ARMY

Ambleve

Spa

Elsenborn
Warche
Malmédy
Büttgenbach

6 Pz ARMY
3 PARA
2 SS PZ
12 SS PZ
1 SS PZ

Stavelot

Ligneuville
Losheim

Salm

Medendorf
Manderfeld

Ourthe

Vielsalm
St.Vith

18 VGD

Schnee-Eifel

62 VGD
Prüm

Laroche

Ourthe
Houffalize

Ouren

560 VGD
116 PZ

5 Pz ARMY

Ardennes

Clervaux

2 PZ

Clerf

Bastogne

26 VGD
PZ LEHR
Bivels

Wiltz
Sure

Vianden

7 ARMY
5 PARA

Diekirch

352 VGD

Sure

276 VGD

Martelange

Echternach

212 VGD

LUXEMBOURG

Luxembourg

Moselle

Legend:

·········· American front on 16 Dec. (evening)
────── " " " 20 Dec. (noon)
⟵ German attacks
▨ Territory conquered 16-20 Dec.

K.C.JORDAN

Miles
0 5 10 15 20

at which the American front penetrated most deeply into German territory; to the north-west—to the left of the arrow and parallel to the Meuse—the plateau of Hautes-Fagnes stretched towards Aix-la-Chapelle and met the wooded foothills of the Hürtgen Forest. To the south-east, near the point of the arrow, the Hautes-Fagnes plateau merged into the Elsenborn massif. The foot of this massif was marked by three fair-sized towns at the key crossing points of the streams flowing into the Ourthe—Monschau, Malmédy and Stavelot. Between these streams and overlooking them, the Elsenborn massif formed a natural fortress barring the route to Liège. To surround the defenders of Elsenborn, Sepp Dietrich proposed to launch a parachute operation on Baraque Michel, the highest point in Belgium (2,000 feet).

At the tip of the arrow lies a cleft, the Losheim Gorge (Losheimer Graben), offering a natural access route into the valleys running along the two wing-tips of the arrow, westwards the Warche and Amblève overlooked by Elsenborn, and eastwards the Our overlooked by the Schnee Eifel. The Hautes-Fagnes was bounded by steep-sided valleys along which ran centuries-old routes avoiding the barren plateau. The towns and villages were generally to be found along the more modern roads which wound their way along the fir-covered slopes, following the streams in the general direction of the Meuse.

I have designedly somewhat over-simplified the picture. It was poor country, a succession of ridges interspersed with marshy areas and barely penetrable woodlands. *A priori* it favoured the defence.

The main offensive effort was to be made by Sepp Dietrich with Sixth Panzer Army. It was for him to set the pace. He was not to allow himself to be held up by isolated centres of resistance and was to carry Fifth Panzer Army on his left along with him; this, in Hitler's view, would ensure that the operation carried on to Antwerp. Dietrich's plan was as follows:

On the right three Volksgrenadier divisions were to carry the whole of the Elsenborn massif and join up with the parachute detachment dropped into the blue on the Hautes-Fagnes plateau. An armoured division, 12 SS Panzer (Hitlerjugend), was then to pass through them and move on to form a defensive front between Eupen and Liège.

In the centre another Volksgrenadier division was given only a few hours to clear the Losheim Gorge, along which was to pass the main attacking force—I SS Armoured Corps led by 1 SS Armoured Division, the crack unit known as the 'Leibstandarte Adolf Hitler' (Adolf Hitler's bodyguard). It was to drive straight through the Americans, who it was assumed would by then be in complete disorder, and carry on to the Meuse between Huy and Liège. The spearhead of the division was an armoured force under the command of SS 'Standartenführer' (Colonel) Jochen Peiper, which would include a high proportion of heavy tanks, supporting

weapons and lorried infantry. It was to be supported on its left by a less
heavily equipped force consisting of six mechanised squadrons under
command of 'Sturmbannführer' (Major) Knittel; the latter was to join
forces with Peiper after crossing the Liège–Bastogne road.

To the south, in other words on the left, of this force lay the area of
Manteuffel's Fifth Panzer Army.

In reserve Sepp Dietrich had II Armoured Corps and the SS Divisions
'Das Reich' and 'Hohenstauffen'. These he proposed to use, according to
circumstances, either to assist I Corps to cross the Meuse or, if necessary,
to take over from it and keep up the momentum of the drive on Antwerp.

Day One with Sepp Dietrich's Army

At 5.30 a.m., whilst it was still dark, Sixth Panzer Army's artillery
opened a forty-five minute barrage on the American lines. It struck
accurately at headquarters and communications. The men in the foxholes
were taken aback by such a resumption of activity and went to ground.
Firing ceased at 6.15 and did not resume until 8.00, this time at longer
range and aimed at the built-up areas in the rear.

Meanwhile, taking advantage of the complete darkness and howling
wind, infantry and pioneer assault units advanced deep into the American
lines, keeping clear of all cross-roads. Silently they did away with the
sentries, cut telephone lines and captured small isolated posts.

The main formations moved off at 7.30. But between Monschau and
Malmédy, along the semi-circle of streams at the foot of the Elsenborn
massif the Americans recovered as soon as it was light. Though harried
and disjointed, the greenhorns of 99 U.S. Infantry Division fell back upon
the veterans of 2 U.S. Infantry Division, which reformed them and turned
them round. This was Sepp Dietrich's first disappointment; he had hoped
to have broken through the weak American front before the veterans could
intervene, for they had been in reserve to V U.S. Corps attacking along
the Roer.

By 10 o'clock, two hours ahead of schedule, the SS General decided
to put in 12 SS Panzer Division, not to exploit the break-through but to
create it and compensate for the failure of the Volksgrenadier. The tanks
were not used, for the snow hid the weak points in the roads, an essential
bridge had been blown and there was no question of moving across
country. These first two hours gave the Germans a foretaste of the difficulties which they faced. In the northern sector of the offensive, the Elsenborn
bastion forced the flood of the German army into a narrow channel.

In the Losheim Gap two German divisions attacked on a 7-mile front
and, in spite of the desperate courage of the American soldiers, scored a
definitive success. The position was ill-defined and lay on the boundary
between V and VIII U.S. Corps. Although it included the exits to the
upper valleys of the Amblève and the Our and covered the approaches to

the Saint-Vith area, this sector had been thought to be relatively safe. Since December 11 it had been defended by 14 Cavalry Group consisting of two 'squadrons', one of which was in reserve at Vielsalm some 20 miles in rear. The other was covering the approaches to Manderfeld, a village overlooking the Our at the last defile on the Saint-Vith road. Also in the area were some mixed tank destroyer and engineer groups specially formed for the forthcoming attack on the Siegfried line.

There was no continuous American front in this sector, no line in the true sense of the word, as there had been in the First World War and as there was now in the Vosges. The U.S. Cavalry had set up fortified strong-points in the main villages on the roads leading into Germany. On their arrival five days before they had dismounted the automatic weapons from their tanks to equip the strong-points. They had been trained for mobility and fast moving long-distance reconnaissance, but having now disarmed their vehicles they were incapable of carrying out their true role and were reduced to patrolling on foot. There were few minefields or road blocks behind them. On their right they were in touch with 422 U.S. Infantry Regiment, which was in position in the old German fortified area of the Schnee Eifel. But on their left on the wooded heights of Buchholz, was a yawning gap, covered only by patrols from an infantry company located at the Losheim Gap cross-roads.

The forward defence of Saint-Vith was, therefore, no more than a thin screen supported by the guns of a 105 mm artillery group located at Medendorf, 3 miles west of Manderfeld.

The 14 Cavalry Group squadron was quickly surrounded at first light by 3 German Parachute Division, but nevertheless, throughout the morning of December 16, it resisted. Two of its troops at Kopfscheid engaged in hand-to-hand fighting, the supporting guns firing over open sights. The remainder blew up their vehicles and disappeared into the woods. A little further north a tank destroyer unit lost seven of its ten guns, five being immediately turned against it. Deprived of their vehicles, the gun crews scattered and set off on a hazardous retreat.

Early in the morning the reserve squadron, No. 32, was called up from Vielsalm and towards midday was put in to plug the gap opening towards the Amblève valley; but by nightfall, threatened with encirclement, it withdrew. Meanwhile on the Schnee Eifel two infantry regiments were completely cut off and under attack by the German Fifth Panzer Army.

The gap was now wide open. During the short winter twilight Colonel Peiper moved his armour forward some 6 miles into a position facing west. The next day, December 17, it was to start its remorseless drive.

'What are these damned bastards of Huns up to?' asked General Gerow, commanding V U.S. Corps. Little information had reached him during the morning of December 16; his task was complicated by the fact that the telephone wires had been cut and the outposts overrun; in the surprise there was general confusion. At least, however, he knew that German infantry only were involved. Then towards midday came the first reports of armoured action. The question was whether the enemy was exerting pressure on Gerow's southern front in order to force him to break off the offensive in progress against the Roer dams.

Judging by the width of front attacked, Gerow came to the conclusion that this was a far larger-scale operation. As early as 1 o'clock he asked his immediate superior, General Hodges, commanding First U.S. Army, for authorisation to break off the Roer offensive. His idea was to withdraw the units engaged in this sector and reinforce the infantry of 2 and 99 Infantry Divisions who were fighting desperately to hold the approaches to the Elsenborn bastion.

Hodges' reply was: 'No. Proceed with the offensive in the north and hold where you are in the south.'

For although his headquarters was at Spa and he could hear the thunder of the guns at the front, General Hodges did not that evening 'believe it'.

There was still an astonishing amount of ignorance in the area directly threatened by Sixth Panzer Army. At Ligneuville, only 12 miles from Honsfeld where the 14 Cavalry had just gone under in hand-to-hand fighting, was the headquarters of an anti-aircraft formation under General Timberlake, whose job it was to protect Liège from the V1s. People there were having a peaceful evening; at stand-down at the end of the day the men of the Headquarters Company, the clerks, medical orderlies and cooks had gone to the cinema. During the film the alert sounded and the rumour went round that there was a German attack somewhere in the Butgenbach direction (at the foot of Elsenborn), where in fact the Volks-grenadier were just renewing their attack against the raw, exhausted American infantry. But the all-clear soon sounded and the Headquarters Company went back to their billets. They were to be chased out of them next day by the SS armour.

Day One with Manteuffel's Army

Judging from the map the country over which Colonel-General Hasso Eckart von Manteuffel's Fifth Panzer Army was to operate offered an easier run than that facing Sepp Dietrich. His first objective was the Meuse in the sector running north to south from Givet through Dinant to Namur.

Along Manteuffel's front ran the valley of the Our; beyond lay a number of obstacles or river lines which might hold up his advance, in particular the valleys of the Clerf, the Lomme and the Lesse, all running generally north–south. On the other hand, starting from the main villages on the Saint-Vith–Luxembourg highway, a number of roads running east and west were available for the movement of his armour.

Bastogne was the key to the area. It was the meeting point, not only of the road from Clervaux and the north–south highway, but also of the routes leading in from the southern Ardennes. During the planning of the offensive Manteuffel had realised that any American counter-attack against his left flank was likely to start from the area of Arlon and Martelange and that its objective would be Bastogne. General Brandenberger's Seventh Army had, therefore, been allotted the task of swinging round to face southwards and counter any such move. Meanwhile Manteuffel, after capturing the focal point of Bastogne, was to move straight on to the Meuse.*

Manteuffel's task was subsidiary to that of Sepp Dietrich. He was given two objectives:

On his right a corps consisting of two Volksgrenadier divisions was to carry the Schnee Eifel, capture Saint-Vith and then protect the southern flank of Sixth Panzer Army.

The centre and left of Fifth Panzer Army with two armoured corps was to cross the Meuse between Huy and Dinant by D plus 3, and move on Brussels. Bastogne was to be taken by XLVII Panzer Corps, commanded by General von Lüttwitz. This corps consisted of a number of well-tried formations all with a reputation to maintain. 2 Panzer Division, with its Trident insignia, was an ex-Austrian division which had been in action throughout the war; it was commanded by General von Lauchert. 26 Volksgrenadier Division was raised in Cologne, with Cologne Cathedral as its insignia, and had been annihilated and reconstituted seven times between June 1941 and September 1944. It had then been cut to pieces yet once more in East Prussia and had just been reformed on the Luxembourg Front with naval and air force personnel. It was commanded by General Heinz Kokott and was to make the break-through for the Panzer Lehr Division. The latter had been formed in the spring of 1944 and led throughout the Normandy fighting and the retreat across France by General Bayerlein, ex-Chief of Staff to Rommel in North Africa.

XLVII Panzer Corps was supported by twenty-three artillery groups and two brigades (twelve batteries) of rocket launchers; as one of the main break-through formations, it had considerable fire power.

On Manteuffel's left Seventh Army had no armoured units. Only one of its corps, LXXXV, was to move; this was to keep pace with the advance of Fifth Panzer Army and cover its southern flank between Saint-Hubert and Neufchâteau. The remaining two corps, one of which was in reserve, were not to advance beyond the Luxembourg frontier.

Now to the events of the day in each of these areas.

In the northern sector of Fifth Panzer Army's front the high ground and the pillboxes of the Siegfried line along the Schnee Eifel had been occupied by two American infantry regiments. They at least knew that an offensive

* The lines of advance between Bastogne and Arlon used by the Fifth and Seventh German Armies in December 1944 were the same as those over which Guderian's XIX Armoured Corps had moved on May 10 1940.

was imminent, but were nevertheless taken by surprise, though by less direct methods than their neighbours further north. The Volksgrenadier divisions, in fact, infiltrated far to the rear of their positions and spent the day of December 16 forcing all the artillery batteries supporting the infantry to withdraw, leaving the two regiments isolated within the German lines.

Before nightfall the Germans swung back against this isolated American-held area and began to carve it up. One of the U.S. regiments, No. 422, withdrew and reformed in the rear. The other, No. 423, was involved in close range fighting from the outset and fought where it stood. Further south the third regiment of the division, No. 424, was overrun at once. The tanks of 116 Panzer passed through the infantry at once and by the end of the day had reached the immediate outskirts of Saint-Vith. Early in the afternoon, however, some American sub-units had reformed behind them and were fighting in hastily organised strong-points. During the evening an ammunition column from Saint-Vith reached them, though even this left them without rockets for their bazookas or ammunition for one artillery group which had fired more than 2,500 rounds during the day.

The three regiments of 106 U.S. Infantry Division were, therefore, isolated, each left to its own resources; they could do no more than hope to regain contact and be reinforced next day. This greenhorn formation had not done badly during its baptism of fire. It had been thrown off balance by the first assault but had then made a brave recovery almost everywhere and its losses were not too high. Both north and south of it the dismounted cavalry units had given ground. Nevertheless, though the Americans had been forced back, the German drive on Saint-Vith had been slowed down from the outset. Talk of panic and precipitate withdrawal does 106 Division less than justice.

On the remainder of Fifth Panzer Army's front the 'storm battalions infiltrated rapidly into the American front like raindrops' as Manteuffel put it to Liddell Hart.

The line of hills between the Our and Clerf was semi-illuminated by A.A. searchlights shining on the low clouds, and the German advance was made all the easier by the fact that forward of these hills there was no real American front, the main road Diekirch–Saint-Vith running to all intents and purposes through no man's land. Some of 28 U.S. Infantry Division outposts, though surrounded, resisted throughout the day and at Hosingen, Buchholz and Munshausen, the Americans held out for two days. At Marnach fighting went on throughout the 16th in spite of two tank attacks by 2 Panzer; other units of this division, however, reached Clervaux, which they occupied during the night. On the southern sector of the German front, in the centre of the Grand Duchy of Luxembourg, two regiments of 5 German Parachute Division advanced without difficulty to the high ground facing them. There they were unexpectedly held up for as long as forty-eight hours by three U.S. strong-points manned by a cavalry unit which sallied out to meet them. For some hours there was panic in 14 German Parachute Regiment. Their assault guns had not come up and the division hesitated. It took two days to get the guns across the Our; there were no bridges or rafts and they were eventually got across on piles of logs. The defence of the town of Wiltz, which contained the headquarters of 28 U.S. Infantry Division, was well organised early on December 16. All the crossing places over the near-by rivers which the Germans must use, and the defiles through which the German attack must move, were covered by heavy artillery. On the outskirts of the town tanks were sited behind the infantry positions but forward of their mortars, blocking the roads from the north and west. Wiltz was not attacked until December 20.

The last town of any size in the sector held by 28 U.S. Infantry Division was Diekirch. As in other cases, the defences were only in moderate order, owing to the unit reliefs which had taken place a few days before. By 6.00 a.m. on December 16, German infantry, supported by a parachute regiment moving in from the north-east, were at the foot of the Herren-berg on immediate outskirts of the Diekirch. By the end of the morning the American garrison had sealed all exits to the town and the unfortunate Luxembourgers were therefore forced to remain under continuous artillery bombardment. To everyone's astonishment, however, the German attack did not materialise. There was no more than intermittent fighting.

No. 276, the other Volksgrenadier division in Seventh Army, crossed the Our on December 16 and surrounded 4 U.S. Infantry Division's posts at the road junctions. They went under one by one but only after very severe fighting; their action was a major factor in blocking the road to Luxembourg. 4 U.S. Infantry Division had just come down from the Aix-la-Chapelle front, where it had been involved in two months of the toughest fighting of the entire European campaign, and was only at half strength. The divisional commander, General Barton, threw into the battle all his headquarters and services personnel. In the city of Luxembourg itself the only force available was the military police whom the garrison commander posted at the exits. Even the Radio Luxembourg military announcers had rifles pressed into their hands.

Reactions at the Higher Levels

Looking back from twenty years away it is comparatively easy to recon-struct the course of events in outline and so reach the conclusion that, all things considered, by the end of the first day, though the Germans had had the advantage of surprise, the Americans had recovered quickly and that they *ought* therefore, on the face of it, to win.

In the swirling snow of December 1944, however, men were prey to agonising uncertainty.

In fact all along the front the initial American resistance was the result of local initiative. The higher headquarters only began to take matters seriously during the afternoon. Hodges, commanding First U.S. Army from Roermond to Echternach, was determined not to play the German game by reacting to what he thought was a diversionary attack, intended to draw off as many American forces as possible preparatory to a main Christmas offensive against the Roer or in the Aix-la-Chapelle area. Throughout December 16, therefore, General Hodges made the mistake of thinking too subtly, and did nothing—absolutely nothing.

The first reaction came from Versailles. Eisenhower's day had started calmly. There was a letter from Montgomery asking for leave to spend Christmas with his son in England. Orders had been issued, he said, for the forthcoming offensive to liquidate the German bridgehead between the Rhine and the Meuse west of Nijmegen. Monty also reminded him that a year before he had laid a bet with him that the war would not be finished by Christmas 1944. Ike owed him £5.

'I'll pay,' Eisenhower said to Butcher. 'But not before Christmas. He can let me have these nine days.'

In reply to Montgomery, Eisenhower assured him that he intended to reinforce the left of Twelfth Army Group to ensure that Bradley's attack and that of the British would be mutually supporting.

Then there came a family celebration. 'Micky', the orderly, was getting married in the chapel of the Château of Versailles. His bride was 'Pearlie', a W.A.C. corporal, history teacher in Minnesota and one of the headquarters drivers. Micky's post-war ambition was to run a saloon. He wondered what Pearlie would say—and the general.

After the ceremony Eisenhower gave a reception for the young couple and his staff in his own villa at Saint-Germain. But Bradley was then announced. Eisenhower returned to Versailles and his headquarters in the Trianon Hotel.

Aircraft being grounded by thick mist, Bradley had left Luxembourg early by car. He had passed via Paris, where it was raining and nobody was about. After lunching at the Ritz he had left for SHAEF.

That he should make this journey at all is somewhat surprising, seeing that a German local counter-offensive was expected against the Roer as soon as V and VII U.S. Corps had crossed the river. In fact it was exactly this operation which was worrying him. In his view it would lead to a 'battle of extermination' which would probably be just as costly in men as the fighting at Hürtgen, and the reinforcements due to fill the gaps were still in the U.S.A. Bradley had therefore decided to send Colonel O'Hare, his G.1 (D.A.G.), to Washington to stir up the War Department and get shipping priority for the troops earmarked for Twelfth Army Group. He hoped that Eisenhower would send a message emphasising the importance of O'Hare's task.

Eisenhower, Bradley, Bedell Smith and some of the staff were considering this problem when, at about 4.00 p.m., a G.2 officer appeared and handed General Strong a message: 'The Germans attacked First U.S. Army front at first light.'

So it had taken nearly ten hours for the Supreme Commander to be informed of the offensive! The SHAEF Intelligence Summary distributed at midday and covering the twenty-four hours from midday on December 15 to midday December 16 merely announced the capture of three small villages on the near side of the Roer. It concluded 'everywhere else the front is quiet'.

Before leaving Luxembourg, Bradley had had no inkling that the Germans were on the move only 20 miles away from him and had not thought it necessary to be present at his own 9.15 a.m. staff conference. At that conference the representative of the operations section had stated: 'No change on VIII Corps front.' The intelligence section had added that 'The northward move of 326 Volksgrenadier division may explain the high rate of vehicle movement opposite the northern sector of VII Corps front.'

Signals difficulties can hardly be the only reason for the senior American headquarters being in such total ignorance. That ignorance was to last another three hours, for the message from General Gerow, commanding V U.S. Corps (in the north opposite Sepp Dietrich) to alert General Hodges, was despatched at 12.44 p.m. but was not registered by the headquarters in Spa until 2.50—more than two hours later! Under these conditions it is remarkable that Versailles should have been informed after only one further hour.*

After receipt of further information, Eisenhower and Bradley concluded 'This is no feint.' At least that is what both of them say in their memoirs. For his part, Bedell Smith merely noted that the initial reports gave few details, not enough to indicate enemy intentions. The fact that the enemy had used tanks was of no special significance; at least it was no proof that armoured divisions were involved, since 'the German infantry divisions often employed a few tanks'.

Bradley considered the enemy objective was a comparatively modest one—a spoiling attack to relieve the pressure exerted by Patton on the Saar and generally slow down the pace of operations. He had envisaged this possibility, he said, among many others and thought it would cost the Germans very dear to break through the Allied lines; in any case they would be stopped on the Meuse. This had been his forecast prior to the offensive. It is the reason he gives in his memoirs for his failure to react. The memoirs of statesmen and the explanations of generals should invariably be regarded with scepticism and one wonders why Bradley took so few precautions at the time to guard against an operation of the imminence of which he was apparently so convinced.

* Forest C. Pogue, *The Supreme Command*, p. 374, note 39.

Bedell Smith states that Eisenhower for his part was doubtful whether the Germans would be content with a minor objective of this nature, but Bedell Smith always kept faithfully to his role of Chief of Staff to the great man to whom he was a sort of preceptor—and undoubtedly also to some extent the brains.

So the Supreme Commander was sceptical. He was also perhaps secretly relieved, for at last the nightmare at which he had vaguely hinted was coming true. Whatever interpretations the staffs may have put upon the information flowing in that autumn, Eisenhower had been haunted by a permanent obsession—that the Germans might repeat the Kasserine operation.

An odd name, Kasserine, and one of ill-omen to Eisenhower; it reminded him of an incident which had nearly cost him his job. He had referred to it as early as September 22 in a letter to Montgomery. The terms in which he compares Kasserine and the Ardennes in his memoirs are eloquent of the reactions of the man who had been through both these crises.

Although with regard to the strength of the forces engaged on both sides the Kasserine affair was a mere skirmish in proportion to the Ardennes battle, yet there were points of similarity between the two. Each was an attack of desperation; each took advantage of extraordinary strength in a defensive barrier to concentrate forces for a blow against Allied communications and in the hope of inducing the Allied High Command to give up overall plans for relentless offensives.*

It is worth recalling the details of the 'Kasserine affair', so prominent in the mind of the Supreme Commander on December 16 1944. Between February 14 and 23 1943 Rommel had launched a general offensive in Tunisia from the Mareth line. The capture of the pass of Kasserine had cost him dear, but he had forced II U.S. Corps to withdraw on Tebessa, where the German advance had been finally halted.

Comparing this affair with that of the Ardennes it almost seems as if the conclusions drawn from that first crisis were so imprinted on Eisenhower's mind that his decisions on December 16 1944 were unconsciously influenced thereby.

As in February 1943, the staffs of November and December 1944 had been 'too prone to take one isolated piece of intelligence in which they implicitly believed, and to shut their eyes to any contrary possibility'. In February 1943 they had decided that the German attack would come through Fondouk, 40 miles north of Kasserine; in December 1944, they were expecting the attack in the Aix-la-Chapelle area and the main American concentration was on this sector of the front, the remainder being only lightly held.

In February 1943 no mobile reserves had been available to intervene

* *Crusade in Europe*, p. 378.

rapidly and in force owing to the hesitations of the local commanders and the mistakes of the intelligence service, which had led to the dispersion of the reserves. In December 1944 once more SHAEF had no immediately available reserves.

Finally, in Tunisia the Americans had thinned out the sector attacked by the Germans in order to concentrate on the protection of Gafsa. What primarily led to the American withdrawal at that period were, according to Eisenhower, 'the inescapable conditions resulting from failure in our long-shot gamble to capture Tunis quickly . . . had I been willing at the end of November [1942] to admit temporary failure and pass to the defensive, no attack against us could have achieved even temporary success.'*

Carrying over this same line of thought into the December 1944 situation, Eisenhower can be imagined regretting having been persuaded into major operations (such as the Arnhem failure) or even the local attacks, before having regrouped his resources—all the resources possible.

There can be no doubt; the man was still the same, laying himself open to the same setbacks and surmounting his crises with the same courage.

Although German intentions were still unclear, Eisenhower took three immediate decisions that evening. He first fixed a stop-line, laying down 'the limit of the penetration that we could, if necessary, permit in that region without irretrievable damage to ourselves'.†

The line followed the Meuse from Liège to Namur and Sedan and thence east to Luxembourg. All of these places were to be held. General Lee, commanding the Services of Supply, was to defend the crossings of the Meuse and ensure that the bridges were blown if necessary.

As immediate reinforcements for VIII U.S. Corps, two divisions were withdrawn from the flanks of the salient now developing. In the south 10 U.S. Armoured Division, located between Merzig and Sierck, was ordered up to Luxembourg, Patton protesting that this removed any hope he might have had of getting through to Sarrelouis in his forthcoming offensive. In the north General Simpson, commanding U.S. Ninth Army, had to make over to Hodges 7 U.S. Armoured Division, moving it due south against the anticipated flank of the German advance.

As for the third decision, the use of the strategic reserves, Eisenhower's hands were tied by the time factor. The difficulty of his situation is in no way concealed by the statement in his memoirs that, 'there now appeared to be developing the very situation which we had felt justified in challenging'. Seeing that the counter-manœuvre took twenty-four hours to prepare, a 'challenge' would have been a most imprudent one.

11 U.S. Armoured Division and 87 Infantry Division were still in the United Kingdom and could not be available for a week. There remained,

* *Crusade in Europe*, p. 163.
† Ibid, p. 377.

therefore, the two airborne divisions, 82 and 101; both were recuperating at Mourmelon after fighting for fifty-eight days to save the British parachute troops from disaster. Re-equipment had not yet been completed and personnel were to a large extent scattered. The third division of XVIII Airborne Corps, 17 Airborne Division, was still in England. Finally, General Taylor, commanding 101 Airborne, was in the United States and his deputy, together with twenty-one senior officers of the corps were in England studying the results of the operations in Holland.

The next question which arose was where to direct the available reinforcements in order to stiffen resistance. General Whiteley, the British Assistant Chief of Staff Operations at SHAEF, proposed Bastogne as the objective. Strong, the head of the intelligence division, agreed. Bedell Smith passed on the idea to Eisenhower, who adopted it. There is some doubt whether the choice of Bastogne as a focal point was made on the evening of the 16th or on the 17th while Bradley was still present (he had stayed overnight with Eisenhower). In any event there was no thought at this stage that the town would form a bastion of the defence; study of the map simply showed that it was the obvious assembly area; there was no inspired foresight here. All the roads leading from the Eifel converged on Bastogne and from it started those leading to the Meuse and France. The town commanded the approaches to the Houffalize–Arlon area whence the main highway Antwerp–Liège–Metz–Strasbourg, the principal supply artery for the Allied front, could be directly threatened by the German offensive.

From the outset Eisenhower was determined to hold Bastogne, and his appreciation seems to have been more pessimistic than that of Bradley. The latter considered Bastogne too far from the front ever to be in immediate danger. Equally pessimistically, Eisenhower urged Bradley to withdraw his tactical command post from Luxembourg to Verdun where the Army Group main H.Q. was situated. Luxembourg, he thought, was so exposed that Bradley was in danger of losing control of his communications. The latter, however, refused to withdraw, saying that he thought such a step might spread panic. The fact that he remained so close to the front, however, largely contributed to the later difficulties and led inevitably to the division of the battle area between Montgomery and himself.

As far as the role to be played by Bastogne was concerned, events were soon to justify Eisenhower's pessimism.

On the northern flank of the break-through Saint-Vith was another focal communications point of decisive importance to the enemy. Six roads and three railway lines met there. 7 U.S. Armoured Division was despatched towards Saint-Vith with the task of holding it and protecting the approaches to Liège.

By midnight on December 16 the picture began to become clearer to American intelligence; one parachute division, ten Volksgrenadier divisions and five Panzer and Panzergrenadier divisions had been identified. There was no sign of any improvement in the temperature and the meteorological service forecast 'very cloudy to thick weather'; it also prophesied an increase in wind strength and patches of fog in central Belgium. The moonless nights were a further factor in the Americans' disfavour; men and vehicles were bogged down by the snow and the movement of reinforcements was as difficult for the Americans as for the Germans.

But that same evening Field-Marshal von Rundstedt's estimate of the situation at Hitler's briefing conference was pessimistic. True, he said, surprise had been achieved during the morning, but the advance guards of Sixth Panzer Army were still held up around Elsenborn. It was questionable whether this army could reach the Meuse and it was already too late to shift the main weight of the attack to the southern axis. The mistakes made in the initial planning were proving irreparable.

Hitler became indignant. The 'main body' of Dietrich's army, he said, had not yet been engaged. As soon as they could get on the move they would crush everything before them.

Chapter 11

THE RACE TO THE SALM

HITLER was indulging in wishful thinking and so made a serious error of appreciation. The offensive had started slowly and in fact it never gathered speed except in the centre, in Manteuffel's sector. From the morning of December 17 Sepp Dietrich found that his forces were running their heads into an elastic-sided pocket. Winter conditions on the sunken roads led to traffic jams and American reinforcements arrived to close the roads in front of them. Nevertheless it was a close race.

During the first two days of the offensive the German armour virtually marked time. The confusion was such that it is difficult to describe the situation other than in broad outline.

Sixth Panzer Army, it will be remembered, had two main tasks: to reduce the Elsenborn breakwater which blocked progress north-westwards, and to break through at all costs towards the Meuse at Huy between Namur and Liège. But all German efforts against the Elsenborn position failed. Between Monschau and Malmédy V U.S. Corps gradually improved its hastily constructed positions, concentrating three divisional artilleries and the guns of VIII Corps as it withdrew. German infantry attacked on three successive days, first towards Monschau, north of the plateau and then towards the village of Elsenborn, but in every case was stopped by the American infantry and the front remained firm. About December 20 a violent artillery duel developed.

The Advance of Peiper Force

Behind the forces attempting to reduce Elsenborn, Colonel Jochen Peiper stood ready to lead his armoured raid westwards 'without worrying about his flanks and leaving the evacuation of prisoners to the infantry divisions following him'.

The Peiper Force moved off at 4 a.m. on December 17, followed by two companies of 150 Armoured Brigade, the special unit formed by Otto Skorzeny, dressed in American uniforms and using captured Allied equipment.*

Peiper was under artillery fire from the start, for all roads leading to Stavelot, his first objective, were within easy range of Elsenborn. He followed a zig-zag route using forest tracks rather than the main roads to avoid the fire from the guns across whose front he was moving. During the morning he encountered no resistance. He himself was with the advance guard in the leading armoured car. Early in the afternoon the

---

* The equipment of this unit will be dealt with in detail later.

column reached the cross-roads at Baugnez on the Liège–Saint-Vith road a few miles south of Malmédy.

At the same moment a convoy of American lorries approached the cross-roads from the north, in other words from the German detachment's right. It consisted of the observation battery of 285 Artillery Group, a unit which did not normally find itself in the front line; the Americans were travelling along without an inkling that the German advance guard could have got so far. In fact the German column was passing between two convoys of 7 U.S. Armoured Division, which had been in reserve behind the Aix-la-Chapelle front and had moved at first light.

The armoured cars and the two leading tanks of the German armoured force opened fire at once. Some of the vehicles burst into flames and the convoy stopped; the men scattered in panic and made for the nearest cover after a few disorderly shots at the German tanks; others gave themselves up, threw down their arms and were collected near the cross-roads. Then an officer collected the fugitives. Meanwhile Peiper's reconnaissance detachment drove on.

A few minutes later the main body of the German advance guard arrived. The Americans were still there, disarmed and waiting in unaccountable inactivity. The leading German tanks fired a burst or two into them and then two revolver shots rang out; this was apparently a signal. One of the tank's machine guns then opened fire on the prisoners. Some threw themselves to the ground, others tried to escape but were pursued by machine-gun fire. Only four got away, one of whom was Lieutenant Lary, who had done his best to organise the little group. The massacre lasted twelve minutes; the result was seventy-one dead. The total convoy had numbered two hundred.

Those who escaped told their story and on December 20 the Allied Radio Station beamed on Germany, 'Soldatensender Calais', denounced the atrocity. This was the beginning of the 'Malmédy Affair'; it did not end until December 1956 when Jochen Peiper came out of prison. In July 1946 an American Military Tribunal sat in judgment on the Waffen SS personnel of the Peiper Force. Peiper himself was condemned to death and then reprieved. There were forty-three death sentences, twenty-two sentences of hard labour for life, and eight sentences of various terms of imprisonment. It was indisputably a war crime; nothing could justify a number of bursts of machine-gun fire at short range on a collection of disarmed fugitives who were hunted down like rabbits in a run. Moreover, a further atrocity was committed by the Peiper Force during the next few days. In Stavelot, where no operation of war in the strict sense of the word took place, ninety-three civilians were massacred.

Leaving the group of prisoners at the cross-roads to their fate, Peiper had turned south towards Ligneuville, where the road crossed the Amblève. His arrival caused General Timberlake—who was still having breakfast—

to move in a hurry. The little German force quickly pushed aside two
companies of U.S. service troops which attempted to block the road to the
bridge. Once across the river, Peiper waited for the main body of his force
to arrive. He then pushed on by the hillside road through the woods overlooking the south bank of the Amblève until he reached the approaches to
Stavelot, where he came under intermittent American artillery fire. After
one or two brushes with isolated American detachments, the force concentrated at nightfall and did not push on further.

This hesitation was one of the dramatic features of that night. Stavelot
and the bridge were wide open to a *coup de main*, but Peiper did not move.

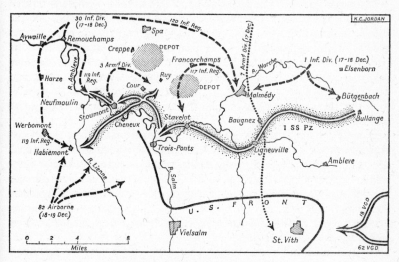

The Advance of Peiper Force

Perhaps he thought that the convoy of which the prisoners he had
massacred formed part, was the forerunner of reinforcements which would
cut his communications. Perhaps he thought that at the end of the evening's
fighting he would come up against a strong delaying position. There is no
knowing. But the simple fact is that Peiper let his exhausted men rest.

The uncertainty at the headquarters of First U.S. Army was equally
agonising. Everyone was wondering what this advance force consisted of
and whether it would turn towards Malmédy and thence Spa.

The balance tipped at about 2 a.m. on December 18, when a battalion
of motorised infantry, a squadron of tank-destroyers, and a battalion of
infantry—the real scrapings of the barrel—ordered to move at 7 p.m. on
the 17th, reached Malmédy and Stavelot. They immediately laid minefields and set up road blocks. At 5 a.m. on December 18 German patrols
made contact. The Stavelot bridge had still not been blown and the main

body of the American reinforcements was concentrated at Malmédy, since it seemed clear that a major armoured column could never get through on the minor twisting roads which had in fact been selected by Peiper.

Everyone expected that he would now turn north, but in fact he continued westwards. Pushing aside a company of infantry and a troop of tanks, he passed through the southern part of Stavelot at 10 a.m. on December 18, but instead of turning north across the Amblève proceeded on towards Trois-Ponts with the object of crossing the Salm. He was uneasy at the fact that his rear was being harried by the American detachments who had fired on him in Stavelot, and he avoided contact.

At Trois-Ponts was a company of American engineers whose sole mission in life was to work the sawmills. Perhaps by chance, however, it was well-equipped; it consisted of 140 men with eight bazookas, ten machine guns and one anti-tank gun. The company waited until the head of Peiper's column had crossed the bridge over the Amblève—yet one more bridge; the Amblève winding along his route at the bottom of a deep gorge was the bane of Peiper's life. The American rear guard then withdrew and blew the bridge over the Salm just as the leading German tanks were beginning to cross.

Peiper later said: 'If only we had taken this bridge intact, we should have had an easy run straight to the Meuse.' Behind this little band of engineers there was nothing, not a tank, not a rifle, nothing but a practically straight main road leading westwards, somewhere along which the German force would meet the American parachute troops hurrying up from the south to intercept it.

Peiper knew nothing of this possible collision, which in any case he would hope to avoid. He had his eyes on the only remaining obstacle between him and a straight run to Huy—the bridge over the Lienne (a tributary of the Amblève running from south to north) at Neufmoulin. This was held by a detachment of 291 U.S. Engineer Battalion.

From early afternoon onwards refugees escaping from the German armoured column came pouring over this bridge. They reported that Peiper had been forced to turn northwards and had plunged into the Amblève gorge. What he had in fact done was to re-cross the Amblève and move up the gorge on to the high ground on the right bank, then turn down into the valley once more and climb the left bank by the forest road, firing broadsides into the woods as he went. It was an improbable route for an armoured column to choose along which to set forth into the blue.

Behind Peiper came the whole of 1 SS Armoured Division, but it was not keeping up. Its interminable columns were spread all along the roads pioneered by Peiper. In Stavelot it was held up by an American infantry battalion which had arrived after Peiper had passed and about midday it was caught on the road running down to Stavelot from Lodomez by American fighter-bombers. The lumbering tanks were easy targets and the attacks spread panic both among the Waffen SS and the Belgian civilians in their cellars.

After reforming with much difficulty during the afternoon, the German column moved off again, but was once more held up in Stavelot by a lucky bazooka shot from an American officer which put a 'Royal Tiger' out of action in the middle of the narrow main street. The traffic jam was increased by the arrival of Knittel's force, which had hitherto been moving south of the main column.

Peiper meanwhile imagined that the main armoured force would have caught up before he had covered the final few miles at the end of which he was certain to encounter serious resistance. But now everything began to go wrong for him. The first set-backs had been the destruction of the Trois-Ponts bridge and the shooting up of his rear elements in Stavelot. Now, having successfully crossed on to the south bank of the Amblève once more and halted in a clearing, he was observed by a Piper Cub of First U.S. Army Artillery. A P.47 patrol was immediately alerted and searched the area for targets. It was followed by three squadrons and for a whole hour the fighters machine-gunned the German armoured column, stationary on the crest of a hill on the edge of the woods between Cheneux and Rahier. On returning to base the pilots reported thirty-two tanks and fifty-six vehicles destroyed. The figure was probably exaggerated; equally untrue was the report that Peiper had been forced to withdraw towards the northern bank of the Amblève.

Every moment lost by Peiper was, however, put to good use by the Americans. While the aircraft kept up their attacks, the engineers at the Neufmoulin bridge placed their charges in position and at about 5 p.m. the bridge was blown. It was the only bridge capable of taking the heavy tanks of 1 SS Panzer and it went up just as Peiper, who was still leading his advance guard, arrived. He could now get no further either westwards or northwards. By nightfall on December 18 the Americans had re-established some sort of position and to force his way towards the Meuse Peiper would have to fight. He probably did not realise this, any more than did General Hodges commanding First U.S. Army, whose appreciation at this moment was that, 'It is not possible to state exactly the line reached by the enemy, the front being extremely fluid, and the situation somewhat obscure.'

Arrival of American Reinforcements

We must now go back two days—to December 16 at Supreme Headquarters, Versailles. On a direct order from Eisenhower, Bradley telephoned his staff in Luxembourg ordering the immediate southward move of 7 U.S. Armoured Division, then in reserve to Ninth Army.

Apart from one combat command holding the line of the Roer the division was resting in its billets to the rear of the Aix-la-Chapelle front.

Its primary concern at the time was its baseball championship. During the day the divisional commander, General Robert W. Hasbrouck, received an order to move from Headquarters First U.S. Army; it gave no timing and no route. Hasbrouck was merely told to get on the road and join VIII U.S. Corps somewhere in the south. During the evening Middleton, commanding this corps, told Hasbrouck that his job was to help repulse 'a small German counter-attack of three or four divisions'. 7 Armoured was still over 60 miles from Saint-Vith, which was to be its concentration area, but with an excess of optimism, Middleton estimated that the entire division could be assembled there by dawn the next day, the 17th.

The division moved off in two columns on two different roads. The first did not leave until 4 a.m. on December 17 and then without its artillery, which was temporarily retained on the Aix-la-Chapelle front. The column reached Vielsalm at 11 a.m. The second column moved at 8 a.m. A section of it was delayed at Malmédy and was overtaken by the observation battery which was the victim of the Baugnez massacre. 7 U.S. Armoured Division in fact took nearly twelve hours to cover 60 miles, crossing convoys of refugees and units retreating westwards. The mud and snow, together with occasional attacks by German reconnaissance aircraft which did little actual damage but had a considerable psychological effect, all contributed to the delays. Moreover the division was expecting to meet German parachutists reported to have been dropped at dawn—a possibility which, as we shall see later, was more real than the Americans suspected.*

During the morning Major New, the divisional intelligence officer, went ahead to Bastogne to get orders from the headquarters of VIII Corps, but found that little was known there about the situation. He then returned to Saint-Vith where he found the headquarters of 106 U.S. Infantry Division; here again he found that General Jones, commanding the division, knew little about the fighting in which his units were involved and was simply keeping up their morale by telling them that armoured reinforcements would be arriving at any moment.

The leading tanks of 7 Armoured were on occasions reduced to a speed of 1 mile an hour. They did not reach Saint-Vith until 5.30 p.m. on December 17, twenty-four hours after receipt of the order to move. This was too late to help the remnants of 14 Cavalry Group; they were withdrawing slowly and in complete confusion along narrow roads jammed with vehicles moving hurriedly westwards with or without orders. Traffic blocks occurred wherever the road was too narrow for two vehicles to move abreast. Knowing nothing except that the enemy was on their heels and outflanking them to the north, the men panicked. By the evening of December 17, apart from one squadron, 14 Cavalry Group had disintegrated. Its commander, Colonel Devine, had a nervous breakdown and his second-in-command took over.

* See p. 187.

7 Armoured also arrived too late to help the two regiments of 106 Infantry Division isolated on the Schnee Eifel. Up to midnight on December 16 the SS armour continued to move past them on the north. At 3 a.m. on December 17 the German Fifth Panzer Army subjected the Americans to a violent artillery and rocket bombardment. At 8.30 a converging attack captured the town of Schönberg, the key to the roads leading westwards from the Schnee Eifel, and the encirclement was complete. 106 U.S. Infantry Division's advanced telephone exchange at Schönberg just had time to announce to its divisional headquarters that the Germans had arrived. There was complete consternation; an hour earlier the headquarters had still been thinking that only some thirty German tanks had got through northwards.

Further south, the arrival of a Combat Command of 9 U.S. Armoured Division enabled 424 U.S. Infantry Regiment—or what was left of it—to disengage. It had held up the German advance for twenty-four hours. Meanwhile, however, the two regiments on the Schnee Eifel felt the German grip tighten around them. As the day wore on the possibility of withdrawal diminished. The colonels commanding the two regiments asked for ammunition to be dropped by air, but General Jones replied from Saint-Vith that 7 Armoured would be arriving at any moment and would counter-attack to clear Schönberg. Early in the afternoon, however, German tanks and infantry moved westwards out of Schönberg and began to infiltrate through the woods. There was not an American aircraft to be seen except for a single Thunderbolt which made no fewer than seven successive runs machine-gunning the enemy armour.

And 7 Armoured still did not arrive. By 10 a.m. Saint-Vith had been put into a state of defence; its garrison consisted of 500 engineers, two troops of tanks and a group of artillery. But General Jones was so full of confidence that he thought the whole situation would change with the arrival of 7 Armoured. He thought that next day, December 18, the two surrounded regiments could take the German armoured column threatening Saint-Vith in the rear. He told them over the radio that ammunition would be dropped during the night along the edges of the woods.

In fact there was no supply dropping and on December 18 the two regiments, one of which had lost 225 men on the first day, attempted to fight their way out. Saint-Vith was outflanked on all sides. The Germans attacked four times, splitting up units, breaking through the lines, but never managing to overcome the main centres of resistance. Petrol ran out; the anti-tank guns were without ammunition. It looked as if Saint-Vith would have to surrender and in fact, it was only saved by the tenacity of 7 Armoured Division. By the evening of December 18 this was the only formation left in this bastion, with the German advance flowing past it on either side; in the north Sepp Dietrich was 25 miles beyond Saint-Vith, and in the south Manteuffel 15 miles. The little town was caught between

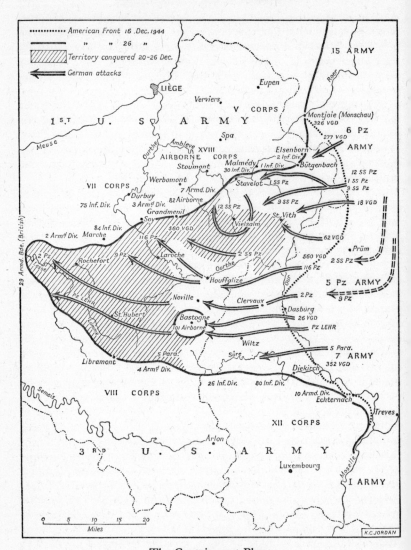

The Containment Phase

the jaws of the pincers of these two armies, but it remained the rock which prevented the jaws closing.

General Hodges, commanding First U.S. Army, was still in his head-quarters in the Hotel Britannique at Spa, where Kaiser William II had signed his act of abdication. 7 Armoured Division having been ordered to move direct by Eisenhower, Hodges initially thought that this would be enough to hold the German offensive. He did not ask the neighbouring Ninth Army for reinforcements until the morning of December 17, when he was given 30 U.S. Infantry Division. Referring to it as 'Roosevelt's SS' the German radio announced its entry into the battle the same evening—a further proof of the ease with which the Wehrmacht's interception service overheard Allied communications.

30 Infantry Division was also out of the line in the Aix-la-Chapelle area and was looking forward to a quiet Sunday. The colonel commanding one of its regiments had departed to London on leave on the afternoon of December 16, and General Hobbs, commanding the division, was preparing to do likewise, when, at 11.15 a.m. on December 17, he received a warning order to move south on temporary detachment.

The division moved off at 4.30 p.m., crossing columns of Belgian refugees and German civilians from the battle area moving towards Liège and Brussels. At the same time another division which had been resting, 1 U.S. Infantry Division, moved up to reinforce the Elsenborn camp defences.

From dawn on December 18, 30 U.S. Infantry Division began to form a screen which was destined to block any northward move by the Peiper Force. One battalion moved into Stavelot, but proved unable to deny the main road to the rear of the German armoured column, though it did block all exits from the town towards Malmédy and Spa; other battalions took up positions on the heights overlooking the Amblève valley parallel to the line of Peiper's advance. Both sides were in fact racing for possession of the hills around Habiémont, where any further advance by Peiper could be blocked. The Americans won, and by nightfall were in contact with German infantry who were searching for a bridge to take the place of that of Neufmoulin.

Just at this moment parachute troops of 82 Airborne Division appeared from the south and linked up with the infantry moving in from the north; they took over from the isolated engineer detachment at the Neufmoulin bridge. Peiper's route was now barred. A thirty-seven-year-old brigadier-general, 'Slim Jim' Gavin, was at Werbomont on the Liège–Houffalize–Bastogne road, and there throughout the night convoys of tired parachutists arrived direct from Mourmelon. They dug in in the woods overlooking the Lienne and two hours after first light on December 19 the whole of 82 Airborne Division was ready to resist any further German advance. In fact, the division held these positions until the time arrived for the strategic counter-offensive, in which it played the primary role.

All this may give the impression of an orderly plan of operations, of parry and riposte to each German initiative and of close co-ordination between the resources available and the object in view; one might think that it had all been worked out by the headquarters of First U.S. Army in Spa in the calm serenity with which generals habitually take great decisions. But the accounts of those who visited that headquarters to get their orders paint a different picture. In his report to the War Department General Gavin stated:

At 09.00 hours [December 18] the situation seemed highly confused [to H.Q. First U.S. Army]. The first reports of contact with the enemy at Stavelot had just arrived; they indicated that an enemy thrust in this area had thrown our troops back across the river, and had succeeded in capturing and destroying a large depot. As they pushed our forces back, the enemy had apparently blown the bridge. The situation south and west of Stavelot was unknown, apart from the fact that the enemy had broken through our front. A large number of American troops were concentrated at Saint-Vith. It seemed that there was a large pocket on the front held by 106 Division.

General Hodges was only 10 miles from the battlefield, but his picture of the situation as given to Gavin was not only 'somewhat vague' in its indications (Gavin's words), but also included inaccurate information. The bridge at Stavelot had not been blown; no depot in this area had been captured; at that moment the enemy had not yet broken through south and west of Stavelot. This was what Hodges' imagination told him might have happened or was likely to happen rather than firm information.

At 1 p.m. on December 18 Lieutenant-Colonel Rubel, commanding 740 Tank Destroyer Battalion, got the same impression. The headquarters of First Army ordered him by telephone to despatch a reinforced squadron to protect the major supply depots at Remouchamps on the Amblève near the main Liège–Bastogne road. The staff officer on the other end of the line said:

The situation is deteriorating in the whole area of the break-through. A considerable proportion of our equipment has already been irretrievably lost. Von Rundstedt is gaining ground rapidly. We do not know exactly the size of the break-through because communications have been cut in many places. The command system is disorganised because unit headquarters have been carried away as if by a tidal wave and as a result of action by German parachutists dropped in the rear areas.

As we shall see, the 'action of the parachutists' dropped at dawn on December 17 was largely a figment of the imagination. Nevertheless, although the size of the force and the area in which it was operating was fairly quickly established, this parachute raid contributed largely to the panic in American rear areas. Many of the sub-units employed on static tasks were dispersed in a useless hunt for imaginary enemy parachutists.

The 'Petrol Depot' Myth

There was another story which emerged from the combination of panic and pre-conceived ideas. This was the famous affair of the petrol depot which Peiper was supposed to have been within a few hundred yards of capturing. It is worth looking at the facts.

The headquarters of First U.S. Army had been located at Spa since October 26, and the little town and its immediate vicinity was bulging with a host of service units incapable of moving at a few hours' notice. There was a bakery company, a counter-espionage section, military police, the headquarters of Ninth Tactical Air Force, a medical battalion, a hospital, a soldiers' canteen—a representative cross-section in fact of all those subsidiary organisations which trail along after an American Army to provide for the soldiers' creature comforts.

In the woods south of Spa, on the edge of the Fagnes plateau, a Gasoline Supply Company (No. 3,814 to be exact) had set up two depots. The first was near the junction of the Andrimont and Borgoumont roads and held nearly 8,000 tons of petrol and 500 tons of oil. The other was on the road from Francorchamps to Stavelot and contained 3,000 tons of petrol and 1,320 tons of oil. From this latter depot, the guard unit had a good view up the valley of the Amblève and along the road running down into Stavelot on which Peiper moved.

Realising that fighting was going on in the town below them and not knowing whether the German armour would not next move up towards their depot, the guards set fire to it early on December 18.

This left the first and larger depot. It was in fact moved jerrican by jerrican on December 18 and 19, a fleet of lorries running back and forth to Spa Station. At no time, apparently, was any order given to set fire to it. Peiper's force moving down the Amblève passed a few miles south of it. Between Peiper and the depot there was nothing but an anti-aircraft battery employed in an anti-tank role guarding the only road along which the German armour might come. The depot would have been a magnificent prize for Peiper; it would have been the complete solution to one of the Germans' main problems—fuel shortage. What more natural than that he should attempt to lay hands on it by a *coup de main*?

Two facts lent colour to the story. A German infantry patrol suddenly appeared out of the mist in front of the anti-aircraft gunners, who were so taken aback that they let it depart without firing a shot. Secondly, somewhat further west, a reconnaissance detachment of two armoured vehicles and two light lorries advanced to within 2 miles of the depot and then withdrew. But both these incidents occurred on the afternoon of December 19, twenty-four hours after Peiper's arrival in the area. Quite clearly, if he had had any inkling that the petrol depot existed, he would have reported the fact by some means or other to the headquarters of 1 Panzer, or to that of Sixth Panzer Army. He would have asked for orders and air support. It seems inconceivable that, whatever his orders, he could have calmly let such an opportunity go by.

There can only be two possible explanations.

The first is so simple as to be somewhat disillusioning. Peiper simply knew nothing about the depot. He was driving on westwards and only reconnoitring the area in his immediate vicinity. The two patrols which moved up from the Amblève were merely reconnoitring the positions of 30 U.S. Infantry Division, which had moved up into the area on the evening of December 18.

The second explanation makes a better story and in the general atmosphere of confusion at the time seemed somewhat reassuring. This is that the fortune of war produced a miracle, that Peiper came within 400 yards of the petrol depot and then vanished without taking any action.

But 400 yards is rather a tall story. The guard unit knew that the enemy was in the area, the other depot having already been set on fire; if the enemy had got so close they must certainly have heard him coming. Surely they would then have set fire to their depot too. A single hand-grenade would have done it.

But the tale apparently grew to incredible proportions with remarkable rapidity. The fact that this most valuable prize had been saved by an apparent miracle was, in the eyes of the war correspondents, proof that the German aggressor had proved incapable of taking it and was therefore at the end of his tether. When they withdrew on December 20, the anti-aircraft gunners reported their silent meeting with the German reconnaissance patrol when not a shot had been fired. This was embroidered into an account of a German *coup de main* which had failed.

This stroke of chance was taken to indicate a revival in American fortunes; it became a factor in persuading the staffs and the press to cease over-estimating their enemy. The battlefield grapevine carried the story across to the Germans. General von Manteuffel recounted it to Liddell Hart, who accepted it and lent the weight of his authority to it. Since then the story has appeared in every account of the battle; it has apparently occurred to nobody that in this case the working of fate was rather too precisely calculated to carry conviction.*

By early afternoon on December 18 Spa was in process of evacuation. Units moving up into the line found every sign of what can only be called panic; secret documents, for instance, were still lying about in the houses evacuated by the staff. Exaggerated rumours were flying round and the Belgian population was in terror, wondering who could protect them against German reprisals. The headquarters of First U.S. Army moved first to Chaudfontaine and then to Tongres, well to the rear of Liège but a focal point on the roads leading to the various sectors of the long army front. Hodges himself remained at Spa up to the last moment, as did the signals

---

* M. Marcel Bovy conducted an enquiry on the spot and then dealt with the point in complete detail in his book *La Batille de l'Amblève*. He states that the History Instructor at the Belgian Military Academy, Colonel Bernard, is entirely in agreement with his conclusion that the petrol depots were never in fact attacked.

centre. Telephone and teleprinter lines were not cut until the night of December 18–19 and communications were functioning from Chaudfontaine by the morning of the 19th. But the headquarters was in fact in touch only towards the rear. Forwards, all lines were cut. Even the wireless operators frequently got no reply. Hodges' knowledge of the situation was in fact very limited. Yet on the morning of December 19 he produced the following astounding appreciation: 'The enemy is continuing his efforts to break through our lines in the south of V Corps sector and the north and centre of VIII Corps sector. Some fairly deep penetrations were made, but our lines have not been broken.'

Nevertheless, from Peiper's point of view, surprise had failed to produce the result expected. On the right bank of the Amblève American infantry was now organising its positions. At dusk on December 18 one of their first patrols came across some thirty German tanks in lager. The tank crews were singing and talking loudly round their camp fires, thinking that they were unobserved. But this illusion did not last long, for shortly after dark one of their armoured vehicles went up on a mine laid by the Americans.

In all probability Peiper did not realise that the last avenue open to his advance had just been blocked. Equally he did not know that he was now faced by a veteran unit comparable to Napoleon's Imperial Guard. The men of 119 U.S. Infantry Regiment had been through the violent fighting of the Mortain pocket, and they had just suffered 50 per cent casualties in front of Aix-la-Chapelle. Now they were holding the approaches to a natural bastion for the defence of which reinforcements were due to arrive, though no one knew when, or what their quality would be. But, as we shall see later, 119 Infantry held firm, and in the process broke an equally élite unit, 1 SS Panzer, the 'Leibstandarte Adolf Hitler'.

Chapter 12

'ALL ROADS LEAD TO BASTOGNE'

Now to the events of December 17 and 18 on the other half of the battle-field, the southern sector where Manteuffel's Sixth Panzer Army was deployed.

One word is enough to evoke memories of all the various actions which took place in this area—Bastogne, the name became the symbol of the entire Ardennes Offensive. In those dramatic days of retreat, something concrete seemed to be required to epitomise the resistance of the G.I.s. Bastogne was turned by the press, the political leaders and later the Old Comrades' Associations into the sacred place where homage will always be done to the 80,000 American soldiers who fell between Monschau and Echternach during this terrible winter. On the Mardasson plateau stands a great monument in the form of a five-pointed star—the white star carried by American tanks and aircraft. Not far away stands the memorial to the first man killed on May 10 1940, perhaps the first casualty of all the Allied Armies after the end of the 'phoney war', Corporal Cady of 2 Chasseurs Ardennais.

Twenty-four Hours of Unconcern

In the early hours of December 17 the silence of Bastogne was shattered by an explosion. Perhaps it was a V1 off course, people thought, but other explosions followed and then on the horizon, somewhere in the direction of Clervaux, three pencils of light appeared and remained stationary—the German anti-aircraft, people thought, switching on its searchlights to intercept American bombers attacking the Siegfried line.

A little later, on the line of the Clervaux road, appeared a whole flood of light; three new clusters of beams appeared so close together this time, that they almost seemed to fuse into one before they swung down towards the ground. At the same time reddish flashes were visible against the sky and the thud of explosions was heard. There could be no doubt now; artillery was in action.*

The people of Bastogne had a rude awakening on the day after Fifth Panzer Army's offensive opened. The town had passed the day of December 16 without a care in the world, the market functioning as usual on either side of the main street. Naturally there were rumours going around; a woman from Saint-Vith had said that she had been forced to evacuate;

* This description is from the account by Abbé Paul Fecherolle in *L'Avenir du Luxembourg*, Arlon, December 1945.

farmers from the neighbouring district had said that at the front the artillery duel was becoming fiercer.

The American headquarters, that of VIII Corps, did not appear to be worried. It had just authorised its men to hold a ball that evening in the big rooms of the French Franciscan monastery which had been requisitioned.

The affair had created something of a scandal; on Sunday, the 17th, the priest officiating at the monastery had inveighed against such frivolities in his sermon at High Mass. 'Heaven', he said, 'has already punished these soldiers. As I speak to you the German troops have reached Clervaux.'

His reasons may have been wrong but his facts were right. During December 16 the scattered American forces had been pinned down in their strong points and 2 Panzer Division had by-passed them and pushed on to Clervaux, entering it at midnight. Throughout the morning of the 17th the armour had been passing through the town, leaving its accompanying infantry to mop up the last centres of resistance in the sanitorium and the new and old châteaux.

The Bastogne congregation was indignant and thought that the Franciscan father had been too hard on the liberating forces, but they had little time to stand about criticising; they had hardly come out of church when the Benedictine fathers from Clervaux Abbey appeared in the midst of a convoy of refugees.

At first the exodus could be passed off as a normal incident of war; the front had become active, that was all, thought the optimists. It was true that clouds of smoke could be seen rising from the Wiltz gap, but Bastogne still seemed a very long way from the front. Then the military police were seen moving to guard the approaches to the town—merely a precaution, everyone said. About midday there was an electricity cut; this was written off as a simple measure of economy. In any case, people thought, the rumours going round were so fantastic that no one could take them seriously; there was even one to the effect that the Germans had dropped 10,000 parachutists. Another piece of news seemed far more likely—that the enemy heavy artillery was in action to break up an American offensive. In any case none of this was enough to interrupt preparations for the ceremonies scheduled for that afternoon. At 5.0 p.m. the entire town was due to celebrate the rehanging of the bells, taken down by the Germans during the occupation.

This serene frame of mind was nevertheless a sign neither of naïvety nor of ignorance. The people of Bastogne 'suspected that something was up'. Close to them though the fighting was, the fact that they knew nothing about it will seem incredible only to those who have never been in the position of civilians lost in the midst of a battle. Civilians are a nuisance in war and all the military ask of them is 'go to ground in your cellars and don't move whether you are on our side or not'.

By midday, however, there were enough disquieting indications to produce the certainty that an enemy offensive was in progress. People were glad to know the worst and the rumour was supported by a whispering campaign to the effect that the offensive had been announced over the radio.*

No one was surprised therefore when at 5.0 p.m. an American staff officer handed the acting Mayor, M. Leon Jacqmin, a curfew order giving no reasons. The people of Bastogne blacked out their houses carefully and stayed at home, puzzled rather than really worried. They sat round by candlelight discussing the situation with the Americans billeted 'in town'. Towards midnight an officer came round calling the men out to join their units. But it was only a short alert; an hour later the soldiers came back and went to bed.

The town was covered by a thick fog through which the searchlights in the east were hardly visible. The rumble of explosions drew nearer. Even so there was so little panic that when the primary school authorities sent children living in the neighbourhood home during the morning of the 18th, the reason given was not the threat of the approaching battle, but the fact that the electricity cut had put the central heating out of action. The great stone building had become little better than an ice-box; life in there was impossible.

The American formation most directly involved was VIII Corps, which the enemy had been battering ever since the Saturday morning; nevertheless its commander, General Middleton, was so expert at concealing any fears he may have had that he had taken to all intents and purposes no defensive measures, or at least very few.

During December 17, however, the wheels set in motion by Eisenhower in Versailles began to turn. 10 U.S. Armoured Division began to move from the Saar area at 1.20 p.m. despite Patton's furious protests at the interruption to his preparations for his offensive. On orders from Bradley, the division was to move to assist 4 U.S. Armoured Division in holding a stop-line to the east of Luxembourg.

Equally on December 17, at 7.30 p.m., General Gavin, commanding 82 Airborne Division in Mourmelon Camp, was alerted. He happened to be the most senior officer available in XVIII Airborne Corps—the other division, 101 Airborne, was at Suippes and Sissonne. General Ridgway, the corps commander, was away in England and so it was up to Gavin to get the corps ready to move within the twenty-four hours laid down. James M. Gavin, nicknamed 'Slim Jim' by his men, was only thirty-seven,

* It seems highly unlikely that this news was in fact given out over the radio just at this moment. As we shall see later, neither side announced the offensive until December 18; the news appeared in the communiqués of the 19th. So no radio station could very well have produced the news on the 17th. It is just possible that by chance the inhabitants of Bastogne had picked up some military communication in English and had understood it. This possibility cannot be altogether dismissed.

exceptionally young for a general even in the parachute troops. He had been commissioned in 1929 and in 1942 was already a colonel commanding a regiment which had been parachuted into Sicily and again at Salerno. On June 6 1944 he had led 82 Airborne Division's attack on Sainte-Mère-Église. He had been commanding the division since August 15 and had led it in the Nijmegen fighting. James Gavin was no publicity-hunter on his own account; he was quite content to let the limelight concentrate on his division. It was a direct descendant of 82 Infantry Division which had fought in the Argonne and at Saint-Mihiel in 1918 and it had given a remarkably good account of itself in Sicily under Ridgway. Its men came from all over the United States and the division had been nicknamed 'The All Americans'. It had provided the regular nucleus for its sister formation, 101 Airborne.

It was upon this latter formation that all the limelight of the Bastogne affair concentrated. The divisional commander, General Maxwell Taylor, who had been the first uniformed American into Rome on September 7 1943 to gain contact with Badoglio, was not present, and his place was being taken by General Anthony MacAuliffe, commanding the Divisional Artillery. At 8.30 p.m. on September 17 arrived a warning order from Gavin: 'Get on the road northwards. Further orders will be issued at Bastogne.'

These were somewhat laconic instructions, but General MacAuliffe got ready to move without even waiting for the return of men on leave in Paris. The shortages of equipment and supplies resulting from the Arnhem battle had not yet been made good and their replacement took a little time. Throughout the night lorries from the 'Oise Base Section' depots near Paris and Rouen rolled in, bringing mortars, unit weapons and equipment.

At 9.30 p.m. the Chief of Staff of XVIII Airborne Corps telephoned to Gavin: 'Hurry! Get up to First Army. The Germans are through near Saint-Vith.' About midnight Gavin decided that 82 Airborne would move one hour after first light on December 18, and that 101 Airborne should follow early that afternoon.

He himself reached Spa during the night in thick fog and rain. He knew nothing of the situation and General Hodges could tell him little. The division got on the move as ordered, but took the entire day to reach Werbomont, whither Gavin had ordered it by radio.

These American radio messages were of immense assistance to the German commanders. When Colonel Eaton, the Chief of Staff of XVIII Airborne Corps, passed the warning order on the evening of December 17, he was not in fact speaking to Gavin alone. The order went through in clear and the German intercept service picked it up. When General von Lüttwitz, who commanded XLVII Corps, the spearhead of Manteuffel's army, returned to his headquarters from a tour of the front, a copy of the message was handed to him.

His first reaction was one of relief: 'If the Americans are having to use two formations which have suffered so heavily in battle, that proves that they will not be undertaking any airborne operations in our rear. They cannot have any reserves left if they have to put their best strategic reserve divisions into the battle.' General von Lüttwitz then studied his map: 'They are moving towards the battlefield. They can have only one concentration area—Bastogne. We shall be there before them.'

During the long night of December 17–18 it was a race for Bastogne. Lüttwitz let loose his two armoured divisions, the Panzer Lehr and 2 Panzer. The former had crossed the Our unopposed on December 17, and was now across the Wiltz; the latter was already through Clervaux.

On December 12 Lüttwitz' instructions to the two divisional commanders, Bayerlein and von Lauchert, had been: 'Bastogne must be taken. If it is not, the town will be like an abscess on our lines of communications. We must start by clearing Bastogne and then we can go forward.' But as the race with the American parachute troops coming up from the south opened, Lüttwitz began to wonder whether the local defences would not necessitate an attack in proper form. So his orders had been categoric: if Bastogne does not fall as a result of direct attack or encirclement, proceed on towards the Meuse leaving the infantry to take the town.

The Americans Win—By a Short Head

There was not much sleep for the inhabitants of Bastogne that night, December 17–18. Next day, though they refused to be panicked, there was no denying that the situation looked threatening. The morning produced unmistakable signs that the American withdrawal was turning into a rout. Luxembourg refugees and the remnants of 28 Infantry Division came tumbling in from the east, the former swearing that the enemy was spending his time burning all villages, and the latter giving vivid descriptions of waves of tanks hard on their heels. The Germans appeared to be converging on Bastogne from all directions. When would they arrive?

Middleton still seemed confident. Military police together with Belgian resisters from the secret army and forces of the interior were patrolling the approaches. They had found no trace of the enemy. The enemy in fact announced his arrival at 3 p.m., when the first German shell fell near the chapel of Saint Teresa. The general outline of the battle became clear at once; the American batteries replied, but the military police detachments and the civil affairs offices prepared to move. The people of Bastogne began to wonder whether they were going to be left to their fate.

Early in the afternoon, M. Leon Jacqmin, the acting mayor, managed with some difficulty to get an exit permit to go to Arlon to collect stocks of flour. On the return journey he passed a column of American armour struggling to make headway against the first columns of refugees leaving

Bastogne. This was a combat command of 10 Armoured Division which Bradley had ordered up from the Luxembourg front during the morning. Its commander, Colonel Roberts, appeared in Middleton's office in Bastogne at 4 p.m., a few minutes after General MacAuliffe, the acting commander of 101 Airborne. The latter had arrived in Bastogne entirely by chance; he had set off during the morning behind his advance parties in a general northerly direction, not with the object of defending Bastogne, but to assist 82 Airborne in covering the roads leading to Liège. On the way MacAuliffe passed the 82 Airborne convoys heading for Werbomont, the agreed assembly area. On reaching the cross-roads at Herbaimont some 10 miles west of Bastogne the general had a sudden thought: why not go and pick up some news from Middleton? Ridgway, the commander of XVIII Airborne Corps, had meanwhile returned to Mourmelon from England and Middleton handed MacAuliffe Ridgway's order for 101 Airborne to remain in Bastogne with VIII Corps. Shortly after nightfall the indefatigable Gavin, after visiting Spa, also arrived in Bastogne from Werbomont. He was followed by Ridgway.

Bradley then telephoned ordering the Airborne Corps to be split, 101 Airborne to fight at Bastogne and prevent the place being surrounded, Gavin to remain at Werbomont. 101 Airborne's convoys were immediately re-routed to Bastogne and charged on through the night, headlights blazing as far as Bouillon (30 miles south-west of Bastogne). The first regiment of the division reached Bastogne at midnight. There was little rest that night either for the drivers or the traffic police, for the roads by which the reinforcements were coming up were jammed with vehicles of retreating units.

East of Bastogne groups of Americans were still resisting in isolated strongpoints at Wiltz and Clervaux. Their action undoubtedly delayed the development of the German assault on Bastogne and gained the few hours necessary to strengthen the defences somewhat. These surrounded men fought on for three days. The short time they gained at the price of their lives was undoubtedly a decisive factor in the eventual German defeat. Their resistance gives the lie to the story which all too soon found its way into Anglo-American polemics — that the men of VIII U.S. Corps were nothing but a mob of fugitives fleeing in terror. A striking example was that of a battery and an armoured detachment from 9 U.S. Armoured Division situated at the Antonius Hof cross-roads on the Bastogne–Saint-Vith road. Throughout the afternoon of December 18 they held up the whole of 2 Panzer which had passed through Clervaux and was intended to form the northern arm of the pincers encircling Bastogne. The Americans fought on until the evening, the last American tanks only being put out of action when the German artillery came up.

By nightfall on December 18 the leading troops of 2 Panzer and the Panzer Lehr were only a few miles east of Bastogne; the former was to by-pass the town to the north and the latter to take it. Behind them

Clervaux was now completely clear, the American garrison holding the old château having surrendered at midday to save the lives of the civilians sheltering in the cellars.

So the Americans and the Germans arrived at Bastogne more or less simultaneously, and during the night they felt their way cautiously towards each other. The Panzer Lehr moved up and 2 Panzer began its outflanking movement; on the American side 10 Armoured Division covered the routes leading eastwards, taking over from combat command R of 9 Armoured Division on the high ground at Longvilly commanding the roads which both the enemy divisions must use.

The fortunes of war certainly favoured the American side that night. Had he acted more boldly, Bayerlein, commanding the Panzer Lehr, could have brushed aside the American armoured detachments facing him and got round Bastogne to the south before the arrival of the American parachute division. But instead of driving on he acted with the utmost caution. Taking over personal command of a small force, he moved forward step by step. In the village of Mageret he interrogated a civilian: 'What is happening? Have you seen the Americans?' The reply was: 'A convoy of some 50 tanks and 40 armoured vehicles passed through in the direction of Longvilly two hours ago.'

This little scene took place at 2 a.m. The convoy described by the Belgian was in fact no more than a patrol reconnoitring the village to check reports that the Germans had infiltrated into it.*

Bayerlein's conclusion from this was that he was in danger of being attacked from the north. He stopped all further forward movement and pushed out a flankguard in that direction. The fact that a German general should react in so timorous a manner on such questionable information is in itself a commentary on the state of German morale.

At Bastogne at this moment MacAuliffe, who had set up his headquarters in the ex-German barracks, was conferring with Colonel Ewell, commanding 501 Airborne Regiment. By chance—chance took a major hand in affairs that night—Ewell had spent two days in Bastogne in November while on leave. He had gone walking in the surrounding countryside and knew the approach roads along which the Germans must come. Ewell said: 'I will move out along the Longvilly road at six a.m., gain contact and attack. That will clear up the situation.'

Bayerlein's pessimism was reflected at Hitler's evening conference at Ziegenberg that night.

---

* In his numerous accounts of this incident Bayerlein attaches great importance to the information given by this Belgian. It is remarkable that the latter has never come forward to take credit for having given false information and is still unknown. The explanation presumably is that in his fear his imagination ran away with him, and he was subsequently unwilling to admit that he had given information to the enemy.

Summarising the results of the first three days, von Rundstedt's conclusion was:

We should abandon the offensive and prepare to defend the area we have gained. Sepp Dietrich's forces are held up between Monschau and Malmédy. Saint-Vith has not been taken. We have only just reached Bastogne, which ought to have been taken on D plus 1. We have not made the most of our initial surprise. The offensive has never gathered speed, due to the icy roads and the pockets of resistance which forced us to lay on full-dress attacks.

Model was cleverer; he pointed out that a chance still remained. Even if Sepp Dietrich was marking time, Manteuffel was still on the move, although behind schedule. The Americans had not been able to re-establish a front in Manteuffel's sector. The weight of the offensive should therefore be transferred to Fifth Panzer Army and Sixth Army put on the defensive. The two Panzer divisions in reserve should be given to Manteuffel and with a total of five armoured divisions he should be able to force his way through.

But the two Panzer divisions in reserve were SS formations and the whole background to the offensive was a political one. For Hitler, therefore, there could be no question of removing the main role from Sepp Dietrich, whatever the strategic considerations might be. So the two SS armoured divisions were allotted to Dietrich to enable him to break through towards Huy and the Meuse.

Political considerations also took priority when Hitler came to lay down the administrative measures to be taken in the area 'liberated from the enemy'. The former 'Reich Commissars', Seyss-Inquart and Grohé, and the Gauleiter Simon were to reassume their positions in Holland, Belgium and Luxembourg and the occupation officials were to be Party members. 'We will never have military government again,' Hitler stated.

On the Allied side, Bradley had held a conference in Luxembourg at 10.30 a.m. on December 18 with the wayward General Patton who commanded U.S. Third Army, the only force capable of acting vigorously against the German flank and driving into the base of the salient. Bradley considered the situation 'fluid' and 'extremely critical'. He ordered Patton to suspend preparations for his offensive in the Saar due to start next day. The latter's annoyance was somewhat mitigated by the prospect of appearing as the indispensable saviour of the situation; he ordered an immediate move of three divisions, 80 Infantry Division from east of Sarregumines, 4 Armoured Division and 26 Infantry Division from reserve in the Metz area.

During the night Bradley reiterated the necessity for speed in the movement of these reinforcements. He ordered Patton to leave Luxembourg next morning and be at Nancy by 11 a.m. when Eisenhower was due to hold a conference at the headquarters of Twelfth U.S. Army Group.

The Supreme Commander was comparatively optimistic as he made ready for this conference. The SHAEF Intelligence Summary issued at midday on December 18 stated: 'The Allies now have the situation under control.' Supreme Headquarters staff continued to think that the previously agreed offensive operations could continue. Patton was to hand over part of his sector to the Vosges Army Group, concentrate six divisions and attack the German southern flank on December 22. Third Army was to take over the remnants of VIII Corps and the reinforcements now in action in the Ardennes. On the northern flank of the pocket First and Ninth Armies were to continue to prepare to counter-attack in the direction of Bonn and Cologne in conjunction with the British operation from Nijmegen.

Chapter 13

THE LAST GERMAN PARACHUTE
OPERATION

IN the autumn of 1944 liberated Europe in general and Belgium in particular were in the grip of a Fifth Column mania equal to that of spring 1940, when in the phrase attributed to Jean Cocteau the general public 'spied nuns doing up their garters' behind every bush.

Based as it was on memories of 1940, the obsession was understandable. The myth of the ubiquitous German drew no distinction between large-scale parachute operations and the infiltration by land or air of a few agents for work behind the Allied lines. Memory of the first major airborne operations in history, the German parachute descent on Rotterdam and the glider landing on the gun turrets of Fort Eben-Emael preparatory to the capture of Liège, still made people shudder and the impression had been heightened by the occupation and the frequent successes of the German police and the Gestapo in penetrating the clandestine organisations.

Enemy Guile

The man in the street would believe anything of the German; he was a wily enemy, up to every trick, floating down from the sky or popping up suddenly out of the shadows. The Allied commanders in Belgium, however, were either less imaginative or less prone to fear the tricks introduced into 'conventional' warfare by stratagem. They tended to shrug their shoulders and set little store by the warnings of the Belgians. Suspicion, when there was any, tended to be misdirected; for instance, some Belgian secret service agents returning from a mission behind the German lines were executed by their liberators and at the headquarters of one American division the Belgian Liaison Officer was arrested by his fellow countrymen. The most obvious subterfuge was the infiltration of German agents in Allied uniform, but equally obviously the stories of operations such as this are the most difficult to unearth. Details are not easy to come by from either side and generally emerge only in the form of very highly coloured stories. Survivors of operations generally held to be contrary to the rules of war or the Geneva Convention tend to refuse to tell their story until they have reached a certain age and are in comfortable retirement.

Little more reliance can be placed on the official announcements; on November 19 1944, for instance, the Belgian Central Information Bulletin announced the following to all Gendarmerie and police posts: 'During the last two days enemy parachutists have been dropped at night in the Ciney area. Search should be made for these men, who may be dressed in American uniform.' During the following weeks similar instructions were given covering the provinces of Belgian Luxembourg and Namur—in other words the entire area in the bend of the Meuse, that of the future offensive.

What part did German agents in fact play in preparation for the offensive? It may be presumed that they were less numerous than the Belgians believed but more active than the Allies imagined. One of the most persistent tales which emerged from the Ardennes offensive and was accepted unquestioningly by many authorities was that strong German detachments in British and American uniforms were parachuted during the night of December 15-16 to assassinate General Eisenhower and other Allied commanders.

The number of actual incidents was small and they soon became known to the Allied commanders, but the war correspondents, forbidden to give any definite information on the course of the battle, embroidered them. Public opinion and the military police were suffering from a bad attack of 'spy-mania', which the press stories reinforced; eventually a complete mythology was built up and kept alive by stories from Belgian civilians.*

In fact the Germans had planned two types of operation into the American rear areas and in neither case was the primary object the collection of intelligence. They formed part of the general plan of the offensive and were intended as distant advanced guard actions in front of the main force.

The first operation was strictly military in purpose; it consisted of the dropping of a body of parachutists in German uniform on December 17 to hold the roads from Eupen and Verviers to Malmédy until December 20.

Contrary to the statement of certain Belgian informants who thought they had seen drops at Beauraing, south-west of Stavelot, on December 24, or at Bastogne, this was the only major parachute operation carried out during the battle of the Ardennes. Subsequent confusion arose because the German 5 and 3 Parachute Divisions were involved in the battle area. The great majority of their personnel, however, were not trained to jump from a Junkers 52 and had arrived on foot or by road transport like any ordinary infantry.

* In 1947 enough of this body of legend remained for the well-known Swiss military writer, Eddy Bauer, to make mention of it in his book *La Guerre des Blindés*. He wrote: 'As regards the Fallschirmjaeger (German parachutists) commanded by the famous Skorzeny, they were employed on sabotage and guerilla missions. Some were captured in American uniform carrying papers stolen from prisoners. In spite of this underhand stratagem they were a total failure.' Bauer is a well-known professor of history at the University of Neufchatel. In July 1962 he produced a new and completely revised edition of his book in which this passage is entirely omitted. The fact that so unquestioned an authority on military history has completely changed his opinion shows how widespread and successful was the deception operation conducted by Skorzeny.

The second operation made use of German soldiers in American uniform. Their training was entirely divorced from that of the normal parachute troops. The unit was commanded by the SS Colonel Otto Skorzeny and had two tasks; to capture the Meuse bridges and to spread panic in the American rear areas. The story that there was also a plan to assassinate Eisenhower is apparently without foundation.

Somewhat naturally the Allies failed to distinguish between these two operations, but from the point of view of the German army there was a great gulf fixed between them. The German parachute troops had a big account to square with Skorzeny and even had they been employed on the same task, the Wehrmacht would never have put regular troops under his command.

With the background of Crete, Tobruk and Cassino — also of the Vercors, where some of them disgraced themselves — the German parachute troops considered themselves an élite force. Their leaders were not likely to forgive Skorzeny the fact that he had snatched all the publicity for the rescue of Mussolini from the Gran Sasso. That operation had been planned by the staff of the parachute division in Rome, which had managed to suborn some Carabinieri officers guarding Mussolini. The raid had been carried out by one company landing near the hotel in gliders while two other companies took up positions in the Assergi Valley at the foot of the mountain. The battalion commander, Otto Harald Mors, went up to the Gran Sasso by the perfectly ordinary method of using the funicular.

Skorzeny was then a captain and his sole job was to discover Mussolini and escort him to Hitler. This he did, taking care that a certain war correspondent, von Kayser, had his camera in the right place.

In Skorzeny's numerous subsequent accounts of the operation the role of the parachute troops was played down and Skorzeny himself was the man represented as demonstrating the fidelity of Hitler, the Nazi Party in general and the SS in particular, to their 'war-time comrade', Mussolini. The part played by Major Mors, who had in fact been solely responsible for the operation, was glossed over and he was eventually told to stop protesting. Skorzeny never allowed the truth of the matter to come out.*

Quite apart from the fact that there was no love lost between the two, the German parachute commanders doubted the utility of despatching men in

---

* The bitter feelings of the German parachute troops persisted long after the war. At the end of March 1952, General Student, the Parachute Commander, stated: 'The liberation of Mussolini by Otto Skorzeny is an historical inexactitude. He was simply a small cog in the wheel of the operation just like all the other soldiers who took part. I believe that Skorzeny knows perfectly well that his story is nothing but a publicity stunt. . . . If I had been in charge of the operation the Skorzeny legend would never have appeared.' See *Le Monde*, April 2 1952.
This is in fact no more than an attempt by Student to clear himself. Although he was not in direct control of it, the operation quite definitely took place under his authority. Even so he did not succeed in preventing Skorzeny getting all the kudos.

M

American uniforms behind the Allied lines. Moreover with the end of the war in sight, these officers would undoubtedly have advised against so questionable a procedure, had their opinion been asked. Skorzeny, however, accepted it without question.

The two operations were therefore entirely different in nature; on the one hand was Operation Greif (Gryphon) under command of SS Obersturmbannführer Otto Skorzeny, on the other operation Stösser (Awk) under command of the regular parachute Lieutenant-Colonel, Baron Friedrich-August von der Heydte.

The Commander for the Final Adventure

Operation Awk was the last true parachute operation of the European war, for the action of the Allied Airborne Forces on March 24 1945, when they took the defences on the right bank of the Rhine north of the Ruhr in the rear, was no more than an airborne landing. For the German parachute troops the wheel was due to come full circle on the Fagnes plateau; they had been the artisans of the Reich's most spectacular victories; they had opened the road to the German armour; now they were to be sacrificed in darkness and snow.

Lieutenant-Colonel von der Heydte's career was a good example of the mixture of revulsion and readiness to fight characteristic of so many German officers when faced with a phenomenon so foreign to all their traditions as Hitlerism. In autumn 1944 von der Heydte was thirty-seven—the same age as James Gavin. He came of a long line of Bavarian Catholic aristocrats and was related to most of the great families of Europe. He would have looked just as much at home in a crusader's helmet or at Charles V's court as he did wearing the parachute troops' flower-pot tin hat and battledress blouse.

Von der Heydte had begun by studying international law and by 1932 was Assistant Professor of Law in Berlin. When Hitler came to power the professor occupying the chair of law, who was a Jew and a Social Democrat, was dismissed and von der Heydte left Germany. He took up a Carnegie Foundation Scholarship and continued to study in Vienna, Italy and Paris. But he found an exile's existence hard. In 1935 he returned to Germany and joined 15 Cavalry Regiment at Paderborn, a unit of 'internal emigrés', almost all of whose officers belonged to the Catholic aristocracy. By the time war broke out von der Heydte had become a regular officer and was in command of a company on the Blies. On graduating from the Staff College early in 1941, he asked to return to troops. By this time he was a captain and was detached to the parachute troops. He took part in the Crete operation as commander of the battalion which captured Canea. This earned him the Collar of Knight of the Iron Cross. In the summer of 1943 he was Chief of Staff to Ramcke's parachute division in Italy and by the spring of 1944 was commanding a regiment in France. One day

Rommel arrived; von der Heydte invited him into his mess, where there were a number of officers and men proudly wearing on their sleeve the black armlet with the word 'Afrika' in white. Rommel was apparently overjoyed at being back among his own people; at the end of the little ceremony he took his host on one side and said: 'Heydte, are you sure of your Regiment?'

'Absolutely.'

'You are sure of every man?'

'Completely.'

'If need be they would obey you alone?'

'Me alone.'

'We want a lot of units like yours,' Field-Marshal Rommel concluded.

In the light of the July 20 plot and the role played by Rommel in the wings of that affair, the implication of his questions was obvious. Von der Heydte was not boasting: his object had been to turn his regiment into a sort of legion, loyal to him personally. As far as possible he accepted into it only volunteers; he was trying to turn his unit into the sanctuary which the Paderborn Cavalry Regiment had once been to him.

His attitude of mind was similar to that of many German officers; morally and spiritually their little military society took the place of their country and provided a short term object for which to fight. The growth of the 'closed circle' as a defence against a distasteful ideology was no exclusive preserve of the Wehrmacht. Other nations have been similarly divided; at this same period, for instance, the French Forces were torn between the F.F.L., the Army of Africa, de Gaulle, Giraud, de Lattre, Leclerc and Monsabert—all names synonymous with various forms of patriotism. The solidarity of armies was being sapped by an exaggerated *esprit de corps*; psychologically men wearing the same shoulder flash formed a little world of their own where the soldier felt at home.

Although a cousin of Colonel Claus von Stauffenberg, who had placed the July 20 bomb, von der Heydte had not been arrested and in the autumn of 1944 was stationed in the Netherlands. His regiment belonged to Student's First Parachute Army, to which it acted as 'fire brigade', despatching a force to any sector of the front which might be threatened. At the end of October he took over command of a training school set up to give basic training to the new recruits who had no experience whatever of the parachute troops' methods of fighting. Officially they were not supposed to be employed on operations, but during the month of November they had been used as infantry and so were parachutists in name only. After the exhausting battles on the Rhine their morale was low.

An Improvised Affair

The curtain rose on operation Awk on December 8, when Student told von der Heydte: 'The Führer has decided to undertake a major offensive in which a parachute detachment will be employed. You are to form and command this force.'

Von der Heydte wondered where the operation was to take place. Student had told him nothing and he was inclined to think that he would be jumping behind the Soviet lines surrounding the German bridgehead over the Vistula. It seemed logical that the Supreme Command should be preparing an offensive to relieve this sector of the eastern front which was under pressure by large enemy forces.

The composition of the force was the next problem. For security reasons von der Heydte was not allowed to take his own regiment, which was to remain where it was. He was permitted to choose only his own staff and the company commanders. Each of the regiments of First Parachute Army were to provide 100 men, if possible with previous parachute experience. But when the 1,200 men were finally assembled, it was found that only 200 to 300 were veterans from Crete, and for the vast majority this risky operation on to the Hautes Fagnes was going to be their first operational jump. One hundred and fifty of his own men managed to get round the regulations and remain with their commander. But von der Heydte was faced with a pretty problem; he had only a few days in which to instil into this assorted collection of individuals that cohesion in face of the enemy without which any unit is useless.

This was only the start of the improvisations. By December 11 von der Heydte had collected all his personnel and had formed a signal section, four parachute companies, one company of heavy machine guns, a section of four 80-mm mortars and one pioneer company. Arms and equipment, however, had not yet been issued on the standard scale and parachutes had not yet arrived.

These German parachutists were in fact hybrids, claimed both by the Army and the Air Force. Even their uniform was a mixture, their trousers being the army field grey and their tunics the light blue of the Luftwaffe. For the moment they were administered by the headquarters of 'Air Fleet West' but operationally they were under the Army. To cap it all, Rundstedt placed them under Sepp Dietrich, who was a general of the Waffen SS, a fact which aggravated both dissension at the higher levels and the usual staff disagreements.

These problems raised their heads as soon as the unit arrived at Sennelager near Paderborn, which it did at 3 a.m. on December 12 in Army Group transport. Sennelager had been designated as the training area by the Air Force, since it was close to the aerodromes from which the parachutists would take off. The army officer commanding the camp, however, had not been warned and refused to accept the order. His huts were full to bursting, he said, and there was no room even for a single additional man.

Lieutenant-Colonel von der Heydte thereupon telephoned to the staff of Münster Air Region. No one there had been told either that the parachutists were due to arrive or of the airfields from which they were due to depart. They therefore refused to help them find accommodation.

The Chief of Staff finally said: 'If this sort of thing goes on, anybody could turn up,' and put down the receiver.

Von der Heydte and his 1,200 men were therefore just left standing in the street at 4 o'clock in the morning. By chance, however, he stumbled across an Oerlinghausen chemist, who was a reserve officer in his former regiment. Flattered at being addressed as 'My dear fellow', the chemist went round waking up the people of the town and they squeezed up a bit to make room for the parachute troops.

The basic questions, however, still remained unanswered—where, when and how was the operation to take place?

Von der Heydte's force was to be transported in 120 Junker 52s of a squadron known as the 'Stalingrad Squadron'. It was the unit which had supplied Paulus' army in 1942–3, but the only man still with it who had taken part in that operation was its commander, Major Erdmann. The experienced crews had all either been posted elsewhere or killed. Their replacements at all levels had come direct from training, had done no night flying and had never dropped parachute troops operationally. This situation, moreover, was not peculiar to that particular squadron; it was generally known that in the Luftwaffe as a whole the transport squadrons were very efficient at everything except parachute training.

Erdmann and von der Heydte had known each other ever since Crete. The commander of the Stalingrad Squadron was dumbfounded when he heard that this was no mere training exercise, but an operation of war. There was no question, he said, of either his pilots, his wireless operators or his navigators being fit for it; the veterans, the survivors of the Stalingrad operation, had long since been removed to serve as infantrymen in the Luftwaffe divisions, out of which Göring had hoped to form his private army.

On December 13 Erdmann and von der Heydte were summoned by the Commander-in-Chief 'Air Fleet West'; they found him more interested in his bottle of brandy than in laying on an operation for which he was only responsible at second hand. He told them: 'The proposed offensive will start from the Eifel and be directed on Antwerp. It will be carried out by Model's Army Group, and the parachute force will be under the orders of that headquarters.'

Erdmann said: 'My unit is not ready.' The general did not reply. Erdmann then asked: 'How will co-operation with the Luftwaffe be arranged?' The reply was: 'You had better go and see General Pelz.'

The latter, who was commander of the tactical air forces, could give them no information, so Erdmann and von der Heydte set off for Field-Marshal Model's headquarters near Euskirchen, where they arrived during the night of December 14.

General Krebs, the Chief of Staff, gave them the overall objectives of the offensive, and then those of the parachute force; it was to clear the way for Sixth Panzer Army and then turn northwards to block the road along which the advance of that army might be threatened. Both Erdmann and von der Heydte objected that their resources were inadequate, but Krebs could do nothing and took them along to Model.

The field-marshal, who was clearly almost at the end of his tether, asked von der Heydte: 'What, in your view, is your percentage chance of success?' 'Ten to twenty per cent,' von der Heydte replied.

'That is good enough,' Model said. 'The operation will therefore take place. Many offensive operations have succeeded which initially had no better chance than that.'

Erdmann and von der Heydte continued their journey, and next appeared at Sepp Dietrich's headquarters at Munstereifel.

General Kraemer, the Chief of Staff, was present throughout the interview with the army commander; he was an efficient officer, detached from the army to the Waffen SS, and he spent his time drumming his fingers on the table and interrupting Dietrich with furious asides: 'Es ist toll! Dummes Unternehmen! (It's crazy! What a lunatic operation!)'

Standing in front of the map, Sepp Dietrich gave von der Heydte the choice of four objectives, two for each of his main tasks.

For the first task, that of clearing the way for Sixth Panzer Army, there were two possible dropping zones: either in the immediate vicinity of the Meuse between Huy and Seraing, with the object of holding the roads and bridges in the area Amay–Ombret Rausa until 1 SS Panzer arrived via Ouffet or, at Ham, in the bend of the Ourthe south of Liège, with the object of securing the east–west lateral road* and the two approach roads to Liège.

Von der Heydte objected, saying: 'I should have to have the whole division if I am to hold this area until the arrival of the armour. These objectives are also too far off.'

This left the second task: to put a temporary block on the roads along which Sixth Panzer Army's flank might be threatened. Again, two dropping zones were proposed: firstly, between Spa and Francorchamps on the Malchamps plateau to secure the roads from Liège and Verviers to Malmédy; second, south-east of Verviers to hold the high ground between Lake Gileppe and the Malmédy road.

This latter dropping zone was finally selected. The force was to drop on December 16, just before the opening of the artillery barrage.

Erdmann and von der Heydte got back to Oerlingshausen the same night, that of December 14–15. The parachutes had just arrived. Among them was a Russian type, the only one in the whole German army; it was a triangular contraption without an opening at the top; this reduced oscilla-

* The road Dolembreux–Esneux–Ehein.

tion, and so the parachutist had to do little to control his swing. Student made a present of it to von der Heydte, since he had hurt an arm in an aeroplane accident in Italy and was going to have to jump with it in a sling.*

Von der Heydte now had less than twenty-four hours to allot objectives, issue equipment and get his unit on the move. The operation broke every one of the hitherto accepted rules for large-scale employment of parachute troops. It was to take place on a pitch dark night, in a wind forecast by the meteorological service as 'fairly strong to strong'. Moreover, instead of being the deciding factor in the operation, as had been the case in Holland, Crete or the plans for Malta and Northern Ireland, the parachute force was playing only an auxiliary role to the land forces. It was not strong enough to hold the enemy for any length of time or to divert him from the main offensive; it was simply going to be frittered away in a minor operation. It could play little part in long-range reconnaissance, since it was without vehicles and was not therefore mobile; it could not put up prolonged resistance on some stop line, since, even though when it left it was issued with twice the normal scale of equipment, its fire power was inadequate and ammunition was in short supply. It is therefore not surprising that von der Heydte had few illusions as to his chances of success.

Now came another problem. Von der Heydte hunted through the files in headquarters Sixth Panzer Army for the essential minimum of information on the opposition which he might meet, but could find nothing. Apart from what he could discover from the map, such as woods and marshes, he was left in complete ignorance of the location of American units, either at the front or in reserve. He did not know what orders they had for dealing with parachute operations; he did not know whether they were expecting airborne landings. The 15 miles which separated his dropping zone from the front might just as well have been unexplored country, a blank on the map. If the wind carried him any distance from the dropping zone, his force might well come down straight on top of an enemy concentration.

Security measures were such that Sepp Dietrich would allow no patrolling and no air reconnaissance over the American rear area. Von der Heydte had great difficulty in obtaining a set of air photographs and maps.

The sole reason for the operation was to open the way for Sixth Panzer Army's armour, and one of the essentials clearly was that communications to the rear should be satisfactory. The parachute troops had wireless sets but von der Heydte knew from experience that modern methods of communication should be backed up by something simpler. There were many reasons why he did not wish to trust solely to radio communications — batteries could run out, the less experienced operators who would take over if the specialists were put out of action were likely to make errors in

* When the Americans captured von der Heydte they were far more interested in his parachute than in him, but they never managed to find it, since he had effectively buried it.

transmission, frequencies were liable to be changed without the out-station being informed and, of course, sets were always liable to damage on landing; he advocated the use of carrier pigeons. But Sepp Dietrich would have none of his arguments. 'What do you think I am?' he retorted. 'Running a zoo?'

He only gave way to von der Heydte on one point; he agreed that an artillery observation officer should drop with the force to direct the fire of the forward batteries on to targets in the American rear area. The effectiveness of this officer clearly depended on the efficiency of radio-communications.

General Pelz, commanding the tactical air forces on the western front, was more co-operative. Indirectly the operation would redound to the credit of the Luftwaffe and the fighter force's *esprit de corps* was not so exclusive that it would refuse to support an operation simply because it was not under full Luftwaffe control.

The Air Force, therefore, laid on quite a scenario, in order to help reduce navigational errors on the part of the Stalingrad Squadron and to deceive the Americans as to the dropping zone.

Between Paderborn and their crossing of the front line, the stream of aircraft would follow a continuous line of light thrown up by the anti-aircraft searchlight batteries. On crossing the front line the aircraft would switch on their landing lights and prepare to drop, extinguishing their lights only after having discharged their men. A quarter of an hour ahead of them a Junkers 88 was to drop four small incendiary bombs to mark the dropping zone, which was approximately 2,000 yards across. One hour, and then two hours, after the drop, fighters would fire slow-burning 'Christmas-tree' rockets to guide any scattered detachments.

All this commotion, lights in the sky and continuous aircraft engine noise was bound to alert the Americans, so measures were taken to mislead them as to the exact area of the dropping zone. German fighters were to mark two other dropping zones with incendiary bombs, one north of Spa in the Staneux woods and near Polleur, the other south-east of Eupen on the Monschau road. Straw dummies attached to parachutes would also be dropped, thus increasing the psychological effect of the real operation. The dropping of dummies was no new trick, the Allies having used it at dawn on June 6 1944 between Rouen and Le Havre to lead the Germans into thinking that an attempt was being made to capture the Seine crossings. It was now to produce the only indisputable German success: the headquarters of First U.S. Army at Spa thought it was being directly attacked and despatched its service units to hunt for the dummies. This gave rise to the rumour, clearly difficult to disprove, that parachutists had been dropped to support Peiper in the Amblève Valley.

A False Start

By 5 p.m. on December 15 the parachute troops were assembled in their tactical groups in the narrow streets of Oerlinghausen. All was ready; the men's chins were buried in their double-padded chin-straps and at each man's feet was his parachute and weapon container. They were to leave from Paderborn and Lippspringe airfields, and were now waiting for the lorries to take them there. The company commanders were standing round the colonel, getting their final orders.

The recruits of the last call-up, mostly half-grown boys or conscripts who had been discharged and then recalled, listened to the old hands talking. They were discussing anything other than the forthcoming drop — Christmas, perhaps a war Christmas in bombed Germany, where there would nevertheless be the nostalgic smell of the Christmas tree and baking apples, and an extra cigarette and rum issue; they speculated where they would spend this Christmas — perhaps in a prisoner of war camp, or perhaps eating a goose requisitioned from some captured farm. In all the armies fighting in Europe at the time the soldiers were thinking of the possibility of leave in the New Year. There was no reason why the young parachute troops should be an exception. With a bit of luck the operation would be over by then.

The transport did not arrive till late at night; the army had only provided enough petrol to get them as far as Oerlinghausen. Since movement from then on was the responsibility of the Air Force, it was up to the Air Force to provide the petrol. By telephoning to every headquarters he could think of, von der Heydte managed to procure an allocation of petrol, but even so the convoy had to move on without its tanks full.

By 10 p.m., only 400 men out of the 1,200 had arrived at the airfield. Von der Heydte wondered whether to wait for those who had fallen behind. To leave without them meant carrying out an already risky operation at only half strength. He was eventually ordered to wait and not to move until the full force was assembled.

The question now was whether to admit that operation Awk was a failure before it had even got off the ground. The only action taken by headquarters, however, was to despatch a legal expert the same night to start an enquiry into the reasons for the delay. Von der Heydte and his officers were treated as suspects and subjected to an interrogation lasting until mid-morning.

They were just beginning to hope for a couple of hours' sleep when Kraemer, Chief of Staff of Sixth Panzer Army, came on the telephone;

The offensive has not progressed as rapidly as expected in our sector [he explained]. We have reached only a very small portion of our objectives. The enemy is still resisting forward of Elsenborn Camp in anticipation of reinforcements arriving from the north. You will therefore drop before dawn tomorrow morning in the area previously agreed with the object of intercepting these reinforcements. Hold on as long as possible—two days as a minimum—and do as much damage as you can to the reinforcements. Your dropping zone has been moved slightly south-eastwards to the Belle-Croix crossroads near the Baraque-Michel.

The new dropping zone was on the second of the highest points in Belgium, overlooking the roads from Verviers and Aix-la-Chapelle to Malmédy.

A Hazardous Drop

On the evening of December 16 the scene of the previous day was re-enacted. This time the transport had enough petrol and arrived at the stated hour beside the 106 Junkers 52, 'Auntie J.U.', the old stagers of many battles. Just before midnight von der Heydte gave his men a final inspection at Paderborn and Lippspringe. In the darkness a priest brought from Oerlinghausen blessed both men and aircraft.

One after another the aircraft started up and lumbered off towards the runways. It was take-off time, and, as they left the ground, both the old stagers and the recruits started up the parachutists' song '*Rot scheint die Sonne*' the words of which were: 'When Germany is in danger there is only one thing for us: to fight, to conquer and assume that we shall die. From our aircraft, my friend, there is no return!'

Von der Heydte was in the pathfinder aircraft. According to tradition he was to be the first to jump. As the column of great aircraft got under way through the night, the searchlights lighting the route came on one after the other, guiding them to the Rhine, which they crossed above Bonn. The front could be seen from a distance—gun flashes, shell-bursts, houses on fire. At last, a quarter of an hour later than planned, came the order: 'Prepare to jump.'

The door opened; the pathfinder aircraft circled above the area marked by the incendiary bombs. Von der Heydte clamped to his side the splint supporting his right arm, and just before dawn on December 17 dived towards the ground.

But the triangular parachute did not fulfil the claims made for it and oscillated just like the rest; von der Heydte could not control his fall and was temporarily knocked out on hitting the ground. Above him the other parachutes were dimly visible in the darkness floating down like gigantic flowers; the aircraft turned for home. In the background was the roar of engines and the incessant thunder of gunfire, interspersed with the chattering of the American anti-aircraft machine guns. In all directions the sky was being swept by searchlights and streaked by tracer bullets.

Von der Heydte was alone. He remained alone for a long time. Having recovered somewhat, he took his bearings and made for his rallying point, the Belle Croix junction, where out of the 1,200 men of his force he found only about twenty.

Some had undoubtedly been killed when their aircraft were hit by the American anti-aircraft and had crashed in the area. But where were the others? Von der Heydte only learnt why they were not present considerably later, after the war; the fact was that out of 106 pilots only 35 had dropped their men in the right place. All the rest had begun to drop their men as soon as they passed Bonn, scattering little groups in the German rear areas and in no man's land, and so—involuntarily of course—giving the impression that a large-scale parachute operation had taken place all along the front. The majority of the men had never jumped before and there were many broken arms and legs among those who fell into trees; in many cases they lost their weapons and equipment, and simply went to ground in the snow; totally out of touch with their unit, all they wanted was to hear some human voice—even that of an enemy. Their lives were saved by capture. Much of the responsibility for this dramatic failure must lie with the meteorological service. They had predicted a wind of 10–12 m.p.h. at ground level, but in fact von der Heydte came down in a gale of twice that strength. This explains both the delay to the aircraft, and the wide dispersion of the men, many of whom came down far from the Hautes Fagnes, nowhere near Belle Croix.

With his miserable little group von der Heydte went to ground in the ditches near the road junction and waited for dawn. In the half-light, when friend and foe are indistinguishable, some vehicles appeared full of sleepy men who waved to the sentries posted at the road junction. Perhaps they thought they were American parachute troops, for the German and American parachute helmets were of roughly the same shape.

These vehicles were the leading elements of 7 U.S. Armoured Division moving from Eupen to Malmédy and Saint-Vith. The Germans crouched down in their ditches and watched from ground level as the U.S. convoys passed at regular intervals; between the convoys individual vehicles from Verviers sped by without security precautions of any sort.

From the German point of view there was no object in starting up a fight; all they could have done was to set one or two lorries on fire and kill a few Americans before being inevitably annihilated themselves. At first light, as the danger of discovery increased, von der Heydte withdrew under cover. He now had 125 men, including the artillery observation officer with his wireless operator and runner who had done well for their first parachute jump. But no one knew where the weapons and supplies containers were. After a prolonged search five or six were discovered; they proved to contain a wireless set which would not work, a mortar with an inadequate supply of ammunition, one heavy machine gun and a number of individual weapons such as sub-machine guns, grenades, revolvers and daggers. So as the time for action approached, von der Heydte had only one-tenth of his personnel and their fire power was practically nil.

In the hope that some others of his scattered force would turn up, von der Heydte remained in the neighbourhood of the road junction until mid-afternoon. He sent out scouts to observe the American positions and the movement of reinforcements. But having no wireless, he could not get in touch with the main German front and it was still too far away for a runner to get the news through in time.

No one else appeared, apart from a lone U.S. armoured car on patrol. This von der Heydte destroyed and then decided to withdraw north-eastwards to get away from the open marshy expanse around the road junction. Only an hour later a U.S. company appeared and occupied the positions the Germans had just left. After marching for some 2 miles von der Heydte came upon a second group of his own men, 150 strong, whom von Kayser, the war correspondent, mindful of his days as a sub-altern, had collected and organised. They had two heavy machine guns. Thus reinforced, the little column halted for the night on the edge of an area protected by marshy ground. Patrols were sent out into the surrounding countryside and came back with some twelve American prisoners swept up from service units; they were more frightened than bellicose.

Von der Heydte handed over to them those of his men who were either too badly injured or too worn out to continue the odyssey and sent them back to their units where they naturally told a highly coloured story of their adventures, thus contributing to the general atmosphere of nervousness. These tales, added to those originating from the dropping of the dummies, quickly went the rounds by the grapevine, lending support to the rumour that there had been a 'mass' parachute drop. As early as that morning, however, Eisenhower's headquarters was reasonably clear. In the SHAEF G.2 Report covering the period from midday December 16 to midday December 17, General Strong stated: 'Enemy parachutists have been dropped behind the lines in an area not yet clearly defined but including Verviers. Their strength is estimated to be about 1500.'

By the end of the day, U.S. Third Army G.2 knew that the parachute operation did not affect their area; their report said:

Paratroop P.W. stated they took off from Paderborn between 2 and 3 a.m. December 17; objective of attack to control the cross roads on Eupen-Malmédy road at Peterhau (?) where they were to prevent reinforcements and disrupt communications. Paratroopers were told to hold out for two days until relieved by 1 SS, 2 SS and 12 SS Panzer Divisions. It is estimated that 350–400 parachutists were dropped. One P.W. stated further landings could be expected night 17–18 December.*

SHAEF Daily Intelligence Summary of December 18 gave further details adding: 'Numerous parachutists are undoubtedly still at large.'

It may well be asked why, with all this accurate information rapidly available to the staffs, panic was allowed to spread to all levels. There

* Third Army G.2 Report, December 17.

seem to be two explanations: in the first place the panic was already there as a result of the enemy break-through and the fact that the American units involved were in the dark as to the overall situation. The only remedy for this was gradual reassertion of control by unit commanders. No one would have listened to an Order of the Day from far distant Versailles to the effect that the parachutist threat should not be over-estimated.

Secondly the Americans at all levels did not realise how scattered the German parachutists were. The figure had first been given as 1,500, which clearly did not tally with the later figure of 350–400; the latter, therefore, gave rise to the notion that there were other groups in greater or lesser strength scattered around the countryside and liable to carry out commando-type raids. The Allied commanders clearly could not know the extent to which von der Heydte's force had been disorganised by the drop and so long as its various groups had not been located, the danger of raids persisted.

Three Days of Wandering

For more than three days the 300 German parachutists wandered around in the area enclosed by the steep-sided valleys of the Soor and Helle which formed natural obstacles. Runners were despatched towards the German lines but there was no reason to suppose that any of them had got through. Headquarters gave no signs of life. From their own air force came no more than the strange scream of a Messerschmitt 262, the first jet fighter, on its way to Liège and Verviers in the night, and on one occasion a solitary Junkers 88 which flew over the area obviously looking for the force. It found it and dropped some containers but the parachutists only recovered one, which proved to be full of brandy and damp cigarettes. This was their third day and they had already eaten their iron rations. They would rather have had a box or two of food and some chocolate than the brandy.

Ammunition was running short and was only used sparingly during the brief encounters with American patrols despatched to hunt them out. There were desultory exchanges of fire as a result of which the parachutists suffered no more than one man wounded in the stomach on the third day. He was brought into the Allied lines the same evening by a group of prisoners released by the Germans. In fact a number of G.I.s fell into von der Heydte's hands every day and he eventually collected a total of thirty-six, including two V Corps despatch riders. An attempt was made to get the orders they carried through to the German lines, but none of the men who volunteered for the job arrived.

So three days passed wandering around waiting. Waiting for what? The attack by the SS armour from the south was clearly making no progress. Each morning continuous gunfire could be heard from the area of Elsenborn Camp, but it never seemed to get any closer, indicating that the American front had still not been broken. Patrols reported increased convoy movement on the Malmédy road; the more the Americans reinforced, the more problematical did the arrival of the SS armour appear.

There could be no question of taking the offensive. It did not seem much good reconnoitring since there was no means of transmitting the resulting information. Equally there seemed to be no object in just staying where they were. After three days the men were at the end of their tether, cold, tired and hungry. There was only one thing to do: to try and break through towards the German lines.

Lieutenant-Colonel von der Heydte decided that it must be done. At dawn on December 21 the parachutists moved off due east; up to their chests in the icy water, they forded the Helle not far from the point at which a little stream called 'Ruisseau de petit Bonheur' (Good luck!) flowed into it. The other side was steep and at the top were American outposts at the exits to the Koenigliches Torf Moor marsh. The Germans were bound to pass through this area in order to reach the Eupen–Monschau road, the only metalled route crossing the Fagnes plateau. The enemy barrier was well sited. After exchanging a few shots von der Heydte withdrew his force under cover and sent out scouts to reconnoitre other points in the American screen. It was found that infantry posts, sometimes supported by tanks, were at every exit from the woods. The Germans had not the resources to mount an attack in force and they would never get through if they remained concentrated.

So von der Heydte gave the order to disperse into small groups of no more than three men. Every man for himself! It was still possible to infiltrate between the enemy positions.

He watched his men disperse through the trees. When the last group had disappeared, he moved off himself, re-crossed the Helle, travelled west for a mile or two, and then crossed the river, once more making for Monschau, which he thought was in German hands. On the way he caught up with a group of young parachutists who tried to join up with him, thinking that with his experience they might avoid being captured. But he sent them packing. 'Each man must try his own luck at getting through', he said. Early on December 22 von der Heydte was captured by American infantry in the outskirts of Monschau. The SHAEF G.2 Report of 12.00 hours December 23 announced: 'He had frost-bitten feet and was suffering from incipient pneumonia.'

The only one on the Allied side to mention this incident is General de Guingand, Montgomery's Chief of Staff. In *Operation Victory* he says:

The Commander of the parachutists was captured after several days, and he was by that time a sick and disillusioned man. His story of the difficulties which he experienced in obtaining his requirements in equipment and aircraft was most interesting. He had to fight at every stage and it was obvious from his remarks that he was anything but satisfied with the role he had been given.*

After his official interrogation von der Heydte was passed on to the war correspondents. For them he was a windfall. Their readers were bored with stories about waiting around in the snow and here was someone totally unusual, a sort of western film hero, a parachute colonel, a Bavarian, an aristocrat and an anti-Nazi. They grilled him, making the most of the 'human' and 'dramatic' aspects, including his career in civil life, his favourite sport and his Carnegie Foundation fellowship. The next day appeared a remark which went the rounds of the Anglo-American press: Someone asked him: 'What do you think of Sepp Dietrich? Is he a great strategist?' Von der Heydte replied: 'He is a cur dog.'

The Confusion with Skorzeny's Operation

The interest aroused by 'Operation Awk' and its commander was, however, soon overshadowed by another raid. Skorzeny's saboteurs in American uniforms were far more exciting to the war correspondents than von der Heydte's parachute troops wandering about on the moors. Very soon, moreover, the two operations were treated as one; on December 27 for instance, the readers of the *New York Times* (and they were among the better informed) were told the following:

A special German task force infiltrated behind the American lines in an attempt to kill the American First Army leaders, it can now be disclosed. The unit, some of which drove through a convoy of British command cars while wearing British uniforms and some of whom dropped by parachute, carried small vials of sulphuric acid in matchboxes which could be thrown into the faces of interceptors. . . . This special German force was part of much larger special sabotage battalions dropped behind the American lines during the current German counter-offensive.

There is an error in practically every line. Lieutenant-Colonel von der Heydte specifically confirmed to me that the two operations were entirely separate. In a letter dated June 27 1954 he wrote:

I only learnt of Skorzeny's operation by chance. People clearly wanted to keep it from me. The code name for the operation to be carried out by my tactical group was 'Unternehmen Stösser'. That of Skorzeny's operation 'Unternehmen Greif'. When I was at the headquarters of Sixth Panzer Army, I asked an N.C.O. for certain routine documents concerning my operation. The fellow mixed up the two operations and gave me the files intended for Skorzeny. Only through this N.C.O.'s mistake did I learn of Skorzeny's plan. After this incident, I naturally asked the officers concerned for details.

* *Operation Victory.* p. 428.

They were extremely reticent. Only after prolonged discussions did I manage to obtain an assurance that Unternehmen Greif would not interfere with my dropping zone and ensure that orders were issued laying down boundaries and pass-words to prevent confusion.

This then, reduced to its true perspective, is the story of the German parachute operation on to the Hautes Fagnes—their last. Although he did not know it, von der Heydte had gained a victory, which might well be called 'a psychological warfare' victory were it not that the words now carry a connotation different from that attributed to them by the staffs at the time. His operation, its effect enhanced by the fact that it was carried out at night, confirmed an obsession to which the Allies were already prone. They did not believe the Germans to be capable of carrying out a major parachute operation and were therefore convinced that the parachutists were being used on the lines of their own commandos, to spread fear and a sense of insecurity. Von der Heydte's 300 survivors wandering around in the marshes succeeded in doing so; they were, in fact, no more than a dispirited set of men thinking of little but their gnawing hunger; but the mere thought of German parachutists spread terror in Europe.

The reader will note that I have been reduced to dealing with Operation Awk from the German side only. This was inevitable. The parachute force was almost entirely isolated and only came into brief contact with Allied units; it is therefore inherently unlikely that there could be any trustworthy account of their doings from the Allied side. The stories which went round among the Americans were based on highly-coloured and somewhat boastful accounts rather than factual military reports.

Baron von der Heydte is now a Professor of Law and an important figure in the German Catholic Integrationist Movement. He has given more than one account of his exploit,* and in 1954 he was good enough to fill out the details for me. There is no good reason to doubt his account of events. Moreover it is supported by the fact that never, either while a prisoner of war nor after the Armistice of May 1945, was he accused of the war crimes attributed to the parachutists, whether in his personal capacity or as a commander. As far as I know he was never even interrogated on the subject—and the American courts of enquiry kept their lists up to date.

As far as the subject matter of his story is concerned, von der Heydte never attempted to gloss over anything, nor did he try to describe actions which could not be checked. This is another indication in his favour. Moreover such scanty information as American documents contain confirms his account. I have therefore considered it inherently likely to be true, taking into account von der Heydte's avowed desire to ensure that his

---

* *Der Fallschirmjäger*, 1953, No. XII, and 1954, No. I, and in his article on parachute operations in *Bilanz des Zweiten Weltkrieges*.

(b) Otto Skorzeny in 1943

Field-Marshal von Rundstedt

Colonel Friedrich-August von der Heydte ▶

Tiger tank burns near La Gleize

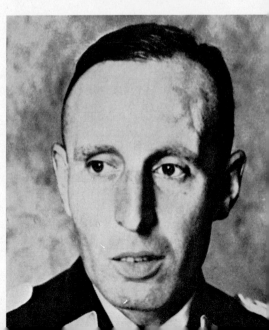

6(a) Eisenhower and Montgomery confer

(b) General Ridgway

(c) General Hodges

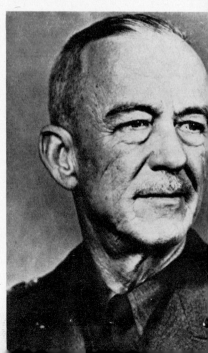

contemporaries should cease to confuse Skorzeny's gangs with his parachute troops, who were simply frittered away on a useless adventure.*

* Since the first edition of this book was published, Professor von der Heydte
has become a brigadier on the reserve of the Bundeswehr and has returned to
German public life in the wings of the case against the weekly paper *Der Spiegel*.
In the course of the resulting arguments certain facts have emerged which throw
considerable doubt on the picture of him which I have painted in this chapter. In
particular it appears that in the spring of 1933, he belonged to the Catholic Conservative Right Wing, led by von Papen, who cherished the illusion that they could
'avert the worst' by penetrating the National Socialist Movement and turning it
into the 'Party of Law and Order' which it pretended to be. At that time Herr von
der Heydte apparently belonged to one of the SA student formations. No doubt his
opinions changed as his knowledge increased but the fact remains that this incident
proves that he had a highly developed sense of opportunism.

N

Chapter 14

SKORZENY'S COMMANDOS

WE now go back to October 26 1944—1 a.m. in the signal centre of the headquarters of German Army Group B at Fichtenheim, near Crefeld. The duty clerk heard the engine of the teleprinter linking the headquarters to that of the Führer start its characteristic maybug-like burr. The carriage began to move, typed one or two meaningless signs, and then the text of a message began to appear: 'The Führer has ordered the formation of a special unit of approximately two-battalion strength for use on the Western Front in special operations and reconnaissance . . .'

It was signed 'Keitel'. Even now it is astonishing that such an order could have appeared; the most elaborate precautions were being taken to ensure the security of the planned offensive, and here was the staff of the Wehrmacht openly distributing an order calling for volunteers to act as partisans, and setting out unequivocally what they were expected to do.

The order was crystal clear. It asked for volunteers from all three Services—Army, Navy or Air Force; they had to be of impeccable physique, experts in hand-to-hand combat, have a knowledge of English and, if possible, of American dialects. 'This order will forthwith be made known to all units and services.'

Volunteers were to be despatched by November 10, to 'Dienststelle Skorzeny' at Friedenthal, near the Oranienburg concentration camp, for an initial examination for suitability. As Reichsführer SS, Himmler was in charge of the operation and was to report to the Staff of the Wehrmacht the number of volunteers accepted.

Had the Allied Intelligence Service laid hands on this document it would have known at once that, under Himmler's authority, Skorzeny was charged with one of the audacious operations through which he had made his name. In fact the order was so widely distributed that by early November the Americans did know of it.

General Westphal, the Chief of Staff to Rundstedt, immediately distributed the order to all units other than the garrisons of the Channel Islands and the 'surrounded fortresses' on the Atlantic coast (Lorient, Saint-Nazaire, La Rochelle, Royan), and non-German units. He laid down that if 'after passing the qualifying examination, volunteers were not accepted, they would not be penalised in any way but special note would be made of their spirit and enthusiasm for the Service'.

Rundstedt and his staff did no more than pass on the order and despatch the volunteers. The object was to use a force dressed in American uniform to capture the Meuse bridges above Liège. When the field-marshal heard of it he told Westphal to ask Jodl whether such an operation was 'fully in accordance with international law', whether, as people were telling him, the Americans had already used German uniforms for certain operations on the western front, what definite proof of this there was, and whether anyone had considered what might happen to any men captured.

Jodl replied:

Since the Field-Marshal has raised the problem we have re-examined the matter. There is no question of any infringement of international law; it is merely a war stratagem, such as the other side has already used on all fronts and with far greater frequency than we have. You need therefore have no scruples.

Moreover, all the men selected are volunteers. They are quite aware of the possibility that they may be treated as partisans. This they have accepted; no-one has forced them into it.

Furthermore, there can be no question of changing the orders already given. They are as sacrosanct as all the other tactical measures laid down for the offensive.*

In spite of Field-Marshal von Rundstedt's reservations, his headquarters inevitably became involved in the operation. All details were sent direct to Skorzeny from Hitler's Headquarters, Wolfschanze, but C-in-C West had to know of it in order to draw up the general operation order for Army Group B. Only after repeated and increasingly insistent orders, however, did Rundstedt hand over some tanks and other captured American vehicles. Even then, the ordnance service purposely worked so slowly that Skorzeny was only provided with two Sherman tanks, ten British or American armoured cars, some fifteen lorries and thirty jeeps. Rundstedt flatly refused to provide uniforms from the prisoner-of-war camps, and Skorzeny had to get them on his own initiative.

The Volunteers' Training

A year earlier, this Otto Skorzeny had appeared on every cinema screen in Europe, an enormous man with a scar stretching from his left ear to his mouth, towering over a dejected Mussolini and looking like a Thirty Years' War Cavalier. He was one of those Austrians who tried to make up by exaggerated Nazism for the fact that physically they did not measure up to SS standards. He had been commissioned to form Allied-type commandos within the German Army, and had made a success of all his raids; he had the further advantage that the Minister of Propaganda had built up a reputation for him.

On October 22 he had been able to report to Hitler the successful kidnapping of Admiral Horthy, the Regent of Hungary, who had been in contact with the Allies. On that occasion the Führer, after his usual heroic

* Statement by General Westphal on June 10 1947.

declamations about the urgency of regaining the initiative in the west, had told Skorzeny that his commandos would have their role to play in the forthcoming operations.

But when Skorzeny received the order giving his name and the assembly area for his volunteers in black and white, he lost his temper, protested to Supreme Headquarters and demanded that this 'secret' mission, now public property, should be cancelled. At least this is what he says in his memoirs.*

He did not, however, pursue the point, and even discovered an ingenious legal subterfuge to justify the use of American uniforms; international law, according to him, explicitly forbade only one thing, use of his arms by a soldier dressed in the uniform of his enemy. The German Commandos were therefore to wear their national uniform underneath the American, taking off the latter when fighting began.

It seems doubtful whether this rule was generally followed. The only firm piece of evidence is a photograph in the American magazine *Signal Corps* showing a young soldier being taken prisoner by four G.I.s. He is wearing German uniform, but various articles of American uniform are lying at his feet in the snow. Other members of the commandos definitely did not clutter themselves up with this conglomeration of clothing, which it would in any case have been difficult to take off at the moment of opening fire. They were not even carrying their German military documents.

The fact that doubt still remains on this small point shows how difficult it is to get at the truth concerning 'Operation Gryphon'. Skorzeny's account is sensational and lacks detail. Its publication in Germany did at least elicit certain further information from one of the survivors of the adventure, Sergeant Heinz Rohde, who had by then become manager of a cinema in Holstein. His corrections to Skorzeny's account in turn produced two other letters from ex-volunteers, one of whom wished to remain anonymous. In all three letters, which appeared in 1951, a certain aversion to publicity was evident—understandable since the Americans might well have arrested and tried the survivors.†

The Americans did not, in fact, take action. Nevertheless it is unlikely that further accounts will appear, since the vast majority of the survivors were killed or captured by the Russians at the end of the war in the Nieder Krönig bridgehead near Schwedt on the Oder.

Allied documents on the subject are based primarily on prisoner interrogations. They are confused and frequently contradictory, but they show clearly that the whole enterprise was an improvised affair, and that a vast number of completely unfounded rumours circulated among the volunteers. Skorzeny moreover stated that he was all in favour of this, as being the best method of preserving secrecy as to his true objective. Excessive

* *Skorzeny's Special Missions*, p. 151.
† The letters appeared in the weekly *Der Spiegel* of January 16 and 31 1951.

publicity distracted people's attention and gave rise to a host of conflicting theories.

Reliable sources of information are therefore limited, and all that can be done today is to extract a number of likely suppositions.

The volunteers had been given all sorts of reassuring promises, but as the gates of Friedenthal and Grafenwöhr camps closed behind them they must have been sadly disillusioned. Some had thought over their decision more deeply than others, but there could be no question of going back on it now, for very soon these men knew far too much to be sent back to their previous units without more ado.* The officers were lavish with explanations and justifications, and Oberregierungsrat Berger made full use of his prestige as a lawyer to prove that subterfuges like the Trojan Horse were not contrary to the rules of modern warfare.

Some of the volunteers had no doubt been attracted by the prospect of breaking the monotony of their military existence, but they must have been bitterly disillusioned to find that—at Grafenwöhr at any rate— sentries were marching slowly up and down at 30-yard intervals around the perimeter of the camp. The guards were all Volksdeutsche, members of the German minorities from abroad, belonged to the SS, and had been recruited as being more secure than their German-born comrades. The volunteers had their German military paybooks removed, and all links with the outer world were completely cut. One of them was shot for having sent home a letter giving too full a description of his existence, in contravention of the oath of complete silence which he had given. Isolation was so rigorously maintained that the sick were not sent to hospital; as a precaution, the others were dosed against influenza and colds.

The primary object of their training was to produce a complete change in the psychology of each individual. The problem was not to toughen up normal soldiers or to train them as guerillas, but to transform these volunteers completely, to inculcate into them a new pattern of behaviour, and almost a new mentality. Nationality is not merely a case of habits of life, gestures or swear-words. It is comparatively easy to learn to whistle instead of clap at a show, to chew chewing-gum like a native of the Bronx or Brooklyn, and to be word perfect on the words of command for arms drill, just like any real 'non-com'. But basic instincts cannot be changed by word of command. These volunteers were cut off from their war-time friends, uncertain of the fate which awaited them and deprived of any fixed

* The O.K.W. War Diary is extremely reticent on the whole subject, but it should nevertheless be noted that it states the opposite: 'So many difficulties arose from the insistence on preserving complete security that many members of the special group had to be released. The deciding factor was the evidence that the enemy already knew of the call for volunteers.' (K.T.B./O.K.W.IV.i., p. 449.)

Heinz Rohde's impression of his first days in the camp should also be noted. He considered that in an effort to form a less numerous but more effective unit, certain superfluous men were released. There can be no certainty on this point.

point around which to construct a normal type of existence; from the outset they were feeling their way in the dark.

No more than some ten or so of these pseudo-G.I.s were really expert in English; they were either ex-sailors or German-Americans by birth, some of whom had even served in the U.S. Army. They were made instructors. Then there were some 150 men who had good school English; they were sent to polish it up in the Limbourg and Austrian prisoner-of-war camps. The rest, who had no English at all, were simply given a list of swear-words and a few key expressions to learn.

Of course not all the 2,000 men, of which the new unit, christened '150 Armoured Brigade', was composed, had to possess advanced knowledge of languages. The brigade was to be an independent unit moving ahead of Sixth Panzer Army and independently of the Peiper Force; it was to seize the three bridges over the Meuse south-west of Liège at Engis, Amay and Huy, making maximum use of the panic which it was thought would reign in the American rear areas.

Otto Skorzeny proposed to divide his brigade into three tactical groups, one infantry and two armoured, with a total of seventy German tanks camouflaged to look like Shermans. Once the break-through had been made, they were to infiltrate past Saint-Vith hoping to be taken for a column of American tanks withdrawing.*

Owing to the slow progress of the initial offensive, the three groups could not move during the first twenty-four hours. In fact, Skorzeny did not put them into action until some time later, in the area of Malmédy.

The entire legend which has grown up around Operation Gryphon in fact refers only to the headquarters company, which was under command of Captain Stielau; he was the last of six company commanders who had followed each other in rapid succession between November 10 and December 16, a fact which in itself shows how ill-prepared the whole enterprise was.

Stielau's company had good American equipment, whereas the rest of the brigade had only German equipment, more or less effectively camouflaged. The company consisted of eighty men, including those with the best knowledge of English; it was divided into two groups: the sabotage

---

* An operation order for Operation Gryphon, captured on December 16 on a captain from 116 Panzer, gave the routes of these three groups. They were to follow different roads and meet between the Ourthe and the main Liège-Bastogne road. The routes given were:

(a) Trois-Ponts, Basse Bodeux, Vilettes, Bra, La Fourche, Harre, Deux-Rys, Roche à Frène.

(b) Recht, Petit-Thier, Ville du Bois, Vielsalm, Salmchateau, cross-roads 500 yards north of Joubleval, Hebronval, Regné, cross-roads 1 mile south-west of Malempré, Manhay, cross-roads east of Grandmesnil, cross-roads 1,000 yards north of Mormont, Roche à Frène.

(c) Roche à Frène, Aisne, Juzaine, Bomal, Tohogne, Oneux, Amas, Ocquier, Vervox.

group in eight jeeps, the reconnaissance group in six. The latter group was in turn subdivided into four short-range reconnaissance teams and two long-range teams. The crew of each vehicle was four men (or in some cases three)—a driver, a commander, a saboteur or radio operator and an interpreter, who was the only one of the team to speak perfect English. In addition to their normal equipment, these men had a phial of prussic acid concealed in the wool of their cigarette lighter, so that if they had the time, they could poison themselves, should they be captured.

The different sections of the brigade left their camps for the western front between December 6 and 12. The trains followed circuitous routes and moved by night only; by day they were camouflaged in forest sidings and special Gestapo detachments 'protected' the men's bivouacs. The brigade eventually concentrated in the Munstereifel–Stadtkyll area where American documents (military paybooks and driving licences) were issued. Stielau's company was kept apart from the main body of the brigade and located on Wahn Airport near Cologne. It was to go through with the German assault units, and then appear as belonging to 5 U.S. Armoured Division from Ninth Army.

The belated German security precautions proved entirely ineffective, for the Allies knew all about the operation from the outset—at least that is what Skorzeny says. During the offensive one of the pseudo-Americans was stupefied to discover in an issue of *Stars and Stripes* an article on the preparation of the volunteers, including photographs of their training camp. On December 2 First U.S. Army's G.2 report referred to the operation order and the routes laid down for Skorzeny's column, together with its indicator sign. The information was repeated on December 10 in the monthly report from the same headquarters.

Nevertheless, events proved that in spite of all this detailed information the staffs did not really believe in the operation. After all, they did not believe that an offensive was imminent either. The only people to become worried were the counter-espionage service. There were so many rumours, so much sabotage and so many reports of agents being infiltrated, that they evacuated the civil population from the Roer area and forbade all movement. A line of check-points was set up between Givet and Visé, and all journeys above 4 miles forbidden. Yet the American security service seemed more preoccupied with its Allies than its enemies. Bradley's staff put it quite clearly. They said: 'No evidence of operations by subversive organisations in liberated countries was encountered. Perhaps the most serious threat to Allied security in this respect came from the resistance groups in Belgium, which remained active and retained their arms in defiance of governmental decree.'*

* Twelfth U.S. Army Group final after-action Report, Vol. IV, p. 195.
This viewpoint may be understandable when it is remembered that the Allied command estimated the Belgian resistance forces at 70,000 men. The Allies had

The Cat and Mouse Game

In so far as it is possible to piece the story together from the welter of conflicting reports, it appears that at dawn on December 16 eight jeeps from Stielau's company infiltrated through the American lines without difficulty. As already pointed out, their recognition signs were known to the Americans, who had published them. They were to paint white spots on houses, trees and roads to indicate the route they had taken; they wore pink or blue scarves, and the second button of their battledress blouse was left undone. Their recognition sign by day was two taps on the helmet; by night they were to raise their right arm and give a series of flashes from a blue torch; the answering signal was the raising of the left arm and a flash from a red torch. Their vehicles carried the letters C.D.X.Y. or Z on the near side of the bonnet.

The moral effect of the operation was out of all proportion to its size. In General Bradley's words 'half a million G.I.s were forced to play cat and mouse with each other each time they met on the road'. Bradley himself was arrested three times by alert sentries—probably only too willing to make the most of the game with him. The G.I.s imagination ran riot; they drew no distinction between the parachutists, parachute dummies and commandos, and ended by thinking that they were not only outflanked by some invisible enemy army, but that he was in their midst.

By a sort of instinctive reaction the Americans invented a method of discovering the impostors, by asking American catch questions—it is a well-known story. Typical questions were: 'What is the man between centre and tackle on a line of scrimmage?' 'What is the capital of Illinois; Chicago or Springfield?'

Another excellent method was to use tricks of pronunciation, such as making a suspect say the word 'wreath'; the effect was almost like a chemical reaction, and the German or German-American was given away by his accent every time.

There were other traps which led to the capture of some of Skorzeny's

---

been trying to get this force disarmed throughout the autumn. The example of the Greek crisis, and still more the inconvenience of having so large an uncontrolled force immediately to the rear of the front, were sufficient explanation for their uneasiness. At the end of November, General Erskine, head of the SHAEF Mission in Brussels, negotiated a disarmament agreement but the Pierlot Government, which was unpopular and tactless, failed to implement it. Tempers continued to rise until the German offensive came, when the 'Independence Front' came out with a proclamation of full support for the Allied Command. The latter, however, made no request for remobilisation of the Resistance Forces and made use only of parts of the regular army.

How worried the Allied commanders were over this situation can be seen from Bradley's words 'the most serious threat'. It seems questionable whether the superlative was justified, but that is another question.

men, though whether they were members of Stielau's company or not is doubtful. On December 18 a group of 'American soldiers' appeared out of the forest north of Poteau on self-propelled guns abandoned by E Troop of 18 Cavalry Squadron. On the way they passed a sergeant of 32 Squadron. The new arrivals' boots looked suspicious to him. Before he had said a word one of the men shouted: 'We are E Company.' But in an American Cavalry group only the tank squadron is designated 'company'. All the other squadrons, including the self-propelled gun squadron, are known as 'troops'. It was the sort of mistake which the German could not possibly suspect, but as a result the Americans opened fire at once, and all the German commandos were killed.*

Another incident occurred at the same time at Aywaille, south of Liège, some 12 miles from the bridge over the Meuse at Engis. A military police-man asked for the password from three men in a jeep. They did not know it and presumably had not the courage to charge the barrier. They were arrested. On them were found German military pay-books, 900 American dollars, £1,000, two Sten sub-machine guns, two Colt 45's, one German revolver and six American grenades.

These three pseudo-privates were members of a long-range reconnais-sance team passing under the names of Charles W. Lawrence, George Sensenbach and Clarence van der Wert. On December 22 they were court-martialled under their real German names of Officer-Cadet Gunther Billing, Corporal Wilhelm Schmidt and Lance-Corporal Manfred Pernass; they were shot on December 23. Their feelings were no doubt the same as those of seven of their fellow-commandos who, some days later, submitted a plea for mercy to General Hodges in the following terms: 'We have been captured by the Americans without having fired a single shot, because we did not wish to become murderers. We were sentenced to death and are now dying for criminals, who have not only us, but also—and that is worse—our families on their conscience.'†

In all, eighteen of the commandos were captured and shot at Henry-Chapelle or at Huy. The last of them was named Corporal Otto Struller, alias Captain Cecil A. Dyer. The American ranks they adopted bore no relation to their German rank. For instance, Lieutenant Guenther Schilz of the navy passed himself off as Corporal John Weller; Engineer Petty Officer Horst Goerlich had turned into Private Walter Verge; on the other hand, Corporals Robert Bollack and Rolf Benjamin Meyer had become Second Lieutenants Sammy Rosner and Charlie Holtzmann.

Only three teams returned intact. One had reached Huy, the second had succeeded in crossing the Meuse near Amay, and the third had patrolled in the Vielsalm area. Two or three other teams got back to the Malmédy area with one or more members wounded. On the whole they had done

---

* See Dupuy, *Saint-Vith, Lion in the Way*, p. 108.
† Shulman, *The German Defeat in the West*, p. 242.

their job; the cutting of telephone lines, marking of false minefields and misrouting of American convoys were in many cases put down to the commandos' action. Nevertheless, it was a double-edged weapon and their own camouflage was often their undoing. For instance, at a bend in a road one of these men came up against an American sentry and gave himself up without any attempt to conceal his identity. Brought up in front of the local commander he was dumbfounded when the latter replied: 'So sorry, but I am a member of Stielau's company too.' And it was true.

On the other hand, the leading scout of a genuine American patrol was suddenly rushed by two men, apparently G.I.s, who announced that he was now their prisoner.

'Damn fools,' the scout replied in perfect German. 'I am on the same job as you. Don't stop me doing it.' He then went back to his patrol and organised an ambush, in which one of Skorzeny's men was killed and the other captured.

Eventually sixteen survivors collected on January 10 at Vallerode, northeast of Saint-Vith, under command of Lieutenant-Commander von Beer. Three new teams were formed, led by Sergeant Heinz Rohde, Lieutenant Schmitt of the navy and Captain Stielau himself. After carrying out certain further reconnaissance tasks on foot in the American rear areas, Rohde and Stielau got their men back intact. Schmitt was killed by an American sergeant to whom he could not give the password.

Was There a Plan to Assassinate Eisenhower?

The aspect of this escapade which looms largest in the less serious historical accounts is the plan to assassinate Eisenhower, but it would seem that this must be classified either as a figment of the imagination or a psychological warfare operation.

One of the sources of rumour was undoubtedly the testimony of the commandos captured near Liège on December 18. They told First U.S. Army intelligence officers that:

Skorzeny is on the way to Versailles to assassinate Eisenhower. He is travelling in an American ambulance full of fake wounded. He is to meet German agents at the Café de la Paix in Paris and they will give him final details of the security arrangements around Supreme Headquarters. Other American generals will be kidnapped.

Harry Butcher noted in his diary that according to information given him by Eisenhower's security service, 150 men had been detailed for the kidnappings, and Skorzeny himself had sixty men. The Supreme Commander became practically a prisoner in his headquarters; he could not move a step without sentries, machine guns and armed escorts. Barriers, patrols and check-points were set up all along the route from Paris to the front, with the result that the speed of movement to the battlefield was reduced; and units in the communication zone were compelled to tighten their security measures.*

The prisoners interrogated at Liège may or may not have been speaking the truth. Corporal Wilhelm Schmidt stated: 'Our unit included a group of sappers, whose job it was to destroy headquarters and kill the head-quarters personnel.' But he may merely have been repeating a well-learnt lesson. German propaganda was quite wily enough to think up that type of story.

But it is also possible that Corporal Schmidt was simply quite truthfully repeating the rumours which had gone the rounds among the commandos during their weeks of training. The men of 150 Armoured Brigade had been subjected to intense conditioning, the effect of which had been heightened by their seclusion. Peter Ackermann, who became 'Captain Murray Eddie O'Connor', stated that: 'At the end of ten days no-one was in any doubt as to our object. The Officers' Mess waiters passed on everything.' One of the rumours circulating, for instance, was that the brigade was to be used alongside the Americans against the Russians. Skorzeny, moreover, was all for allowing rumour to add to the legendary halo surrounding his name: for the 'liberator of Mussolini' there was nothing impossible in kidnapping Eisenhower, carrying out a parachute raid on his headquarters or assassinating him. To overheated imaginations such an idea came naturally. In any case, Skorzeny has never denied that he was in favour of the spread of such rumours.

Eisenhower's entourage was certain that they 'had complete and positive proof of the existence of such a plot'. But when told of it, Eisenhower considered that 'this story was greatly exaggerated'. He said that he would 'consider it miraculous if any ambitious German murderer could determine in advance that he would find his prospective victim on a particular railway train at a given moment at a given spot in Europe'.

The most unexpected reaction was that of Montgomery. He saw in this an opportunity of getting himself a new status. He declared that he was uneasy over the reactions of American sentries who might not recognise British identity papers, and demanded American documents from the commander of Ninth U.S. Army in order to avoid being mistaken for a German spy disguised as Montgomery. He got his papers, in spite of formal orders from Washington to the contrary.

Allied gullibility was perhaps accounted for by Skorzeny's reputation. More sober consideration, however, would have shown that Eisenhower's

* In order to mislead any possible enemy agents, Lieutenant-Colonel Baldwin B. Smith of Chicago, who was a perfect double of Eisenhower, appeared in various sectors of the combat zone in the uniform of the Supreme Commander, and with the Supreme Commander's escort.

reaction was at least equally realistic. Skorzeny seemed capable of undertaking the craziest of adventures, always provided that it had some possibility of success. In this instance, however, what hope could he have had of getting through an area alive with American convoys, or of making his way along roads jammed with columns moving to the front? It is hardly conceivable that the German general staff ever considered such an operation.

This operation was the primary subject of Skorzeny's first interrogation in early May 1945 after his voluntary surrender. He was so successful in convincing the American security service of his innocence that Colonel Henry G. Sheen, the head of SHAEF counter-espionage service, made a statement to the Allied war correspondents in Paris, giving an unconditional denial of the rumours circulating in December. 'There was not, and there never was, a plot against Eisenhower's life', he said. He further declared that the official statements of the Supreme Headquarters spokesmen were 'cancelled'.*

Astounding though this denial was, no further reference was made to it on the Allied side and it passed into oblivion. The case for the prosecution before the International Tribunal in Nuremberg was—at least from the historian's point of view—full of gaps and omissions, but had there been any reason to think the plans attributed to Skorzeny to be probable, the prosecution could hardly have failed to mention them, particularly when Skorzeny himself appeared on July 31 1946. But in fact he was only subjected to a somewhat vague interrogation on his activities as Head of the SD Training Group; yet in that capacity he had been responsible for organising the espionage and counter-espionage commandos. Moreover when plans for attacks against other generals, such as Weygand and Giraud, said to have been ordered by Hitler personally, were under discussion, no reference was made of a plan to assassinate Eisenhower.

On August 18 1947, when Skorzeny was tried before the American military tribunal in Dachau, his Counsel, Colonel Robert Durst, began to question him about the plot against Eisenhower. There was no reply, and the President passed over the question.

Skorzeny was finally acquitted after evidence had been given by Lieutenant-Colonel Yeo Thomas, the famous 'White Rabbit', to the effect that he also had used procedures similar to those of which Skorzeny was accused. Nevertheless the 'assassination of Eisenhower' will remain as one of the 'Loch Ness Monsters' of the Second World War. Later, in the spring of 1961, Skorzeny was accused of having planned to assassinate Stalin by means of a pistol with poisoned bullets. This was probably a case of confusion with another piece of evidence given at his trial, one of his men

* See also the *New York Times* headline, May 22 1945: 'Nazi Plot against Eisenhower was Hoax.'

from Friedenthal Camp having stated that poisoned bullets had been distributed to the men of Operation Gryphon, a statement which proved to be untrue.

The operation as a whole was certainly not without precedent during the two world wars; nevertheless, Operation Gryphon was outstanding in its scope, originality, audacity and the publicity given to it throughout. The main error on the part of both Hitler and Skorzeny was their fatal underestimation of their enemy; the Americans showed that they were definitely not just 'bank clerks in uniform'.

Skorzeny held 150 Armoured Brigade in readiness in the Losheim area, waiting for the break-through to open up his road to the Meuse bridges. As the opportunity appeared to be getting more and more remote, the brigade was put under the command of I SS Panzer Corps, which sent it into action in front of Malmédy. Having no heavy equipment or artillery, it failed to capture the town, and on December 28 Skorzeny withdrew.

Even then, however, the German High Command did not altogether give up such Trojan Horse operations. On January 18 1945 a secret order was distributed to the units of 257 Volksgrenadier Division on the Saar front. It ordered the formation of long-range, three-man reconnaissance teams. They were to wear white battledress blouses without belt or overcoat, and keep their steel helmets on at all times; they were to leave behind their personal papers and military pay-books. The order stated that 'a few words of American will be enough to get past the American soldiers, and prevent sentries asking for the password.'

The order continued:

At the very least, the following questions and answers will suffice to gain time to allow the men to fire first if need be, or seize a favourable moment to escape. As a rule the sentry will ask for the password by saying 'Who goes there?' The reply should be: 'It's O.K., Joe' or 'It's O.K. Joe. Don't mind me.' If the sentry continues to ask for the password, reply: 'Go on, don't bother me' or 'Lay an egg', or even 'Come up and see me sometime', or again 'So is your ole' man.'

The attempt to deceive by appearing as American soldiers was not, however, so deliberate in this case as in that of Operation Gryphon. The long-range reconnaissance teams were to do no more than spend two nights reconnoitring the American fall-back position; they were not intended to carry out sabotage or to spread panic; in fact, their success depended upon their non-discovery. They did no more than borrow certain technical tricks from Skorzeny's repertoire.

Chapter 15

FROM VERDUN TO VERSAILLES

VERY early on December 19 Eisenhower left his Trianon-Palace head-quarters for Verdun, whither he had summoned Bradley, Patton and Devers to consider the situation created by the first three days of the German offensive.

Only the day before, when a group of French generals and senior officers, led by General Juin, had visited the Supreme Commander, one of them had said to Bedell Smith in a tone of astonishment: 'What! Aren't you packing your bags!' On the face of it Eisenhower and his staff had perhaps been slow to react, the result possibly of the distance separating them from the front, lack of experience of ground conditions in Belgium, lack of imagination or simply the scrappy nature of the information reaching Versailles from the various sectors.

The Supreme Commander's temperament played its part too. Once he had taken a decision, Eisenhower was not one to gnaw his fingernails waiting for results; just as Joffre would take a good night's sleep, he would read a Western thriller. In this case the decisions he had taken on December 16 were beginning to pay off; the flanks of the German salient were holding and resistance was firm at the vital communication points. In the centre there was still a gap of 25 miles between the two airborne divisions and the German armour was pouring through it. But already there were signs that the offensive was running out of steam. It was true that American troop movements were not proceeding exactly with peacetime precision, and the exodus of civilians was increasing the confusion between units moving up and others withdrawing; 200,000 Belgians and Luxembourgers had spontaneously taken to the road to avoid the enemy. In addition the Americans had ordered the evacuation of the displaced persons left behind by the Germans (2,000 in the area of Eupen, Malmédy and Saint-Vith and 4,000 in Luxembourg) and they were wandering aimlessly around.

'I Wish to See Only Cheerful Faces'

Eisenhower travelled to Verdun in an armour-plated car with an escort of military police in machine-gun-carrying jeeps. In spite of all this he was stopped several times at check points, and did not arrive until 11 a.m. The meeting was held in the main hall of the barracks where Bradley had established his headquarters. There was only a solitary stove to take the edge off the cold. Apart from Eisenhower, only his deputy, Air-Marshal Tedder, together with Bradley, Devers, Patton and Bedell Smith, were at the table. Behind them sat a number of staff officers.

General Strong opened the discussion with a summary of the situation. Then Eisenhower spoke. He said:

The present situation is to be regarded as one of opportunity, and not of disaster. There will be only cheerful faces at this conference table. By coming out of the Siegfried Line, the enemy has given us a great opportunity which we should seize as soon as possible. Instead of having to take the Siegfried Line pillbox by pillbox, we can now beat them by defending the Meuse, while at the same time preparing our own offensive.*

Then the Supreme Commander traced the course of events. He had been well aware that the Germans were likely to take advantage of the Allied failure to seize the initiative in the autumn. But before attempting to drive deep into Germany, he wished to reach and consolidate the entire west bank of the Rhine, at least as far south as Bonn; he thought it desirable, though not essential, to go as far as Frankfurt. All Allied action had, however, been delayed by bad weather, inadequacy of stocks, the length of the lines of communication and the shortage of man-power.

Here, however, was an opportunity to manœuvre; it should be possible in one fell swoop to put out of action a considerable proportion of the enemy's resources, instead of the exhausting process of wearing him down by slow and costly local offensives.

Patton broke out with: 'Hell! Let's have the guts to let the —— —— —— go all the way to Paris. Then we'll really cut 'em off and chew 'em up.'

Eisenhower calmed the impulsive Patton down, saying that the Germans would not be allowed to cross the Meuse. The immediate problem was to plug the holes north of the salient and attack its southern flank.

The entire early part of the conference consisted of a dialogue between Eisenhower and Patton. In retrospect it is remarkable that both Eisenhower and Bradley were able to exert their authority over this extraordinary specimen of an American general, a character so different from either of them. Patton was wild, impulsive and tyrannical, something of an iconoclast and yet, according to the experts, an excellent theoretician. He was George Patton II. His grandfather, George Patton I, was an attorney who had organised the first regular unit of the Confederate Army, the 'Kanawha Riflemen' of Virginia—black and green uniform bespattered with gold. George Patton I had reached the rank of general at the age of twenty-eight; he died in 1864.

Judged by his record, the grandson, George Patton II, was the typical cavalry officer. He had entered West Point in 1904, determined to become a top-rank football player and the first man of his year to reach the rank of general; he became a copy-book cavalryman and took part in the Stockholm Olympic Games of 1912; the following year he went to Saumur to learn French methods; while there he made various trips to Normandy

---

* A few days later Churchill wrote to Field-Marshal Smuts: 'The tortoise has thrust his head out very far.'

and Brittany, passing through Saint-Lô, where he was later to make his name. In 1916 he fought against Pancho Villa under Pershing. He returned to Europe in 1917 still only a subaltern, but charged with the formation of the American army's tank units. One year later, as a temporary colonel, he fought his first armoured battle in command of a brigade in the Saint-Mihiel pocket, where he was wounded.

On the outbreak of the Second World War he was posted to California in command of an armoured division selected to study desert warfare. He had read Guderian and Rommel and made a detailed study of their campaigns, which stood him in good stead. In November 1942, on the way to Casablanca, he read the Koran. George Patton, with his cowboy pistol on his hip, was the subject of innumerable stories, many of them pure invention, but all illustrating his impulsiveness. He thrived on publicity and was sometimes vain; he surrounded himself with yes-men. Yet his staff at Third Army alternated between exasperation and hero-worship.*

Unfortunately he was not the only general in the American Army—to say nothing of the British. In his view all of them were in league to do down George Patton and prevent him winning the war on his own. They did not want merely his share of the cake, but the whole cake. Patton shouted and swore in such coarse terms that in spite of all his genius, the British could not stand him. He would have made a wonderful Napoleonic Marshal. His men had nick-named him 'Old Blood and Guts'. But he knew how to handle troops, so the experts said, and they were right, for in six days he now withdrew six divisions from the Saar front, swung them through ninety degrees and moved them 75 miles without a hitch.

This was exactly what Eisenhower was asking him to do, and Eisenhower knew what to expect.

'How many troops can you concentrate? When will you attack? When can you get to Luxembourg to take command of the battle?'

VIII Corps, which had been disorganised by the German offensive, was to be transferred temporarily from First Army to Third Army.

'I can go to Luxembourg this afternoon,' Patton replied.

'To launch a counter-attack in force against the southern flank,' Eisenhower said, 'you must have six divisions. No attack for a week, therefore.'

Patton's reply was: 'I will attack in three days' time, in other words, December 22, with three divisions which are already on the move or about to move. Don't let's lose the advantage of surprise in our counter-attack.'

As Eisenhower expected, Patton was envisaging 'impossible objectives'. He had at the time four corps available: VIII Corps (101 Airborne at Bastogne, 10 Armoured Division, the remnants of 28 Infantry Division

---

* 'A mediaeval character transplanted into our century by accident. Victor Hugo would have said of him "Everything about him was contradictory, and he must be accepted as such." He loved making war just as did Gaston de Foix.' (H. Bernard in *Revue d'histoire de la seconde guerre Mondiale*, October 1958, p. 89.)

(_a_) Infantry of 4 U.S. Armoured Division clearing a way towards encircled Bastogne

(_b_) General Omar Bradley, commander of Twelfth U.S. Army Group

(_c_) General MacAuliffe, defender of Bastogne

8(*a*) General Patton   (*b*) General Juin, French Chief of Sta

(*c*) General de Lattre de Tassigny, commander of the First French Army, and Ge
Marshall, American Chief of Staff

and 9 Armoured Division); III Corps, which was to counter-attack towards Arlon; XII Corps, which was to move up from the Saarguemines–Saaralbe area to hold the hinge of the salient between Echternach and Luxembourg, and XX Corps at Thionville. The latter Patton proposed to direct towards Trier and beyond across the Palatinate, since in his view the elimination of the German salient would be a rapid business.

Eisenhower had to point out to Patton that in the immediate future there could be no question of driving across the base of the bulge towards Saint-Vith. His tasks were, first to ensure that the hinge of the salient at Echternach was securely held, next to hold the enemy advance towards the Meuse and finally to despatch to Bastogne III Corps, consisting of the three divisions concentrated on the previous day.

'Be methodical and sure,' he told him.

Bradley was in agreement with this programme; it was identical with what he had proposed to Patton on the previous day. The immediate objective was clear: to hold Bastogne until the arrival of Third Army on December 22 or 23.

On the northern flank of the salient Montgomery was moving up XXX British Corps towards Louvain, but there were no other possibilities of reinforcements. Ninth U.S. Army, holding the Aix-la-Chapelle front had already had to transfer four divisions to First Army, which was directly involved against Sepp Dietrich. All Ninth Army transport had been mobilised for the movement of reinforcements and the withdrawal of stocks of ammunition and equipment. Its reserves had run so low that one of its artillery groups had just been re-equipped with German 105-mm guns and two others with British twenty-five pounders. The Army might well have to face a second German offensive either north of Aix-la-Chapelle or at Monschau. It was ordered to consolidate its positions and prepare to destroy all stocks, such as ammunition and electrical equipment, which could not be moved at the last moment. It was to put Maastricht into a state of defence and carry out local offensives all along the front in order to gain depth.

To round off these instructions to Ninth Army, Eisenhower asked Montgomery—and confirmed his request next day—to consider 'the possibility of giving up if necessary some ground, in order to shorten our line and collect a strong reserve for the purpose of destroying the enemy in Belgium'.*

In the meanwhile First Army was to do its best to hold on, but was not to count upon receiving any immediate reinforcement.

* Pogue in *The Supreme Command* says that this request was made on December 19; in his memoirs Eisenhower puts it on the following day. Both quote official sources. From this I infer that the request was made twice. The point is of importance, since it was the background to the interpretation Montgomery placed upon his powers.

o

It remained to find the reserves to take over the Saar front which Patton would have to abandon. These could only come from General Devers' Sixth Army Group, which was ordered to detach part of Seventh U.S. Army. This operation necessitated shortening the front. It may well be, therefore, that December 19 was the day on which the question of evacuating Strasbourg first arose, for the line in that area was longer than it might have been primarily due to the Colmar pocket, and withdrawal to the Vosges was the obvious method of shortening it. In his memoirs Eisenhower links to the Verdun conference his disagreements with the French government on this subject. It seems, however, that he did not seriously consider withdrawing the Alsace front before December 26.

The Situation Deteriorates

While the Allied rebound was thus being prepared at Verdun, the Germans were renewing their attack and the Americans improvising some sort of counter to it as best they could.

The Schnee Eifel, now far behind the German lines, was a scene of drama. At dawn the remnants of the two surrounded American regiments were still waiting for a supply drop of rations, ammunition and water, without which they could not hold out. The previous day all aircraft had been grounded by bad weather, but on December 19 a few fighter-bombers appeared over the area. All transport aircraft were still grounded by fog in England, but one would have thought that these fighter-bombers could have done some improvised dropping. The Ninth Tactical Air Command Liaison Officer with VIII Corps stated with some reason: 'Somebody in First Army should be court-martialled for the delay which was involved'.*

The surviving units of these abandoned regiments put up a last fight in an attempt to break out westwards. 423 Infantry Regiment, now at only 50 per cent strength, fought all day in an effort to reach Schönberg, but was eventually broken up. As 422 Infantry Regiment moved westwards, the Germans followed up closely and occupied the positions it evacuated. The individual battalions were eventually surrounded and forced to surrender. Thanks largely to the resistance of these two regiments, three days had been gained for the defenders of Saint-Vith; they had undoubtedly fought with great courage. Over the next forty-eight hours small groups of men who had managed to escape capture continued to get through to their own lines or to the garrison of Bastogne.

Saint-Vith was given some respite during this day, owing to lack of co-ordination between the German Fifth and Sixth Panzer Armies. To the north, the SS Armour was already some 25 miles past the town, but

---

* Quoted by Colonel R. E. Dupuy, *St. Vith—106 Infantry Division in World War II*, p. 135; he adds that in his opinion this affair ought to have been the subject of a Congressional investigation.

their supply columns became jammed on the narrow forest roads, blocking the routes of the next-door army.

In the south, Manteuffel had pushed his leading armour up to Saint-Vith and 15 miles beyond it. He kept up considerable artillery activity in order to prevent 7 U.S. Armoured Division and the two engineer units consolidating their positions. He was clearly preparing for an attack in force. Meanwhile the remnants of 9 U.S. Armoured Division, which had been hustled off the Our, streamed back towards the town.

To turn to Bastogne, 101 Airborne was engaged in fighting with the Panzer Lehr from first light onwards. As the day went on, Bayerlein found that whatever way he tried to outflank the town, he encountered resistance; his enthusiasm for battle began to wane. It waned even further when early in the afternoon he was slightly wounded and found himself being cared for by an American nurse, who had been captured with an advanced surgical team. She was so pretty, and the look in her eye so disturbing to Bayerlein that the general remained in the vicinity of the First Aid Post until the evening.

On the other side, however, Middleton, commanding VIII U.S. Corps and the troops defending Bastogne, had few causes for optimism. During the morning 2 Panzer coming in from the north, had driven a parachute battalion and a small force of tanks off the high ground at Noville. This clearly heralded a full-dress attack from that direction next day. Only one reinforcing unit arrived, 1705 Tank Destroyer Battalion from the Aix-la-Chapelle front.

In the east the parachute troops withdrew during the afternoon, step by step and suffering heavy losses. During the evening a 'glider' regiment took up positions south and west of the town, to forestall any attack developing from that direction and taking the main body of the parachutists and armour fighting on the eastern outskirts in the rear.

There was no hope of any further reinforcement. During the day, 250 fugitives arrived from Luxembourg. (The total was to rise to 600 during the following weeks.) But they had neither equipment nor transport. Moreover their morale was appalling, as would be expected with men who had become used to victory, and suddenly found themselves overrun in a quiet sector; they clearly could not be put into the line. The prospects of further ammunition supply did not appear much better; a small number of lorries came in along the Neufchâteau road, and delivered 1,500 105 mm rounds. An hour later the road was cut by the Germans; it was clear that that would be all.

Part of the civil population of Bastogne, terrified by the return of the Germans, had rushed off along the roads to Neufchateau, Saint-Hubert and Marche, with no clear idea of where they were going. Those who remained, however, seemed, according to the Americans, completely impervious to danger. They walked about in the streets quite unconcerned, looking at the damage caused by the artillery fire. During the afternoon, however, MacAuliffe, who had meanwhile been appointed garrison commander, knowing from experience the difficulties caused to military movement by a flood of refugees, forbade anyone else to leave the town. Civilians were also forbidden to leave their cellars except between midday and 2 p.m. to buy food. The Germans might begin infiltrating into the town at any moment, and if there were no civilians on the streets it would be easier to pick up any enemy scouts who might come in in civilian clothes. The American authorities were so afraid of the appearance of German irregulars that shortly afterwards they forbade movement even of the small Belgian detachments employed to prevent looting.

On the other side, von Lüttwitz, commanding the German XLVII Corps, was as despondent as Bayerlein. None of his divisions was making noticeable progress; of his two armoured divisions, the Panzer Lehr was not making headway against Bastogne, and in the north 2 Panzer had failed to break through towards the Meuse. He reported to Manteuffel: 'We shall not break through the parachute troops unless we use the entire Corps; it is no good leaving the whole job to 26 Volksgrenadier Division.' But that evening Manteuffel turned down von Lüttwitz' request.

On the southern flank of the salient, facing the German Seventh Army, the Allied centres of resistance were either giving way in face of repeated attacks or being surrounded. Wiltz surrendered on December 20; the Americans evacuated Diekirch on December 19, and it remained in no man's land until the Germans entered it next day. Patton took full advantage of the delay to get matters under control. At Ettelbrück, an objective of the first importance on the Luxembourg road, there was a similar delay; the low grade Volksgrenadier divisions hesitated and so one of the vital routes for Third Army's movement was saved.

Further east, 4 U.S. Infantry Division, exhausted though it was, disputed every inch of ground, and the Volksgrenadier failed to capture the Luxembourg–Consdorf–Berdorf–Echternach road.

On the northern flank, the situation in First U.S. Army area stabilised during the day. In thick mist which lasted throughout the morning, 30 U.S. Infantry Division was involved in heavy fighting on the high ground above the Amblève with the Peiper Force armour trying to break through northwards. At midday the Germans withdrew, but the American battalion most heavily engaged had lost 250 men out of 450. It was then reinforced by another battalion and a tank destroyer battalion which had never been in action. The Germans resumed their attack but by nightfall it had been brought to a halt and the American infantry had recovered some 2,000 yards of ground.

While this fighting was going on around Stoumont another battalion of 30 U.S. Infantry Division was in Stavelot, engaged in an attempt to eliminate the small area through which 1 SS Panzer transport was moving. Heavy fighting went on from dawn to midnight. Meanwhile Oberführer Möhnke, commanding 1 SS Panzer, made ready for a new attempt to cross the Salm and the Amblève to reinforce Peiper.

At the same time, 10 miles further west, 82 Airborne was consolidating on a line north and south. Ridgway arrived and set up his headquarters at Werbomont. XVIII Airborne Corps, consisting for the moment only of 82 Airborne Division (101 being in Bastogne), was to cover the centre from the Amblève on the north to Houffalize in the south. Towards the end of the afternoon the parachute troops moved cautiously eastwards, to close the pocket now forming around Peiper.

On their right 116 Panzer, one of Manteuffel's formations, reached Houffalize and by-passed it. Only the fact that the bridge over the Ourthe north of Bertogne had been blown prevented the Germans reaching La Roche and Marche that evening. 116 Panzer was now the spearhead of the German offensive, and in front of it there was nothing—nothing but its objectives, including the most important of them all, the Meuse.

The Versailles Decisions

Faced with this development in the situation on his return to Versailles that evening, Eisenhower was forced to admit that the decisions taken at Verdun had already been overtaken by events. Rundstedt still had six Panzer and Panzergrenadier divisions not yet engaged; if he pushed these through the Houffalize gap there was nothing to prevent him reaching Dinant, Givet and Namur, and then swinging back against Liège, which was still thought to be his primary objective.

The latest prisoners' statements showed that the aim of the operation was more ambitious than Liège, and that Antwerp was the ultimate objective. It seemed likely that the German High Command would try to get there by using the method Manteuffel had employed so successfully, a series of enveloping movements designed to split the Allied front. The main German effort seemed to be directed northwards.

It was not yet clear where the ultimate stop-line should be, whether between Liège and Roermond, or at the mouths of the Rhine, or along the Meuse. In any case, however, the fresh divisions capable of putting up the necessary resistance were north of the German salient and these divisions were under Montgomery's command. While they were being concentrated the field-marshal had sent forward covering detachments to the bridges from Liège to Givet, and was keeping the roads leading to Brussels under observation in order to stop any German reconnaissance detachments.

If the Germans continued to push on energetically, Bradley would be quite unable to control both flanks of the salient. To get from one to the other by road would entail a long journey over dangerous roads; telephone and radio communications went straight across the battlefield—there was one direct buried telephone cable, which was cut on December 23, and three radio relay stations, at Jemelle, Ettelbrück and Aubange; the Germans allowed these to continue to function for several days after they had captured them, since they could thus intercept all messages.*

Eisenhower was forced to the conclusion that under these conditions Bradley would not at all times be able to control First and Ninth Armies.

There was only one solution, and early that night Bedell Smith telephoned to Bradley: 'Ike thinks it may be a good idea to turn over to Monty your two armies in the north and let him run that side of the bulge from 21st Group. It may save us a great deal of trouble, especially if your communications with Hodges and Simpson go out.'

Bradley replied: 'If Monty's were an American command I would agree with you entirely.'

The question of prestige was at the root of his objection. If Eisenhower's suggestion indicated that he had been disowned, he would have to be sent back to the United States; otherwise American commanders would be entirely discredited in the eyes of the British. In any case, what had the British done since the start of the offensive? Hodges was holding on in the north and in the south it was Patton who was going to attack.

But on the morning of December 20 Eisenhower confirmed Bedell Smith's instructions: 'Those are my orders, Brad.'

Bradley bowed to the inevitable. Shortly afterwards, he discussed Eisenhower's motives with Patton; either, he thought, Eisenhower was simply lacking in confidence in him or he had been stampeded. To make over to Montgomery a part of the American forces (eighteen divisions in all) would put Montgomery a long way on the road to his ambition ultimately to take over command of all Allied land forces.

All Patton's old grievances revived: ever since September Ike had always favoured the British, he said; he had allocated to them so much transport and fuel that the victorious career of Third Army had been halted.

Eisenhower did all he could to soothe his old friend Bradley's wounded *amour propre*, laying down that the division of the front was to be temporary only and limited strictly to the period of the counter-offensive. He asked Marshall to promote Bradley immediately, and made a public statement that the withdrawal of the two armies constituted no reflection upon him, but was purely an operational necessity. He admitted that mistakes had been made prior to the German offensive, but stated that the offensive had not been foreseen primarily because air reconnaissance had been stopped by bad weather.

None of it did any good. Bradley's and Patton's staffs were already giving vent to the most bitter reproaches, calling Eisenhower a weakling, under

* Twelfth Army Group Final After-action Report, Vol XI, p. 204, signal section.

the thumb of British officers who were always afraid of some threat to
Antwerp. It was through these officers, they said, that Montgomery was
exerting his pressure, and the division of the battlefield he had now
managed to achieve was an undreamed of present for the Germans.

It is a fact that Montgomery considered it urgent to take a grip of First
and Ninth Armies; in a telegram to Field-Marshal Alan Brooke, despatched on the evening of the 19th, he stated that he had impressed upon
Whiteley that he should be given the job. It is also true that both General
Whiteley, Assistant Chief of Staff Operations at SHAEF, and General
Strong, Head of the Intelligence Division, were British officers. During
the discussions in the early evening of December 19, it was Strong who
had emphasised how difficult it would be for Bradley to conduct operations
both north and south of the bulge. He and Whiteley had spoken to Bedell
Smith, who in turn had convinced Eisenhower.

Eisenhower took the decision on his own, merely reporting the matter
to the Joint Chiefs of Staff in Washington, without asking for authorisation. On the morning of December 20 he informed Montgomery, who
immediately telegraphed to Alan Brooke: 'I am to assume command of the
northern front. That was all I wanted to know.' When Churchill telephoned to Eisenhower during the afternoon to ask him to divide the front
the Supreme Commander was able to tell him that he had already
anticipated his wishes.

The American generals, who considered that they had been betrayed
by Eisenhower, failed to take into account the timing of these various steps.
They forgot, moreover, that Eisenhower's staff was truly 'integrated', and
that Whiteley and Strong were merely giving proof that in their view the
interests of the alliance outweighed any national consideration.

In fact the basic difference between Bradley and Eisenhower lay in their
general attitude of mind. Bradley merely thought the situation 'unpleas-
antly vague'; the important point in his eyes was that the flanks of the
salient were holding, and in his heart he was convinced that the Germans
would be exhausted before they ever reached the Meuse. He believed that
the enemy had lost the initiative and that the Allies therefore had freedom
of manœuvre. Eisenhower, on the other hand, felt that German energy
was not yet exhausted and that they still had surprises in store, that urgent
preventive action must therefore be taken, although in principle the
decisions taken at the Verdun conference still held good.

The Three-Day Blackout Lifted

On the morning of December 19 an Allied communiqué dated December 18 was issued to the press; the impression it gave was that Supreme
Headquarters was in no way anxious and considered the offensive merely
a manœuvre by the enemy designed to gain time and to interfere with

possible Allied plans. Although it gave little away, it marked the end of the complete three-day silence imposed by Eisenhower.

It is only fair to say that the German communiqué showed an equal optimism and similar discretion; it said: 'The major offensive battle is pursuing its course.' It too appeared three days after the events concerned.

The war correspondents had become used to knowing practically everything, and so they were furious to discover that their first despatches had been delayed in transmission. Some of them, invoking their sacred duty to keep their readers informed, demanded seats on aeroplanes in order to return to the United States and give an uninhibited account of what they had 'established', which was that the front was breaking down, that it was being submerged by floods of German parachutists disguised as G.I.s, that a fifth column in France had risen, that Paris and Versailles were directly threatened, and that Eisenhower was under permanent threat of assassination.

SHAEF merely replied, 'No space will be available for weeks, either on ships or aircraft.'

The war correspondents were stuck in Europe.

Such a news black-out was no innovation. It had been an accompaniment of all previous major operations. But then it had been a question of offensive action, of keeping the enemy in ignorance of the direction and strength of the next blow. Under those conditions the journalists had accepted the fact that they were only allowed to know the minimum. In December, however, the atmosphere was such that they suspected the object to be the concealment of bad news and, even worse, the evasion of responsibility.

Basically, however, there were good reasons for Eisenhower's step. Experience had proved that any information given out was reproduced within an hour by the BBC and the Press Agencies. The Germans admitted that the best—and the most frequently used—source of information concerning the situation at the front was the British wireless.

Nevertheless the Allied staff would have been better advised to give the journalists—who were doing no more than their job—a little carefully selected information. With nothing available from official sources both the war correspondents and the military critics were reduced to embroidering upon the rumours brought back from the front by liaison officers or picked up from the headquarters clerks. An editorial in one of the more sober British newspapers, for instance, contained references to 'the capture of Malmédy' (which was in fact never taken), 'a German offensive towards Givet, Mezières and Sedan', 'successful action by German heavy tanks', 'Rundstedt's determination to economise his forces as far as possible', 'the absolute and permanent superiority of the German soldier over the American'. The tone of the popular press, which daily demanded some 'human drama' feature, can therefore easily be imagined. It was hardly surprising that New York began to hear the rustle of a breeze reminiscent of Pearl Harbour.*

The fact remains, however, that as a result of this black-out, on the evening of December 19 Eisenhower did not have to worry about the reactions of the war correspondents, through whom he might have been able to sense the emotional reactions of the peoples they represented. If the waves of protest from British and American public opinion had entered into his calculations, Eisenhower would never have decided to divide the battlefield or to give way, even on the surface, to Montgomery.

Through being held in check for a time these reactions were all the more vigorous when they came. This is a long way from saying, however, as Bedell Smith did in 1946 in his eulogy of 'Eisenhower's six great decisions', that the press alone was responsible for the fear felt by the entire free world at this period. Smith went so far as to say that he and Eisenhower had only learnt subsequently from the newspapers how great was the danger from which the Allied armies had escaped. The Germans, he said, had never been able to advance with any real speed; they had never gained more than 5 miles in a day, whereas during the race from the Channel to the Ardennes the Allied divisions had been covering 30 miles a day.

If these statements are taken literally, they merely prove that the information available to the Supreme Commander's staff must have been very incomplete.

In fact this was probably only a belated explosion of ill humour, resulting from the very differing treatment accorded to different generals by journalists, who obviously had their likes and dislikes.

The fact remains also that a good argument leads to good reporting, and whenever a spokesman states that he is giving the press simply 'facts, true facts', he must expect his audience to become highly critical.

* As soon as the danger was over the American command showed that its intentions towards the press were still good: 'Briefing correspondents should be at a high level and, subject to varying circumstances, correspondents should be given the entire story to provide a background in which a true overall picture can be written. . . . Facts, the true facts, have been considered the prime weapons of psychological warfare.' (Twelfth Army Group After-action Report, Vol. XIV, p. 68.)

Chapter 16

MONTGOMERY THE ORACLE

AT 1 p.m. on December 20, Montgomery arrived at Hodges' headquarters at Chaudfontaine 'supremely confident and cheerful', in the words of General de Guingand, his Chief of Staff.

Another of his staff officers said that he entered like 'Christ about to cleanse the Temple'. The evening before he had telegraphed to Alan Brooke, 'There is a definite lack of grip and control; no one seems to have a clear picture as to the situation . . . I have heard nothing from him [Eisenhower] or Bradley . . . I have myself had no orders or requests of any sort.' But before this telegram had even arrived at its destination, the Supreme Commander had come to take counsel of the oracle, the British field-marshal, the saviour.

As soon as Whiteley's telephone call arrived the previous evening Montgomery had despatched liaison officers and he had their reports before going to Chaudfontaine. Perhaps because he was better informed, he saw things more clearly than Hodges. In any case he knew what he wanted. He was so sure of it, that had General de Guingand not been there to pour oil, this first contact might have been a sour one.

The Defence Balance Sheet

Hodges was convinced that the German offensive was aimed at Liège and so clung to his initial concept—to resist at all costs between Monschau and Stavelot, to attack eastwards from Werbomont to take the enemy in flank as he moved north, and then to join up with the defenders of Saint-Vith. He apparently took no account of the possibility of a resumption of the enemy offensive, nor would he consider even the smallest alteration to his plan.

Montgomery was convinced that Liège was of only secondary interest to the Germans and that their primary objective was the Meuse between Liège and Namur. The Luftwaffe, after all, had been ordered not to bomb bridges in this area. In his view the main Allied effort must be made forward of Huy and Namur, and a reserve formed in the Durbuy–Marche–Ciney area, ready to counter-attack in any direction.

This reserve, however, still had to be assembled. Montgomery proposed that VII U.S. Corps should disengage from the Roer front, leaving that to Ninth Army, and move to the Marche area. First Army should also shorten its front by withdrawing from the salient between Monschau and Malmédy, bringing back its most severely mauled divisions.

'No,' Hodges replied. 'The American troops will not withdraw.'

No argument could shift him. His determination was reinforced by the arrival of a letter from General Hasbrouck in Saint-Vith, announcing that as from the next day he would be completely cut off. This seemed no moment to abandon this garrison and leave it within the German lines.

Montgomery gave way. That evening he reported to Eisenhower 'I see no reason for the moment to give up an inch of the territory we have won at the price of severe fighting in recent days.'

He approved Hodges' directive to Ridgway, ordering XVIII Airborne Corps to 're-establish the line Malmédy–Saint-Vith–Houffalize, and gain contact with the units in Bastogne'. The immediate task of this corps was to advance simultaneously both east and south-east, and to form a firm screen in front of the German advance, behind which VII Corps would concentrate around Marche.

Further back, beyond the Meuse, XXX British Corps would await developments in the area between Namur and Liège; it was not to come into action unless the enemy established bridgeheads, since any move on to the right bank of the Meuse would merely have created traffic blocks and complicated the American supply arrangements.

General Lee, commanding the Services of Supply, had been in charge of measures to defend the river since December 17. It was now covered by two main and six secondary zones of obstacles.*

None of the bridges over the Meuse had been blown, but throughout the battle area 257 bridges had been prepared for demolition and 70 bridges over the tributaries of the Meuse had been blown as a precaution. Each of the Meuse bridges was guarded by a detachment equipped with searchlights and machine guns; the bridge piles were surrounded by barbed wire to keep off frogmen, who at Nijmegen had come down with the stream pushing explosive charges in front of them. The sentries were to fire on sight at anything floating or apparently floating which came near

---

* The main zones were:

(a) Eupen to Butgenbach and thence Malmédy, then following the Amblève and Ourthe down to Hotton and Marche, and thence to the Meuse between the Lomme and Lesse.

(b) Along the left bank of the Meuse from Maastricht to Givet.

Secondary zones:

(a) Along the Salm from Trois-Ponts to Bovigny.
(b) Along the Ourthe from Hotton to Ortho and Sibret, and thence to the Sure.
(c) North-east of Bastogne.
(d) To the rear of Spa from Remouchamps to Limbourg.
(e) A final stop-line along the Vesdre from Eupen to Chêné and thence to the lower Ourthe.

the bridges. This order proved sound: at Visé a steel helmet was seen floating downstream. At the eleventh bullet it blew up only a hundred yards from the Bailey Bridge. The explosion did considerable damage to houses on the river bank.

When the engineers drew up their balance sheet after the battle they announced that in First Army area alone 505 minefields, comprising 115,000 anti-tank mines, had been laid; 120,000 other mines had been issued to units and 370 light construction pillboxes had been built at the main cross-roads.

This list of obstacles made reassuring reading for the staffs, but in fact the engineers were frequently compelled to withdraw or go into action before they had completed their job. Moreover in the frost-hardened ground and with the protection of the snowdrifts, the minefields were frequently of very doubtful value, and on many occasions more dangerous to the Allied side than the enemy. Corridors through them had to be left free for retreating units, and the Germans frequently followed hard on their heels.

*   *   *

After seeing Bradley at Luxembourg, Patton spent the day of December 20 going round his corps. He was in command of the entire front from Givet to Prum, and the tasks he laid down were: III Corps to attack on December 21 from Arlon towards Saint-Vith; VIII Corps to continue to hold the area Neufchâteau–Bastogne and to reorganise with a view to attacking northwards.

It was completely immaterial to Eisenhower whether the situation was saved by Patton or Montgomery. He simply knew that the battle would now be got under control without further intervention by him; he returned to Versailles, where in effect he became a prisoner. Indirectly he was a prisoner of Skorzeny and his forty commandos; directly of Supreme Head-quarters security services. On the insistence of his staff, the Supreme Commander left von Rundstedt's old villa in Saint-Germain; the possi-bility of an ambush on the road was thought to be too great! Everywhere were barbed wire, double guards, tanks and stringent security checks. The Trianon-Palace was in a state of siege, and the atmosphere there was tenser than at either Chaudfontaine or Luxembourg. Even Kay Summersby and Ruth Briggs, Eisenhower's other secretary, were incarcerated within the security enclosure. They knew too much about the Supreme Commander's business to be allowed to run the risks of the Versailles or Paris streets.

Eisenhower champed at the bit; he was the only one who did not think that there might be some German sharpshooter concealed in the garden of the Palace of Versailles watching him take his daily walk.

Consolidation of the Northern Flank of the Salient

Except in the immediate area of the Meuse, the boundary between Montgomery and Bradley was the same to within a few miles as that between Sepp Dietrich and Manteuffel.*

The battle therefore now fell into two sectors, which can logically be dealt with separately. It was in the days up to December 25 that the period of doubt and hesitation was to come to an end, the German offensive was finally to run out of steam, and the Allied line was to be stabilised.

The courageous defence of Saint-Vith was a major factor in the success of Montgomery's plans. It will be remembered that during December 20 General Hasbrouck, commanding 7 U.S. Armoured Division, together with the small garrison of Saint-Vith, had asked for urgent assistance. He clearly did not realise what the overall situation was, and the instructions he received from his immediate superior, General Middleton, VIII Corps Commander, did little to enlighten him. They were dated December 19 but arrived only on the evening of the 20th, and described the German front as consisting merely of 'pockets' which should be eliminated. First Army Situation Report of the same day also merely stated: 'Small enemy groups are in rear of our line' — a singularly euphemistic way of describing the situation, showing how inadequate the available information was.

Saint-Vith was now the bottleneck preventing the deployment of the SS armour of II Armoured Corps. Both Sepp Dietrich and Manteuffel spent the day of December 20 moving into position the forces necessary to capture the place. Three divisions were already on the ground; to these Sepp Dietrich added the Führerbegleitbrigade (the Führer's Escort Brigade), an independent unit formed from Hitler's Guard Battalion. It was commanded by General Otto Remer, who only six months previously had been a battalion commander. His promotion was no doubt due to the fact that, together with Goebbels, he had played a decisive role in crushing the revolt of July 20. Once the town had been captured, 9 SS Panzer, an 'O.K.W. Reserve' like the Escort Brigade and therefore under Hitler's direct orders, was to exploit westwards.

For a time the two sides waited, probing each other's positions in small local actions. The American engineers laid minefields on the edge of the woods and the cavalry dug in their tanks to strengthen their positions. The Germans kept themselves hidden. In places they infiltrated and their artillery hammered the surrounding villages.

On the morning of December 21 the German artillery fire increased and fighting became more severe. During the afternoon the Germans blazed away for two hours with everything they had. Only one American artillery group was available, and that could not reply owing to lack of ammunition.

* The line in fact ran from Givet, south of La Roche, north of Houffalize, south of Saint-Vith to Prum and Cologne.

The assault came at 6 p.m. along the Schönberg road, which in order to leave open the possibility of an American counter-attack, was the only one which had not been mined. The Germans poured down by every track, followed by lorried infantry detachments and mortars mounted on tracked vehicles. They overran the centres of resistance on the eastern outskirts

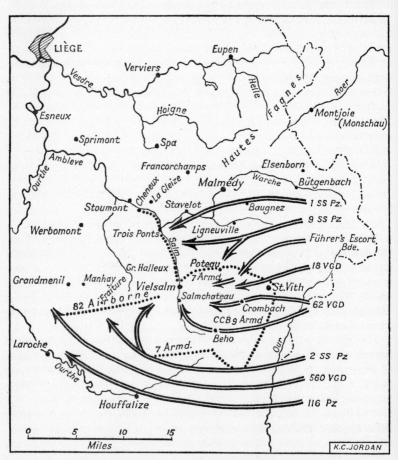

The Elimination of the Saint-Vith Salient. December 17–23

and penetrated into the town. Groups of Americans continued to resist for a further few hours, before attempting to withdraw towards their own lines. Some fifty engineers succeeded in getting through to Vielsalm, where General Hasbrouck had just set up the headquarters of the remnants of 7 Armoured Division and 106 Infantry Division.

Manteuffel later told the American historian Robert Merriam: 'I wanted to have Saint-Vith on December 17. Although I had expected that Bastogne would be defended, I did not think that the Americans would be able to defend Saint-Vith.'

So the Germans were now five days behind schedule, their armoured divisions were marking time and their supply echelons were piling up on top of each other; they took two further days to deal with the American remnants between Saint-Vith and Vielsalm. All this can be put to the credit of the defence of Saint-Vith. It had gained the time necessary to establish U.S. First Army on a new line, behind which the British reserves were moving into position. There was still plenty of punch left in the German offensive, but the 'Battle of the Bulge' legend gives too much credit to the defenders of Bastogne at the expense of those of Saint-Vith. Without the latter, Bastogne could probably not have been held, for Manteuffel would quickly have widened the gap and outflanked the Allies as they moved up to contain the German salient.

While II SS Panzer Corps marked time in the Saint-Vith area, Sepp Dietrich's route westwards was blocked; his advanced guard, the Peiper Force, could find no way out of the valley of the Amblève for its advance on Huy.

119 U.S. Infantry Regiment reinforced by a combat command of 3 Armoured Division was now established on the high ground north of the Amblève between La Gleize and Stoumont. Peiper spent three days trying to break through them. During the night of December 20–21, however, he was cut off from the rear. A group of U.S. engineers, though under fire, succeeded in manhandling a thousand pounds of T.N.T. through to Stavelot and blew up one span of the bridge. The next night Peiper had to be supplied by parachute.

The Waffen SS dug in around Stoumont Sanatorium, a strongpoint against which all American attacks broke with heavy losses. By the evening of December 21 General Harrison, the local American commander, was losing heart, having suffered 200 casualties. On December 22, however, he succeeded in capturing the village of Stoumont, thus dividing the German force in two. One half was immediately attacked by 82 Airborne between Cheneux and the Amblève; the other concentrated in La Gleize and fought a delaying action throughout the 23rd.

Peiper was now running short of supplies and his position was hopeless. He was ordered to withdraw towards the German lines. His petrol being exhausted, he could do no other than set fire to his vehicles and try to get through the American front on foot.

Peiper told Major MacGown, a 119 Infantry Regiment battalion commander whom he had captured two days earlier, that he now had no more than 800 men.

At about 3 a.m. on December 24 the column collected in a bend of the

Amblève near the hamlet of La Venne and crossed the river—in Mac-Gown's words, 'on a small footbridge underneath the railway'. Two hours later, just before dawn, the whole force was across and had reached the area of Brume. The Germans looked back; a tank blew up and all the abandoned vehicles caught fire. At 10 a.m. that morning American infantry moved into La Gleize, setting free 140 American prisoners and some wounded from both sides who were under the care of a German medical officer.

Throughout the day of December 24 Peiper reconnoitred the valleys leading down to the Amblève, with his prize prisoner, MacGown, in tow between two guards. He knew he was in no man's land but could not locate the American positions with any accuracy. As night fell, he moved off silently south-eastwards towards Trois-Ponts. MacGown reported: 'We could have passed within two hundred yards of an outpost without detection.' On two occasions the advance guard exchanged shots with American outposts and then the column arrived in the area which was being hammered by the artillery of both sides. MacGown gave his SS guards the slip, and 200 yards further on came upon a patrol from the U.S. Airborne.

The La Gleize-Stoumont pocket having been reduced, there remained a strong German bridgehead above the point at which the Salm flowed into the Amblève, on the high ground overlooking Stavelot. Below it in the river gorge a 3 U.S. Armoured Division detachment had been unwise enough to install itself. Fighting between this detachment and the SS infantry went on for two days. The latter were not dislodged until Christmas Day, and then only by three battalions and some tanks. The sky having cleared, they were supported by Thunderbolts; unfortunately the fighting in the valley was so confused that targets were difficult to distinguish, and they earned themselves the name of 'U.S. Luftwaffe' from the men of the tank troop. The remnants of 1 SS Panzer then withdrew across the Amblève, along which the German line now ran.

The situation was therefore slowly turning in favour of the Allies, though this was hardly discernible when, on December 22, Eisenhower published one of his rare Orders of the Day—the only one between August 14 1944 and April 20 1945. It showed insistent optimism and was couched in a sober style, but to those at the front still in the height of the crisis it must have had the ring of the illusions to which those in the rear were subject. They were just reeling under the blow of the loss of Saint-Vith and were still racing to plug the holes in front of the German advance, and so were somewhat bitter at being invited to 'rise now to new heights of courage, of resolution and of effort'.

Recalling that the Germans were playing their last card and that their plans had already been checkmated by the valour of the Allied troops, Eisenhower stated: 'We must not be content purely and simply to push the enemy back. By rushing out from his fixed defences the enemy may give us the chance to turn his great gamble into his worst defeat.'

In the end the Supreme Commander was justified by events. At the time they hardly seemed to accord with his forecast.

Gavin to the Rescue

The only other fresh troops on the northern flank of the salient were 82 Airborne of Ridgway's XVIII Airborne Corps, commanded by 'Slim Jim' Gavin. This division, now on a north–south line, had been given the task of finally bringing Sixth Panzer Army to a halt. On December 20 Montgomery authorised Gavin to 're-establish the line Malmédy–Saint-Vith' and 'eliminate any German pockets west of this position'. By the next day it was already too late; it was the Germans who were eliminating the American pockets between Saint-Vith and the Salm, and there was no possibility of preventing them. 82 Airborne therefore moved up to the Salm with two tasks: to establish contact with the units cut off in the Saint-Vith–Vielsalm area, and—with the support of a combat command from 3 Armoured Division—to throw out a screen on their flank to stop Manteuffel's advance east of the Ourthe.

The object was to fight a rearguard action long enough to enable VII U.S. Corps to concentrate behind the Airborne Division and counter-attack the head of the German advance.

On the right bank of the Salm the American salient was contracting under the pressure of three German divisions and Remer's brigade. Exhausted and short of both equipment and supplies as these last American units were, they did their utmost to stop the enemy infiltrating forward, as long as was necessary to enable the airborne troops hurrying up to reinforce them to consolidate their positions. Throughout December 21 and the following night the latter moved up towards the Salm.* This meant carrying out a manœuvre most distasteful both to Gavin and to Ridgway —withdrawal. In his operational report Gavin stated: 'The Division had never withdrawn throughout all its battles.' Both generals were confident in the capabilities of their men and did not share Montgomery's caution. The latter was convinced that the German offensive must be allowed to exhaust itself and should be countered by an elastic defence.

Ridgway had told Hasbrouck to hold on in Saint-Vith as long as possible, but had nevertheless reconnoitred for fall-back positions. He did not, however, intend to occupy them unless forced to do so.

Once Saint-Vith had fallen, however, Hasbrouck reiterated his view to Montgomery, and during the night December 22–23, was ordered to withdraw. At dawn that day, in a snowstorm, he began a movement which,

---

* 82 Airborne's front ran along an arc of a circle from La Gleize via Cheneux-Trois-Ponts–Grand Halleux–Vielsalm–Salmchâteau to Hebronval.

in spite of German pressure on the rear-guards, ended by getting 22,000 men across the river to Vielsalm and Salmchâteau over three bridges. After covering the withdrawal of the last detachments, the airborne troops also crossed back on to the left bank. Guided by refugees from the Eifel, whom the Americans had evacuated to this area, the first German tanks entered both places on the heels of the airborne troops.

82 Airborne was now faced by four German divisions and was in danger of being outflanked on its right by 2 SS Panzer which had just reached the area. During December 24 the division withdrew, although according to Gavin the men 'did not understand why' and occupied a position facing south-east from Trois-Ponts to Manhay. During Christmas Day one of its regiments, No. 505, 'withdrew through the enemy'. The Germans concerned probably formed part of the Peiper Force. One wonders why there was no fighting. In fact the caution exercised on both sides was probably due to exhaustion, anxiety, pressure of time and a noticeable sinking of morale.

Gavin's second task, to block a section of the gap still open at the point of the salient, also meant that he must fight a delaying action while the reserves were being concentrated. Sepp Dietrich's problem was similar: he had failed to capture Elsenborn and the Amblève valley was blocked; he must therefore, take advantage of Manteuffel's break-through on his left, sidestep through the gap and outflank 82 Airborne. To do this he had to make good the Houffalize–Liège road (with the key road junctions of Baraque-Fraiture and Manhay) before moving towards the Ourthe and Marche or north-westwards. He detailed 2 SS Panzer for the task.

At Baraque-Fraiture strong points held by a few tanks and the remnants of an artillery group which had made its way back from 106 Infantry Division, held out from December 20–23 against increasingly violent attacks. On December 23 they were reinforced by one Airborne Company but were forced to withdraw the same day by a converging attack. This left open the flank of XVIII Airborne Corps.

On Christmas Eve Sepp Dietrich made a fresh attempt to break through, capturing Manhay and Grandmesnil, where 2 SS Panzer dug in. Throughout the 25th, two U.S. battalions made violent attacks on both villages, losing many men from point blank machine-gun fire. Fighting continued during the night and eventually the American infantry recaptured Manhay. At dawn on December 26, reinforced by parts of 75 Infantry Division which had just arrived from Normandy, the Americans counter-attacked from three directions. For eight hours, the 'Greenhorns' together with the survivors from the Schnee Eifel and Saint-Vith gnawed their way into the German positions and captured them, recovering 3 miles of ground and finally denying the Houffalize–Liège road to the enemy.

This sector of the front then calmed down, but Sepp Dietrich's fourth attempt to break through had forced Lawton Collins, Commanding

VII U.S. Corps, to put in one of the units destined for the counter-offensive.

During December 26, Sepp Dietrich launched one final attack all along the front of 82 Airborne, which was now facing south-east. There was very severe fighting between 9 SS Panzer and 508 Airborne, but when night fell the American main line of defence was still intact. The front was now stabilised and Ridgway began to suspect that under cover of a violent artillery bombardment, Sixth Panzer Army was preparing to withdraw. On Ridgway's right, however, 83 Infantry Division only arrived at Rochefort in the nick of time on December 27. It was immediately attacked by 9 Panzer, which Manteuffel had despatched to assist 2 Panzer, now the leading German formation but thoroughly disorganised.

The Unhappy Affair of the Bombing of Malmédy

At the northern tip of his front Sepp Dietrich had put in four divisions in a final assault on Elsenborn on December 23 and 24, but the attack had failed. Sixth Panzer Army then handed over the area to the neighbouring army, the Fifteenth, which remained on the defensive up to the end of January. To free his northern flank and assist his attack on Elsenborn, Sepp Dietrich planned to draw American reinforcements towards Malmédy. The outskirts of the town were held by 30 U.S. Infantry Division, which anticipated that the enemy would attack its right flank in order to assist Peiper, struggling in the Amblève Gorge. On December 19 and 20, however, American patrols found no sign of any German preparations to attack; Sixth Panzer Army's activity seemed to be concentrated between Trois-Ponts and Vielsalm.

During December 20, a prisoner (some accounts refer to him as a Belgian or Dutch deserter from the Waffen SS) gave away the fact that an attack was about to come in along the Stavelot road. It came before dawn on December 21 along the valley of the Warche and was made by one company of Germans in American uniform. It came up against an American battalion and fighting did not last long. Prisoners stated that their objective was the high ground above Malmédy, whence the American artillery was firing on German columns moving towards Stavelot. At 7 a.m. a second wave appeared; this consisted of two companies and ten tanks led by a Sherman carrying the American white star. There was a sharp engagement but as the day wore on the American artillery was able to intervene.

The next day a further and equally fruitless attempt was made to capture Malmédy from the east.

Both attacks were carried out by Skorzeny's force, which had become available owing to the fact that no break-through towards the Meuse had arisen for them to exploit. The fact that the attack was made by Germans in American uniform was probably the reason for one of the most dramatic incidents of the entire Ardennes offensive: the three-day bombing of Malmédy by the Allied strategic air forces.

The bombing began on December 23, the first day of good weather. The mistake was probably due to contradictory information, uncertainty as to the exact positions held by the two sides and the fact that SS commandos had appeared at Malmédy. The soldiers, however, knew the truth even though the airmen did not.

On the evening of the bombing the spokesman at First U.S. Army's press conference read the daily communiqué: 'The Germans having entered Malmédy our air force bombed the town'. Peter Lawless, the *Daily Telegraph* war correspondent, blew up: 'There were no Germans at Malmédy,' he said, 'you have been bombing your own troops and killed three hundred Americans.' But the communiqué was unchanged.*

The next day, despite the frantic efforts of 30 Infantry Division to convince headquarters in the rear that friendly forces occupied Malmédy,† another wave of bombers came over the town and Saint-Vith and Stavelot were similarly attacked. On December 25 Malmédy was the heavy bombers' target for the third time. During these three days 125 Belgian civilians were killed by the air forces of their allies, to say nothing of the American troops' losses, the figures of which were never published.

The first error of this nature was made by a German squadron on May 10 1940 when it bombed Freiburg mistaking it for Mulhouse. Since then there had been many such errors on both sides, and it is just possible that on this occasion, Malmédy was mistaken for Stavelot.

But the fact that in spite of all the army's protests, the raids were carried out on three successive days raises doubts. One wonders whether they were not the result of some deliberate plan. Six months earlier other towns had suffered a similar fate, witness Caen, Saint-Lô, Aunay-sur-Odon, Vire, etc.

Like Malmédy these towns were built around vital communication points. It seems possible in the light of the details of this unhappy affair that the object of the American High Command in bombing Malmédy on three days running was simply to block the junction of the roads from Eupen and Spa, the point at which two important valleys converged, and so prevent German reinforcements launching a new attack northwards. Perhaps these could be called prophylactic bombings. It could be. For on December 25, far from being sure that the Germans were exhausted the Allies had every reason to fear that they might resume their attack at this vital point of the northern front. Malmédy, Stavelot and Saint-Vith were the main communication points in the area. The fact that all these

* Marcel Bovy, *La Bataille de l'Amblève, December 18 1944 to January 28 1945*, p. 91.

† R. L. Hewitt, *Workhorse on the Western Front—the story of the 30th Infantry Division*, p. 189.

three places were attacked simultaneously on December 24 and 25 makes it look as if this must be the true background to a ghastly tragedy.*

* On p. 91 of his excellent book referred to above M. Bovy mentions an explanation of the incident which appeared in a number of Belgian publications. It consists of three points:

(1) It is 'morally certain' that on December 24 Germans disguised as Americans spread out on the roofs of buildings the red recognition panels used by the American Army to mark their positions for the air force.

(2) The Americans therefore concluded that 'the whole valley was infested with Germans in disguise'.

(3) As a result 'in order to avoid a catastrophe they laid down a barrage in front of the only line of defence of which they were sure, the high ground north of the town'.

This explanation does not hold water. It is difficult to see why 'Germans in disguise' should have displayed recognition panels. They would be more likely to have wished to draw American fire on to the town which they had not yet captured.

On the other hand, there were plenty of American units in the town to warn the air force of their error. It could be that Skorzeny's Commandos had produced such an atmosphere of mistrust that the aircraft crews thought the panels were traps designed to prevent them carrying out their assigned bombing mission. The reason why the attacks were ordered at all, however, remains a mystery.

Chapter 17

THE OFFENSIVE LOSES MOMENTUM

DURING this same period of December 20–25 all operations on the southern flank of the Bulge revolved around the resistance of Bastogne. Not only did it constitute an obstacle to the westward movement of Fifth Panzer Army but it acted as a spur to the counter-offensive by the Third U.S. Army moving up from the south to take the Germans in flank and relieve the town.

Any account of the development of the situation on the southern flank is therefore tantamount to a description of the vicissitudes of the siege of Bastogne.

The Grip on Bastogne Tightens

December 20 was a day of thick fog and increasing cold during which the Germans tightened their grip around the town but the Americans emerged from the stage of improvisation. The U.S. parachute troops and armour had so far been thrown into the battle as they arrived; though fighting side by side, the only commander to whom both owed allegiance was General Middleton of VIII Corps and he had moved his headquarters to Neufchâteau, too far away to effect the necessary co-ordination. The establishment of a proper defensive system was being hampered by an exaggerated sense of *esprit de corps* which had led to certain highly inopportune manifestations of prickliness.

While there was one road still open General MacAuliffe, the artillery commander of 101 Airborne who was temporarily in command of the division in the absence of General Maxwell Taylor in the United States prior to the offensive, went to Neufchateau. He found Middleton somewhat sceptical as to the possibility of prolonged resistance: the town was already being attacked by three divisions and there was now a danger that it would be outflanked from the north by 116 Panzer. VIII Corps commander was perhaps influenced by the fact that the evening before Patton had given him an order to evacuate the town.*

* This is mentioned only by Colonel (later General) S. L. A. Marshall, *Bastogne*, p. 209, note 4. Accounts of the doings of Patton and Third Army (the majority written in a vein of rapturous hero worship) obviously do not refer to this sign of 'weakness' usually so uncharacteristic of Patton.

The probable explanation is that he was apprehensive that the Germans would swing not towards Antwerp, but into the area Givet-Bouillon, towards Sedan and Verdun. With this in mind, Patton may have been thinking of withdrawing and consolidating his front, just as Montgomery did on the northern flank.

Reference to much the same idea may be found in the French General Staff

MacAuliffe apparently reassured Middleton, stating that he could hold Bastogne 'for another forty-eight hours and perhaps longer'. He returned to his headquarters in the evening half an hour before the encirclement of the town was complete, having been given command of all the troops therein. He reached a *modus vivendi* with Colonel Roberts commanding 10 Armoured Division Combat Command B, whose tanks were to be concentrated as a mobile reserve in accordance with the tactical doctrine on which he insisted. No attempt was to be made by any parachute commander to use them for purposes of static defence. The agreement in fact gave MacAuliffe the reserve essential to him; at the same time Roberts, although under command of the parachute troops, was guaranteed his autonomy in practice. Susceptibilities were therefore respected.

On the other side Lüttwitz, commanding XLVII Panzer Corps, spent December 20 and 21 completing the encirclement of Bastogne. In the north, 2 Panzer, leaving covering detachments behind, pushed on with its main body towards Champlon and Marche. In the south, on the left of the corps, 5 Parachute Division held the roads along which the American relieving forces might come. Between the two came 26 Volksgrenadier Division, which was to take Bastogne, and the Panzer Lehr. The latter disengaged on December 21 and joined 2 Panzer in the race to the Meuse leaving one Panzergrenadier regiment in front of Bastogne.

As the Germans closed around them Belgian civilians and American soldiers found themselves sharing a common fate. MacAuliffe appointed M. Leon Jacqmin as Mayor; he was assisted by the only three officials still in Bastogne, together with two doctors. Cellars had been reinforced during the preceding months' flying bomb offensive against Liège and were adequately warm. There was a stock of coal at the railway station enabling rudimentary cooking arrangements to be made. The shelters, passages and basements of the major buildings were uncomfortably congested but fortunately the town was under siege in the proper sense of the word for a comparatively short period only; the re-opening of the roads at the end of December came before the supply problem had reached crisis proportions.

For his 3,500 inhabitants Jacqmin had some seven and a half tons of flour, which he shared with the American garrison; the daily bread ration was fixed at half a pound. Meat was provided by the animals abandoned in the surrounding farms. The main supply centres, however, were on the outskirts and the intermittent artillery fire made movement there dangerous; the majority of families were therefore compelled to live off their own

---

Bulletin No. 9 (para. headed 'Operations', No. 133). This is dated December 22 and deals with the situation on December 20. It asks the question: 'Antwerp or Verdun?' the reply being, 'the latter objective appears the more probable since it would open up the rear areas of Patton's army'. But it was nevertheless pointed out that the enemy would first have to cross the Meuse.

stocks. Two tons of biscuits were available from the *Secours d'Hiver* (Winter Help) and these had not been entirely eaten up even when the siege came to an end, in spite of being shared with the Americans.

M. Jacqmin told me later: 'People were very provident.'

No doubt they were. It should be added that as soon as supply columns got through to Bastogne once more the Americans made a generous distribution of 'K' rations. The people of the villages isolated near the front had a much harder time than the inhabitants of Bastogne.

M. Jacqmin also told me: 'For four or five days we lived in a sort of dream. We did not lack anything; there was just one agonising question: would the Germans succeed in taking the town?'

This fear grew as the sound of battle drew closer, its ups and downs shrouded in the fog. At 6 p.m. each day a German heavy gun in the entrance to Kautenbach tunnel sent over a salvo of six shells. Fear of artillery fire was, however, a minor matter compared with the general obsession with enemy infiltration. The G.I.s said that they had found Germans dressed in American uniform in the outskirts of the town. No one bothered to ask how they were recognised as Germans; the general atmosphere of nervousness increased. Belgian and Allied flags were taken down and the urge to take to the road mounted.

The American Medical Service was in considerable difficulties, since the advanced medical depot at Mageret had been captured. Fortunately stocks of German drugs and dressings were found in the seminary. This also proved to contain some coils of barbed wire and these were immediately put up wherever a forest track crossed the lines; owing to the snow the woods could not be set on fire, and in the darkness and fog, German patrols were finding it easy to infiltrate.

The inhabitants of Bastogne alternated between mortal fear and confidence; their attitude was a mixture of over-concentration upon their daily vexations, and oblivion as to the real danger. In fact they lived in a 'dream' —M. Jacqmin's phrase is a good description of the fever of doubt and uncertainty into which the inhabitants of a besieged town are plunged, at least in the early days. But their courage was unfailing. The steadiness of their morale upheld the Americans as they fought. On their side the civilians appreciated the friendliness and courage of soldiers who could laugh between two spells at the front. Distance no doubt lends enchantment, but it does seem that during these few days Bastogne went through a unique experience: a real bond was formed between men drawn from all over the United States of America and these Belgians of whom they had never heard, the inhabitants of this Ardennes town, hitherto so comfortably convinced that the war would pass over it without deigning to stop.

Patton's Attack

Patton kept his Verdun Conference promise, and on December 22 attacked along the whole 25 miles of the southern flank of the German salient. By a *tour de force* which will long be the admiration of the experts, he withdrew three army corps from the Saar front, swung them through ninety degrees and put them into battle. On the east was XII Corps, which was to hold the enemy in Luxembourg forward of the line Echternach–Ettelbrück. III Corps moved up between Ettelbrück and the Bastogne–Arlon road, along which 4 Armoured Division was to drive to relieve the town. Finally, the collection of composite units making up VIII Corps were to act against the western tip of the salient in the area Saint-Hubert–Libramont.

On the German side this front was held by 5 Parachute Division. Its equipment was mediocre, its men inexperienced and the Luftwaffe was nowhere to be seen. It took up a position 12 miles south of Bastogne, putting its best regiment and all its fifteen assault guns to bar the road to 4 U.S. Armoured Division. In spite of the action of Allied fighter-bombers German resistance was to last until December 26. Patton still had to consider two possible threats: an attack in eastern Luxembourg and a southward move by the German divisions which had reached Saint-Hubert. Bradley allotted him 11 Armoured Division and 17 Airborne, which had hitherto been in general reserve. They were to move up to the Meuse between Givet and Verdun. But the best method of countering both these threats still lay in the earliest possible relief of Bastogne.*

On both sides the height of the Bastogne crisis was reached on December 22. General Heinz Kokott, commanding 26 Volksgrenadier Division and the forces surrounding the town, was at his wits' end to know how, with his available strength, he was going to take the place; on his side, MacAuliffe was drawing up a rather dismal balance sheet of his remaining resources. Kokott did not think he could take the town without reinforcements; MacAuliffe did not think he could defend it for long without supplies. After the fog, snow had been falling since the 21st. Germans and Americans dug in a little deeper; there were patrol clashes. Both sides waited uneasily.

Late on the morning of the 22nd, Kokott tried to break the deadlock. At 11.30 a.m. a German deputation of four appeared in front of 327 Airborne Infantry Regiment's positions on the Arlon–Bastogne road; they carried a white flag and an ultimatum:

Unconditional surrender is the only method of avoiding complete

---

* On December 24, Third Army Intelligence Section estimated that west of the Moselle the army was faced by eleven German divisions, totalling 88,500 men, whereas First U.S. Army was opposed by eight divisions, totalling 63,000 men. See Third Army After-action Report, Vol. 1, p. 179.

annihilation of the surrounded American units. Two hours' grace is granted hereby. Should this offer be refused an artillery corps and six groups of heavy anti-aircraft guns stand ready to annihilate the American forces.

The appeal ended by invoking the 'well-known American humanity', urging them to spare the civil population further suffering.

'Aw, nuts!' MacAuliffe exclaimed involuntarily while trying to think of a reply more worthy to go down in history and more in accord with military convention.

'Why not just that—nuts!' one of his officers said.

The word was written down, and the German plenipotentiaries took some time to work out its meaning and realise that the Americans had no intention of surrendering.

The remark made MacAuliffe's reputation in a day. The locals thought that he was referring to the Nut Fair held at Bastogne about this period of the year. MacAuliffe at Bastogne was turned into a modern version of Cambronne at Waterloo.

It seems doubtful whether Kokott had had the agreement of Lüttwitz and Manteuffel to his action. It was an obvious ineptitude; the American garrison drew the conclusion that he was coming to the end of his tether, and searching round for a loophole. On the return of the flag of truce the threatened storm of shells did not descend on Bastogne. Late in the afternoon two attacks were put in against the southern front, and the following night the Luftwaffe began a series of raids lasting four days. In spite of this morale-booster, MacAuliffe's situation was none the less critical. He now only had an average of twenty rounds per gun, and some of the armoured units were down to ten. His only hope lay in the arrival of 4 Armoured Division, which was only starting to move that day, and a supply drop, which was dependent on an improvement in the weather. It seemed to be a question of days, if not of hours. However, although his fire power was falling, his positions were being nibbled away and he was anxious over the possible arrival of fresh German forces, MacAuliffe had one or two valuable trumps in his hand on the psychological side: the civil population was showing no signs of panic, and a sudden spirit of co-operation had sprung up between the parachutists and the cavalry, in place of their traditional rivalry.*

The German commanders, on the other hand, seemed to be afflicted by paralysis and lack of confidence in their resources. Lüttwitz was in a

---

* Marshall, op. cit., p. 143. The spirit of comradeship was such that at the end of the siege Marshall heard a number of officers of both arms say that they wished all the defenders of Bastogne could be kept in the same tactical formation. 82 Airborne, and 740 Tank Destroyer Battalion felt the same way after having fought together in the counter-offensive on the Salm. Their first contacts had also been extremely chilly.

continual state of indecision, caused no doubt by the general lack of progress of the offensive, fear of an American counter-stroke, which the 1944 campaign in France had shown might be formidable, and an uneasy scepticism over Germany's prospects. General Kokott, whom Marshall found after the war 'a temperate man in his action and judgments', launched only sector attacks, thereby giving the garrison the opportunity of concentrating against each threatened point. A combined infantry and armoured offensive all round the perimeter, which was what MacAuliffe feared, never came. When the German commanders finally made up their mind to pay the price necessary to capture Bastogne it was to be too late.

On December 23 the sky cleared and there came the event which heralded the end of the siege—the first supply drop, twice cancelled on the previous day. Its moral effect was far greater than its material results. At 10 a.m. in brilliant sunshine, marker flares were dropped west of the town, along hedges patrolled by the Germans. Towards midday arrived the first of 241 C.47 transport aircraft, and with no opposition from the Germans they continued to arrive until 4 p.m., dropping 144 tons with such accuracy that an hour later 95 per cent of the containers had been recovered and the equipment distributed to units. In addition to 17,000 K rations, the drop consisted primarily of ammunition which was unfortunately unbalanced and did not meet requirements. The doctors got 300 blood plasma units, but this, too, was inadequate and they remained anxious over the condition of their wounded, the number of whom was increasing as fighting became more severe.

These deficiencies were to some extent made good on December 24. 160 aircraft dropped 100 tons, consisting of half the previous quantity of ammunition but a better assortment, batteries for the wireless sets, a small quantity of petrol and 20,000 K rations. Even with those of the previous day, these rations provided little more than one day's consumption; the rationing of military supplies had to be tightened, and some of the civilian stocks requisitioned.

On Christmas Day there could be no dropping owing to weather conditions in Great Britain where the transport group was based, but dropping was resumed on the 26th and 27th, though this time seriously hampered by violent German anti-aircraft fire. 962 aircraft and 61 gliders dropped or landed 850 tons, but 19 were shot down, 211 damaged and 50 seriously hit.

The pilots of the great transport aircraft remained unmoved, and the groups of fighter-bombers escorting them had, in the words of one of their pilots 'better hunting than the Falaise pocket'. They were directed from the ground by a Ninth Air Force officer, Captain Parker, who had arrived in the town on December 19 with a high frequency radio set. The fighters made up for the lack of artillery ammunition, and wrought havoc among the German armoured columns hidden in the woods north of the town.

The Allied Air Force was also a thorn in the flesh of the German infantry. Parker called up patrolling fighter-bombers from all directions, and they sprayed the enemy positions with incendiary bombs.

General Heilmann, commanding the German 5 Parachute Division, later said:

this day (December 24) was the day of the Air Force, but unfortunately it was not ours. Not a single German aircraft appeared over Bastogne. What had happened to the air support we had been promised for vital sectors? When night fell a glow could be seen stretching back right to the Westwall. The roads were marked by lines of flaming vehicles.

Even ten years after the event, all the civilians I spoke to beamed as they recalled the sky full of parachutes emerging from the transport aircraft as they went slowly on their way. Leon Jacqmin said: 'The American soldiers were in raptures. Soldiers and civilians hugged each other. There was an explosion of feeling and a marked rise in morale; it is still an unforgettable memory. That day we were given the certainty of victory.'

The issue was, however, by no means settled. Bastogne was still the main objective for the third phase of Fifth Panzer Army's offensive. Throughout the night of December 23–24 the American cavalry and airborne troops had to fight hard. Manteuffel had arrived to urge Kokott to take the town before Christmas, since without it all his movement was paralysed. Fifth Panzer Army commander was in fact about to propose to Hitler a new plan, aiming merely at reaching the Meuse. Its sole chance of success, however, lay in the capture of Bastogne.

The Tip of the Offensive Blunted

The leading German formation was now 116 Panzer of LVIII Panzer Corps. But the offensive was losing momentum as a result of the hesitations and delays which had characterised the advance during December 20. As 116 Panzer moved down from Houffalize towards the main Bastogne-Marche road, it was ordered to return to Houffalize and advance on La Roche via Samrée.*

This it had done on December 20; it had captured Samrée together with an American petrol and supply depot, and sent forward a detachment to Hotton to seize the bridge over the Ourthe.

But it was too late. Ridgway had despatched a combat command of 3 U.S. Armoured Division to protect the flank of 81 Airborne, and it reached Hotton before the Germans. On the 21st therefore Manteuffel withdrew the Panzer Lehr from Bastogne and sent it to Rochefort to search for a way through westwards. 116 Panzer was meanwhile to hold the defenders of Hotton. General von Waldenburg, commanding the latter

* General de Cossé-Brissac in *Revue Historique de l'Armee* 1955, No. 2, p. 141, calls this an 'inexplicable order . . . The detour via Houffalize certainly led to a loss of three days.'

division, tried to by-pass the town and cross the Hotton–Marche road, hoping then to have a free run northwards. Once again he was frustrated; he came up against 84 U.S. Infantry Division, which had just disembarked from its trucks.

General Bolling, commanding this division, had gone ahead of his troops to Marche, where he arrived during the night of December 20–21. He found it evacuated, with the Germans on the outskirts and expected in the town at any moment. A solitary engineer battalion was preparing to defend itself at the junction of the Hotton and Champlon roads. A regiment of infantry arrived before dawn and with this Bolling organised the defence of Marche.

84 Infantry Division was the advance guard of VII Corps, which Montgomery was keeping in hand to counter-attack the head of the German salient. Its commander, General Lawton Collins, had been ordered to concentrate his corps by midnight on December 23 in the area of Marche, Hotton and Modave, and be prepared to attack either east or north-east against the flank of the German advance on Liège. He had under his command 84 Infantry Division from Ninth Army; 75 Infantry Division from Normandy, which had not yet been under fire, and General Harmon's 2 Armoured Division, nicknamed 'Hell on Wheels'. This last had been in action continuously since the North African landing, had fought at Kasserine and Anzio, and had just come from the violent position warfare fighting in the north of the Aix-la-Chapelle pocket under Ninth Army. It had been alerted on December 21 and moved down to control the roads leading north from the salient towards Huy.

For three days running 84 Infantry Division stood like an island in a rising tide, while the rest of the corps moved up. On its left 75 Division went forward to cover the Ourthe. On its right, however, was a yawning gap, which two German armoured divisions were doing their best to exploit.

116 Panzer was still bogged down in front of Hotton, but 2 Panzer and the Panzer Lehr pushed forward side by side towards the Meuse, with nothing to oppose them but a thin screen of cavalry along the right bank of the river Lomme between Marche and Éprave. Moving up from Saint-Hubert, Bayerlein with the Panzer Lehr reached Rochefort on the 22nd with some thirty tanks, but then took thirty-six hours to deal with a battalion which 84 Infantry Division had sent forward to reconnoitre.

2 Panzer, on its right, seemed likely to break through. On December 23 it reached Hargimont, between Rochefort and Marche. Before dawn on December 24 a force of Panther tanks was sent forward as advance guard, and reached Celles on the high ground overlooking the Meuse, above Dinant. There the leading tank went up on a mine. Once more, if the local stories are to be believed, the fate of the German advance was decided by a civilian. As Bayerlein had done at Bastogne, the detachment commander asked a café owner, Marthe Monrique: 'How far from here to Dinant?'

Bravely she replied: 'Six miles, but the Americans have mined all the roads.'

Fearing a trap, the Germans did not go down the hill to the river, but withdrew into the woods and waited for the main body of the division to arrive. At 9 a.m. they were attacked by a British squadron from 9 Royal Tanks of the Guards Armoured Division, which had moved up two days earlier to guard the approaches to the bridge at Dinant. The Germans were pinned down in Foy-Notre-Dame, where they were hammered by British guns from Onhaye on the far bank of the Meuse and American batteries in position around Ciney.

To be precise, therefore, Celles was not the extreme limit of the German advance, nor Marthe Monrique the decisive factor. Foy-Notre-Dame is a mile north-west of Celles on the road to Dinant, the road from which the good woman had tried to divert the enemy tanks. Dinant was therefore in fact saved by the Guards Armoured Division rather than Mme Monrique.

At midday 2 U.S. Armoured Division came to the rescue, moving up between Ciney and the area south-west of Marche and putting in a converging attack on 2 Panzer, its 'opposite number' which it had already met in Normandy. Meanwhile the British Household Cavalry Regiment attacked between Celles and the Meuse, pushing the Germans into the jaws of 2 Armoured Division. Bitter fighting went on for four days, at the end of which 2 Panzer had run out of both fuel and ammunition and was in ribbons. American fighters did the rest. On Boxing Day the Panzer Lehr arrived, not to support 2 Panzer, but to rescue its 1,500 survivors. 2 Armoured Division's bag was 81 tanks, 7 assault guns, 405 trucks, 74 guns, 1,200 prisoners and twice that number of men put out of action. 2 Panzer had set forth on December 16 with 88 tanks and assault guns. It had ceased to exist.

9 Panzer, hitherto in reserve, was sent to the rescue, but ran out of fuel around Rochefort. Panzer Lehr withdrew to hold Saint-Hubert, and with 9 Panzer formed the tip of the German salient. Both went on to the defensive, waiting for the Allies to resume their advance.

Victory for the Allied Air Forces

Around Christmas the sky cleared, and the action of the Allied Air Forces became a major factor in bringing the German offensive to a halt. Innumerable German accounts testify that no vehicle, whether motor or horse-drawn, whether in convoy or isolated, could move by day other than from cover to cover. In the Rhineland to the rear of the German salient Allied fighter-bombers destroyed all the bridges; air battles took place over the battlefield, for the Luftwaffe was reacting more strongly than usual; the sight of British and American aircraft in action was a morale-raiser for the divisions as they moved up into the battle.

The panegyrics launched after the German tide had receded hardly did the Air Forces justice.

Eisenhower stated that in the early days they had been grounded by 'cloud and impenetrable fog', thus giving the enemy 'an ally worth many additional divisions'. The facts were that from December 16 to 19 there was fog over England, grounding the heavy bombers. Over the Ardennes a low cloud ceiling kept the number of sorties down: on December 17 the Allies made 1,100 and the Luftwaffe 600. On December 18 each side made 600. On December 19, 20 and 21 the fog moved from England to the Continent, and not a single aircraft took off. But on December 23 the Allies made 700 fighter sorties and 1,300 bomber. These figures are, of course, small compared to those of the three decisive days December 24, 25 and 26 when 5,000 sorties were made.

The Belgian Royal Meteorological Institute stated that during the first three days visibility was good, that there was little rain or mist, and the cloud moderate to thick.*

The Allied Air Forces were therefore limited to harassing action which could not be decisive in stopping the enemy offensive, and as usual, the infantry on the ground were unable to 'appreciate' the role played by the air. The fact remains that nowhere did the Luftwaffe establish air superiority, and it had little, if any, effect on the Allied lines of communication, though it was frequently successful in intercepting bombers on their way to Germany. The German air effort collapsed on December 19, when they lost 124 fighters in the air and 105 shot down by anti-aircraft. The same afternoon, a major formation of seventy German aircraft was broken up in the area of Trier. Thereafter the only German air activity was around Bastogne on December 22, and the raid of January 1 was its last major action.

By January the Luftwaffe had practically disappeared from the sky, and the Allies had complete air mastery. The ratio of losses is a good indication: during that month the Luftwaffe lost thirty-four aircraft, as against sixty-four Allied, the majority by anti-aircraft fire.

Hitler's Obstinacy

Unexpectedly and paradoxically, the description of this period given in the O.K.W. communiqués was accurate, almost prophetic. One would have expected them to make much of the great prospects held out by the German advance. Instead they were reserved, almost modest in so far as such a thing is possible in compositions of this sort. Their wording left the impression that the sequel might just as easily be disillusionment as the triumphant announcement of final victory. As before, they were drafted by Major Ritter von Schramm, who also, as we know, was frequently the author of the paraphrase given in the *Völkischer Beobachter*, the official

* Marcel Bovy, *La Bataille de l'Amblève*, p. 167.

National Socialist newspaper. On December 21, for instance, the *Völkischer Beobachter* carried this warning:

> In the forthcoming fighting we shall have to exploit our tactical success ... We know that this attack is no walkover. The enemy is strong; in fact, he is very strong. On the first day of our general offensive he was taken by surprise, but he will now try to reorganize ... It is clear that we are only at the beginning of severe fighting, and that this battle will not be decided for some time.

The military, then, were giving vent to barely concealed pessimism. What were the political leaders, responsible for maintaining the morale of the nation and the armed forces, saying? At Christmas-time Goebbels had refused to comment on the operations in the west, saying that he would do so 'on a more favourable occasion and at a more propitious period'. He found it easier to remain in the stratosphere of heroics than to give his readers the information for which they were waiting. To comfort the 'brotherhood of the isolated', he revived the theme of the post-Stalingrad period:

> This war is no more than a crisis in world evolution; it is not a catastrophe ... The German people is not destined to destruction, as our enemies try to make us believe, but on the contrary to a great future. This future will be ours to the extent that we merit it.

In Germany there were other no less remarkable statements during this Christmas season. At Aix-la-Chapelle, Oppenhof, the mayor installed by the Americans and murdered in March 1945 by an SS commando, announced to his fellow-citizens: 'Today there comes a repetition of the Carolingian phenomenon; a new spirit is spreading over Europe from Aix-la-Chapelle, the Christian spirit.'

At the front a subtle propaganda war was the accompaniment of battle. Radio Luxembourg had been requisitioned by the American Psychological Warfare Service, and was being used for purposes similar to those of the Germans in the early war period. It gave accurate information on the location of enemy units and their movements, thereby sowing mistrust and creating a spy mania.*

Radio Berlin replied by transmitting on a wavelength close to that of the B.B.C., in order to confuse not only foreign listeners, but also German officers, who now made no secret of the fact that they they kept their situation maps up to date by listening to information from London. A mysterious

---

* As early as September, 'Operation Annie' had been launched; it consisted of a transmission lasting a quarter of an hour, with the call sign '1212 calling', given each night between 2 a.m. and 6.30 a.m. Its information was aimed primarily at the Rhinelanders, and was given in Rhineland dialect. The commentators were careful to avoid any open anti-Nazism, and even the Wehrmacht communiqué was read. See Twelfth Army Group After-Action Report, Vol. XIV, p. 190.

bulletin called *Scorpion* began to circulate within the Wehrmacht; it deliberately adopted an anti-Nazi line and gave an able description of the consequences of defeat. It carried a Field Post Number, a somewhat elementary piece of deception, calculated to trace any naïve reader who might be interested in such pseudo-clandestine activity. *Scorpion* had probably originally been a genuine tract put out by opposition circles; with considerable ability an official agency run by Himmler or Goebbels turned it into a periodical bulletin and unobtrusively changed its tone. A further aspect of the psychological battle was the shooting by the Allies into the German lines of shells full of tracts, or even of safe conducts for surrender. They do not, however, appear ever to have had any great effect.

During the counter-offensive the Allies captured a number of German mailbags, which gave a good indication of the fluctuations in the morale of the German infantryman.

On December 22, for instance, a lieutenant named Rockhammer wrote: 'Our soldiers still have the old zip. Always advancing and smashing everything. The snow must turn red with American blood. Victory was never so close as it is now.... We will throw them into the ocean, the arrogant big-mouthed apes from the New World.'

But at Christmas another was writing: 'We have been on our way through Belgium from December 11 to 24 without a break. No rest or sleep at all. My Christmas presents consisted of washing, shaving and five hours' sleep.... We cleared an enemy supply dump.... I took only chocolate. I have all my pockets full of it ... The worst is behind me. Now this is just a hunt.'*

On January 5, however, yet a third wrote: 'I have just got my New Year's present—two frost-bitten feet.'

As for the generals, they were under no illusions. On December 22, Field-Marshal von Rundstedt intervened for the second time—and with equal lack of success—asking for the offensive to be called off immediately. He left the talking to General Guderian, who, as Chief of Staff of the Army, was in charge of the eastern front. Guderian besought the Führer to 'bar the road in the east before it was too late'. A gigantic offensive, he said, was threatening in Poland and 750 miles of front were held by only twelve and a half divisions.

Guderian still clung to the idea that for the long term good of the Fatherland it was better to lose the Ruhr and save Silesia. If the western front were stripped, it would be possible to take the offensive against the Russians north of the Carpathians, in a war of movement; this would gain time for Germany's western enemies to turn into allies and come to the aid of the Wehrmacht in stopping the Soviet armies flooding across central Europe. Improbable though this conception may seem, it was the background of many of the German generals' ideas.

* Shulman, *The German Defeat in the West*, p. 356.

Q

But Hitler regarded Guderian's proposals as stupid; he was convinced that nothing would happen in the east. Supported by Jodl, he could think of nothing other than exploiting the results of the recapture of the initiative in the west. The fact that surprise had failed meant nothing to him. The essential point in his and Jodl's view was that they had got a jump ahead of the enemy, thrown him back on the defensive and made it impossible for him to launch the offensive which he was preparing. On December 24 Rundstedt proposed that the offensive should be halted on the line of the Salm–Houffalize–Bastogne, and should await the American counter-offensive. Hitler refused, and ordered two subsidiary operations to assist the main sector, one in the Saar to threaten Patton's rear and force him to relax his pressure on Bastogne, and the other against the Aix-la-Chapelle salient, to draw the British forces in that direction.

At the same time he ordered that the drive towards the Meuse should continue along the narrow corridor forced by Manteuffel, disregarding all the problems which had already made even the generals' 'limited solution' impracticable.

Manteuffel nevertheless did his best. He kenw that all Hitler's hopes were still centred on Sepp Dietrich, and so, telephoning to Adlerhorst on December 24, he made much of his determination to 'assist Sixth Panzer Army', but suggested that he should himself take over the task given to Sepp Dietrich. He laid down three conditions: that he should be given the four divisions still in reserve, a guarantee of full support from the Luftwaffe and rapid re-supply in petrol—nothing so extraordinary, after all. With these he considered he was capable of swinging round behind First U.S. Army in the direction of Liège–Verviers, to meet another German offensive which should start from the north of the Aix-la-Chapelle pocket. This was the movement which, that very morning, 2 Panzer and 116 Panzer, together with 2 SS Panzer, had begun to carry out when they came up against VII U.S. Corps.

Hitler would not have it, and refused to make up his mind until December 26, by which time the situation at the head of the German salient had degenerated catastrophically. Then, and only then, did he approve Manteuffel's plan, envisaging the capture of Bastogne, the annihilation of enemy forces still resisting between the Ourthe and the Meuse, and the encirclement of the northern flank. He had already, on December 23, given Manteuffel 9 Panzer and 15 Panzergrenadier Division, and to these he now added three SS Armoured Divisions from Sepp Dietrich's Army. To assist in re-establishing the southern front facing Patton, Rundstedt proposed an operation from the Saar towards Metz; Hitler, however, announced that there would be two offensives, one against Bitche and Wissembourg, and the other against Strasbourg.

These last operations were to be conducted by Himmler, who had just taken over command of the Upper Rhine Front in addition to his other numerous duties; he would at least spare the Führer the necessity of listening to further recriminations from his generals.

The German communiqué of December 26 stated: 'The main effort will now be made in the Luxembourg sector. Enemy attacks at Bastogne have been repulsed'. There was only one small reference to the northern front: 'West of the Ourthe our leading troops resumed their advance after having beaten off numerous enemy counter-attacks.'

That same afternoon, 4 U.S. Armoured Division entered Bastogne.*

* The Americans were, however, most uneasy over the morale of their troops. This was clear with the confirmation on December 23 by Eisenhower himself of the sentence on Eddie Slovik, who had been condemned to death for desertion. The Supreme Commander was probably determined to make an example. Such a thing had not happened in the American Army since the Civil War. This was one of the best kept secrets of the time, and only came out into the open when the Pentagon agreed to tell the story to the journalist William Bradford Huie.

Chapter 18

ALLIED DRAMA—THE FRENCH TAKE A HAND

EISENHOWER'S decision to divide the responsibility of command on the evening of December 19, may have settled matters from the strategical point of view, but it left, and in some ways increased, a serious feeling of uneasiness. Bradley had been temporarily deprived of command of the northern front, but he was quite prepared surreptitiously to encourage General Hodges, commanding First U.S. Army, to follow his own inclinations and take the offensive, contrary to the orders of his new commander, Montgomery.

The American press gave a good illustration of this attitude of mind when it reported a conversation between Hodges, Lawton Collins, commanding VII Corps, and Harmon, commanding 2 Armoured Division. This was supposed to have taken place on December 23 or 24, just when 2 Panzer was threatening to move down on Dinant.

Collins: 'The boss [Monty] says I can withdraw across the Meuse and give up the east bank to those so-and-so's, but I don't want to.'
Hodges: 'It's up to you to call the next play. Do what you want to do.'
Collins: 'Give me General Harmon and his 2 Armoured Division. [to Harmon] I want you to jump off tomorrow morning, and take the "Panzer" out of that 2 Panzer Division.'
Harmon: 'Hell, yes.'

The military correspondent concerned would hardly have invented this; although the report may not be word perfect, the general tenor of the conversation is undoubtedly correct. It is moreover confirmed, if confirmation is necessary, by the accusations of timidity made against Montgomery by the American generals. Finally it is a fact that Harmon's attack on 2 Panzer was made, to all intents and purposes, on his own initiative.

Montgomery Resumes his Offensive

Since December 20 Montgomery's outlook had changed from one of cool optimism to definite pessimism, but this hardly seems to merit the epithet timidity. He had unbounded confidence in his own abilities—on December 20 for instance, before taking over command of the northern front he had written to Alan Brooke, 'The situation must be taken firmly in hand'; he had quickly appreciated that material and man-power shortages made any attempt to regain the initiative a hazardous business at least as long as the German offensive still retained its momentum.

The majority of American accounts are so taken up with polemics that they omit to mention British material assistance which was in fact given on a considerable scale. Montgomery took from the tank park with which Eisenhower had provided him in Normandy 254 tanks for First U.S. Army (which had lost 263) and 97 for Third Army (which did not make up for its loss of 300). The shortage of infantry and bazooka ammunition and of mines was highly critical and it was only just made good in the closing days of the year by the arrival of convoys from the United States. When the snow began to fall on December 21 and 22 it was found that there were no stocks of white camouflage clothing and the deficiency had to be made good from local resources. The Germans, of course, had ample stocks intended for the Russian front.*

The cold became so severe that motor transport was paralysed and, like the Germans, the Allies were compelled to requisition horses. Infantry frequently had no weapons other than those they could manhandle.

Man-power seemed to represent an insoluble problem on both sides. On December 24 Hitler promised Model 2,400 men, to be provided by taking ten per cent of all units on the western front; similarly on January 1 Eisenhower assured First and Third U.S. Armies that they would get 17,000 men produced by 'cannibalisation' of the rear services, a measure which Patton had already enforced on a considerable scale.

Montgomery's plan consisted of three main features, for the preparation of which he estimated he required a week from Christmas Day:

Firstly to bring the enemy, who would shortly run out of fuel, finally to a halt; this was to be done by positioning XXX British Corps along the right bank of the Meuse, in case it should prove impossible to re-organise and consolidate the American front.

To prepare for a counter-offensive, the conditions of which could not yet be exactly foreseen.

Thirdly, to assemble the reserve essential for any manœuvre.

Montgomery was in full agreement with Eisenhower on these points and he was encouraged by a message from Churchill received on December 22 assuring him of his full confidence and, in the Churchill manner, announcing the despatch of 25,000 men. In preparation for the counter-offensive the Supreme Commander ordered that the number of replacement

---

* At Hemroulle, near Bastogne, the American officer in command had the church bells rung to summon the inhabitants and asked them for sheets from which to make snow clothing, promising to replace them after the war. The villagers did as they were asked, though without much faith in the promise of replacement. Some years later the officer returned with a whole consignment of sheets. As a sign of its gratitude Hemroulle presented its church cross to the officer's home town. It now adorns a church of a different persuasion.

tanks should be made up to 2,000, accelerated the movement of divisions in transit from the United States and moved over to the Continent four divisions located in the United Kingdom.

These measures were, of course, too long-term to affect Montgomery's plans. To constitute his reserve, therefore, he demanded as an immediate measure that the front as a whole be shortened by withdrawing from the salients in other sectors, including that in the south, which was no concern of his. On Christmas Day he gave Bradley a most pessimistic picture in terms only too well calculated to raise his opposite number's hackles; Patton records it as follows 'Montgomery stated that the First Army could not attack for three months and that the only attacks that could be made would be made by me but that I was too weak. Hence we should have to fall back to the line of the Saar-Vosges or even to the Moselle to gain enough divisions to permit me to continue the attack.'*

That evening Patton was dining with Bradley, who told him of Montgomery's ideas. Both were furious, as had been Hodges, to whom Montgomery had left the final decision. In the eyes of the American generals, the defeat of the Germans was almost an accomplished fact: all that was necessary was for the northern front to get on the move in its turn; Montgomery's slow cautious approach seemed to them entirely out of place. The fact that the leading troops of 4 Armoured Division reached Bastogne on December 26 merely increased their determination to resume the offensive.

They did not, however, wait for this before taking action to counter what seemed to them the excessive influence exerted by Montgomery at Versailles. That same day Patton sent to Supreme Headquarters an *aide-mémoire* by his Chief of Staff, stating that the operations of Third Army then in progress threatened the German lines of communication through the salient. This was premature to say the least. The *aide-mémoire* continued that any withdrawal of the Allied front would merely allow the enemy time to re-constitute his reserves and above all that there was a risk of a catastrophic reaction on the part of the American troops.

'Third Army troops', Patton wrote, 'know and understand the attack. They do not know or understand the retreat or general withdrawal . . . A withdrawal . . . to the Saar-Vosges mountain line would perhaps at most yield two American divisions . . . Withdrawal to the Moselle is not considered advantageous in any way.'

Telephoning to Bedell Smith, Bradley went even further; he demanded that First and Ninth Armies should immediately revert to his command. He stated that he was ready to move his headquarters to Namur. As re-

* Patton, *War as I knew it*, p. 203. Neither Montgomery nor Bradley referred to such proposals in their memoirs but it should be noted that in the U.S. official history *The Supreme Command*, p. 383, note 71, Pogue accepts them as correct; this makes Patton's account look less exaggerated than it appears.

gards the three fresh divisions which SHAEF had just brought up from Reims into general reserve, these, he said, should be allocated to Patton.

The latter was proposing to use these divisions to take over his left flank and then without further ado carry out an attack via Echternach in the general direction of Bonn.*

This was clearly premature and although Bedell Smith did allot the three divisions to Third Army, he laid down that they should be kept on the Semois. The German offensive did not yet seem to be played out; the possibility that it would swing round southwards could not yet be excluded and in the south there was now nothing except the lowest grade battalions of the French army, units which the Allies had hitherto refused to equip and which found themselves on the old battlefields of spring 1940, now covered with snow for the fourth time.

We shall shortly be dealing with the role played by this French army but we must first consider the further developments in the Allied command crisis.

On December 28 Eisenhower went to Hasselt to settle with Montgomery the details of the counter-offensive which was to eliminate the German salient. On the same day Hodges moved forward all along the northern front and Patton struck out to meet him, giving Houffalize and Saint-Vith as the objectives for the forces which had just relieved Bastogne.

Montgomery was planning his riposte for the first days of January. No doubt encouraged by Eisenhower's approval, he followed up his advantage, stating that unified command of all the land forces on his front was essential for success and that the key to future victories lay in keeping this unified command in being. He asked that once the front had been re-established, he should be given command of all American divisions in order to carry out the offensive north of the Ruhr.

So Montgomery was seizing the opportunity to revert to his plans of September. Whatever the strategic advantages, this persistence looked to Eisenhower like a manœuvre, almost an act of disloyalty. Montgomery moreover soon committed his views to paper, making matters worse.

On December 29, as might have been expected, he reiterated his proposals in a letter to Eisenhower without, however, stating that the unified command should be given to him.

Eisenhower had already agreed that one American army should be under Montgomery's command for the proposed offensive towards the Rhine and Montgomery's letter seemed to him a poor reward for his concession. Not only had he no intention of going further, but even had he wished, the furious reaction of his American generals would have dissuaded him from any such idea. Marshall cabled to him from Washington: 'Under no circumstances make any concessions of any kind whatsoever.

* Patton, op. cit., p. 205. The divisions in question were 11 Armoured, 17 Airborne and 87 Infantry.

I am not assuming that you had in mind such a concession. I just wish you to be certain of our attitude. You are doing a grand job and go on and give them hell.'

Reassured by this, Eisenhower wrote to Montgomery that he would be sorry to have to submit their opposing ideas for a decision by the Combined Chiefs of Staff since this would be tantamount to asking for a choice between the two of them. Via de Guingand, he let Montgomery know that 'It is you or me. If one of us has to give up his job, I do not think that it will be me.'

De Guingand told Montgomery of Marshall's telegram to Eisenhower and so Montgomery compromised. This was all the easier for him since Eisenhower's official reply, which was a masterpiece of understatement, had attached to it a plan for operations subsequent to the reduction of the Ardennes salient, giving Montgomery 'all he wanted, except in the realm of operational control'.

On January 4, however, Winston Churchill visited 21 Army Group headquarters and put to Montgomery one of his surprising ideas: 'Alexander,' he said, 'is now doing no good in Italy, since we shall never undertake an offensive from the Po Plain into Austria. Let us recall Tedder to the Air Ministry and put Alexander in his place as Deputy Supreme Commander. He will help to keep Eisenhower on the rails.'

Montgomery's loyalty to Eisenhower thereupon revived. Though expressing polite approval, he barely concealed his opposition to a plan which, on pretext of partially relieving Eisenhower of control of the land forces, would in fact turn Montgomery into No. 2 British general on the western front.*

A month later Churchill and Alan Brooke raised the question once more. This time Montgomery made much of the criticism to which the arrival of Alexander would inevitably give rise among the Americans. In reality, he was basically opposed to the idea.

In his memoirs he says, 'In so far as I was concerned, the "ground force commander" problem was closed by the end of 1944.'

This final battle of words between the senior British and American commanders adds spice to the telegram sent to Roosevelt by Churchill on his return from the front:

His Majesty's Government have complete confidence in General Eisenhower and feel acutely any attacks made on him . . . He and Montgomery are very closely knit and also Bradley and Patton and it would be disaster which broke up this combination which has in 1944 yielded us results beyond

---

* See Arthur Bryant, *Triumph in the West*, p. 374. In this account, Field-Marshal Alan Brooke relates this proposal to the Prime Minister's visit of January 4. Montgomery only refers to it in connection with the occasion on which Churchill made the proposal for the second time.

the dreams of military avarice. I have not found a trace of discord at the British and American Headquarters.

This telegram was despatched on January 6 and Churchill put the responsibility upon the everlasting scapegoat: 'Should there be any difficulties with the Press. . . .'

On January 7, however, Montgomery summoned the war correspondents and made a series of statements, the effect of which was to rub salt into the wounds of the American generals. He seemed to be saying to the press 'Look what a good boy I am!' This forthwith sparked off the inter-allied crisis once more; it was to reach unheard-of heights.

The French Intervene

At the end of December there came another crisis, this time with another ally, all of whose requirements and problems Eisenhower would have been quite ready to meet provided that he was not expected to overstep the limits of his powers in trying to solve them. This time the ally was France and her appearance on the scene was destined to force the Supreme Commander in self defence to pronounce on two questions, both of which were equally vexatious: the despatch of French forces to the Meuse front and the question of Strasbourg.

During the first days of the offensive the thought of calling upon the French army for assistance had never entered the Supreme Commander's head. Major Fournier, head of the French Forces of the Interior in the Department of the Ardennes, had re-positioned his men so that they could carry out 'mopping up patrols against German irregulars supplied by parachute' and guard fixed installations; but he had done so on his own initiative.

Some French units were already fighting as an integral part of the Allied forces: Third U.S. Army, for instance, included parts of 16 and 30 Chasseurs battalions; 2 Parachute Regiment, commanded by Major Puech-Samson and consisting of 200 commandos, was under the British Special Air Service. It had carried out certain operations in central France and for the last two months had been in reserve in Champagne. On December 21 it was ordered to move to the area west of Bastogne to 'fill the gap'; it was based first at Bertrix and then at Libin and Raumont and was engaged up to the end of January in maintaining some form of liaison between 87 U.S. Infantry Division (on the northern front) and 6 British Airborne Division and later MacAuliffe's troops. At nightfall on January 10, two of its patrols captured Saint-Hubert in a surprise attack just as Bayerlein moved out.

Up to Christmas, in other words until the fresh American divisions arrived on the Semois, the Meuse above Sedan was covered only by French forces. On December 21, General Thrasher, commanding the 'Oise Base Section', on orders from General Lee, commanding the Services of Supply, asked General Préaud, commander of the Saint-Quentin military district, to take over the defence of the Meuse bridges from Givet to Verdun. At the same time, at the request of SHAEF, the French General Staff alerted the Lille, Saint-Quentin, Rouen, Nancy and Metz military districts, ordering the officers in command to 'hold themselves ready to carry out without delay and with all the resources at their disposal, any specially urgent tasks requested by the Allied authorities whatever might be the state of equipment of their troops'.*

General Préaud positioned three battalions (from Mezières, Beauvais and Chauny) between Givet and Mouzon; they came under orders of VIII U.S. Corps. He kept one battalion in reserve. They could hardly be called military formations. Although it had its full establishment of weapons, only one of them had received its British equipment and that for only three-fifths of its personnel. That night the detachments despatched to guard vulnerable points up to 5 or 6 miles east of the Meuse were withdrawn.

Three further battalions were located between Mouzon and Verdun and at midday on December 24 General Dody, the military governor of Metz, took over command of the 'Security Formations North-East', with the task of 'setting up between the Sambre and Meuse and along the Meuse from Givet to Commercy, a security screen to guard against enemy thrusts and infiltrations'.

This was far more than the motley collection of units euphemistically known as 'Security Formations', had ever thought of being called upon to do. The first battalions, as indeed the later ones, were to all intents and purposes without uniforms. The men in the Lille battalion for instance, had either a battledress blouse or an overcoat but never both. Their armament was as heterogeneous as would be expected at this period. Four days after taking over command General Dody noted that some units were 'still in civilian clothes, and merely had sky-blue overcoats unrecognised by the Allies'.

Inevitably Dody labelled them 'not fit to fight'. At least, however, in his view, they could undertake the task of 'controlling civilian traffic'. General Dody was sent as reinforcements certain other units which had been in training for three months—parts of 1 Spahis Brigade which had a full complement of anti-tank guns and mortars, the Somua Tank Squadron of 13 Dragoons and a half brigade of Chasseurs. Nine foreign legion battalions were alerted. Finally, four battalions of 5 and 24 Infantry Regiments from 10 Infantry Division, the Paris secret army division, were located in the area of Laon.†

---

* In the actual text of the telegram the last phrase had been added and then struck out.

† In his book *Salvation*, p. 144, General de Gaulle puts the total of men under General Dody at 50,000; he does not say what additional units went to make up this number.

General de Gaulle reviewed this 'completely new formation' near Fontainebleau. He claimed that it proved that 'skilful gardeners can always restore the military stalk to full bloom'.*

This was a remarkably euphemistic way of putting it. General de Gaulle can hardly have been ignorant of the fact that this particular division's 'gardeners' were either worn out after years of fighting with the Free French Forces, or thinking nostalgically of their friends in their old units. In any case they were bitter. No less bitter were their men; they had seen nothing but a short period of service in the Colmar pocket; they had not volunteered for service in order to gather nuts in the Chevreuse Valley, to moulder in the sugar-beet fields of Seine-et-Marne or finish the war with a glorious campaign among the wines of Anjou. This period produced plenty of ludicrous stories but that of 10 French Infantry Division is undoubtedly one of the most ludicrous of all.†

The 'gardeners' were old soldiers who had been through every action fought by the French army over the previous four years, starting with Bir Hakeim; they did their best, but with a formation so high a proportion of whose men felt that opportunity had passed them by, the 'military stalk' was a wilting one. The state of the division merely demonstrated the fact that, apart from the original French First Army divisions under de Lattre and Leclerc's 2 Armoured Division, there was no real French army.

On January 4, the battalions of 10 Infantry Division were withdrawn to be moved to the Vosges. Their movement produced an American protest; at Amagre-Lucqy station on the way to Laon, one of the regiments of the division had looted a train full of Christmas presents for the American troops. The affair made quite a stir at the time.

Meanwhile the French forces were located behind the three Allied reserve divisions and used for guard and police duties. There were many foreigners moving round in the area, particularly Poles who said that they had been deported by the Germans for forced labour. Among them could well be hidden some of the east Germans who had come to take over French farms in the early days of the occupation, when the Reich was embarking on the 'colonisation' of the Ardennes. These people formed a sizeable proportion of the population and were obviously extremely suspect; they were both a nuisance and a menace.

It has sometimes been alleged that these foreigners provided safe houses

* General de Gaulle, *Salvation*, p. 141.

† Marcel Vigneras in *Rearming the French*, p. 347, gives the following report on 10 French Infantry Division: 'Its strength was approximately 14,000 men. Its material, consisting largely of enemy-captured equipment of assorted types, was wholly inadequate. American inspecting officers considered that the unit would not be in a condition to be used in an offensive role until it had received suitable equipment and had been trained for a period of not less than four months.' (Message Sixth AGp to SHAEF, January 6 1945).

for German agents parachuted into the country or for infiltrating enemy patrols. The story can neither be denied nor confirmed. The same can be said, moreover, of the rumours which went round about French nationals who were supposed to have gone over into Germany in the summer of 1944 and been parachuted back into France as agents.

So at the end of December 1944 these Paris units found themselves simply patrolling cold sleepy villages watching for 'parachute drops'. U.S. Sixth Army Group went so far as to alert General de Lattre stating that 'parachute commandos had been dropped at various points in rear of the western front'. There seemed to be a general fear that a further von der Heydte operation might take place. It proved unfounded, but it does seem that at this period O.K.W. had in mind a parachute operation to the rear of French First Army to cut its lines of communication in the Belfort gap.

The Strasbourg Affair

In General Eisenhower's mind French intervention during this period was invariably connected with the 'Strasbourg question which was to plague him throughout the duration of the Ardennes battle'.*

Even writing months after the event, his memories of the incident were still tinged with ill-humour, though this did not prevent him accepting without comment Winston Churchill's glowing tribute to him in August 1949: 'That great American soldier who was willing to assume additional risks rather than expose the people of Strasbourg to German vengeance.'

Matters were not quite so simple as that. The memoirs of those directly involved have effectively blurred the issue by putting forward contradictory versions and the historian has to make a comparison of all the various accounts: those of the two main antagonists, Eisenhower and General de Gaulle, those of the witnesses, General Juin and Field-Marshal Brooke, that of the semi-official American history of the war, which does not always tally with Eisenhower's version, and the accounts of the affair by the intermediaries, Winston Churchill and Duff Cooper, then British Ambassador in Paris. All the historian can do is to construct a workable hypothesis in answer to the only question of real importance, which was this: how and for what reasons was the Supreme Commander induced to cancel the order for withdrawal of the American and French forces holding the Alsace Plain? In other words, what pressure was exerted on him to induce him not to abandon Strasbourg?

First the facts: On December 26, Eisenhower was visited by General Devers, commanding U.S. Sixth Army Group (Seventh U.S. Army and French First Army), in the Vosges and along the Saar. Devers' object was to inform Eisenhower of rumours, taken seriously by his intelligence section, to the effect that the Germans were preparing an offensive into Upper Alsace for the period January 1–3. Hitler had in fact ordered this

* Eisenhower, *Crusade in Europe*, p. 385.

diversionary attack forty-eight hours previously; it was known as Operation North Wind. Eisenhower ordered Devers to prepare purely and simply to withdraw to the line of the Vosges. The German attack in fact came at 11 p.m. on December 31. On January 3, by which time it had not been necessary even to begin to carry out his order for withdrawal, Eisenhower agreed that Sixth Army Group should maintain its position and General de Lattre should be left defending Strasbourg.

The Supreme Commander had visualised the possibility of withdrawal on December 19 at the Verdun Conference at which Devers was present; the object of so doing was to make forces available to allow Seventh Army to take over the Saar front which Patton would have to abandon in order to launch his counter-attack against the southern flank of the German salient in the Ardennes. The French First Army, being involved in the Colmar pocket and therefore unable to 'hold the line of the Rhine from the Swiss frontier to the Saar,' could not free the neighbouring Seventh U.S. Army to side-step northwards. There was, therefore, no possible solution other than withdrawal.

On December 19, however, the idea was no more than a hypothesis, known to a few only. It pre-supposed that General de Lattre would fail. Eisenhower made no secret of this fact, since he hinted that the French 'would only have themselves to blame' if it became necessary to evacuate Strasbourg.

In Eisenhower's memoirs the sequence of events is telescoped and it is hard to believe that this was not done of set purpose. The result is to leave the impression that the French High Command was warned of the possibility as early as December 19 or 20 and that when General Juin came to visit Eisenhower, it was to persuade him to defend Strasbourg to the end. The Supreme Commander can hardly merely be in error here, but the fact is that General de Lattre only learned of the plan for withdrawal to the Vosges on December 27 when summoned to Vittel by Devers; it was confirmed next day by Sixth Army Group Letter of Instruction No. 7.*

Equally, it was not until December 28, during a liaison visit to Versailles, that General Juin, Chief of the French National Defence Staff, in his turn learned of Eisenhower's intentions; these were, moreover, put to him as a purely hypothetical possibility such as 'staffs are in the habit of considering, particularly in a defensive situation'.†

Eisenhower's memory is therefore 'at fault' on this point and the reason is clear: his intention is to relate the strategic reasons governing his decision to the main crisis period.

On December 31, General de Lattre told General Touzet du Vigier, Military Governor of Strasbourg Designate, whom General de Gaulle had sent on a 'reconnaissance', that 'the plan was no more than a study of a

* General de Lattre de Tassigny, *History of the French First Army*, p. 303.
† Marshal Juin, *Mémoirs*, pp. 76–7.

certain hypothesis in which no one could believe under present circumstances'.*

In saying this, de Lattre was obviously referring to the famous Letter of Instruction No. 7 in which Devers had not gone as far as Eisenhower. He had laid down three successive lines of withdrawal back to the Vosges, but had stated in so many words: 'Efforts compatible with integrity of forces will be made to hold Strasbourg and Mulhouse. These must be such as will not jeopardise the integrity of forces in a withdrawal to a rearward position.'†

The proviso is not very clearly expressed in the French translation of the order, but at least the phrase 'Efforts . . . to hold Strasbourg and Mulhouse' is unequivocal. Devers was perhaps discreetly leaving a door open to de Lattre. At least he appeared to accept the possibility of some watering down of the 'strategic necessities' laid down by Versailles.

This was the situation on January 1, therefore, when General Juin reported to General de Gaulle. Juin having already stressed to Devers the importance of defending Strasbourg, de Gaulle as head of the French provisional government threw all his political weight into the scales. To Eisenhower he stated: 'whatever happens the French will defend Strasbourg' and he suggested that 10 French Infantry Division should be moved there. He directed General de Lattre to 'take matters into your own hands and to guarantee the defence of Strasbourg'.‡ From the tone of these letters the situation was still thought of as hypothetical and their expressions both of anxiety and determination therefore had a ring of contingency about them. For on the afternoon of January 1 the French Government was still in ignorance of something which Eisenhower knew already: *a German offensive had been launched at 11 p.m. on December 31.*

According to Juin, this news only became known in Paris on the following morning — January 2 — when General Touzet du Vigier returned; he had heard of it the previous evening in Devers' headquarters in Vittel.

This time lag is astonishing; one would think that Versailles was nearer to the Saar front than to Paris. It is difficult not to conclude that the Supreme Commander had no wish to warn the French government that his hypothesis was about to turn into fact. He ordered Devers to 'withdraw promptly to the main Vosges position'; as far as de Gaulle was concerned, however, Eisenhower left knowledge of the order to percolate through official channels and reach the head of the French government 'for information'. In any case, Eisenhower clearly had no intention of informing him by the most rapid possible means.

But there is even more. Devers' order laid down that withdrawal was to be completed by dawn on January 5, but de Lattre did not receive this order until 10 p.m. on January 2, in other words, *nearly thirty hours after*

* Juin, op. cit., pp. 76–7.   † De Lattre, op. cit., p. 304.
‡ General de Gaulle, *Salvation*, p. 145.

its issue. General de Lattre himself says, 'the secret of the withdrawal was kept even from our liaison mission'.*

There seems to be no explanation for the time-lag other than a desire to face the French with a *fait accompli* and compel de Lattre to carry out the 'emergency' instructions without giving him time to refer back to Paris.

There is a mystery as regards de Gaulle here. In his memoirs he reproduces the letter of instruction from Devers to de Lattre which the latter received on January 2. It contains the definite order to withdraw to the Vosges with no reference to this being a hypothetical possibility. General de Gaulle, however, gives its date as December 28, clearly confusing it with the Letter of Instruction No. 7 referred to above, which dealt with a contingency only.†

Whether the general confused the two texts (which however, are dissimilar) or made a mistake in date, the fact remains that in his account it is this order which is the starting point for all his subsequent action; it was the categorical order for withdrawal which caused him 'to take action'. His actions were as he described them, but the circumstances were not. To judge by his memoirs, he was intervening in opposition to an Allied decision already taken, but not to be put into operation until the German attack developed. In fact, de Gaulle got his information from Juin and not from some letter of instruction despatched on January 1 and received on January 2. Until Touzet du Vigier returned from Vittel, the general had nothing to go on except the opinions of his officers, which may have been disturbing but were necessarily based on supposition only.

His object seems to have been to prove that he was not caught short, whereas in fact he was, and was also within an ace of being out-manœuvred by Eisenhower, but this hardly affects the 'thread of the story'. As de Gaulle himself said when Eisenhower's *Crusade in Europe* was published, however eminent the authors of memoirs may be, each has his own view of the truth.

When, however, on January 2, de Gaulle decided to 'take action', he did not lose an instant. Juin went straight off to Versailles to try to talk Bedell Smith round. He pointed out that from Christmas Day onwards the German offensive in the Ardennes had been effectively contained, so there seemed no good reason to build up reserves for the battle there. Persistence in withdrawal to the Vosges would be tantamount to yielding up Alsace in order to win back in the Ardennes what the Allies had already conquered before. This was something that would lead to severe criticism of the Supreme Commander.

Then he began to bargain:

'General de Gaulle has ordered de Lattre to take responsibility for the defence of Strasbourg.'

* De Lattre, op. cit., p. 305.   † General de Gaulle, op. cit., p. 145.

'If that is so,' replied Bedell Smith, 'it is bordering on insubordination pure and simple and the French First Army will not get a single further round of ammunition or gallon of petrol.'

'All right,' retorted Juin, 'in that case, General de Gaulle will forbid American forces the use of French railways and communications.'

Before leaving, General Juin arranged a meeting between de Gaulle and the Supreme Commander for the following day.

During the night General de Gaulle, who was only too conscious of his responsibilities as political leader, despatched two telegrams, one to Roosevelt and one to Churchill. In that to Roosevelt he gave an outline of Eisenhower's decision and added, 'The French Government cannot accept . . . a withdrawal of this nature, which does not seem to be strategically justified and which would be deplorable, both from the point of view of the overall conduct of the war and from the French national point of view . . .' The telegram to Winston Churchill simply passed on a copy of that to Roosevelt, adding: 'I ask you to support me in this serious matter.' Three lines—that was all. Via the U.S. ambassador, Jefferson Caffery, Roosevelt replied that, the question being purely military, he would leave it to be settled by Eisenhower. Churchill, on the other hand, in spite of the terseness of de Gaulle's telegram, acted at once: he went straight over to Versailles arriving at midday on January 3.

During the morning General de Gaulle took his third step. He despatched a further letter to Eisenhower dealing purely with the military aspect of the affair. He proposed discussion of the 'strategic grounds' for evacuating Alsace and part of Lorraine; he then referred to the 'overall conduct of the war, which is a matter above the level of the military command and, from the French national point of view, is the concern of the French Government.'

The implication was clear; de Gaulle knew that the French as a whole were solidly behind him in his refusal to give up Alsace, but he was ready to find a compromise formula to relieve Eisenhower of his embarrassment provided it did not affect his own authority.

This was the atmosphere in which the conversations between de Gaulle, Eisenhower and Churchill took place. Over these again, no two accounts agree.

Churchill states: 'I chanced to be in Eisenhower's Headquarters.'

Eisenhower also refers to chance, saying: 'Mr Churchill was by chance in my Headquarters when de Gaulle came to see me.'

De Gaulle, however, says: 'Mr Churchill, alerted by my message, had also decided to come and was apparently disposed to use his good offices.'

This is the only reference in any account to de Gaulle's telegram. Eisenhower, however, had been informed of Roosevelt's reply by Jefferson Caffery, and therefore must have assumed that de Gaulle had also asked Churchill to intervene.

The first question is whether there was any real discussion between the two principals, Eisenhower and de Gaulle. Churchill says nothing, de Gaulle gives a long account, Eisenhower a short one and according to Juin: 'there was not even a discussion'.

The next question is, what role was played by Churchill. His record is very short: 'Eisenhower and Bedell Smith listened attentively to my appeal. Eisenhower cancelled his instructions.'

Eisenhower says: 'Churchill sat in with us as we talked, but offered no word of comment. After de Gaulle left he quietly remarked to me: "I think we've done the wise and proper thing." '

Juin says: 'As soon as we entered the room Churchill indicated that everything had been arranged, that Strasbourg would not be abandoned and this was confirmed by Eisenhower.'

Field-Marshal Brooke, who accompanied Churchill, strikes the same note: 'Eisenhower let de Gaulle do the talking, but he had already decided to leave his forces where they were.'

Eisenhower's memory must definitely have failed him when writing his memoirs, for in his report to Marshall, sent that same evening, he referred to an intervention by Churchill mentioned only by General de Gaulle: 'All my life I have known what significance Alsace had for the French. I agree with General de Gaulle that this fact must be taken into consideration.'

As for the reasons which led Eisenhower to cancel his decision, he has himself given differing accounts. In November 1945 he said he wrote to Churchill that 'he had been convinced by General de Gaulle that the political developments which would follow a partial withdrawal in Alsace would lead to a deterioration of the situation in the rear areas far in excess of the value of getting one or two divisions for the SHAEF reserve.'[*]

In his memoirs, however, he merely takes refuge in the fact that 'by the date of this conference the crisis in the Ardennes was well past'.

General de Gaulle's account shows that he emphasised the political arguments asserting that 'armies are created to serve the policy of the states concerned'.

Eisenhower would no doubt have agreed with this, provided that political and military considerations were kept separate. General de Gaulle's argument, according to him, seemed 'to be based upon political considerations founded more on emotion than on logic and common sense'—a statement characteristic of its author.

At the end of December the enemy was still capable of reacting, either in Alsace or towards Liège or towards Sedan. Eisenhower therefore felt himself forced to do something to restore his reputation—the British were not giving him an easy ride, particularly in the Combined Chiefs of Staff Committee. Public opinion in his own country, every whisper of which reached him, was already accusing him of having given way to the

* *The Supreme Command*, p. 401, note 122.

R

British. Was he now to yield to the demands of the French, allies whom he found 'lacking in spirit'? He was as careful not to interfere in the political field as Roosevelt was in the military, and was there any military reason to inform the French of his intentions beforehand? The care with which he covered up, however, suggests that he realised how the French national front would react, but preferred to postpone the crisis until the decision had already been taken.

Eisenhower was not in the position of Foch, forced constantly to appear before a Supreme War Council; he did not have to render a day-to-day account of his decisions. So he simply took refuge behind his duty as a soldier. It seems, moreover, that even five years later when writing his memoirs, he did not appreciate the psychological shock which the evacuation of Strasbourg would have given, not only to France but to the European Allies of the United States.

The British, on the other hand, did their best to make him see the light. As early as December 26 his deputy, Air-Chief-Marshal Tedder, who seldom interfered in the conduct of land operations, 'questioned the wisdom of the action' (the evacuation of Strasbourg).*

On January 2 Charles Peake, Eisenhower's British political adviser, went to Duff Cooper and told him of the decision. They agreed that this was 'one of those blunders which are so easily made when supreme power is in the hands of the military who lack political experience'.†

The ambassador forthwith sent a personal telegram to Churchill, emphasising the consequences which he foresaw.

Peake and Duff Cooper presumably had the news via the British generals on SHAEF staff. Peake's action—a serious one for a diplomatic adviser—and Duff Cooper's telegram, produced an immediate reaction from Churchill. Had the circumstances been different he might have thought twice before going over to Paris in person in reply to de Gaulle's extremely terse message. He may not yet have realised the price which France was capable of exacting for the abandonment of Strasbourg, but at least he knew de Gaulle, and he knew, too, that the more restricted his possibilities of retaliation, the more obstinate would the head of the French provisional government become. France may have been in very low water, but a break with her at this juncture would seriously affect the position of the Allies from many points of view. Eisenhower therefore had to be convinced.

During the morning of January 3 Eisenhower held a staff meeting to consider the 'grave political repercussions of the withdrawal'; the conclusion was that he should await the arrival of Churchill, in order that the Prime Minister might be 'briefed on the necessity for the withdrawal'.‡

After lunch the Prime Minister and Eisenhower went into conference,

---

* *The Supreme Command*, p. 398.   † Duff Cooper, *Old Men Forget*, p. 343.
‡ *The Supreme Command*, pp. 400–1.

Bedell Smith, Field-Marshal Alan Brooke and Generals Whiteley and Strong also being present—four British versus two Americans.

It was clearly at this point that the Prime Minister made his impact. The only certain fact which can be extracted from all these contradictory accounts is that his intervention was decisive. This is moreover confirmed by Pogue in *The Supreme Command*, who adduces as proof Eisenhower's report to Marshall, drafted immediately thereafter.

There remains a final enigma. If this was in fact the course of events, why have all those involved made such a mystery of it? Why did Churchill show such unaccustomed modesty? Why did he suggest to Eisenhower in November 1945 that the latter should issue a statement that no pressure had been brought to bear on him? Why did he refer to 'chance' as the reason for his being at the conference? Why, in 1949, did he place such emphasis upon the somewhat questionable merits of the decision, using terms which deceived no one?

Eisenhower's attitude is more understandable. He would have us believe that during the morning the military reasons for withdrawing from Strasbourg seemed to him so overriding that he was in duty bound to ride roughshod over the political disadvantages, although the only military reason for withdrawing was the containment of the Ardennes offensive. But during the afternoon he executed a complete volte-face, for in his memoirs he states that as the Ardennes crisis was over, he decided to hold on to Strasbourg. No one is likely to believe that this change of opinion was due to anything other than Churchill's political arguments. In four hours the military situation could hardly have changed from catastrophic to reassuring. When presenting a picture of himself to history, however, the ex-Supreme Commander could hardly contradict himself or suggest that it was the British Prime Minister who had been instrumental in causing him to bow to the inevitable. In describing his meeting with de Gaulle, therefore, he pictures Churchill merely as a bystander in the background. To explain his own reaction, Eisenhower clings to the military reasons, the only ones which in his view should weigh with a military commander.

Churchill's game clearly required him to keep his own counsel after the meeting. On January 5, in a telegram to Roosevelt, he merely said:

the CIGS and I have passed two very interesting days at Eisenhower's Headquarters at Versailles. Quite by chance, de Gaulle arrived at the same time on the business about which he has sent you and me, as heads of Government, a telegram concerning the Southern Sector (Strasbourg). We had an informal conference and the matter has been satisfactorily adjusted as far as he is concerned. Eisenhower has been very generous to him.*

The explanation seems to be this: at a moment when he and Roosevelt were doing their best to calm down a crisis in Anglo-American relations,

* Churchill, *Triumph and Tragedy*, p. 296.

Churchill had no wish to add fuel to the fire by preening himself on the role which he had played. The eulogy of Eisenhower is all the more understandable when it is remembered that Washington was still smarting from the criticisms voiced by the British press.

Even this, however, does not explain why Churchill felt it necessary to maintain this attitude when writing his memoirs in the early 1950s. But this can no doubt be explained by the post-war climate of the relationship between Great Britain and the United States. The polemics of the final phase of the war continued through the period of memoir-writing, and were affecting the continuance of the 'war-time alliance', at the time the backbone of Western policy. To reveal that Eisenhower had been on the point of giving up ground and that the British Prime Minister was the one who stopped him, would inevitably have affected Eisenhower's prestige, and for little purpose.

Moreover, when Churchill's memoirs appeared, he had once more become Prime Minister, and Eisenhower stood at the head of the forces of the Atlantic Alliance. His halo as the liberator of Europe was the only strong card in his hand, both personally and internationally. By refusing to expose the most monumental blunder of Eisenhower's career, Churchill undoubtedly prevented a loss of face which would have been most inopportune in 1951.

As for General de Gaulle's reasons, they are self-explanatory. Although he was far more aware of the role played by Churchill than was Eisenhower, when describing his own actions he refers to him only in passing. As we know he has never been one to give his allies much credit for their assistance, even on the occasions when he has asked for it.

So although it was a good dramatic scene, such as Churchill enjoyed, like a wise old statesman he kept his counsel. In the few lines which he devoted to it, however, he could not help introducing a touch of that humour which he knew how to use as delicately as he did a magnificent phrase; 'de Gaulle', he said, 'expressed his gratitude'. The true implication of this remark becomes clear when it is compared with Marshal Juin's detailed account; he says:

On getting back into our car, I could not help remarking to de Gaulle that Churchill had some right to expect at least a word of thanks. 'Bah!' he said, and relapsed once more into apparently gloomy contemplation. He was obviously vexed with everything connected with this unhappy incident.

In the wings of this scene of Franco-American tension, the discussions on re-armament of the French forces continued. On November 30 the French general staff had put forward a plan envisaging the raising of 120 security battalions and a call-up of 207,000 men to be formed into eight divisions. Five were to be ready to fight by May 1, and the remaining three by August 1.

The Ardennes offensive having shown up both the Allied shortage of man-power and the resources still available to Germany, Eisenhower abandoned his hostile attitude to these ambitious plans. The war might now well last long enough to make it necessary to use these young Frenchmen, something which in September he had considered out of the question. He supported the plan, and within twenty-four hours obtained the approval of the Combined Chiefs of Staff. The programme met everybody's point of view; the British and Americans were jointly to provide the re-resources to equip at least the first five divisions. But in his letter of thanks to President Roosevelt, General de Gaulle went a step further: fifty 'good divisions' could be raised, he said, by the end of 1945. Eisenhower screamed to high heaven: expansion on this scale, he said, was beyond French resources and did not accord with American intentions. General de Gaulle's purpose was to recreate a standing army capable of dealing with France's post-war problems in Europe and elsewhere; Eisenhower would not recognise any requirements other than those of an auxiliary force to the American and British armies.

From March 1945 onwards, however, operations moved at such a speed that both points of view were overtaken by events.

Chapter 19

FIVE MONTHS FROM THE END

THE launching of operation North Wind in Alsace did not bring with it any relaxation of the German effort in the Ardennes salient. By the end of December the Americans had regained the initiative, but they could advance only step by step, pushing the enemy slowly in front of them. On January 3 a final co-ordinated German assault, lasting two days, was made on Bastogne. On January 8 Hitler ordered the southern front to withdraw to the line Bastogne–Echternach; on January 10 he withdrew Sixth Panzer Army into reserve under his personal control. He had given it the designation SS at the turn of the year. On January 16, exactly one month from the start of the German offensive, a Third U.S. Army squadron joined hands with First Army infantry at Houffalize. The northern and southern pincers had therefore closed without the expected battle of annihilation. By the end of January Manteuffel had succeeded in getting both his infantry and armour back to the December starting line.

This last convulsive German effort had cost both sides dear: 24,000 killed, 63,000 wounded and 16,000 prisoners for the Germans; 8,000 killed, 48,000 wounded, 21,000 prisoners for the Allies. The figures testify to the severity of the fighting.

Hitler Still Clinging to His Hopes

Although by Boxing Day the failure of the offensive was clear, Hitler was as determined as ever that this was no reason to give up the struggle. On December 28 he said to General Thomale: 'We have had remarkably bad luck', and then returned to his standard theme of 'holding on'.

> The one who must hold out the longer is the one who has got everything at stake . . . If America says 'We are off. Period. We've got no more men for Europe', nothing happens; New York would still be New York, Chicago would still be Chicago . . . But if we were to say today 'We've had enough' we should cease to exist. Germany would cease to exist.

To counter this extraordinary 'bad luck' he now placed all his hopes in the forthcoming offensive in Alsace, intended as the fore-runner of a resumption of the initiative in the Ardennes. At about the same period, sensing that the morale of his generals was cracking, Hitler collected them all at Ziegenberg and treated them to a long dissertation on familiar lines:

> The Ardennes operation achieved one result: the Anglo-Americans were forced to abandon their offensive plans and engage in slow, costly fighting. This fighting has also cost Germany dear. The armies of the Reich can only

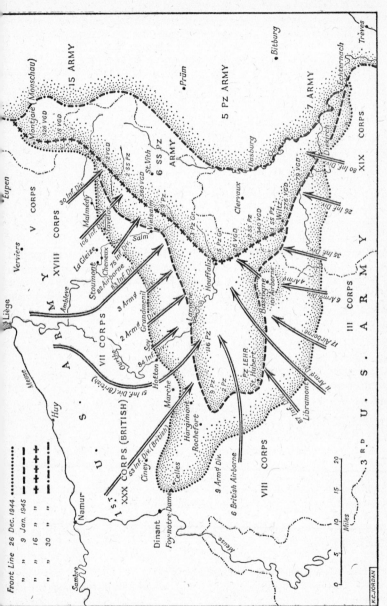

The Allied Counter-offensive

succeed if they move once more into the attack to annihilate the enemy forces, which is more important than gaining ground. We are struggling continuously for arms, for men, for material, for fuel, for God knows what. This cannot go on for ever. The offensive must therefore succeed.*

What further proof was needed to convince Hitler that Germany was defeated? If we are to believe Jodl, the Führer was not prone to self-deception. 'The Führer realised the situation as a whole as well as we did, and probably much sooner than we did. Therefore we did not need to say anything to him in this connection.'†

It would be pleasant to think that Hitler was as lucid as that, if only because it would bring him into the category of normal, sensible human beings. But it must be remembered that when putting forward this theory, Jodl was in prison in Nuremberg and engaged in writing the outline of a study of the strategical role played by Hitler. His view of the reasoning which had led his late Supreme Commander to refuse to draw the logical consequences from the facts was as follows:

It is often said that Hitler's military advisers ought to have opened his eyes to the fact that the war was lost. This is a naïve idea. Before any of us, he sensed and knew that the war was lost. But can anyone give up a nation, particularly his own people, for lost if there is any way out? A man like Hitler certainly could not. It is said that he should have fallen in battle, rather than choosing to cheat fate by suicide. That was his wish, and he would have done it, had he been physically capable. His choice of death was not therefore the easiest, but the most sure. He acted as all heroes throughout history have acted, and always will. He buried himself among the ruins and with the hopes of his Reich. Let those who so wish condemn him—personally I cannot.‡

This 'lucid' strategist apparently could not hear the squadrons of heavy bombers passing over every night to pulverise towns in the heart of Germany, already crowded with refugees from both East and West. The O.K.W. War Diary contained a daily paragraph on the subject:

1 January.
1,300 four-engined aircraft over Hamburg. 39 shot down. Own losses 49. 200 bombers, 900 British fighters against Düsseldorf.

4 January.
1,000 U.S. aircraft over Cologne–Fulda–Aschaffenburg. 480 British aircraft over Dortmund.

---

* *Hitler's Lagebesprechungen.* Fragment No. 27.

† *I.M.T.*, Vol. XV, p. 428/9. Note however, that when on December 24, Guderian submitted to him General Gehlen's forecast of Russian offensive potentialities, Jodl exclaimed angrily: 'This is the biggest bluff since Genghis Khan!' This savours of an irresistible urge to hide his head in the sand.

‡ K.T.B./O.K.W., IV, ii, 1721.

6 January.

1,000 U.S. bombers, 550 fighters against Hanover and Berlin. 40 shot down.

7 January.

1,000 four-engined U.S. aircraft on Düsseldorf–Mannheim. 200 British on Stettin and Danzig.

This was indeed total war, burying the German people in ruins before it buried Hitler himself.*

On January 1 came a final effort by the Luftwaffe to support the Führer's hallucinations; 1,035 German fighters took off to destroy the Allied air forces on the ground; it was the last German mass raid. But as they crossed the front the German formations were broken up by U.S. anti-aircraft fire, and only sixteen aerodromes were hit; 200 British and American aircraft were set on fire on the ground against a German loss of 300.

The Third Reich was now no longer in a position to undertake major operations, for however profitable they might be, they were bound to be costly. Hitherto, by a remarkable *tour de force*, Speer had contrived to keep German production abreast of the destruction caused by Allied bombing, but that period was now coming to an end. Rumania and its oil had been lost, and Silesia with its oil and coking coal, was shortly to go the same way; so, even if constructed, vehicles could not move. But Hitler lived on in his dream world, implicitly believing the figures produced by technicians who knew that they could never be checked. One day he would order the manufacture of 1,500 tanks and assault guns for January, the next he would predict an end to the war in late 1945, or even 1946. One wonders what he thought he could do with the time thus gained.

The German High Command now knew the Anglo-American peace plans. They had laid hands on a copy of 'Plan Eclipse', which summarised the Allied proposals drawn up in November 1944 for the enforcement of unconditional surrender and the control of conquered Germany. Hitler had referred to some of its provisions in his December 28 speech to the generals: 'Victory by our enemies would involve the temporary bolshevisation of Europe. . . . The Russians would drive seven, ten, eleven million men from the territory they would take over. . . . Churchill counts on exterminating six to seven million by bombing meanwhile.'

There seemed now to be no alternative to unconditional surrender or a senseless continuation of the struggle—less so even than in the summer.

---

* The value of the results achieved by the air offensive against Germany is a hotly debated subject. It cost the Allies 80,000 American and 80,000 British casualties and 18,000 American and 22,000 British aircraft. 2,700,000 tons of bombs were dropped, resulting in 300,000 German dead, 800,000 wounded and 7,500,000 homeless. These fantastic figures bear little relation to the actual damage inflicted on German industry.

Ideas were, however, becoming slightly clearer. At the Nuremberg trial Jodl stated:

Unconditional surrender meant that the troops would cease to fight where they stood and be captured by the enemy facing them. The same thing would happen as happened in the winter of 1941 at Viasma. Millions of prisoners would suddenly have to camp in the middle of winter in the open. . . . Above all, the men still on the Eastern Front, who numbered about 3½ million, would have fallen into the hands of the enemy in the East. It was our endeavour to save as many people as possible by sending them into the western area. That could only be done by drawing the two fronts closer together. These were the purely military opinions we held in the last stages of the war. I believe that in years to come there will be more to say about this than I can say or wish to say today.*

Jodl was bold enough to refer to the 'eastern enemy' even in front of General Rudenko, the Soviet prosecutor, but in fact, apart from certain other equally unsupported and somewhat less cautious statements, little more was said on the subject in the years that followed. The fact remains that in his choice of the theatre in which surrender should be made—the only choice now open—Jodl was adopting a 'pro-western' attitude, if any meaning could be attributed to that word at the time.

In similar vein there seem to have been some final efforts at diplomatic soundings. Von Papen, ex-ambassador in Ankara and, with Schacht, one of those primarily responsible for putting Hitler into power, is said to have emerged from retirement near Frankfurt and proposed to Ribbentrop that he should act as intermediary to the Americans and British; the Wehrmacht, he suggested, should offer only token resistance and allow the Allies to cross the Rhine and occupy Germany as far to the east as possible, so as to hold the U.S.S.R. away from the heart of Europe. Von Papen never received a reply to his proposal. At this time Ribbentrop was in fact thinking of exactly the opposite—negotiations with Moscow. After Stalingrad, he had heard Hitler refer to Stalin on several occasions with a certain admiration. Why, Ribbentrop suggested, should not he go to Moscow with his family as volunteer hostages and living proof of a genuine German desire for peace? Hitler gave him no answer. But at the same time Ribbentrop summoned Otto Abetz, the ex-ambassador in Paris, and charged him with the formation of a resistance group in the Black Forest to act in the rear of the French forces. Meanwhile Abetz was to try to gain contact with the Anglo-Americans via Switzerland.

There is seldom much firm evidence regarding hare-brained schemes of this sort, but it is clear that the background to all of them was the conviction of the leading Nazis that there was rivalry between Churchill and Roosevelt on one side and Stalin on the other. Anglo-American reactions during the Ardennes offensive had confirmed the idea—witness a note in

* *I.M.T.*, vol. XV, p. 429.

the O.K.W. War Diary, dated January 10 1945 stating that: 'Roosevelt proposes to go to England on January 20. It is also reported that the delay in the Russian offensive is the result of the present tension; it is possible that the war may carry on into 1946.'*

This terse note seems to attribute a causal relationship between the supposed crisis in inter-Allied relations and the launching of the Soviet offensive. It is significant of a climate of opinion preoccupied with far longer-term objectives than the immediate advantages to be drawn from the supposed crisis. This attitude of mind also showed itself in Hitler's midday conference of January 27:

Hitler: 'Do you think the British invariably look on all these Russian advances with enthusiasm?'

Jodl: 'No, certainly not. The two sides have very different plans. We shall probably only be able to see how far-reaching this difference is very much later.'

Göring: 'They certainly won't have been expecting us to hold firm on their front and allow the Russians to conquer the whole of Germany. If things continue this way we shall get a telegram in a few days' time.'

Hitler: 'The National Committee (Free Germany) might be of some importance. If the Russians were in fact to proclaim a German National Government, that would give England the shakes . . . I have given orders that the word should be passed through that the Russians are raising 200,000 Germans under the command of fully communist-indoctrinated German officers, and that they are going to bring this force into Germany with them. A story like that should be like a needle in the pants to the British.'

Göring: 'They came into the war to prevent us marching east, not to bring the east to the Atlantic.'

Hitler: 'Of course. It's all so crazy. British newspapers are already saying bitterly: what's the point of this war?'

Göring then referred to the possibility of the Allied Air Forces operating in support of the Soviet land forces. Hitler's reaction was: 'That is tactically impossible. Moreover, even we do not know exactly where the Russians are and exactly where we are. How could the British know?'†

To the others present at the conference, ideas such as these interjected into the midst of a diffuse discussion must have seemed like the ravings of a madman, as if the great ones of the regime were issuing a challenge to

* The note also confirms how well-informed the Germans were; proposals for President Roosevelt's journey were in fact only revived at the beginning of January, and Churchill was pressing him to come to London. The German information was, however, very incomplete; for instance, it made no reference to the Big Three meeting, the reason for Roosevelt's journey, and a delay in the Russian offensive was reported, whereas in fact Stalin had just put the date forward.

† *Hitler's Lagebesprechungen*, Fragment 24/25 and Nuremberg trial document PS.3786.

themselves as much as to the British. One of the features of Hitler's policy had always been a capacity to turn improbable theories into facts; ever since June 22 1941, and especially since Stalingrad, he had been prepared to take the most unbelievable gambles. This latest notion, however, was the gamble of all gambles. There could be no possible rational explanation for his attitude.

Nevertheless the idea was in the air. The British and American press made only cautious allusions to it, obviously wishing to avoid any appearance of suspicion of Soviet sincerity. On January 4 1945, however, Jean Heer made open reference to it in the *Gazette de Lausanne*. He had been a close observer of German affairs ever since Hitler's seizure of power, and as a neutral was free to express his sympathy with the British and Americans, a fact which had led to his expulsion from Germany a few weeks earlier. He still had good sources of information, however, and his comments were therefore not simply the fruit of his own imagination. He wrote:

Information issuing from Germany is to the effect that there are now many Germans who do not think that they can trust the 'capitalist bloc'. Diplomats and foreign journalists tend to do business with the intellectual élite, which corresponds to their own social class and which is opposed to the regime, but which represents only a fraction of German public opinion. In the present struggle, this bourgeois section of the population has no means of asserting its views. It is a group which undoubtedly tends towards Anglo-Saxon ideas, but since the failure of the plot of July 20, its influence has diminished, and it is now clearly only a minority.

Is Germany looking towards the East? The question is worth asking and for this reason the Ardennes offensive may well be a matter of great political significance, irrespective of its military success or failure. The Germans attacked in the West and not in the East. The flying bombs were used against the West and not against the Russians. The German is becoming less and less 'capitalist'. According to one theory, the Third Reich, being anti-capitalist, would have nothing to gain from an alliance with the high finance of London and New York, particularly with American industry intact. Post-war Germany would have no ships and no raw materials, and German industry would therefore be in danger of being submerged by American products. Finally, agreement with the West would mean the loss of Japanese support.

To the Germans, the Russian problem appears in a different light. It is possible to be anti-Bolshevist without being anti-Russian; the 1939 Pact is proof of that. Exhausted by the war, Russia will need German industry working with Russian raw materials. So if they are given the choice, there is every possibility that the Germans will turn east rather than west.

Events were to prove that there were certain contradictions in this theory, but basically the tendency to which it referred was no figment of the imagination. It has still to be proved, however, that it was based on more than the tempting prospect it seemed to hold out to Hitler and his gang—for Hitler himself, the attraction of springing one last surprise by allowing the Russians to invade Germany, for Himmler and others of the regime, the possibilities thought to be offered by these senseless schemes. For this was the moment chosen to constitute 'Vlassov's Army' as an independent force; this consisted at the time of about 50,000 men, ready at any moment to desert or turn into highway bandits. Its recognition came too late to enable it to form the foundation for any policy. The general lines of a Russo-German rapprochement of the traditional German type had already been indicated by Colonel Count von Stauffenberg and General von Treskow, but they had then turned to plotting against Hitler and with their execution the project had died.

On the Soviet side all interest in such flights of fancy had long since disappeared. In 1943 the 'Free Germany Committee' may have been thought of as the tool which would fashion a pro-Soviet regime, but by the end of 1944 its value was nil. The more conservative elements, led by General von Seydlitz, had lost all influence in it, and the Catholic General Vincenz Müller, who was a convert to Stalinism, was no longer capable even of serving as a figurehead for the sorely tried German communists preparing to administer the future Soviet zone. Ilya Ehrenburg was writing in *Pravda* 'the only innocent beings in Germany are the dogs and unborn children'. The launching of the greatest of all the Soviet offensives, employing vast resources, was sufficient to show that the time for compromise, if it had ever existed, was now past. There was nothing left for Germany but to return to the time-honoured game of playing off East against West.

The Allied Crisis at its Height

Public opinion in the Allied countries was so preoccupied with the latest enemy success that it had no inkling of the imminence of German disintegration, or of how complete it was destined to be. Seen through the eyes of the press, Anglo-American relations were verging on irreconcilable family rift. Walter Lippmann was one of the few to refuse to indulge in the search for a scapegoat. 'What we have to do now is to . . . adjust our political ideas', he wrote, 'to the realities of a long, hard war', and he embarked on a campaign for national service, saying that: 'We [the United States] alone among the great powers in this war have been too soft with ourselves to enact it.' In his State of the Union message on January 7, President Roosevelt took up the proposal, but was unable to obtain the approval of Congress.

Comparison between the respective war efforts was the background to the press war which broke out in early January and its first subject was the surprise of December 16. The columnists and leader writers were unanimous that the Ardennes offensive ought not to have taken the Allied

High Command unawares. Led by Liddell Hart, they chorused that it ought in any case to have been foreseen; each side looked for its scapegoat. Oddly enough, the most violent polemics appeared in the section of the press reputed to be the most serious, or at least the most balanced and moderate. The *Economist*, for instance, pointing out that the Allied forces were strung out all along the frontier of Germany instead of being concentrated for a break-through at a single point, referred to Eisenhower's strategy as one of 'equal pressure along a very extended front—the strategy of an elephant leaning on an obstacle to crush it'. If the *Economist* could write in this vein, the tone of the popular press can well be imagined.

The Americans, however, replied that the reason for Eisenhower's inaction was probably the Arnhem reverse at the end of September, which had deprived the Supreme Commander of his airborne troops. After Arnhem it had not been possible to carry on the offensive towards Cologne. Moreover, with all due respect to the British, Bradley was the only real proponent of offensive action; it was he who wished to use 'envelopment tactics' against Germany. The *Washington Post* stated that 'when the history of this war comes to be written it might be found that the stumbling block to the Bradley plan was the cautious and recalcitrant Montgomery'.

Up to this point there had been no more than an exchange of sharp comment. But the long knives came out with a forceful article from the *Daily Mail* Washington correspondent:

This Xmas the slogan in some quarters seems to be: 'War on earth and ill-will towards men, particularly Englishmen.' We are being abused by the extreme left for Churchill's policy in Greece, condemned by the extreme right for Churchill's policy regarding Poland, vilified by isolationists and nationalists for being British, and condemned by certain big businessmen and dollar diplomats for not knuckling under in aviation, communications and shipping.

On December 30 the *Economist* said:

The fat was really in the fire with the outbreak of fighting in Greece and the Prime Minister's latest speech on Poland redoubled the fury ... What makes the American criticisms so intolerable is not merely that they are unjust ... To be told by anyone that the British people are slacking in their war effort would be unsufferable enough to a people struggling through their sixth winter ... but when the criticism comes from a nation that was practising cash-and-carry during the Battle of Britain, whose consumption has risen through the war years, which still is without a National Service Act, then that is not to be borne ... It is not reasonable to suppress legitimate British interests simply because they offend American susceptibilities ... If British policies and precautions are to be traded against American promises, the only safe terms are cash on delivery. And if the Americans find this attitude too cynical or suspicious they should draw the conclusion that they have twisted the lion's tail just once too often.

The *Yorkshire Post*, over which Anthony Eden, the Foreign Secretary, still had considerable influence, struck a cooler but more effective note:

In short, the European peoples are expected to refrain from making such arrangements for their security and prosperity as they can make at this moment, and to wait until the foundation of a Security League is possible. But when they ask whether America can be relied on to help with the building up of this Security League, it appears that America will only do this if she thinks fit in her own interests and if in the meantime we have behaved well according to her ideas. In other words, the nations of Europe are being asked to deny the attainable substance for the distant shadow.

Political controversies were therefore overlapping and reacting upon each other; the two sides were talking on different wavelengths. The Americans kept to the military field: 'We are providing the basis of the Allied war effort'; the British kept to the political arguments: 'Faced with the uncertainties of American policy, Europeans are forced to insist on some guarantees of their security.'

This was the situation when, on January 6, came the announcement of Montgomery's appointment to command the northern flank of the Ardennes salient. Even before the news had become official, Hanson Baldwin had written in the *New York Times*: 'If such a move has been made ... it will ... mark up another political psychological asset for the Nazis as a result of their offensive.' Other columnists referred to 'a slap at General Bradley' and 'justification for the anglophobe school of thought in our country'.

In return, the general theme of the British press was: 'The only man who foresaw von Rundstedt's attack, and the man with the best knowledge of German tactics has been called in to save the Americans.'

With the object of reducing the violence of the British press campaign against Eisenhower, Montgomery summoned a press conference on January 7. The only result, however, was to add fuel to the fire. Yet the views expressed by Montgomery were unexceptional: 'I shall always feel that Rundstedt was really beaten by the good fighting qualities of the American soldier and by the teamwork of the Allies ... I salute the brave fighting men of America; I never want to fight alongside better soldiers.' Montgomery then paid tribute to Eisenhower, 'the captain of our team to whom I am absolutely devoted ... he needs our fullest support, he has a right to expect it'. He ended in terms of obvious sincerity by asking the British war correspondents to cease their campaign of criticism against the Supreme Commander.

From all that Montgomery said, the Americans picked out only one thing: Montgomery had given it to be understood that American forces had been pulled through by him and the British troops, because he had said that: 'national considerations were thrown overboard'. At no time did he say that command of First and Ninth U.S. Armies had ever been handed over to him other than temporarily.

To cap it all, the German radio intercepted the account of the press conference sent to the B.B.C. by Chester Wilmot. They produced an embroidered version which was picked up in Luxembourg by Bradley's headquarters. Without consulting Eisenhower, Twelfth U.S. Army Group published a supplementary statement next day, forcing Versailles to keep the promise which the British seemed so ready to forget—that the American armies had only been handed over to Montgomery temporarily. Eisenhower was now threatened with a resignation by Bradley, and Patton would have followed suit; so he acted, and at midnight on January 17, a few hours after Patton's and Hodges' armies had joined hands at Houffalize Bradley was given back one of his armies, the First. As had been agreed prior to the Ardennes offensive, Ninth Army remained under Montgomery for the 'concentrated blow' north of the Ruhr.

Finally Winston Churchill intervened, in an attempt to heal Allied wounds. On January 18, in the House of Commons, he deployed all his eloquence to soothe public opinion on the other side of the Atlantic:

> The Americans have engaged 30 or 40 men for every one we have engaged and they have lost 60 to 80 men for every one of ours ... Care must be taken ... not to claim for the British Army an undue share of what is undoubtedly the greatest American battle of the war and will, I believe, be regarded as an ever-famous American victory ... We must not forget that it is to American homes that the telegrams of personal losses and anxiety have been going during the past month, and that there has been a hard and severe ordeal during these weeks for our brave and cherished Ally.

Roosevelt, in his New Year's Message, had also emphasised Anglo-Saxon solidarity. Both he and Churchill sensed the danger which might spring from a misunderstanding, aggravated by the fact that the resulting press campaign, coming well after the crisis which had caused it, was prolonging the crisis itself. Before the Ardennes offensive Anglo-American disagreements had reached a new climax when Churchill had come out in the Commons in support of the Curzon Line as the future frontier of Poland without having obtained prior agreement from the United States. The divergence had further been underlined by Churchill's Christmas Day journey to Athens, and the British veto on the inclusion of Count Sforza in the Italian Government. Neither incident, however, had provoked an actual crisis.

Now, at this dangerous juncture, Eisenhower did not hesitate to appeal to Montgomery, and Roosevelt made a gesture towards Churchill. Meanwhile public opinion reached new heights of acrimony in both countries. The explosion of wrath in the press and the fury of the great prima donnas, only too faithfully reported by their favourite war correspondents, would have been grist to the German mill, if only Hitler and Goebbels had been able to make as good use of them as they would have in the great days of Nazi propaganda. The situation was aggravated by the fact that the memory of the hard words used was only too likely to linger on in the parliaments which exerted so powerful an influence both in England and the United States, and to cast a long-term shadow over their diplomatic relations.

But Winston Churchill was a big enough man to keep a cool head. As far as one can see he neither approved nor took advantage of the wave of anti-Americanism in the British press. On the American side, the reaction was more violent even than the anti-British opposition thought wise.

Counsels of moderation were soon to be heard and were all the more willingly heeded since the Allies were now pushing the Germans back once more, the Russians were on the move at the same time and the meeting of the Big Three was approaching.

The plan for a meeting was of long standing: on July 17 1944 Roosevelt had suggested to Stalin that they should meet in Scotland. The Russian had, however, twice turned down the invitation, alleging that his health would not permit such a thing. Then Churchill visited Moscow, but was unable to commit Roosevelt. In mid-October Harry Hopkins apparently took it upon himself to sound out Gromyko, the Russian ambassador in Washington, on the possibilities of a conference at the end of November. Stalin refused to go further than the Black Sea. Churchill feared that once they got there he and Roosevelt would be invited to proceed on to Moscow, and at his suggestion the American President expressed a preference for Malta or Cyprus. On November 14 he proposed a meeting in Rome or on the Italian Riviera, suggesting a postponement to the end of January to allow Stalin to make arrangements to go by train.

Stalin's doctors seem indeed to have been a most powerful body, however sceptical the U.S. ambassador, Averell Harriman, may have been about the poor state of the Generalissimo's health. Once more he refused to leave the Soviet Union. On January 3 the *Daily Mail* announced that there would be a meeting, though only between Churchill and Roosevelt, but by an extraordinary coincidence, on the very same day came a telegram from Roosevelt: 'I shall arrive at Yalta from Malta by air on February 1 or 2'. On January 10 Stalin issued the official invitations. On the 12th, Churchill simply replied: 'O.K. and best wishes.'

It was thus O.K. for 'Argonaut', the code name suggested by Churchill for this Black Sea meeting. The Big Three did not invite France to join them, and Georges Bidault, the Minister of Foreign Affairs, let them know that France would not feel herself bound by any decision taken without her, and that she desired to participate in the discussion of problems concerning the overall conduct of the war and the peace settlement. There was apparently never a reply to this message.

The groundwork for the Yalta Conference having been laid six months

S

before, the timing alone is enough to show that it was not an outcome of the Ardennes offensive. One question, however, remains: should that offensive be considered as one of those 'realities of the military situation' which 'affected the negotiating position of the Western Powers at Yalta'?*

The point is in fact vital, and an attempt to answer this question must form the concluding chapter of this story.

* Forrest C. Pogue, 'The Struggle for a New Order' in Snell (ed.) *The Meaning of Yalta*, p. 26.

Chapter 20

FROM BASTOGNE TO YALTA

THE legend of the Yalta Conference first made its appearance in the hurly-burly of the American electoral campaign of 1946, but Eisenhower only became directly involved during the Presidential campaign of 1952. President Truman, a Missouri politician who pulled no punches during a political battle, was quite prepared to lend his weight to attacks on the ex-Supreme Commander, now a dangerous political rival. The Democrats, who had long since disowned Roosevelt, represented Eisenhower's military errors as being responsible for the position of weakness in which the Allies had to face Stalin in February 1945.

Eisenhower never forgave Truman these criticisms; they were reinforced by others, coming this time from the MacArthur clique and concerned with the general conduct of the war, particularly the Ardennes surprise and the Bastogne affair. Some people went so far as to say that Marshall had sent Eisenhower so sharp a message that logically it should have led to the sacking of the Supreme Commander. This was a pure figment of the imagination but it tallied with Montgomery's insinuations.*

Eisenhower's attitude, his refusal to react or even to reply, might lead one to think that there was something in these criticisms, all the more so since the Yalta Conference, coming immediately after the Ardennes surprise, is generally considered as the overture to a disastrous phase of Roosevelt diplomacy. The story runs that in view of the President's natural tendency to make continuous concessions and the reverses suffered by Eisenhower, who was little better than a beaten general, Stalin had an easy time; no wonder that faced with an ally labouring under such disadvantages, he extracted everything he wanted.

This became the American legend, and it was systematically embroidered and exploited by McCarthyism. Paradoxically it is in line with the 'official historical truth' put out by the Soviet Union, which in spite of all changes since the death of Stalin, has never varied on this point since 1945. It is woven around two themes. First, that the Ardennes offensive was no more than a 'sortie with limited objectives made to cut the ground from under the feet of a major Allied offensive'.†

Secondly, that 'to avert the danger of a second Dunkirk' the Red Army came to the assistance of its Allies; 'out of pure loyalty to its obligations and in contrast to the example of the Anglo-American leaders', it advanced

* Marquis Childs, *Eisenhower, Captive Hero*, p. 84.
† *Conferences at Malta and Yalta*, Ambassador Harriman's Despatch, January 10 1945.

the date of its offensive from January 20 to January 12 1945, in spite of the fact that, as a result of the inaction of its Allies on the western front during the autumn, it was facing the bulk of the German armies.

According to the McCarthyists, the result of the political and military errors committed by the Allies was to enable the Russians to boast that they had saved the Americans. For the Soviet historians, this interpretation of events fits logically into the theory that the U.S.S.R. alone won the war, thanks to the directions of the Communist Party (no longer thanks to Stalin) and without any real contribution from the West; Western economic assistance 'only constituted 4 per cent of Soviet war production.'*

Both theories amount to a deliberate distortion of the facts and a failure to appreciate the atmosphere of the time.

Eisenhower's Appeal to Stalin

In late 1944 there was an almost complete absence of co-ordination between the two fronts which were slowly crushing Germany. Both in the east and in the west there had been a pause in the offensives since the autumn, and the two Supreme Commanders, Eisenhower and Stalin, quite naturally wished to know the general lines of each other's plans in order to try and synchronise them, even if only to a degree.

On December 5, therefore, the Supreme Commander asked Marshall to get Harriman to approach Stalin. Eisenhower was worried over reports of movement of German divisions from Hungary and East Prussia towards the western front. When the American ambassador raised the subject, Stalin's reply was to demand in his turn information on Eisenhower's plans. He did, however, promise that a winter offensive would be launched shortly, saying that it had so far been delayed by bad weather. He stated that he would give his own reply within a week.

Harriman's report reached the War Department at Washington on December 17. Apparently Eisenhower was not informed, for he returned to the charge on December 21:

The arrival of these German divisions obviously influences the events in my area [he cabled], and if the trend continues it will affect the decisions which I have to make regarding the future strategy in the West. If for instance it is the Russian intention to launch a major offensive in the course of this or next month, knowledge of the fact would be of the utmost importance to me and I would condition my plans accordingly.

He proposed to send an information mission to Stalin under Air Chief-Marshal Tedder.†

Eisenhower's telegram, it must be admitted, was somewhat ambiguous. He was not definitely calling for an operation in the East to assist him,

* See *Red Star*, the Soviet Army newspaper, quoted by *Die Welt*, February 19 1962.
† *The Supreme Command*, p. 405.

nor, however, did he reject the idea. His request could equally well refer to the short term and therefore be a direct consequence of the German operation in the Ardennes, or to future co-ordination in connection with the offensive towards the Rhine which he was still planning.

On December 23 Roosevelt wrote to Stalin supporting the proposal to send Tedder, and putting the matter quite clearly: 'The situation in Belgium is not bad, but it is time to talk about the next phase.' Churchill also intervened in his turn, suggesting closer co-ordination: 'It is Eisenhower's need to know in outline what you plan to do.' Stalin gave his agreement immediately (on December 25), but he did not indicate the extent of the 'exchange of information' which he would have with 'the accredited officer sent by General Eisenhower'. Clearly he was letting matters take their course.

The exchange of letters was resumed after Churchill's visit to Eisenhower on January 6. The Prime Minister had found the Supreme Commander 'acutely anxious to know whether the Russians could do anything from their side to take off some of the pressure against us in the West'. He thereupon wrote to Stalin:

The battle in the West is very heavy, and at any time large decisions may be called for from the Supreme Command. You yourself know from your own experience how very anxious the position is when a very broad front has to be defended after the temporary loss of the initiative ... I shall be grateful if you can tell me whether we can count on a major Russian offensive on the Vistula front or elsewhere during January.

So there was no doubt that in Churchill's mind the problem was connected with the battle in the Ardennes and not with the preparation of future offensives. Churchill's letter was quite clear and Stalin's reply on January 7 was equally explicit:

Taking into account the position of our allies on the Western Front, G.H.Q. of the Supreme Command has decided to accelerate the completion of our preparation and, regardless of the weather, to commence large-scale offensive operations against the Germans along the whole central front not later than the second half of January. You may rest assured that we shall do everything possible to render assistance to the glorious forces of our allies.'

Churchill's comment is: 'It was a fine deed of the Russians and their chief to hasten their vast offensive, no doubt at a heavy cost in life.'

Eleven years later Churchill fully confirmed this reading of the facts by giving the Commons the text of a telegram which he had sent to Stalin on January 16 1945:

On behalf of his Majesty's Government and from the bottom of my heart I offer you our thanks and congratulations on the immense assault you have launched upon the Eastern Front. You now no doubt know the plans of General Eisenhower and to what extent they have been delayed by

Rundstedt's spoiling attack. I am sure that fighting along the whole front will be continuous. The British 21st Army Group under Field Marshal Montgomery have today began an attack in the area south of Roermond.

In his memoirs Eisenhower says not a word about this background to the approach to Stalin, an approach, moreover, in which Roosevelt did not join. He refers to Tedder's journey to Moscow, but only in relation to the preparation of plans for offensive action in late winter and spring. In any case, when the Soviet offensive opened on January 12 the German retreat in the Ardennes salient had definitely begun. Hitler had just ordered the withdrawal of Sixth SS Panzer Army, which clearly helped the Americans to recover the lost ground. That army was given fifteen days' rest before being sent to Hungary, and neither Stalin nor Eisenhower could have dreamed that their enemy would let two weeks go by before putting it into battle. Guderian's memoirs prove clearly that one of the main reasons for the withdrawal of Sixth SS Panzer Army was the threat and then the launching of the Russian offensive. The move may have come too late to relieve the western front, but the fact remains that both Stalin and Eisenhower were assisted by Hitler's obstinacy and refusal to listen to the advice of his generals.

When Air-Marshal Tedder and his mission arrived in Moscow on January 14, having been held up in Malta by bad weather, the Ardennes problem could be considered as being over. There remained, therefore, only the second part of their task, and in Eisenhower's view the more important—plans for the future.

Eisenhower was quite clear that his future strategy fell into three phases: destruction of the main body of enemy forces between the Rhine and the German frontier, the capture of bridgeheads between Emmerich and Karlsruhe, and an advance on parallel lines into north Germany and towards Frankfurt. He was apprehensive that the Germans might make available some one hundred divisions from Norway and Italy and forestall his spring offensive. His whole plan, therefore, depended upon the progress of the Soviet army. It is of little consequence whether his calculations were based upon a persistent overestimation of German resources—he had some excuse for it since December 16; the fact remains that two weeks later, at the Malta Conference, the Combined Chiefs of Staff Committee reached the conclusion that 'co-operation' between the two fronts was now more necessary than ever. This meant that on the military level it was the Allies who were asking for something from Stalin.

When the discussions at Yalta opened on February 4 1945, the Soviet offensive was in full swing. The Vistula had been crossed, Warsaw captured, Upper Silesia encircled, the German forces in East Prussia split into three fragments and Budapest was under siege. All the Western Powers had to set against this list of concrete achievements was a series of paper plans.

Stalin the Altruist

The contrast between Russian successes already achieved and Anglo-American goals—mere hopes—set the tone for the first meeting of the Yalta Conference, which opened at 5 p.m. on February 4, following an hour's desultory discussion between Roosevelt and Stalin. General Antonov, First Deputy Chief of Staff of the Soviet Armed Forces, and General Marshall described the situation on their respective fronts. Antonov was cold and precise, reeling off colossal figures for the resources used in the Soviet offensive: over 100 guns to the mile, over 300 miles covered in eighteen days, 100,000 German prisoners, 300,000 Germans killed and wounded. Stalin confirmed that the Russians had used 180 divisions—100 more than the Germans—together with 9,000 aircraft and 9,000 tanks. Antonov added that he was expecting German offensives in front of Vienna and Berlin, and the arrival of 35 to 40 German divisions from the western front.

Marshall's figures were modest by comparison. He stated that 79 German divisions were facing 78 Allied, announced that Montgomery would attack towards Düsseldorf on February 8, and that the crossing of the Rhine should be possible from March 1 onwards. He expressed some fear of a possible intensification of the submarine war, and explained that supply difficulties limited future operations.*

The conclusion which emerged from the military exposés was that neither side was envisaging the final offensive before the summer. The Western Powers emphasised the difficulties of a large-scale crossing of the Rhine. Antonov demanded an offensive in Italy to hold as many German divisions as possible, which otherwise might be moved to the eastern front. But he seemed very sure of himself and of the Soviet army's plans and capabilities. In comparison, Marshall clearly cut a 'poor relation' figure.

No mention was made of the Ardennes offensive, the military exposés being entirely devoted to the future. Stalin, however, raised the question in a subsequent exchange of views, and it is significant of the political importance of the affair that Charles Bohlen, President Roosevelt's interpreter and a diplomat with long experience of distinguishing the important from the unimportant in statements from Soviet leaders, devoted a long passage to it in the Minutes. In contrast the Chiefs of Staff *aide-mémoire* passed over the subject in a few lines.

Stalin only intervened after Churchill had expressed Allied gratitude for the scale and initial success of the Soviet offensive.

Marshal Stalin replied that this offensive was not a desire. Marshal Stalin then said that the Soviet Union was not bound by any agreement at Teheran

* *Conferences at Malta and Yalta*, p. 574 et seq.

to conduct a winter offensive and despite what some people had thought, no demand or request had been received from the President or Prime Minister in regard to such an offensive. The President had asked him to receive a representative, Air Marshal Tedder, from General Eisenhower's staff to discuss the situation and he had of course immediately agreed. He said that he mentioned this only to emphasise the spirit of the Soviet leaders who not only fulfilled formal obligations but went further and acted upon what they conceived to be their moral duty to their allies. He said Air Marshal Tedder had explained the desire, which he presumed was that of the President and Prime Minister, that the Soviet army continue their offensive operations until the end of March. Marshal Stalin said that they would do it if the weather and road conditions permitted.

Roosevelt replied somewhat feebly: 'At the Teheran Conference it had been merely agreed that each partner would move as quickly and as far as possible against the common enemy. He said that at that time he personally was facing an election and that it had been impossible to make detailed plans far into the future.'

Churchill attempted to gild the lily:

The Prime Minister remarked that the reason no request had been made on Marshal Stalin was because of the complete confidence which the President and he felt in the Marshal, the Russian people and the efficiency of the Russian military and therefore there had been no attempt to strike a bargain. He had always been thoroughly confident that when an offensive was possible the Red Army would attack. The Prime Minister added that no matter what discussions Air Marshal Tedder had had in Moscow, he felt that it was of the highest importance that the three staffs which were assembled here for the first time should really work out together detailed plans for the co-ordination of the joint blows against Germany.

This is the only reference in the Minutes of the Yalta Conference to the repercussions of the Ardennes offensive and the assistance of the Soviet army. But it is easy to guess what each of the Big Three was in fact feeling.

No Bargaining

Stalin's phrase about 'moral obligations' was well calculated to have an effect upon Roosevelt, but no one present—except perhaps Roosevelt himself—was under any illusions as to the Generalissimo's real views. He had, moreover, made no secret of them a few weeks previously when speaking to Air-Marshal Tedder. He had said that 'although he had no treaty with the Western Allies, he considered it a proper, sound and selfish policy for all of them to help one another in time of difficulties. It would be as foolish for him to stand aside while the Germans annihilated the Allies, as it was wise for the Allies to prevent the enemy from crushing the Russians'.*

This was the language neither of a Communist nor of a Russian, but

* Pogue, *The Supreme Command*, p. 407.

simply of a prudent nationalist statesman. It is true that the reference to moral obligations was capable of an entirely different interpretation: it could be taken to mean that Stalin was asking for nothing in return for the assistance given to the Western Allies which Churchill had so explicitly requested. Why this generosity? The explanation clearly lies in the 'sound and selfish policy'.

This policy, moreover, was based upon a definite principle: from the outset Stalin had always been anxious to preserve his liberty of action. He had carefully avoided being drawn into a system of formal treaty obligations. He had been encouraged in this attitude by the American policy of non-reciprocal aid to the Soviet Union. In a despatch to Marshall General Deane, Head of the American Military Mission, had stated: 'Each transaction forms a separate whole, unrelated to aid in the past.' Moreover, in spite of his insistence, he had had to wait for eighteen months for the opening of the second front, which could not but confirm him in his view that the Big Three were conducting parallel but separate wars, a system which suited him admirably.

By asking for no reward for having met the wishes of Churchill and Eisenhower, Stalin built up for himself a credit balance, of which he intended to make full use when the moment for major bargaining arrived. The balance, however, was small, for it could not honestly be said that the Soviet offensive on the Vistula had made any decisive contribution to the relief of the western front. The offensive had only been launched on January 12, when the German withdrawal in the Ardennes was already well under way. Hitler's decision to withdraw Sixth Panzer Army had been taken for other reasons, and neither Eisenhower nor Stalin could claim the smallest credit for Hitler's decision to keep it idle for two weeks, a decision which made the task of his enemies on both fronts easier.

In fact, detailed discussion might have brought out the point that the Ardennes offensive had played a considerable part in assisting Russian plans from the autumn onwards. Marshal Zhukov later said: 'When we reached Warsaw we could not see how we could get beyond the Vistula unless the German forces on our front were considerably weakened.'*

As we have seen, in preparation for the Ardennes offensive and against the advice of his staff, Hitler had moved large-scale reinforcements both in men and equipment to the western front. The 'considerable weakening' which Zhukov wanted therefore took place, but to Eisenhower's disadvantage. The two Panzer Armies which he was shortly to have to face were given priority both for men and equipment from the beginning of November onwards.

The acceleration of the Russian offensive by eight days cannot have given rise to any very serious problems, for preparations had been in train for several months without noteworthy opposition. In fact it may well be

* Chester Wilmot, *Struggle for Europe*, p. 630.

that it was because he found that the Germans were still tied down on the western front that Stalin seized the opportunity to launch his offensive earlier than planned.

So the balance of services rendered by each side was approximately equal. Neither Churchill nor Roosevelt made the case for the advantages which Stalin had reaped from the Ardennes offensive; on his side Stalin did not over-insist on the value of the Red Army's offensive. The moment would in any case have been ill-chosen for such a discussion; it would inevitably have been sterile and might well have ended in a mutual cross-examination regarding motives.

The Real Issue at Stake

One problem, however, they all had to solve, and for that it was essential that the atmosphere should remain favourable: how to finish off Germany, now being attacked from all sides.

More than the repercussions of the Ardennes offensive, more even than those of the Russian offensive, it was the views of the Chiefs of Staff which weighed with Roosevelt and Churchill. They were demanding full co-ordination of land and air operations, and the continuance of the Soviet effort; they pressed their political masters to lose no opportunity of 'encouraging the Russian military effort' (Churchill's words). The American Chiefs of Staff were primarily preoccupied with finishing the war against Japan, which they foresaw continuing for another eighteen months. They were sceptical as to the effectiveness of the atomic bomb, although Roosevelt knew of the prospects which it held out as early as December 30; their major fear was to see Stalin relapse into neutrality, or even go off on a policy of his own and ally himself with Japan.

These considerations meant that yet once more the Western Allies were coming cap in hand. The Ardennes offensive was no more than a past interlude, and there were better things to do than argue about a squaring of accounts between Allies. It was the future which was important, and without Soviet collaboration victory was still a chancy affair.

The Yalta Conference cannot be judged in isolation. Any attempt to do so would be to give too little weight to extraneous political considerations with their own driving imperatives. Foster Rhea Dulles took up the cudgels on Roosevelt's behalf, saying that he 'did not give anything away which the United States really had or controlled. He was hardly in a position—nor was Churchill—to bring decisive pressure on Russia for any broader concessions than those that were actually made.'*

Stalin was already master of eastern Europe and what he was given in the Far East he would have laid hands on in any case. He did not show himself intransigent on every point, in particular not on policy for the occupation of Germany or procedure in the United Nations. Roosevelt's

* F. R. Dulles, *America's Rise to World Power*, p. 217.

error undoubtedly lay in his failure to realise that European balance of power considerations must inevitably come into play. He and Churchill were obsessed by fear of a separate Russo-German peace. Both were perhaps over-influenced by the example of recent history. They had to pay for the American refusal to 'subordinate and to relate military plans to political considerations'. Yet, all things considered, 'granted that it was a retreating action, what else could they do'?*

The critics of the Yalta Conference are in the same position as those of the Treaty of Versailles: if justice is to be done the atmosphere of the time cannot be deliberately ignored. It must not be forgotten that in the eyes of the entire world Germany carried a crushing burden of responsibility, not only for having plunged the world into war but for the ruthless nature of the war itself. The treatment meted out to the peoples of occupied Europe was present in everybody's mind, and Russia was one of the greatest sufferers: millions of Soviet citizens had died in battle, and in face of that fact niceties of foreign policy seemed out of place. Though the ghastly truth of the extermination camps was as yet hardly suspected, enough was known to make it clear that the SS and the Gestapo deserved nothing less than total and pitiless elimination. In the light of experience, it also seemed clear that this time the Allies must go all the way to Berlin and refuse all compromise, if they did not wish to see the farce of peace treaty revision recommence.

Churchill realised more clearly than anyone the results which might flow from this shotgun alliance. But who other than Hitler and what nation other than Germany carried the final responsibility for having produced the conditions which made the alliance necessary? In any sober judgment of this period, Churchill's warning to the Commons on his return from Yalta should not be forgotten: 'We are now entering a world of imponderables, and at every stage occasions for self-questioning arise. It is a mistake to look too far ahead. Only one link in the chain of destiny can be handled at a time.'

There is a final question. Even if it was not hanging like a shadow over the Yalta Conference, did not the Ardennes offensive deprive the Allies of an opportunity of driving into the heart of Germany and forestalling the Russians?

In fact the offensive came so late that there can be no question of the Allies having missed an opportunity. At the end of the summer offensive there was a period of at most two weeks when a bolder commander might perhaps have tried to keep up the momentum of his offensive. But Eisenhower was bound by his instructions from the Combined Chiefs of Staff Committee, and it was not in his nature to use military operations to force a political decision. Even supposing he had had available the material resources required—which is highly doubtful—it seems questionable

* J. B. Duroselle, *From Wilson to Roosevelt*, p. 409.

whether the resistance which he would have encountered on the territory of Germany itself could have been broken in late summer without serious fighting. Speculation on the question could be endless.

On the other hand there is no doubt that by the autumn the moment had passed. Allied weakness was only too obvious, for the supply services had not been able to keep pace and the armies were running short. The man-power problem was serious and apparently insoluble, for both British and Americans were treating it as if it was one merely of keeping an expeditionary force up to strength. The result was the failure of December. The British and Americans were taken by surprise and caught off balance, because they had failed to adjust their war effort, great though it was, to the realities of the struggle. They had thought that they could conduct a colossal colonial war, but found that they were faced by a continental war curiously reminiscent of its predecessor, a fact which Stalin had fully grasped.

What then were the results of this last bluff by Hitler? They seem to amount to this: fear at all levels and in all circles, 150,000 dead and missing and an inexhaustible subject of discussion for the generals who have studied and will long continue to study this operation described by Montgomery as 'most interesting; I think possibly one of the most interesting and tricky battles I have ever handled'.

On the Wehrmacht side, if it did nothing else, it exhausted the stock of decorations. On February 4 1945 a Volksgrenadier division submitted the following report:

47 VGD
OPERATIONS SECTION.
Third Bureau.
Reference: 221/45 Secret.
To: H.Q. LXXXIX Corps   *4 February, 1945*

The division reports that no result has been achieved by the distribution of signed photographs of Field-Marshal von Rundstedt as individual rewards for services in battle. No request for these has been received. The division does not consider that this type of reward has any effect in encouraging the infantry to fight.

The divisional commander considers that the choice of this reward is unfortunate. The soldier cannot carry the Field-Marshal's photograph around with him when in the line. The majority of men cannot send it home, since many families have been evacuated, owing to the bombing. In those cases where it does reach home it is more than likely to be forgotten.

The division considers that better results would be achieved by the grant of special leave for bravery, and by the distribution of some visible decoration to individual infantrymen.

On March 11 Field-Marshal von Rundstedt was relieved of his command on the western front. This time it was for good. The Germans went on fighting, but not because of signed photographs from the field-marshal. War was now being waged on German soil.

BIBLIOGRAPHY

Page references given in the footnotes to the text apply to British editions of the works cited and are not necessarily valid for American editions.

Abetz, Otto, *Ein Rückblick auf zwei Jahrzehnte deutscher Frankreich-Politik*, Greven, Cologne 1951.

Allen, Col Robert S., *Lucky Forward: The History of Patton's Third U.S. Army*, Vanguard Press, New York 1947.

Aron, Robert, *The Vichy Regime*, translated by Humphrey Hare, Putnam & Co., London 1959; Dufour Editions, Philadelphia, Pa., 1966.

—— *De Gaulle before Paris: The Liberation of France*, translated by Humphrey Hare, Putnam, London 1962; as *France Reborn: The History of the Liberation*, Scribner, New York 1964.

Bauer, Major Eddy, *La guerre des blindés*, Payot, Paris 1947.

Baumbach, Werner, *Zu Spät?*, Pflaumverlag, Munich 1949.

Bernard, H., *Leçons d'histoire militaire*, Vol. III, Imprimerie medicale et scientifique, Brussels 1951.

Bertin, F., *La ruée de von Rundstedt à travers nos Ardennes*, Brussels 1945.

Betbeze, A., *Qui ose gagne* (le 2me R.C.P.), Paris 1946.

Blumentritt, General Günther, *Von Rundstedt, the Soldier and the Man*, translated by Cuthbert Reavely, Odhams Press, London 1952.

Borchert, Wolfgang, *The Man Outside*, translated by David Porter, Hutchinson, London; New Directions, New York 1952.

Bormann, Martin, *The Bormann Letters*, edited by H. R. Trevor-Roper, translated by R. H. Stevens, Weidenfeld & Nicolson, London 1954.

Bovy, Marcel, *La bataille de l'Amblève*, Liège, n.d.

Bradley, Omar, *A Soldier's Story*, Eyre & Spottiswoode, London; Henry Holt, New York 1951.

Bryant, Arthur, *Triumph in the West*, Collins, London 1959.

Bullock, Alan, *Hitler: a Study in Tyranny*, Odhams Press, London; Harper & Bros, New York 1952.

Bush, Vannevar, *Modern Arms and Free Men*, Heinemann, London 1950; Simon & Schuster, New York 1949.

Butcher, Harry C., *My Three Years with Eisenhower*, Heinemann, London; Simon & Schuster, New York 1946.

Childs, Marquis W., *Eisenhower, Captive Hero*, Hammond & Hammond, London; Harcourt, Brace, New York 1958.

Churchill, Winston S., *Triumph and Tragedy* (*The Second World War*, Vol. VI), Cassell & Co., London 1954; Houghton Mifflin, Boston 1953.

Clostermann, Pierre, *The Big Show*, translated by Oliver Berthoud, Chatto & Windus, London 1951.

Cole, Col H. M., *The Lorraine Campaign*, Office of the Chief of Military History, Department of the Army, Washington 1950.

Cooper, Alfred Duff, *Old Men Forget*, Rupert Hart-Davis, London; E. P. Dutton, New York 1953.

Corta, Henry, *Les bérets rouges*, Paris 1952.

Crouquet, Roger, *La bataille des Ardennes*, Editions 'Libération 44', Brussels 1945.

Dawson, W. Forrest, *Saga of the All Americans*, Albert Love, Atlanta, Ga., 1946.

Delaval, Maurice, *La bataille des Ardennes*, Brussels 1958.

Desonay, F., *Maquis des Ardennes et de chez nous*, Brussels 1946.

Deuerlein, Ernst, *Die Einheit Deutschlands*, Metzner, Frankfurt 1957.

Donnison, F. S. V., *Civil Affairs and Military Government, North-West Europe* (*History of the Second World War*), H.M.S.O., London 1961.

Draper, Theodore, *The 84th Infantry Division in the Battle for Germany*, Viking Press, New York 1946.

Ducrocq, Albert, *Les armes secrètes allemandes*, Paris 1947.

Dulles, Foster R., *America's Rise to World Power*, Hamish Hamilton, London; Harper & Row, New York 1955.

Dupuy, R. E., *St Vith: Lion in the Way*, Infantry Journal Press, Washington 1949.

Duroselle, J. B., *From Wilson to Roosevelt*, translated by Nancy L. Roelker, Chatto & Windus, London 1964; Harvard University Press, Cambridge, Mass., 1963.

Ehrman, John, *Grand Strategy* (*History of the Second World War*, Vols. V–VI), H.M.S.O., London 1956.

Eisenhower, Dwight D., *Crusade in Europe*. Heinemann, London 1949; Doubleday, New York 1948.

Feis, Herbert, *Churchill-Roosevelt-Stalin*, Princeton University Press, Princeton, N.J., 1957.

Foley, Charles, *Commando Extraordinary*, Longmans Green & Co., London and New York 1954.

Forny, A., *Ruée SS en Wallonie*, Paris 1946.

Fuller, J. F. C., *Second World War—A Strategical and Tactical History*, Eyre & Spottiswoode, London 1948; Duell, Sloan & Pearce, New York 1962.

Galland, Adolf, *The First and the Last*, translated by Mervyn Savill, Transworld Publishers, London 1957; Henry Holt, New York 1954.

De Gaulle, Charles, *Salvation*, (*War Memoirs*, Vol. III), translated by Richard Howard, Weidenfeld & Nicolson, London; Simon & Schuster, New York 1960.

Gilbert, G. M., *Nuremberg Diary*, New American Library, New York 1947.

Görlitz, Walter, *Der Zweite Weltkrieg*, Steingrüben Verlag, Stuttgart 1951.
—— *Keitel*, Musterschmidt Verlag, Göttingen 1961.

Greindl, Baronne Renée, *Noël 1944 à Isle en Hesse*, Brussels, n.d.

Guderian, H., *Panzer Leader*, translated by Constantine Fitzgibbon, Michael Joseph, London; E. P. Dutton, New York 1952.

Guillaume, General A., *La guerre germano—soviétique*, Payot, Paris 1949.

De Guingand, General Sir F., *Operation Victory*, Hodder & Stoughton, London 1947.

Hausser, Paul, *Waffen SS im Einsatz*, Göttingen 1953.

Heagy, *Quand l'offensive von Rundstedt menaçait Verviers*, Verviers 1945.

Heiber, H., *Hitlers Lagebesprechungen*, Stuttgart 1960.

Hewitt, Robert L., *Work Horse on the Western Front*, Infantry Journal Press, Washington 1946.

Huie, William B., *The Execution of Private Slovik*, Jarrolds, London 1954; E. P. Dutton, New York 1956.

Ingersoll, Ralph, *Top Secret*, Harcourt, Brace, New York 1946.

International Military Tribunal, *The Nuremberg Trial*, English version, 1947–9.

Ismay, Hastings L., *Memoirs of General Lord Ismay*, Heinemann, London; Viking Press, New York 1960.

Juin, Marshal, *Mémoires*, Vol. II, Fayard, Paris 1960.

Keilig, Hans, *Rangliste des deutschen Heeres, 1944–45*, Podzun, Bad Nauheim, 1955.

Kennan, George F., *American Diplomacy: 1900–1950*, University of Chicago Press, Chicago 1951.

Kleist, Peter, *Auch Du warst dabei !*, Vowinckel, Heidelberg 1952.

De Lame, G. R., *Spa et les Américains*, Liège 1948.

De Lattre de Tassigny, Marshal, *The History of the First French Army*, translated by Malcolm Barnes, Allen & Unwin, London; Macmillan, New York 1952.

Leahy, Admiral William D., *I Was There*, Victor Gollancz, London; Whittlesey House, New York 1950.

Leasor, James, and Hollis, Sir Leslie, *War at the Top*, Michael Joseph, London 1959; as *The Clock with Four Hands*, Reynal, New York 1959.

Lévy, Paul M. G., *Les heures rouges des Ardennes*, Brussels 1946.

Liddell Hart, Basil, *The Defence of Britain*, Faber & Faber, London 1939.

—— *The Other Side of the Hill*, Cassell & Co, London 1948; as *The German Generals Talk*, William Morrow, New York 1948.

Lombard, Laurent, *Stavelot: cité héroïque et martyre*, Liège, n.d.

Lusar, Rudolf, *Die deutschen Waffen und Geheimwaffen*, Lehmann, Munich 1956.

McCann, Kevin, *America's Man of Destiny*, Heinemann, London 1952; as *The Man from Abilene*, Doubleday, New York 1952.

Maertz, J., *Luxemburg in der Rundstedt Offensive*, Luxembourg 1948.

Marshall, S. L. A., *Bastogne: The First Eight Days*, Infantry Journal Press, Washington 1946.

Maycock, T. J., and others, *The Army Air Force in World War II*, Vol. III, Chicago 1951.

Meissner, B., *Russland, die Westmächte und Deutschland*, Nölke, Hamburg 1954.

Melchers, Lt-Col E. T., *Les deux libérations du Luxembourg*, Luxembourg 1959.

Merriam, Robert E., *Dark December*, Ziff Davis, Chicago 1947.

Montgomery, Field-Marshal Viscount, *Memoirs*, Hutchinson, London 1947.

—— *Normandy to the Baltic*, Hutchinson, London; Houghton Mifflin, Boston 1947.

Moorehead, Alan, *Eclipse*, Hamish Hamilton, London; Coward–McCann, New York 1945.

Morison, Samuel E., *Strategy and Compromise*, Little, Brown, Boston 1958.

Mourin, Maxime, *Les tentatives de paix dans la seconde guerre mondiale*, Payot, Paris 1949.

Patton, General George S., *War as I Knew It*, W. H. Allen, London; Houghton Mifflin, Boston 1947.

Ploetz, K., *Geschichte des zweiten Weltkrieges*, Würzburg 1960.

Pogue, Forrest C., *The Supreme Command* (*The U.S. Army in World War II*), Office of the Chief of Military History, Department of the Army, Washington 1954.

Rapport, Leonard, and Northwood, A., *Rendezvous with Destiny*, Washington 1948.

Reitlinger, G., *The SS: Alibi of a Nation*, Heinemann, London 1956.

Ribbentrop, Joachim von, *The Ribbentrop Memoirs*, translated by Oliver Watson, Weidenfeld & Nicolson, London 1954.

Riess, Curt, *Josef Goebbels*, Hollis & Carter, London 1949.

Rose, U. D., *Die unheimlichen Waffen*, Munich 1957.

Rubel, Lt-Col George K., *Daredevil Tankers*, Göttingen 1945.

Rumpf, Hans, *Das war der Bombenkrieg*, Oldenburg 1961.

Schellenberg, Walter, *The Schellenberg Memoirs*, André Deutsch, London 1956.

Schramm, P. E., *Kriegstagebuch des OKW*, Vol IV, Bernard & Graefe, Frankfurt 1961.

Semmler, Rudolf, *Goebbels—The Man Next to Hitler*, Westhouse, London 1947.

Sherwood, Robert E., *The White House Papers of Harry L. Hopkins*, Eyre & Spottiswoode, London 1954; as *Roosevelt and Hopkins: An Intimate History*, Harper & Row, New York 1948.

Shulman, Milton, *The German Defeat in the West*, Secker & Warburg, London; E. P. Dutton, New York 1954.

Skorzeny, Otto, *Skorzeny's Special Missions*, Robert Hale, London 1957.

—— *Secret Mission*, E. P. Dutton, New York 1950.

Snell, John L., and others, *The Meaning of Yalta*, Louisiana State University Press, Baton Rouge, La., 1956.

—— *Wartime Origins of the East-West Dilemma over Germany*, Hauser Press, New Orleans 1959.

Stettinius, Edward R., *Roosevelt and the Russians*, Jonathan Cape, London 1950; Doubleday, New York 1949.

Stimson, Henry L., and Bundy, McGeorge, *On Active Service in Peace and War*, Harper & Bros, New York 1947.

Summersby, Kay, *Eisenhower was my Boss*, Werner Laurie, London 1949; Prentice-Hall, New York 1948.

Telpuchowski, B. S., (German translation) *Die sowjetische Geschichte des grossen vaterländischen Krieges*, Bernard & Graefe, Frankfurt 1961.

Tippelskirch, Kurt von, *Geschichte des zweiten Weltkrieges*, Athenäum Verlag, Bonn 1951.

Toland, John, *Battle: The Story of the Bulge*, Random House, New York 1959.

United States Official Publications
The Conferences at Malta and Yalta, 1955.
Twelfth U.S. Army Group, *Report of Operations: Final After Action Report*.
First U.S. Army, *Report of Operations*.
Third U.S. Army, *After Action Report*.
Seventh U.S. Army, *Report of Operations*.

United States Formation and Unit Histories
Conquer: The Story of the 9th Army.
Roll out the Barrel (7th Armored Division).
The Thunderbolt across Europe: A History of the 83rd U.S. Infantry Division.
Call me Spearhead: Saga of the 3rd Armored Division.
The Road to Germany: The Story of the 5th Armored Division.
Lightning: The History of the 78th Infantry Division.
Second Armored Division.
The Story of the 11th Armored Division.
Brest to Bastogne: The Story of the 10th Armored Division.
Brest to Bastogne: The Story of the 6th Armored Division.
The 4th Armored from the Beach to Bastogne.
18 Airborne Corps.

Vigneras, Marcel, *Rearming the French*, Office of the Chief of Military History, Department of the Army, Washington 1957.

Wagner, Wolfgang, *Die Teilung Europas*, Deutsche Verlags-Anstalt, Stuttgart 1960.

Wellard, J., *The Man in a Helmet*, Eyre & Spottiswoode, London 1947; as *General George S. Patton, Jr.: Man under Mars*, Dodd, Mead, New York 1946.

T

Westphal, General Siegfried, *The German Army in the West*, Cassell & Co., London 1951.

Wheeler-Bennett, Sir J. W., *The Nemesis of Power*, Macmillan, London; St Martin's Press, New York 1953.

Williams, Mary H., *Chronology 1941–45*, Office of the Chief of Military History, Department of the Army, Washington 1960.

Wilmot, Chester, *The Struggle for Europe*, Collins, London; Harper & Bros, New York 1952.

Woodward, Sir Llewellyn, *British Foreign Policy in the Second World War*, H.M.S.O., London 1962.

INDEX